DIGITAL DIPLOMACY AND INTERNATIONAL ORGANISATIONS

D1719250

This book examines how international organisations (IOs) have struggled to adapt to the digital age, and with social media in particular.

The global spread of new digital communication technologies has profoundly transformed the way organisations operate and interact with the outside world. This edited volume explores the impact of digital technologies, with a focus on social media, for one of the major actors in international affairs, namely IOs. To examine the peculiar dynamics characterising the IO–digital nexus, the volume relies on theoretical insights drawn from the disciplines of International Relations, Diplomatic Studies, Media, and Communication Studies, as well as from Organisation Studies. The volume maps the evolution of IOs' "digital universe" and examines the impact of digital technologies on issues of organisational autonomy, legitimacy and contestation. The volume's contributions combine engaging theoretical insights with newly compiled empirical material and an eclectic set of methodological approaches (multivariate regression, network analysis, content analysis, sentiment analysis), offering a highly nuanced and textured understanding of the multifaceted, complex, and ever-evolving nature of the use of digital technologies by international organisations in their multilateral engagements.

This book will be of much interest to students of diplomacy, media, and communication studies, and international organisations.

Corneliu Bjola is Associate Professor in Diplomatic Studies at the University of Oxford and Head of the Oxford Digital Diplomacy Research Group, UK.

Ruben Zaiotti is Jean Monnet Chair in Public Diplomacy, Director of the European Union Centre of Excellence, and Associate Professor in the Political Science department at Dalhousie University, Canada.

ROUTLEDGE NEW DIPLOMACY STUDIES

This series publishes theoretically challenging and empirically authoritative studies of the traditions, functions, paradigms, and institutions of modern diplomacy. Taking a comparative approach, the New Diplomacy Studies series aims to advance research on international diplomacy, publishing innovative accounts of how "old" and "new" diplomats help steer international conduct between anarchy and hegemony, handle demands for international stability vs international justice, facilitate transitions between international 'orders, and address global governance challenges. Dedicated to the exchange of different scholarly perspectives, the series aims to be a forum for inter-paradigm and inter-disciplinary debates, and an opportunity for dialogue between scholars and practitioners.

Series Editors: Corneliu Bjola, *University of Oxford*, and Markus Kornprobst, *Diplomatic Academy of Vienna*

China's Cultural Diplomacy
A Great Leap Outward?
Xin Liu

Diplomacy and Borderlands
African Agency at the Intersections of Orders
Edited by Katharina P. Coleman, Markus Kornprobst, and Annette Seegers

Diplomacy and Ideology
From the French Revolution to the Digital Age
Alexander Stagnell

Digital Diplomacy and International Organisations
Autonomy, Legitimacy and Contestation
Edited by Corneliu Bjola and Ruben Zaiotti

For more information about this series, please visit: https://www.routledge.com/Routledge-New-Diplomacy-Studies/book-series/RNDS

DIGITAL DIPLOMACY AND INTERNATIONAL ORGANISATIONS

Autonomy, Legitimacy and Contestation

Edited by Corneliu Bjola and Ruben Zaiotti

Routledge
Taylor & Francis Group

LONDON AND NEW YORK

First published 2021
by Routledge
2 Park Square, Milton Park, Abingdon, Oxon OX14 4RN

and by Routledge
52 Vanderbilt Avenue, New York, NY 10017

Routledge is an imprint of the Taylor & Francis Group, an informa business

British Library Cataloguing-in-Publication Data
A catalogue record for this book is available from the British Library

Library of Congress Cataloging-in-Publication Data
Names: Bjola, Corneliu, editor. | Zaiotti, Ruben, editor.
Title: Digital diplomacy and international organisations: autonomy, legitimacy and contestation/edited by Corneliu Bjola and Ruben Zaiotti.
Description: Abingdon, Oxon; New York, NY: Routledge, 2021. | Series: Routledge new diplomacy studies | Includes bibliographical references and index.
Identifiers: LCCN 2020023757 (print) | LCCN 2020023758 (ebook) | ISBN 9780367470012 (hardback) | ISBN 9780367469993 (paperback) | ISBN 9781003032724 (ebook)
Subjects: LCSH: International agencies. | Communication in international relations. | Internet and international relations. | Social media–Political aspects. | Diplomacy–Technological innovations.
Classification: LCC JZ4850 .D546 2021 (print) | LCC JZ4850 (ebook) | DDC 352.3/842110285–dc23
LC record available at https://lccn.loc.gov/2020023757
LC ebook record available at https://lccn.loc.gov/2020023758

ISBN: 978-0-367-47001-2 (hbk)
ISBN: 978-0-367-46999-3 (pbk)
ISBN: 978-1-003-03272-4 (ebk)

Typeset in Bembo
by Deanta Global Publishing Services, Chennai, India

CONTENTS

FIGURES

TABLES

CONTRIBUTORS

Corneliu Bjola is Associate Professor in Diplomatic Studies at the University of Oxford and Head of the Oxford Digital Diplomacy Research Group. He also serves as a Faculty Fellow at the Center on Public Diplomacy at the University of Southern California and as a Professorial Lecturer at the Diplomatic Academy of Vienna. His research focuses on the impact of digital technology on the conduct of diplomacy with a focus on strategic communication, digital influence, data analytics, and methods for countering digital propaganda. He has authored or edited six books, including the twin volumes on *Countering Online Propaganda and Violent Extremism: The Dark Side of Digital Diplomacy* (2018) and *Digital Diplomacy: Theory and Practice* (2015). His work has been published in *the European Journal of International Relations*, *Review of International Studies*, *Ethics and International Affairs*, *International Negotiation*, *Cambridge Review of International Affairs*, *Global Policy*, *Journal of Global Ethics*, and *the Hague Journal of Diplomacy*.

Caroline Bouchard is an Assistant Professor in International Communication at the Université du Québec à Montréal (UQAM). She previously held a Research Fellow position at the University of Edinburgh, Scotland. She has worked on various research projects studying international organisations in the age of globalisation including Designing UN Women, and the MERCURY project – Multilateralism and the EU in the Contemporary Global Order. Her research experience is complemented by professional experiences at the Council of Europe (Strasbourg, France) and the International Development Research Centre (IDRC) (Ottawa, Canada). Her current research focuses on the United Nations in the digital age.

Matthias Ecker-Ehrhardt, Ph.D., is Visiting Professor for International Relations at Universität Leipzig. His research focuses on the politicisation of international organisations, public communication, and cosmopolitanism. Previous publication appeared in *International Studies Quarterly*, *Review of International Organizations*, *European Journal of International Relations*, *International Theory*, *International Political Science Review*, *Review of International Political Economy*, *Global Society*, *Zeitschrift für Internationale Beziehungen*, and *Politische Vierteljahresschrift*.

Nabeel Goheer is the Assistant Secretary-General at the Commonwealth Secretariat in London. He joined the organisation in December 2010, and provides leadership in the areas of strategy, governance, innovation, transformation, evaluation, and partnerships. He brings to the position 25 years of experience in development, democracy, diplomacy, and diversity promotion. Earlier, he worked with multilateral organisations such as the ILO, World Bank, UNDP, USAID, as well as the Government of Pakistan at senior levels. Nabeel holds a Ph.D. in Management from Cambridge Judge Business School. He is a Distinguished Fellow with the Hull University Business School and a Board Member of the International School of Government of Kings College London.

Natalia Grincheva is the Assistant Professor in the Department of Media at the National Research University "Higher School of Economics" in Moscow, Russia. She is also an Honorary Research Fellow at the Digital Studio of the University of Melbourne. She pursues her career in the field of digital humanities focusing on development of new computational methods to study museums as important players in creative economy and actors of soft power. Dr Grincheva is also a Lead CI and Conceptual Designer of the award-winning digital mapping system Museum Soft Power Map. She is holder of numerous academic awards and fellowships, including Fulbright (2007–2009), Quebec Fund (2011–2013), Australian Endeavour (2012–2013), SOROS (2013–2014), and others. She has successfully implemented a number of research projects on new forms of contemporary diplomacy developed by the largest internationally recognised museums in North America, Europe, and Asia-Pacific. Her publication profile includes over 30 research articles, book chapters, and reports published in prominent academic outlets. The most recent publications are two monographs: *Global Trends in Museum Diplomacy* (Routledge: 2019) and *Museum Diplomacy in the Digital Age* (Routledge: 2020).

Mike Habegger is an instructor and Ph.D. candidate in the Department of Political Science & International Relations at the University of Delaware. His research lies at the intersection of democracy and the internet, broadly, and social media practices and the concepts of subjectivity and the public sphere, specifically. His work is influenced by the democratic political theory, internet politics, political communication, and social movements literatures. He has co-authored work with Tobias Lemke that pushes his theoretical contribution to audiences in IR theory, specifically, the English School.

Matthias Hofferberth, Ph.D., is Associate Professor for Global Governance at the University of Texas at San Antonio. He is interested in non-state agency and the provision of order beyond nation-states. He has published two books on multinational enterprises in world politics as well as several articles in journals such as *International Studies Review*, *Journal of International Relations and Development*, *Millennium: Journal of International Studies*, *Business and Politics*, *Global Society*, and *Palgrave Communications*. Dr Hofferberth regularly teaches courses on global governance, international organisations, and related themes.

Michał Krzyżanowski holds a Chair in Media and Communication Studies at Uppsala University, Sweden as well as a research appointment as a Chair in Communication & Media at the University of Liverpool, UK. In 2018–2019 he was also Albert Bonnier Jr. Guest Professor in Media Studies at Stockholm University, Sweden. Michał is one of the leading international experts in critical discourse studies of media, political, and organisational communication. His key research interests are in discursive dynamics of right-wing populism, diachronic analyses of constructions of crisis in European and transnational media, and the role of discourse in organisational communication and institutional change in Europe. He is the Editor-in-Chief of the *Journal of Language and Politics* and a Co-editor of the *Bloomsbury Advances in Critical Discourse Studies* book series.

Tobias Lemke is Instructor of Political Science and International Relations at the University of Delaware. He is also the Program Coordinator for Faculty Development and Assessment at the English Language Institute's Academic Transition Program, where he teaches courses in Global Politics to international students preparing to matriculate at the University of Delaware. His research focuses on the intersection of domestic politics and foreign policy with a special focus on how nationalist movements and parties can shape international relations and order. He has also written about the role of collective identity, strategic narratives, and digital communication networks in both historical and contemporary international relations, and he is currently working on several projects that examine the role of Russia-linked news outlets in the distribution of disinformation campaigns on social media platforms like Twitter. His most recent article has been published in *International Relations*.

Ilan Manor is a digital diplomacy scholar at the University of Oxford. His research focuses on the use of digital platforms during times of geopolitical crises. His book *The Digitalization of Public Diplomacy* was published in 2019 by Palgrave Macmillan. He has contributed to *The Hague Journal of Diplomacy*, *Place Branding & Public Diplomacy*, *The Cambridge Review of International Affairs*, *Internet & Policy*, and *Media, War & Conflict*.

Ruben Zaiotti, Ph.D. Toronto, MSt Oxford, B.A. Bologna is Jean Monnet Chair in Public Diplomacy, Director of the European Union Centre of Excellence and Associate Professor in the Political Science department at Dalhousie University (Halifax, Nova Scotia). His main areas of interest are European Union politics, social media and public diplomacy, border control and immigration policy, and transatlantic relations. Ruben Zaiotti is the author of the monograph *Cultures of Border Control: Schengen and the Evolution of European Frontiers* with University of Chicago Press and editor of books on language and globalisation and on migration policy. He has published articles for *Review of International Studies*, *European Security*, *Journal of European Integration*, *Journal of Borderland Studies*, *International Journal of Refugee Law*.

ACKNOWLEDGEMENTS

The present volume is based on contributions at a workshop held at Dalhousie University (Halifax, Canada) on April 24, 2019. The event was hosted by Dalhousie University's Jean Monnet European Union Centre of Excellence (JMEUCE) and the Jean Monnet Chair in Public Diplomacy. We would like to thank all the workshop participants and those who contributed to the organisation of the event. A special mention goes to the workshop coordinators, Madeleine Coffen-Smout and Alanna Taylor. Their professionalism and dedication were instrumental in making the event a success. We are also grateful to the graduate students who helped before and during the event: Nafisa Abdulhamid, Amy MacKenzie, and Ksenia Mykula. This project was made possible thanks to the generous financial contribution of the European Union' Erasmus+ Programme and the institutional support provided by Dalhousie University. Corneliu Bjola is grateful to the Department of International Development at the University of Oxford for granting him two sabbatical terms to conduct research, including for this project. Lastly, special thanks to the editorial team at Routledge, including Bethany Lund-Yates and Andrew Humphrys, who provided excellent support and guidance throughout the publication process. In addition, we would like to thank the three anonymous reviewers whose useful criticisms and constructive suggestions helped strengthen the volume.

Ruben Zaiotti and Corneliu Bjola
Halifax and Oxford

1

GOING DIGITAL

Choices and challenges for
international organisations

Corneliu Bjola and Ruben Zaiotti

Introduction

The global spread of new digital communication technologies has profoundly
transformed the way individuals, states and businesses operate and interact with
the outside world. The present volume explores the impact of digital technologies, with a focus on social media, for one of the major actors in international
affairs, namely international organisations (IOs). IOs such as the European
Union, the Commonwealth Association, and the United Nations have increasingly embraced social media as tools to manage their internal and external communication. Whether as organisations or as individuals representing them, IOs
have established an active digital presence on the most popular social media platforms, from Twitter to Facebook and Instagram. In turn, a growing number of
private users and groups around the world are virtually engaging with IOs, following their social media accounts, sharing information about them, and commenting on their actions. As a result of these developments, IO bureaucracies,
which until recently have been perceived as rather obscure and impenetrable,
have become more visible and "sociable" on the global digital stage.

Due to their rapid spread and potential impact on the management of global
affairs, digital technologies have started to attract the attention of International
Relations scholars (Jackson 2018; Carpenter and Drezner 2010; Copeland 2013;
Bjola and Holmes 2015; Hocking and Melissen 2015; Pamment 2016). These
scholars recognise that the dynamics that characterise the current "global information age" (Simmons 2011), an era defined by "the ability of individuals to
create, transfer, and access information *globally*" (ibid, 595, emphasis added), have
created new opportunities for international actors to enhance their power on
the international stage. Simply put, digital technologies are perceived to act as
"influence amplifiers," helping governments and IOs to increase their diplomatic

clout in a manner that they might not otherwise be able to achieve. Social media, as a popular form of communication, enhance these opportunities thanks to their global reach and ability to connect a broad spectrum of private and public actors (Ghannam 2011, 6).

One of the most promising areas of research on the role of social media in international politics is the emerging subfield of "digital diplomacy," which has been broadly defined as the use of social media for diplomatic purposes (Bjola and Holmes 2015, 4). Studies on digital diplomacy have examined how political leaders and foreign policy officials use new technologies to increase their engagement with foreign audiences, highlighting how social media platforms have become an influential foreign policy tool (Khatib, Dutton and Thelwall 2012). These works show that the adoption of digital technologies has transformed the traditional practices of diplomacy, especially those involving communication with local stakeholders (or what is known as "public diplomacy"; Melissen 2005; Cull 2019). With social media, public diplomacy is no longer restricted to the relay of information, promising instead "the interactive construction and leveraging of long-lasting relationships with foreign publics" (Bjola and Jiang 2015; Kampf et al. 2015). With the emergence of digital diplomacy, foreign policy officials have become directly involved in the shaping of public opinion and advocacy activities. The digital diplomacy literature has also examined the role that social media has had in shaping national images and "brands," and the efforts that democratic and authoritarian regimes have deployed to manage their country's reputation on the world stage (Manor and Segev 2015; Bulovsky 2019).

By focusing on foreign affairs ministries and officials, the digital diplomacy literature has thus far analysed the role of social media in world politics through the prism of states and their interactions (Pelling 2016; Hocking and Melissen 2015; Spry 2019). The state-centrism of research on digital diplomacy is apparent from the dearth of studies on IOs and other actors digitally active on the world stage, such as NGOs (Seo et al. 2009; Thrall et al. 2014; Pagovski 2015; Hocking and Melissen 2015). The literature on digital diplomacy has also paid less attention to the organisational implications of the emergence of new communicative technologies for international politics. These issues have been addressed more explicitly by works in the field of Communication and Media Studies (Watson and Hill 2015), and, more specifically, the subfield of Organisational Communication (Livingstone and Lievrouw 2006). This literature emphasises how social media are part of a "communications technology revolution" that has "redefined the relationship between producers and receivers of online information" (Carpenter and Drezner 2010, 256).

One of the key insights of this scholarship is the recognition that the flow of information is a source of power (Marlin-Bennett 2013). This insight is valid for social media as well. Social media, as tools of direct communication, allow for circumventing traditional media organisations, thus providing more control over public communication (Van Dijck and Poell 2013). Social media also inspire organisations to articulate network connections within and outside their boundaries (DeNardis and Hackl 2015, 762; Jackson 2018). The organisational communication literature also highlights how the impact of digital technologies for organisations is not limited to its public relations dimension. Social media influence the functioning of organisations in all the phases of the policy-making process, from agenda-setting to decision-making, planning, implementation and policy evaluation (Bjola 2017; Bjola and Ren 2019).

While mainly focused on the role of communication in "domestic" settings, the organisational communication literature has branched out to examine "global" communicative dynamics beyond national borders (Thussu 2009/2018; Alleyne 2016; Murphy et al. 2003). When IOs have been explicitly addressed, however, the focus has been until recently on the role of traditional media and communication tools (Gilboa 2005; Dimitrov 2014; Risso 2014). Works in this field have started to expand to include IOs' use of digital technologies, highlighting the growing role of social media within these organisations' public relations strategies (see, for instance, Ecker-Ehrhardt 2018b; Dimitrov 2014; Corrie 2015) and their "operational" functions in crisis management situations and the provision of public services (e.g. disaster relief; Gao et al. 2011).

These works, however, are not yet part of a coherent research program and lack systematicity. Moreover, there is still limited engagement with debates occurring within the International Relations-inspired literature on digital diplomacy; despite the apparent overlap in terms of themes addressed in both literatures, these bodies of scholarly work have not been in dialogue with each other yet. In bringing together these two literatures, the present volume seeks to fill the gaps in the existing literature by offering a theoretically grounded and empirically driven analysis of the impact and implications of the emergence of digital technologies as communicative tools for international organisations. The volume's premise is that IOs' engagement with social media, while sharing some of the experiences of other "domestic" public and private organisations (e.g. national governments, NGOs), raises a series of unique theoretical and empirical questions about the role of communication, technology, and power in global affairs, questions that to date have not been the object of in-depth academic scrutiny (Jackson 2018).

These questions, in turn, stem from some of IOs' key distinguishing features as organisations and the context in which these entities operate, namely the international system. IOs, like other public organisations, are complex bureaucratic structures of different sizes and resources that operate according to specific decision- and policy-making procedures. What distinguishes IOs as public organisations is their status as semi-autonomous entities created to address specific common global problems, and that operate in a setting (the international system) characterised by the lack of central authority (Simmons and Martin 2002). The following sections elaborate on these issues, focussing on four analytical themes that will inform the contributions to this volume: 1) the nature of the IOs' "digital universe"; 2) IOs and digital autonomy; 3) IOs and digital legitimacy; and 4) IOs and digital contestation.

International organisations' "digital universe"

The first theme addressed in the volume relates to the structure and dynamics that characterise IOs' presence on social media. The broad reach of IOs' presence and activities means that the community of social media users engaging with IOs is global, and it encompasses a multitude of individuals and groups that are active both within and outside these organisations around the world. This global network involves a multitude of users and accounts active both within and outside these organisations. Within IOs, accounts are run by secretariats, agencies, member states' delegations, and by staff members in their personal capacity. Outside IOs, the network comprises accounts run by various stakeholders such as NGOs with consultative status, pressure groups, companies, individual citizens (journalists, experts, advocacy organisations, corporate lobbies) in countries around the world. These actors play different roles and have different influences on IOs' social media communication practices. In the organisational studies language, these actors function either as "gatekeepers" or "liaisons" or "bridges," depending on whether they mediate interactions with the outside world or convey communication upward within the organisation (Thussu 2018). The ongoing digital communication that occurs among these actors create the IOs' global network. This network's spatial configuration, "thickness," and location of major "nodes" vary due to IOs' different sizes and degree of presence and penetration on social media, the activity of its users, and the salience of the global issue IOs are addressing at a particular time.

This unique configuration of the IOs' digital universe is reflected in the structure, form, and content of the communicative practices that take place within it. These practices take place between organisations, downward from the organisation to the stakeholders, and upward from stakeholders to the organisation (Mumby and Kuhn 2018). These practices can take different forms (textual and/or visual) depending on the platform used (e.g. tweets, FB posts), and their content can be either formal or informal. The informality of communication is one of the most significant innovations of social media for IOs, as these entities have traditionally been quite cautious and restrained in their external communication. As Cornut states (2019):

> Traditionally, diplomats are expected to uphold a certain level of decorum, but this tweet crosses the boundaries of propriety. In the digital era, it is socially acceptable to present information in non-formal ways on social media as long as the message is clever and – to the point ... The ability for a diplomat to have a cheeky/clever outlook on current events has a positive effect as it aids in promoting his/her country's position. Not only does a clever response effectively summarize complicated events, making it easier for regular citizens to understand, but its humorous nature also contributes to the popularity of the Tweet itself – resulting in a more widespread message.

Besides mapping IOs' digital universe, the volume also seeks to examine its origins and evolution. The exponential rise and expansion of IOs' reliance on social media raise questions about the rationales and the conditions under which international organisations have adopted and used social media. One of the most prominent arguments is that IOs have become digitally active because of the mimicking of norms and practices developed within domestic politics and outside (Cho 2014, 381). In this reading, IOs are replicating what other public and private organisations have been doing domestically in their public relations efforts. Another potential reason for why social media have become so popular in IOs is the result of the emerging trend towards the personalisation of international politics and diplomacy (another example of "spilling over" from domestic politics; see Marlin-Bennett 2013), a trend that has emphasised the role of the personal(ised) communication in promoting a particular message on behalf of an organisation. In the IO's context, this is encapsulated in the rise of the phenomenon of "celebrity IO ambassadors" (Adler-Nissen 2016).

These arguments about IOs' digitalisation, however, do not take into account that bureaucratic organisations are unlikely to invest resources in a new communication strategy without a modicum of planning and assessment of its value and impact, and without the structures in place to manage new digitally based initiatives. Indeed, over the last decades, IOs have enhanced and professionalised organisational capacities for public communication (Ecker-Ehrhardt 2018a). The role of new media has become prominent in IOs' communication strategies, and additional resources have been deployed to reinforce IOs' digital presence. How different IOs have implemented these strategies, however, has not been examined in depth. Moreover, while social media have been hailed as having a positive impact on private and public organisations in terms of meeting their mandates and performing their functions (Collins and Bekenova 2019; Sandre 2015), less is known about their impact on IOs. This volume assesses whether and how social media have improved the ways in which IOs work, make decisions, and engage with stakeholders. At the same time, it also questions whether digital tools are providing added value to IOs' communication strategy and diplomatic practices, or whether, instead, they might hinder them.

Addressing these questions, Matthias Ecker-Ehrhardt argues in Chapter 2 that the widespread use of social media opens entirely new opportunities for international organisations to directly communicate with and engage an increasingly aware and assertive public. Using a time-series cross-section regression methodology for a stratified-random sample of 49 IO accounts on Facebook and Twitter, Ecker-Ehrhardt finds that the application of social media for public communication purposes is informed by multiple factors. First, external contestation and the opening of IO bodies for representatives of transnational civil society is strongly associated with the adoption of social media, which suggests an underlying imperative for self-legitimation. Secondly, organisational mandates shape IOs' demands for social media, for example, by calling for the direct implementation of multiple policy programs on the ground. Lastly, centralised public communication also facilitates the adoption and extensive use of social media.

In Chapter 3, Michał Krzyżanowski addresses the question of how IOs accommodate and integrate digital technologies into their analogue patterns of public communication. The chapter looks at how social/online media – using the example of Twitter – were used by the European Union for communication at a critical time (2014–2015), when the organisation faced multiple crises and was in acute need of effectively engaging with the European demos. Proposing a critical discourse framework for the analysis of the politico-organisational use of Twitter, the chapter shows that the new digital platforms did foster change or "modernisation" of EU political communication patterns. At the same time, social media helped sustain some of the deep-seated dispositions of EU communicative and organisational practices as well as political discourses. As deployed by the EU's – and specifically by the European Commission's – spokesperson service, social media helped solidify some controversial patterns of EU political communication.

In Chapter 4, Natalia Grincheva examines the efforts undertaken by the International Council of Museums (ICOM), a non-governmental international organisation under formal relations with UNESCO, to update its mandate and restructure itself. To this end, the chapter focuses on the case of the 2019 online global crowdsourcing campaign that ICOM launched in the search for a new museum definition capable of bridging internal divides and political expectations regarding the future role of the organisation. Employing content analysis, Grincheva's research examines the multitude of museum definitions submitted to the ICOM platform from different corners of the world and demonstrates how digital activities have collided with traditional procedures and bureaucracies of large international organisations. The case is important as it offers valuable insight into the role of digital technologies in facilitating vs undermining democratic systems of global governance.

International organisations and digital autonomy

The second theme that the volume addresses concerns the role that social media plays in shaping international organisations' autonomy as actors on the international stage (Haftel and Thompson 2006, 255). In the case of IOs, autonomy is "the ability to operate in a manner that is insulated from the influence of other political actors – especially states" (Haftel and Thompson 2006, 256, Kenneth Abbott and Duncan Snidal 1998, 9). Since states create, support, and direct IOs, the latter's independence is, by design, constrained. IOs nonetheless can make autonomous decisions and have a degree of discretion in their actions (Barnett and Finnemore 2004). Moreover, since the 1990s, IOs have expanded their authority and, as a result, the scope of their activities (Hooghe and Marks 2015; Zürn, Binder, and Ecker-Ehrhardt 2012, 107–112). This trend, which has started to reverse more recently, is to a large extent the result of states' growing willingness to delegate their power, which involves the offloading of control of fundamental tenets of the policy-making process at the international level, including agenda setting, decision-making, implementation, and enforcement (Haftel and Thompson 2006, 256).

Communication, and new media in particular, is playing an increasingly central role in facilitating and, in some cases, expanding IOs' autonomy. This state of affairs is due to the way IOs exercise and project their power. IOs' power can take different forms, but it is typically not direct. IOs do not dictate their will or rules on other international actors; instead, they tend to act as "orchestrators" (Abbot et al. 2015). Orchestration entails the use of persuasion and incentives, and the reliance on intermediaries (e.g. NGOs), which are induced to collaborate in achieving a particular goal or in shaping the policy process. An international organisation's ability to be a successful orchestrator is premised on the existence and projection of a unique and coherent corporate identity vis-à-vis relevant stakeholders (Cho 2014; Mumby and Kuhn 2018). A corporate identity refers to the consistent and durable set of values that an organisation possesses, and that differentiates it from other entities. IOs develop a corporate identity by building a "narrative" about who they are and what they represent, a narrative that is typically outlined in internal strategic documents, and it is articulated publicly by their official representatives.

IOs' identities, however, are not static, and they are shaped by an organisation's interaction with its environment (Cho 2014, 377). In turn, over time, IOs adjust their original identity to reflect the (sometimes negative) feedback they receive from their environment (Cho 2014, 378). NATO's communication strategy, for instance, has evolved as a result of its alleged "image problem," stemming from the perception in the popular imagination of being a "global policeman," "a tool of the U.S. to achieve its end," and "an unnecessary post-Cold war leftover" (Pagovski 2015, 13). As they have done for private companies, social media have provided an invaluable tool to IOs to collect information about themselves and to reformulate their identity narratives accordingly, making them potentially more effective and coherent.

Crucial in the exercise of "soft" power is the role of communication, as IOs need to proactively establish channels of communication, convey relevant information, and engage in dialogue with relevant stakeholders in their effort to cajole and persuade them to collaborate towards the achievement and implementation of IO-sponsored policy goals or initiatives. In this context, digital technologies have become a popular new "baton" deployed by IOs' officials to lead their orchestrating efforts. Social media, in particular, have expanded IOs' ability to exert their power by helping them define and consolidate their digital autonomy in different ways. First, by offering a platform to directly engage with stakeholders, thus circumventing official channels, especially if member states are involved. Second, by signalling their intentions, a particularly valuable feature during negotiations. Thirdly, by coordinating actions, especially with intermediaries during campaigns, but also for crisis management. Finally, by calling out stakeholders or shaming them in order to influence their behaviour. While social media platforms promote a more visible digital presence, their decentralised, informal, and personal nature, combined with their capacity to multiply the number of voices within IOs who speak on behalf of these organisations, means that the message they convey can come across as inconsistent and confusing, and, as a result, it weakens their efforts at projecting a coherent identity. In this way, social media can exacerbate an inherent tension that characterises and IO's identity, namely that between an IO's collective identity and states' individual identities (Cho 2014, 376).

The chapters in this section explore the different ways in which social media have become tools to promote IOs "brand-making" and considers whether these practices are consistent with those of other private and public organisations. The volume also assesses whether new digital tools provide a viable platform to increase IOs' digital autonomy vis à vis states, or whether they merely reproduce this subordinate relationship, thus testing the claim that "digital orchestration" helps IOs increase their power in international affairs.

In Chapter 5, Caroline Bouchard investigates how and to what extent the introduction and adoption of new digital communication and information technologies (ICTs) have affected UN processes. Changes have been observed both in the ways UN actors interact within the organisation and the ways the organisation communicates with external audiences. Drawing from the International Relations (IR) literature on UN processes, studies on new media, and research on the diffusion of innovations theory, the chapter presents results from a case study analysis that focuses on a key UN entity: the Department of Global Communications of the UN Secretariat. Bouchard argues that digital ICTs have affected three UN processes: rules of procedures, strategic interactions, and informal relationships. The chapter shows how specific UN actors played key roles in the integration and diffusion of digital tools in the UN process. It also contends that new digital ICTs have created unintended and undesirable consequences for the organisation that the UN has to grapple with.

Noting that IOs were established during the height of the industrial age, in Chapter 6 Nabeel Goheer examines four challenges – relevance, efficiency, effectiveness, and visibility – that have haunted international organisations since the dawn of the digital era. As bureaucracies, IOs were designed and tuned by their political masters to respond to the exigencies of the industrial age that worked like a CLOCK – Complicated, Logical, Ordered, Closed, and Kinetic. They have struggled to adapt to the digital reality, which is Complex, Large, Open, Unpredictable, and Dynamic (CLOUD). Drawing on the case of the Commonwealth Secretariat's digital transformation journey since 2015, the chapter discusses the strategic, structural, and systemic shifts that have helped morph the organisation from a bureaucracy to a network by unleashing its digital power in the form of data, display, delivery, and discovery. The chapter provides ex ante assessment and ex post evaluation of the digital reform process, and makes a case that a networked redesign, an innovative outreach, interoperable processes, and value-creating visibility are the digital ways to recalibrate IOs' autonomy in a CLOUD world.

International organisations and digital legitimacy

The volume's third theme relates to the role of social media in boosting (or undermining) IOs' legitimacy. Like other public organisations, IOs need legitimacy, namely a set "beliefs of audiences that an IO's authority is appropriately exercised" (Tallberg and Zürn 2019, 4) in order to perform their functions effectively. Stakeholders' support (or lack thereof) determines the degree of IOs' relevance as primary forums where global problems are addressed (Morse and Keohane 2014). This support also influences the ability of IOs to introduce and implement new policies and ensure compliance with legal and normative commitments (Sommerer and Agné 2018). Moreover, legitimacy helps IOs counter the charge that they lack fundamental democratic credentials (Held and Koenig-Archibugi 2005). With few exceptions (e.g. the European Union's elected parliament), IOs do not formally obtain their legitimacy directly from citizens, as is the case with other public organisations at the national level.

Because of the lack of direct, bottom-up sources of legitimisation, IOs typically rely on the assessment of their "output," namely what they do, and how, to determine their legitimacy (Steffek 2015). IOs' output is, in turn, evaluated based on how they are perceived to conform to established procedural and performance standards (Tallberg and Zürn 2019, 18). Procedural standards refer to features such as efficiency, legality, and expertise. Performance standards refer to effectiveness but also the protection of democratic rights and processes. The latter element points to the fact that IOs are not just technocratic entities created to solve common problems, but also carry a more normative mandate (Tallberg and Zürn 2019, 19). Whether it is assessed based on procedural or performative standards, IOs' legitimacy is never constant, as it changes depending on the particular audience and timeframe (ibid., 9).

Since IOs have traditionally been shielded from popular scrutiny, until recently their legitimacy has been relatively invisible as a subject in public and academic debates. Of late, however, attention to their actions has increased, and, as a result, IOs have become more sensitive about their public perceptions and more active in seeking support from stakeholders. These stakeholders – be it within the organisation or outside – can increase the support for IOs through a series of "legitimation practices" (Gronau and Schmidtke 2015).[1] These practices are inscribed in official texts and public statements, and they include "public justifications of institutional reforms, framing of IO policies, use of value-laden symbols, and other rhetorical measures aimed at nurturing beliefs in the legitimacy of an IO" (Tallberg and Zürn 2019, 13). The form these legitimation practices takes is communicative since it involves the relaying of information to an audience (ibid., 9).

As a popular means of communication, social media represent a novel and authoritative source for the discursive practices of legitimation involving IOs

(Denskus and Esser 2013). These digital practices can range from individual posts to full-fledged social media campaigns. IOs can actively employ social media to improve their image among targeted audiences. By communicating directly with these audiences, IOs have the opportunity to showcase their accomplishments and signal their continuing relevance. At the same time, social media offer a channel for audiences to engage directly with IOs and express their opinions on these organisations. The content of these opinions can, in turn, be used by IOs to adjust their narrative.

As an interactive platform to engage citizens, social media can represent a democratic tool that fosters a more open, inclusive, and participatory policy process involving IOs. Social media can increase IOs' accountability, as they "facilitate the articulation of complaints and grievances" (Buchanan and Keohane 2006). By directly reaching their targeted audience, social media also increase the ability of IOs "to effectively raise public awareness for global problems, publicly shame governments for not complying with international commitments teach norms and knowledge to citizens," obviating for the lack of "hard" power (Pamment 2016). This volume expands on these themes to explore how social media influence IOs' legitimacy and the challenges IOs face in their efforts to boost their digital legitimacy.

Looking at the UN and its use of Twitter, in Chapter 7 Matthias Hofferberth advances a theoretical account of how international organisations use social media to reach out to their potentially global constituencies and maintain their legitimacy as global governors. Drawing on the normative dimension of Habermas' theory of communicative action and its applications in International Relations, the chapter examines how different stakeholders and actors, both individual and institutional, within and towards this global organisation communicate through tweets. More specifically, Hofferberth employs qualitative content analysis of UN tweets from the 73rd UN Session in 2018 to reconstruct the UN Twittersphere and to determine how and whether this global organisation engages its public audience. He also assesses the communicative action potential of this engagement with the purpose of articulating a new line of normatively informed IO research on digital communication. In so doing, the chapter calls attention to the understated normative dimension of digital technologies in shaping public perceptions of the legitimacy of IO actions and activities.

Ilan Manor's chapter connects the question of IO legitimacy to the ability of member states to use IO's fora to enhance their digital influence relative to their peers. To this end, he examines how digital diplomacy provides opportunities for diplomatic actors lacking in material resources to overcome prestige deficits. The study adapts approaches used in earlier studies to calculate the material and ideational components of diplomatic prestige to the online sphere – in terms of presence, centrality, and reputation. By analysing the Twitter accounts of 67 foreign ministries and 33 United Nations missions, he finds that the traditional markers of diplomatic prestige do not automatically translate online and that significant effort is required to maintain prestige in online diplomatic networks. He also finds that the flexibility and transience of online networks do allow diplomatic actors a degree of prestige mobility. Nations with limited diplomatic networks may use Twitter networks to gather information from their peers, thus anticipating policy changes or shocks to the international system. Moreover, nations may attract many of their peers on Twitter, enabling them to assess possible objections to their own policy agenda. Hence, this study is highly significant for understanding how prestige is managed and strategically influenced in digital diplomacy and the extent to which this competition for online prestige may indirectly contribute to the legitimacy of IOs.

In Chapter 9, Ruben Zaiotti examines the role that social media plays in shaping international organisations' reputation in international affairs, using the European Union and its handling of the refugee crisis as a case study. To study reputation, Zaiotti adopts what in organisation theory is called an "outside in" approach (Manning et al. 2012). In this perspective, the main source to determine an organisation's reputation is the feedback from individuals not affiliated with the organisation, rather than just what the organisation says about itself. Moreover, to redress the existing literature's reliance on traditional media as sources of data, the chapter focuses on how the European Union's reputation is built and evolves on social media. The findings of this study show that the impact of the refugee crisis on the EU's reputation is more nuanced than it has been presented in existing accounts. First, the EU's reputation was only marginally tarnished, if at all. Second, the crisis, while challenging the Union's reputation, has simultaneously increased the organisation's salience and visibility to the global public, thus contributing to the strengthening of its identity as independent actor on the world stage. Crucially, this outcome has occurred despite the lack of efforts on the part of the EU to pro-actively manage its reputation online.

International organisations and digital contestation

The fourth theme in the volume has to do with the role of social media in challenging IOs' authority and how IOs may respond to these challenges. IOs' recent growth in authority has increased their visibility, and with it, the potential for criticism and politicisation (Zürn et al. 2012; Ecker-Ehrhardt 2018b). As a popular means of expressing opinions, social media have become a powerful tool of political contestation. This state of affairs is true for IOs as well. Social media can be deployed to monitor IOs performance and keep IOs accountable. They can, for instance, highlight mismanagement or scandals. IOs can be publicly challenged because their conception of the public interest is outdated, or because their claim to public interest orientation itself has become doubtful (for instance, through charges of corruption). This contestation can take the form of actions against IOs, such as street demonstrations (Gregoratti and Uhlin 2018). For the most part, however, they are discursive, such as NGOs "publicly criticizing IOs for being undemocratic or for pursuing policies that make the poor worse off, as well as state representatives criticizing IOs for unfair decision-making proce-dures" (Tallberg and Zürn 2019, 15).

Contestation of IOs can also involve more malicious efforts. In an era of real or alleged "fake news," social media have increasingly become the target of criti-cism because of their (mis)use by political agents with a mission to manipulate public opinion (Gronau and Schmidtke 2015). These practices include digital disinformation campaigns and trolling (Bjola and Pamment 2018). Social media have also been used for surveillance and repression (Trottier 2016). Whether because of their mandate and activities, which could impinge on an actor's core interests (be it state or a terrorist group) or because of ideological reasons, IOs have become a target of this digital warfare, and they are likely to face a more significant number of digital threats in the future.

The chapters in this section explore the benign and malign ways in which social media have contributed to IOs' contestation and their impact on IOs' del-egitimation. They also look at IOs' responses. When faced with open contesta-tion, IOs, like other organisations in similar situations, are compelled to respond to avoid further negative backlash, and their task is to rebuild the trust of their audience. IOs thus move from routine to crisis mode of governance (Smith and Elliot 2007, 348–52). Responding to critical situations is particularly needed for organisations such as IOs since they rely heavily on output legitimacy. Yet, the core component for a successful response to a crisis is to focus on its communica-tion strategy, which involves being open to external feedback and adjustments of actions to reflect the public mood (Steffek 2015, 275). Indeed, there is evidence to suggest that contestation has led IOs to prioritise public communication (e.g. NATO's Information Service, Risso 2014), but much less is known about how digital contestation manifests itself in the case of IOs, with what results, and what type of strategies of digital response could prove most effective to contain the more malign effects of digital contestation.

Addressing these questions, Lemke and Habegger point out in Chapter 10 that diplomacy rests on the idea that a limited number of vetted actors interacts with one another while following a strict set of behavioural rules. In contrast, digital communication is driven by almost countless numbers of actors—many of whom remain anonymous—who interact irregularly and without much oversight or rules to guide their interactions. Their chapter thus argues that the diplomatic and digital practice represent two distinct systems of political communication, which differ not only in scope (i.e., the number of participants) and process (i.e., how these participants interact), but have produced two very different commu-nicative *logics*. For diplomacy, this is the amelioration of international conflict by peaceful means. Digital communication, in contrast, thrives on affect (i.e., grati-fication) and emotion (i.e., outrage). To test these claims, the authors analyse the Twitter activity of NATO and the Russia embassy in the U.K. They find that @NATO and @RussianEmbassy are not only engaged in quite distinct activi-ties online, but the latter's tendency to espouse a much more contentious and outrageous style of communication suggests that Russian digital staff recognise the peculiarity of the digital communication environment and are willing to take full advantage of it despite (or maybe because of) the damage it can do to diplomatic relations.

In Chapter 11, Corneliu Bjola notes that, in the past decade, digital disinformation has become the tactic of choice for many state and non-state actors simply because the gains of engaging in such a practice are perceived to far outweigh any possible risks. Amidst these developments, a glaring gap of significant relevance for the already besieged liberal international order continues to be overlooked in the academic literature: the use of digital disinformation in multilateral contexts, especially against international organisations. To bridge this gap, the chapter draws on the case of the disinformation campaign against the UN Global Compact for Migration (UNGCM) and argues that the potential challenge the UN and IOs, in general, may face as a result of digital disinformation is "manufactured delegitimation." Drawing on Twitter data collected between September 2018 and January 2019, the study shows that the disinformation campaign against the Global Compact has been successful in shifting public attention away from the UN's agenda, increasing epistemic confusion about the objectives and provisions of the Global Compact, but without causing a negative escalation of attacks on the UN institution as a whole. The study also calls attention to the empirical difficulties researchers may face when trying to distinguish between legitimate political contestation and disinformation, hence the need for identifying reliable metrics (e.g., corrupted tactics, polarised themes, toxic escalations) for unpacking the unique pathways by which digital disinformation may help engineer legitimacy crises for international organisations.

The volume concludes, in the final chapter, with a discussion of the digital blind spots that IOs may develop and which could prevent them from taking full advantage of the opportunities of digital transformation or, by case, from protecting themselves from the inevitable challenges generated by this process. Epistemic blind spots pose a problem for decision-making as they imply that certain courses of action could be taken without those affected being able to assess the full implications of the available information. Decision-makers may thus miss important signals, form a distorted view of the unfolding events, delay their reactions, or draw the wrong lessons from their experience. IOs are particularity vulnerable to developing weak and strong digital blind spots since the main features of the process of digital transformation (data, intensity, speed, and sustainability) are not easy to reconcile with the traditional ways by which IOs operate. However, if international organisations manage to overcome their blind spots, then there is a real possibility for them to become full-fledged "digital organisations" based on the same core principles that underlie digital technologies themselves: built around personnel with the ability to self-manage and to operate within a non-hierarchical chain of command, relying on resources that are collectively owned and shared among its members, and adopting rules and infrastructures that encourage connections and collaboration among their members, both internally and externally.

To conclude, the volume brings together a multidisciplinary group of scholars and practitioners to tackle important questions regarding the impact of digital technologies in international affairs and to explore the current debates surrounding IOs' use of social media and the future of digital diplomacy. These different disciplinary perspectives offer a nuanced and textured understanding of the multifaceted, complex, and ever-evolving nature of the phenomenon under investigation and highlight its wide-ranging policy implications. These contributions combine engaging theoretical insights with newly compiled empirical material that is analysed using an eclectic set of methodological approaches (e.g., multivariate regression network analysis, content analysis, sentiment analysis). The combination of empirical and theoretical insights thus provides a solid analytical foundation for policy-relevant prescriptions concerning the use of digital technologies by international organisations in their multilateral engagements.

Note

1 Legitimation practices are those involving "actors deliberately seek(ing) to make a political institution more legitimate, by boosting beliefs that its rule is exercised appropriately" (Tallberg and Zürn, 2019: 9).

References

Abbott, K. W., and D. Snidal. "Why States Act through Formal International Organizations." *Journal of Conflict Resolution* 42, no. 1 (1998): 3–32.

Abbott, K.W., P. Genschel, D. Snidal, and B. Zangl. *International Organizations as Orchestrators*. Cambridge: Cambridge University Press, 2015.

Adler-Nissen, R. "Diplomatic Agency." In *The Sage Handbook of Diplomacy*, edited by C.M. Constantinou, P. Kerr, and P. Sharp. London: Sage, 2016.

Alleyne, M. *International Power and International Communication*. Houndmills, Basingstoke, Hampshire: Macmillan, 1995.

Alleyne, M.D. *International Power and International Communication*. London: MacMillan, 2016.

Barnett, M., and M. Finnemore. *Rules for the World: International Organizations in Global Politics*. 1st ed. Ithaca, NY: Cornell University Press, 2004.

Bauer, M., Christoph Knill, and Steffen Eckhard. *International Bureaucracy: Challenges and Lessons for Public Administration Research*. London: Palgrave Macmillan, 2017.

Bjola, C., and M. Holmes. *Digital Diplomacy: Theory and Practice*. Abingdon: Routledge New Diplomacy Studies, 2015.

Bjola, C., and L. Jiang. "Social Media and Public Diplomacy: A Comparative Analysis of the Digital Diplomatic Strategies of the EU, US and Japan in China." In *Digital Diplomacy: Theory and Practice*, edited by Corneliu Bjola, and Marcus Holmes, 71–88. Abingdon and New York: Routledge, 2015.

Bjola, Corneliu. "Adapting Diplomacy to the Digital Age: Managing the Organisational Culture of Ministries of Foreign Affairs." 2017. https://www.swp-berlin.org/fil eadmin/contents/products/arbeitspapiere/WP_Diplomacy21_No9_Corneliu_Bjola _01.pdf.

Bjola, Corneliu, and James Pamment. *Countering Online Propaganda and Extremism: The Dark Side of Digital Diplomacy.* Abingdon and New York: Routledge, 2018.

Bjola, Corneliu, and Yuanzhe Ren. "Digitization and the Transformation of Contemporary Diplomacy – Based on the Perspective of Organizational Culture Theory." *Foreign Affairs Review* 1 (2019): 1–27. doi:10.13569 / j.cnki.far.2019.01 .001.

Buchanan, A., and R.O. Keohane. "The Legitimacy of Global Governance Institutions." *Ethics & International Affairs* 20, no. 4 (2006): 405–37.

Bulovsky, A. "Authoritarian Communication on Social Media: The Relationship Between Democracy and Leaders' Digital Communicative Practices." *International Communication Gazette* 81, no. 1 (2019): 20–45.

Busch, P.O., and A. Liese. "The Authority of International Public Administrations." In *International Bureaucracy. Public Sector Organizations*, edited by M. Bauer, C. Knill, and S. Eckhard. London: Palgrave Macmillan, 2017.

Carpenter, C., and D.W. Drezner. "International Relations 2.0: The Implications of New Media for an Old Profession." *International Studies Perspectives* 11, no. 3 (2010): 255–72.

Cho, S. "An International Organization's Identity Crisis." *Northwestern Journal of International Law & Business* 34, no. 3 (2014): 359–93.

Collins, Neil, and Kristina Bekenova. "Digital Diplomacy: Success at Your Fingertips." *Place Branding & Public Diplomacy* 15, no. 1 (2019): 1–11.

Copeland, D. "Digital Technology." In *The Oxford Handbook of Modern Diplomacy*, edited by A.F. Cooper, J. Heine, R. Thakur, and R. C. Thakur, Oxford: Oxford University Press, 2013.

Cornut, J. "Digital Diplomacy in Practice: Implications for IOs". *Paper Presented at the workshop Digital diplomacy going Global.* Halifax (NS): Dalhousie University, April 24 2019.

Corrie, Karen L. "The International Criminal Court: Using Technology in Network Diplomacy." In *Digital Diplomacy*, edited by Corneliu Bjola, and Marcus Holmes, 159–77. New York: Routledge, 2015.

Cull, Nicholas John. *Public Diplomacy: Foundations for Global Engagement in the Digital Age.* Cambridge: Polity Press, 2019.

Dellmuth, L., and J. Tallberg. "The Social Legitimacy of International Organisations: Interest Representation, Institutional Performance, and Confidence Extrapolation in the United Nations." *Review of International Studies* 41, no. 3 (2015): 451–75.

DeNardis, L., and A. M. Hackl. "Internet Governance by Social Media Platforms." *Telecommunications Policy* 39, no. 9 (2015): 761–70.

Denskus, T., and D.E. Esser. "Social Media and Global Development Rituals: A Content Analysis of Blogs and Tweets on the 2010 MDG Summit." *Third World Quarterly* 34, no. 3 (2013): 405–22.

Dimitrov, R. "Bringing Communication up to Agency: UNESCO Reforms Its Visibility." *Public Relations Inquiry* 3, no. 3 (2014): 293–318.

Duffield, J. "The Limits of 'Rational Design.'" *International Organization* 57, no. 2 (2003): 411–30.

Ecker-Ehrhardt, M. "International Organizations "Going Public"? an Event History Analysis of Public Communications Reforms 1950–2015." *International Studies Quarterly* 62, no. 4 (2018a): 723–36.

Ecker-Ehrhardt, M. "Self-Legitimation in the Face of Politicization: Why International Organizations Centralized Public Communication." *The Review of International Organizations* 13, no. 4 (2018b): 519–46.

Ellis, D.C. "Theorizing International Organizations: The Organizational Turn in International Organization Theory." *Journal of International Organizations Studies* 1, no. 1 (2010).

Gao, H., G. Barbier, and R. Goolsby. "Harnessing the Crowdsourcing Power of Social Media for Disaster Relief." *IEEE Intelligent Systems* 26, no. 3 (2011): 10–4.

Ghannam, J. "Social Media in the Arab World: Leading up to the Uprisings of 2011." *Center for International Media Assistance* 3, no.1 (2011): 1–44.

Gilboa, E. "The CNN Effect: The Search for a Communication Theory of International Relations." *Political Communication* 22, no. 1 (2005): 27–44.

Gregoratti, C., and A. Uhlin. "Civil Society Protest and the (De) Legitimation." *Legitimacy in Global Governance: Sources, Processes, and Consequences*, 134 (2018).

Gronau, J., and H. Schmidtke. "The Quest for Legitimacy in World Politics – International Institutions' Legitimation Strategies." *Review of International Studies* 42, no. 3 (2015): 535–57.

Haftel, Y., and A. Thompson. "The Independence of International Organizations: Concept and Applications." *Journal of Conflict Resolution* 50, no. 2 (2006): 253–75.

Hall, N., and N. Woods. "Theorizing the Role of Executive Heads in International Organizations." *European Journal of International Relations* 24, no. 4 (2018): 865–86.

Held, D., and M. Koenig-Archibugi, eds. *Global Governance and Public Accountability.* Oxford: Blackwell Publishing, 2005.

Hocking, B., and J. Melissen. *Diplomacy in the Digital Age.* Clingendael, Netherlands: Institute of International Relations, 2015.

Hooghe, L., and G. Marks. "Delegation and Pooling in International Organizations." *The Review of International Organizations* 10, no. 3 (2015): 305–28.

Hopke, J., and L. Hestres. "Visualizing the Paris Climate Talks on Twitter: Media and Climate Stakeholder Visual Social Media During COP21." *Social Media Society* 4, no. 3 (2018). Social Media Society, July 2018.

Howard, P., and M. Hussain. "The Role of Digital Media." *Journal of Democracy* 22, no. 3 (2011): 35–48.

Jackson, S.T. "A Turning IR Landscape in a Shifting Media Ecology: The State of IR Literature on New Media." *International Studies Review* 46 (2018): 518–34.

Kampf, R., I. Manor, and E. Segev. "Digital Diplomacy 2.0? A Cross-National Comparison of Public Engagement in Facebook and Twitter." *The Hague Journal of Diplomacy* 10, no. 4 (2015): 331–62.

Khatib, L., W. Dutton, and M. Thelwall. "Public Diplomacy 2.0: A Case Study of the US Digital Outreach Team." *The Middle East Journal* 66, no. 3 (2012): 453–72.

Livingstone, S., and L. Lievrouw. *Handbook of New Media: Social Shaping and Social Consequences.* London: Sage Publications, 2006.

Macnamara, J., and A. Zerfass. "Social Media Communication in Organizations: The Challenges of Balancing Openness, Strategy, and Management." *International Journal of Strategic Communication* 6, no. 4 (2012): 287–308.

Manning, Harley, Kerry Bodine, Josh Bernoff, and Mel Foster. "Outside." In *The Power of Putting Customers at the Center of Your Business.* New York: Forrester Research, 2012.

Manor, I. *Are We There yet: Have MFAs Realized the Potential of Digital Diplomacy?: Results from a Cross-National Comparison.* Eiden/Boston: Brill, 2016.

Manor, I. *The Digitalization of Public Diplomacy.* Basingstoke, UK: Palgrave Macmillan, 2019.

Manor, I., and E. Segev. "America's Selfie: How the US Portrays Itself on its Social Media Accounts." In *Digital Diplomacy*, edited by Ilan Manor, and Elad Segev, 103–22. London: Routledge, 2015.

Marlin-Bennett, R. "Embodied Information, Knowing Bodies, and Power." *Millennium* 41, no. 3 (2013): 601–22.

Melissen, J. *Wielding Soft Power: The New Public Diplomacy.* The Hague, Netherlands: Netherlands Institute of International Relations, Clingendael, 2005.

Melissen, J. "Public Diplomacy." In *Diplomacy in a Globalizing World: Theories and Practices,* edited by P. Kerr, and G. Wiseman, 192–208. Oxford: Oxford University Press, 2013.

Morse, J.C., and R.O. Keohane. "Contested Multilateralism." *The Review of International Organizations* 9, no. 4 (2014): 385–412.

Mumby, D.K., and T.R. Kuhn. *Organizational Communication: A Critical Introduction.* London: Sage Publications, 2018.

Murphy, P., M. Kraidy, and M.M. Kraidy, eds. *Global Media Studies: Ethnographic Perspectives.* Hove: Psychology Press, 2003.

Ness, G.D., and S.R. Brechin. "Bridging the Gap: International Organizations as Organizations." *International Organization* 42, no. 2 (1988): 245–73.

Pagovski, Z. Zach. "Public Diplomacy of Multilateral Organizations: The Cases of NATO, EU, and ASEAN, CBD." *Perspectives on Public Diplomacy* (2015). Paper No.4.

Pamment, J. "Digital Diplomacy as Transmedia Engagement: Aligning Theories of Participatory Culture with International Advocacy Campaigns." *New Media & Society* 18, no. 9 (2016): 2046–62.

Pelling, Jon. "Public Diplomacy in the Age of Networks: Midwives4all." *Place Branding & Public Diplomacy* 12, no. 2 (2016): 201–9.

Risso, L. *Propaganda and Intelligence in the Cold War: The NATO Information Service.* Abingdon: Routledge, 2014.

Rogers, E. *Diffusion of Innovations.* 5th ed. New York: Free Press, 2003.

Sandre, Andreas. *Digital Diplomacy: Conversations on Innovation in Foreign Policy.* Lanham: Rowman & Littlefield Publishing Group, 2015.

Seo, H., J.Y. Kim, and S.U. Yang. "Global Activism and New Media: A Study of Transnational NGOs' Online Public Relations." *Public Relations Review* 35, no. 2 (2009): 123–6.

Simmons, B.A., and L.L. Martin. "International Organizations and Institutions." In *Handbook of International Relations,* edited by Beth Ann Simmons, and Lisa L. Martin, 192–211. London: Sage, 2002.

Simmons, Beth Ann. "International Studies in the Global Information Age." *International Studies Quarterly* 55, no. 3 (2011): 589–99.

Smith, D., and D. Elliott. "Exploring the Barriers to Learning from Crisis: Organizational Learning and Crisis." *Management Learning* 38, no. 5 (2007): 519–38.

Sommerer, T., and H. Agné. "Consequences of Legitimacy." In *Legitimacy in Global Governance: Sources, Processes, and Consequences,* edited by J. Tallberg, K. Bäckstrand, and J.A. Scholte. Oxford: Oxford University Press, 2018.

Spry, D. "Facebook Diplomacy: A Data-Driven, User-Focused Approach to Facebook Use by Diplomatic Missions." *Media International Australia* 168, no. 1 (2018): 62–80.

Spry, Damien. "From Delhi to Dili: Facebook Diplomacy by Ministries of Foreign Affairs in the Asia-Pacific." *The Hague Journal of Diplomacy* 15, no. 1–2 (2019): 1–33.

Steffek, J. "The Output Legitimacy of International Organizations and the Global Public Interest." *International Theory* 7, no. 2 (2015): 263–93.

Tallberg, J., and M. Zürn. "The Legitimacy and Legitimation of International Organizations: Introduction and Framework." *The Review of International Organizations* 1, no. 4 (2019): 581–606.

Thrall, A.T., D. Stecula, and D. Sweet. "May We Have Your Attention Please? Human-Rights NGOs and the Problem of Global Communication." *The International Journal of Press/Politics* 19, no. 2 (2014): 135–59.

Thussu, D.K., ed. *Internationalizing Media Studies*. Abingdon: Routledge, 2009.

Thussu, D.K. *International Communication: Continuity and Change*. London: Bloomsbury Publishing, 2018.

Treem, J., and P. Leonardi. "Social Media Use in Organizations: Exploring the Affordances of Visibility, Editability, Persistence, and Association." *Annals of the International Communication Association* 36, no. 1 (2013): 143–89.

Trottier, D. *Social Media as Surveillance: Rethinking Visibility in a Converging World*. London: Routledge, 2016.

Van Dijck, J., and T. Poell. "Understanding Social Media Logic." *Media & Communication* 1, no. 1 (2013): 2–14.

Watson, J., and A. Hill. *Dictionary of Media and Communication Studies*. London: Bloomsbury Publishing, USA, 2015.

Zürn, M., M. Binder, and M. Ecker-Ehrhardt. "International Authority and Its Politicization." *International Theory* 4, no. 1 (2012): 69–106.

PART I

International organisations' "digital universe"

2

IO PUBLIC COMMUNICATION GOING DIGITAL? UNDERSTANDING SOCIAL MEDIA ADOPTION AND USE IN TIMES OF POLITICIZATION

Matthias Ecker-Ehrhardt

Many IOs are "going digital."[1] They increasingly use social media such as Facebook and Twitter for disseminating a variety of information about, for example, recent speeches of organisational leaders, symposia of affiliated experts, the meetings and decisions of intergovernmental bodies, or the launch of major policy programs. What is more, they share related posts by other organisations in the respective policy field or those of governments heralding progress in the implementation of national policies coordinated by the respective IO or projects funded with its grants or credits. This trend to use social media is part and parcel of a broader trend of "going public." Over the last decades, IOs have codified public communication as organisational task, departmentalised this task into well-staffed departments, and finally intensified strategic planning of public communication as indicated by the release of a multitude of strategy documents (Ecker-Ehrhardt 2018a). They target a widening array of audiences – such as journalists, experts, advocacy organisations, corporate lobbies, as well as citizens – and have diversified communication channels to reach them.

Social media are most fascinating ingredients of the recent trend for more ambitious public communication. Enhancing the capacities for social media may increase the ability of IOs to, for example, effectively raise public awareness for global problems, publicly shame governments for not complying with international commitments, or teach norms and knowledge to citizens. As tools of direct communication, social media allows for circumventing classical media organisations as highly selective gatekeepers of general publics. In this way, social media offer some new degree of organisational control over public communication. Relatedly, the more IOs develop direct channels, the more we should expect citizens to experience them as autonomous voices and not merely as remote arenas of international diplomacy (Archer 1983). Therefore, important questions regarding the public recognition of IOs as "governors" of significant epistemic, moral, or political authority are intimately related to how and why IOs might develop and exploit new opportunities to directly reach and interact with citizens (cf. Barnett and Finnemore 2004; Avant et al. 2010).

Relatedly, the study of social media is critical for addressing important normative questions. The opening up of IOs towards civil society has fostered wide-reaching expectations regarding citizens' direct participation in global governance (Steffek et al. 2008; Bexell et al. 2010; Scholte 2011). Enhanced channels for direct communication may allow IOs to better inform citizens about internal processes and make IOs more transparent (Florini 2000; Grigorescu 2007). What is more, social media invite to "produse" (Bruns 2008) content by liking, sharing, and commenting. At a minimum, social media can facilitate the articulation of complaints and grievances bottom-up, thus, enhancing public accountability at the output-side of the policy process (Buchanan and Keohane 2006). In a more ambitious reading, social media communication suggests new possibilities for dialogue or even "user-generated democracy" (Loader and Mercea 2011) across levels of governance in an emerging global polity. However, social media use should also concern scholars to the extent that it may enable IOs to more effectively manage and manipulate societal perceptions of what they do and don't (Dingwerth et al. 2015; Gronau and Schmidtke 2016). Social media may allow IOs to more effectively intervene in processes of social mobilisation, either by effectively supporting (or even "orchestrating," Abbott et al. 2015) transnational action or by deflecting it (Ecker-Ehrhardt 2018b).

Given the multiple ways in which social media is relevant for better understanding the future of global governance it is striking that mainstream scholarship has by-and-large ignored social media activities of IOs. Research has repeatedly investigated the remarkable rate with which NGOs, and governments have started to use social media for self-presentation and strategic campaigning worldwide as well as across issue areas (e.g. Nah and Saxton 2013; Bulovsky 2019). However, research on IOs has almost exclusively focused on classical communication tools such as annual reports or press releases, mostly with regard to major IOs such as EU (Brüggemann 2008; Meyer 2009), the UN (Alleyne 2003; Lehmann 1999), UNICEF (Aghi and McKee 2000), UNESCO (Defourny 2003; Dimitrov 2014), WHO (Servaes 2007), and NATO (Risso 2014). Notable exceptions address digital communication (Ecker-Ehrhardt 2018b) or social media activities (Dimitrov 2014; Corrie 2015) but only with regard to single cases. It follows that we still have very limited knowledge about how and why IOs try to reach citizens directly by adopting and using social media.

This paper seeks to address this lacuna by means of Large-N comparative analysis of social media presences on Facebook and Twitter. Original data on social media activities of a stratified-random sample of 49 IOs is employed to describe and explain the main characteristics of respective pages across time and covered IOs. IOs are complex organisational systems as research has repeatedly theorised and empirically illustrated (Jacobson 1984; Koch 2009). To increase analytical leverage, the main level of analysis is the IO body, that is, IOs are split up into a diversity of 290 constitutive units including intergovernmental bodies (councils, plenaries, committees), administrations, courts, parliaments, and semi-autonomous agencies to understand variation in their use of social media.

Results suggest that multiple causal processes shape the application of social media for public communication purposes: First, increased external contestation and the opening IO bodies for representatives of transnational civil society, which seem to increase social media use as a tool for self-legitimation directly addressing non-state audiences. Secondly, organisational mandates shape IO demands for social media, for example, by calling for direct implementation of multiple policy programs on the ground. Thirdly, centralised public communication substantially facilitates the adoption of social media.

The paper begins by mapping the variation of social media use across IO bodies and over time. In the second part, I discuss alternative explanations, before these explanations are put to the test empirically by using negative binomial regression analysis. The final part concludes by laying out a number of implications of these results for further research.

Descriptive analysis

To what extent do IOs use social media? The following empirical analysis is based on information about Facebook pages and Twitter accounts of 49 IOs from 2008 to 2018. The selected IOs constitute a stratified-random sample drawn by the TransAccess project (Tallberg et al. 2013) – net the WEU that ceased to exist in 2011 – and include general and issue-specific IOs of regional and global reach that are still active at the end of 2018 (see Appendix for a comprehensive list of covered IOs). For these IOs we reviewed institutional homepages for hints at social media activities and used search functions of Facebook and Twitter for allocating additional presences. Pages generated by Facebook autonomously ("social community pages") were excluded. Presences attributed to individuals where included only if an organisational backing was clearly indicated. We carefully crosschecked whether presences were functional and minimally active. In total we were able to identify 385 Facebook pages and 861 Twitter accounts that could be attributed to one of the sampled IOs for the years 2008 to 2018. From these 49 IOs, 38 (which equals 78%) have at least one Facebook page by the end of 2018; 40 IOs (that is, about 82%) use Twitter.

Both platforms regularly provide the date of creation of pages and accounts. Additionally, information about most recent posts or comments indicate to what extent the respective presence is still active or fell dormant at some point in the past. Assuming that older accounts were not deleted to a significant extent, this allows a dynamic analysis of institutional adoption and use. Figure 2.1 reflects frequencies of social media presences by year of creation. The first pages on Facebook covered by this data are from 2008 and belong to the UN, Worldbank, and OECD. These three IOs also started Twitter accounts in the same year – the

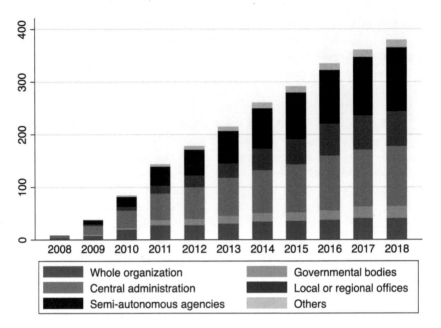

FIGURE 2.1 Number of Facebook pages across years and types of IO bodies

notable "early adopters" of this organisational field. Over time, we see a steady increase of social media presences created each year, with a decreasing slope over recent years, which may suggest some process of saturation.

To better understand what kind of activities we see, Figures 2.1 and 2.2 further categorise all presences by kinds of bodies to which the respective page or account is said to belong to. Note that such "belonging" needs to be qualified: The "whole organisation" category comprises those that are devoted to the IO as such, simply labelled "Comunidad Andina" or "ASEAN."[2] Quantitatively, these main presences do play a minor and decreasing role over time as can be read from Figures 2.1 and 2.2. Nevertheless, we see a clear organisational history of creating a main page or account first in most IOs, before more focused outlets come to be added. According to Figure 2.3, 51 pages have been created on Facebook if we focus on all first years of adoption, that is, the year in which the respective IO has first used Facebook as a tool of public communication. Of these "first year pages," 27 – a share of 53% – have been devoted to the whole IO. These numbers only slightly increase to 34 over the following four years despite the fact that the overall number of pages increase to 214. Similarly, of 46 Twitter accounts attributed to the whole organisation, 32 accounts – a share of 43% – have been created in the first year of adopting Twitter by the respective IO, while the overall number of accounts have increased to 410 accounts across all IOs using Twitter (Figure 2.4).

A relative majority of social media presences that come to dominate the picture of later years belongs to *the central administration* or its subordinate units

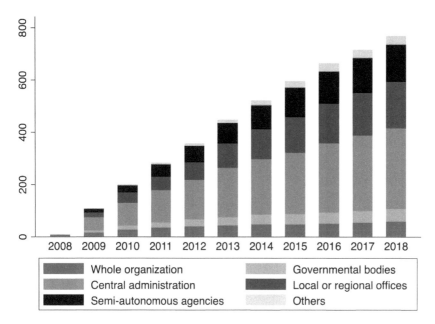

FIGURE 2.2   Number of Twitter accounts across years and types of IO bodies

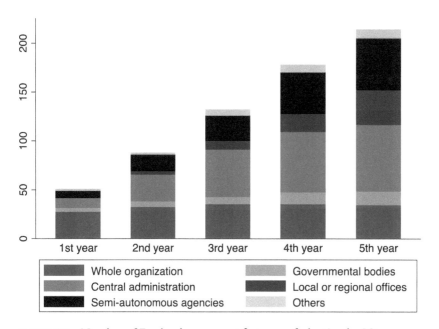

FIGURE 2.3   Number of Facebook pages post first year of adoption by IOs

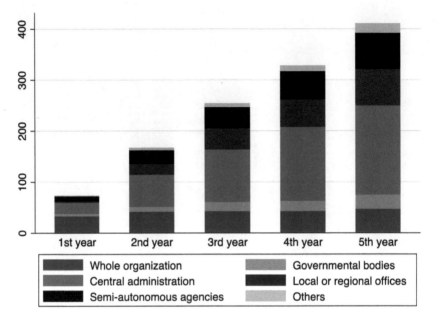

FIGURE 2.4 Number of Twitter accounts post first year of adoption by IOs

concerned with specific policy areas (e.g. human rights unit, office for development issues, energy policy department) or administrative functions (e.g. public complaints unit, program evaluation mechanism, publication office, human resource department). Presences by semi-autonomous *agencies* (e.g. the OECD Development Centre or UNEP, the UN Environmental Program) constitute the second most common type; local or regional bodies (like the Worldbank office Moldova or the OSCE Programme Office in Dushanbe) come third in quantitative terms across social media platforms.

Compared to these, we found presences of *intergovernmental bodies* to be a striking exception even in recent years. This is remarkable, because member states are the main principals of IOs. Thus, intergovernmental bodies are not only a necessary feature of all IOs per definition but also still stand out in terms of decision-making power and overall political relevance. Nevertheless, in case of social media activities (as well as public communication in general), they do not seek a high-profile (despite the fact that individual governments have shown to adopt social media with an impressive rate, see Barberá and Zeitzoff 2017; Bulovsky 2019).

Comparatively rare are activities attributed to *parliamentary assemblies* (N = 12) as well as *courts or court-like bodies* (N = 6). However, these kinds of entities are not regular features of IOs, therefore, only a subset of covered IOs are "at risk" of creating such pages. Set in perspective, of the 20 Courts or court-like bodies in the analysis we could identify six Facebook pages and eight accounts on Twitter (including those of the Caribbean Court of Justice[3] and the European Court of Human Rights[4]). In the case of the 12 parliamentary assemblies existing in the IOs covered, we did find eight related pages on Facebook and even 12 Twitter accounts – for example of the Pan-African Parliament (as part of the African Union[5]) and the Parliamentary Assembly of the Council of Europe.[6] Thus, while relatively rare, such bodies show a remarkable interest in using social media.

Facebook and Twitter allow for social networking and dialogic communication. Nevertheless, existing research suggests that social media use by political organisations (Bortree and Seltzer 2009) or governmental elites (Barberá and Zeitzoff 2017, 4) tends to be far more uni-directional than dialogical. The same seem to hold for IOs, which use social media predominantly to promote a variety of organisational activities – major gatherings of delegates, speeches of secretary-generals, public symposia with experts, the publication of reports in order to raise awareness for pressing problems or to herald successes in solving them. However, even if IOs may disappoint hopes for a more participatory global governance on average, the *reach of activities* on social media is significant, validating the basic assumption that its use is an important activity worth a thorough investigation. The median Facebook page run by IOs in the sample has about 7,400 likes (Figure 2.5); similarly, their median Twitter account draws about 3,900 followers (Figure 2.6). There is a notable variation in how much attention IO activities on social media draw. The Northwest Atlantic Fisheries Organization (NAFO) received 227 likes on Facebook and has 426 followers on Twitter, despite being online since 2011 on both platforms. Over the same timespan the International Coffee Organization (ICO) triggered 6,976 likes and

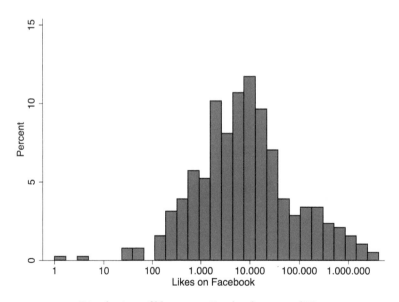

FIGURE 2.5   Distribution of likes across Facebook pages of IOs

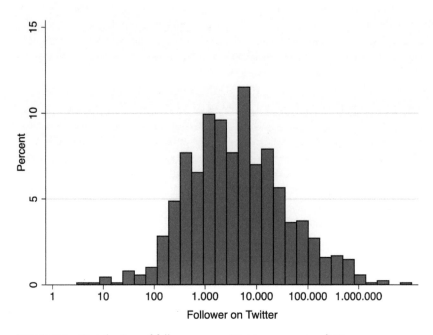

FIGURE 2.6 Distribution of followers across Twitter accounts of IOs

6,268 followers. The UN leads the pack with about 4.2 million likes for its main page on Facebook and 11 million following their main Twitter account. Even if social media presences have been created across the board of IOs, though, they significantly vary in reach, pointing to important questions of citizens' cognitive and social mobilisation for international governance (Dellmuth 2016). In any case, the social resonance suggests a remarkable success in expanding direct links to public audiences.

Theories and hypothesis

Why do some IOs use social media earlier or more intensively than others? Why do we find variation not only across different IOs but also across different bodies of the same IO? Existing research suggests a couple of alternative factors that may explain social media activities in the IO organisational field or beyond.

Social media as a tool of IO self-legitimation in times of politicisation

Existing evidence suggests that expanding public communication in the IO organisational field is intrinsically linked to IO politicisation, that is, rising levels of public awareness and contestation of international governance (Gronau and Schmidtke 2016; Ecker-Ehrhardt 2018c; Dingwerth et al. 2019).

To start with, research has provided ample evidence for the empirical significance of IO politicisation (Zürn et al. 2012). Public opinion studies now reveal a remarkable attitudinal awareness of major global and regional IOs in terms of structured beliefs and evaluations accessible to citizens across continents (Norris 2000; Boomgaarden et al. 2011; Johnson 2011; Dellmuth and Tallberg 2015; Dellmuth 2016). Scholars of social movements and NGO advocacy have extensively studied how IOs have become a new focus of transnational activism (Keck and Sikkink 1998; O'Brien et al. 2000; Tarrow 2001; della Porta 2007). Similarly, research on parliamentary debates (de Wilde 2011), party manifestos (Ecker-Ehrhardt 2014), and mass media communication (Bennett et al. 2004; Nullmeier et al. 2010) suggests that a couple of prominent IOs have become major reference points of political discourse.

Such politicisation increases the organisational need to manage societal contestation in order to avoid involuntary defections by governments (Odell and Eichengreen 1998), organisational crises induced by the withdrawal of resources (Cárdenas 2000; Smith 2004), or immediate societal resistance that obstructs operations on the ground (e.g., Moulin and Nyers 2007). Thus, non-state actors constitute relevant social constituencies that have to be addressed and accommodated in order to make many IOs work smoothly (Dingwerth et al. 2019). Increased levels of politicisation suggest that at least those IOs directly addressed require social legitimacy, that is, a "generalized perception or assumption that actions ... are desirable, proper, or appropriate" (Suchman 1995, 574). While systems of political rule show a general tendency "to cultivate the belief in its legitimacy" (Weber 1978, 213), politicisation drives IOs to engage in strategic communication in order to manage legitimacy.

Tellingly, a core aim of the World Bank External Affairs department as well as NATO's Public Diplomacy Division is to increase "public support" for their organisations (World Bank 2011, 41; NATO 2009, 2). APEC's "Communications and Public Affairs Strategic Plan for 2014–16" asks its communications team to "identify and highlight APEC success stories and concrete benefits and distribute these through appropriate vehicles" (APEC 2014, 3). In the same vein, the OAS Department of Press and Communications has been explicitly tasked with "project[ing] the image of the OAS as a hemispheric forum for policy discussion with ... a meaningful role to play in the solution of any crises that occur in the Americas and the Caribbean" (OAS 2006, 26). Empirical evidence further suggests that imperatives for self-legitimation have a substantial imprint on the output of the UN Department of Public Information (Ecker-Ehrhardt 2018b).

However, the extent to which politicisation may explain social media activities remains unclear. I assume three related processes to define an enhanced need for self-legitimation, which also may increase the propensity of IOs to adopt and use social media:

First, we should expect that *waves of contentious politics addressing a specific IOs* foster internal perceptions of a popular legitimacy deficit and make it much more imperative to effectively manage public discourse by improving means of communication. A number of case studies suggest a causal link between social movement activities and the fact that public communication has become an organisational priority in the case of NATO Information Service (Risso 2014, 132f) and Asian-Europe Meetings (ASEAN, Gilson 2011, 216). Similarly, Jennifer Gronau and Henning Schmidtke argued that protest activism against the G8 and the IMF has led both organisations to stress self-legitimation as an operational goal – including strategies addressing the general public (Gronau and Schmidtke 2016, 553). Large-N evidence corroborate these results with regard to the degree of centralisation of public communication capacities (Ecker-Ehrhardt 2018c) as well as the timing of respective reforms in an event history perspective (Ecker-Ehrhardt 2018a). These results suggest that we may assume public contention to substantially enhance organisational demands for self-legitimation, and, relatedly, an organisational propensity to use social media.

Hypothesis 1: Social media adoption and use is more likely after waves of contentious politics addressing the IO in question.

Secondly, the organisational demand for self-legitimation should substantially increase with the frequency and salience of *scandals, which are* defined as instances of public debate where bureaucratic leaders or staff members are accused of transgressions, that is, gross misconduct that is widely deemed unethical (cf. Thompson 2000, 12). Empirical cases include allegations of corruption (oil-for-food at the UN), patronage (Paul Wolfowitz's "Rizagate" at the World Bank), sexual harassment (Ruud Lubbers at UNCR), or organised sexual exploitation and abuse (UN peacekeepers in Bosnia, DRC, and elsewhere). In these and similar cases, individual behaviour has been deemed damaging for the reputation of the affected IO to the degree that misconduct was perceived to indicate systematic deficiencies by relevant audiences (Brändström and Kuipers 2003; Boin et al. 2009). In any event, case study evidence illustrates how effective scandalisation may have a disruptive impact on organisational life (Meyer and Califano 2006; Lehmann 2011) and trigger substantial reorganisations of communication capacities (Meyer 2009). Beyond single-cases, quantitative evidence suggests that public scandals significantly account for enhancing institutional transparency (Grigorescu 2007) and public communication (Ecker-Ehrhardt 2018c). According to this evidence, profound experiences of public scandalisation seem to substantially increase the organisational need for self-legitimation. By implication, therefore, we should expect to find scandals to significantly account for variation in social media activities.

Hypothesis 2: Social media adoption and use is more likely to arise after political scandals at the IO in question.

Thirdly, a notable trend to give institutional access to non-state actors has significantly intensified the degree to which transnational demands have become relevant for specific IOs (Tallberg et al. 2014). A global sphere of advocacy organisations has emerged in recent decades, "inserting themselves into a wide range of decision-making processes on issues from international security to human rights to the environment" (Florini and Simmons 2000, 3). The inclusion of representatives from organised transnational civil society into IO bodies has been shown to work as a (highly selective) "transmission belt" for societal demands from the bottom-up (Steffek et al. 2008). In any event, the flourishing and inclusion of transnational civil society has arguably increased the organisational need for more effectively managing public legitimacy – if only to avoid public delegitimation when transnational civil society is mobilised to challenge IOs in the public sphere. By implication, if self-legitimation drives public communication in general, and social media activities more specifically, the flourishing and inclusion of transnational civil society should significantly account for variation in social media activities over time and across IOs.

Hypothesis 3: Social media adoption and use is more likely if transnational civil society organises in an IO's environment and finds access to its internal processes.

Alternative explanations

Nevertheless, the need for self-legitimation is but one plausible explanation in a wider debate of why actors in global governance might invest in public communication in general, and their usage of social media more particularly.

Democratic membership: There is substantial evidence that democratic governments tend to use social media more than their authoritarian counterparts (Bulovsky 2019; Barberá and Zeitzoff 2017). From what we know about IOs, the degree to which their membership is made of democracies is an important factor of IO institutional design and operational activities. In a "liberal" tradition of theorising international politics, this can be attributed to democracies' tendency to "externalise" domestic institutions to the international level, as it has been argued, for example, with respect to states' propensity to support freedom-of-information such as transparency provisions (Grigorescu 2007). Accordingly, we might expect democratic governments to push IOs towards adopting social media tools – to make them more effective in reaching out to societal constituencies as well as to accommodate growing domestic expectations of transparent and accountable global governance.

Hypothesis 4: Social media adoption and use is more likely the more democratic an IO membership is.

Organisational mission to govern societal discourses: A common explanation in the field of social media research relates observed variation in applying communication technologies to different missions that organisations pursue (Nah and Saxton 2013). On his view, choices for investing in public communication are more likely if organisations define advocacy for certain ideas or policies as part of their mandate. It is striking in this regard that IOs have famously been described as vocal "teachers of norms" (Finnemore 1993) as well as influential "knowledge producers" (Nay 2014) of global politics. Major campaigns of IOs suggest that such mandates do indeed motivate IO public communication to some important degree. For example, the Strategic Communication Division of the UN Department of Public Information (DPI) focuses on activities that aim at putting specific issues, such as global poverty and human rights violations against women, on public agendas (Alleyne 2003). Similarly, some important campaigns by issue-specific IOs such as the WHO (Servaes 2007), UNESCO (Finnemore 1993; Defourny 2003), UNICEF (Aghi and McKee 2000), FAO (Coldevin 2001), or the World Bank (Mefalopulos 2008; Odugbemi and Lee 2011; Nay 2014) seek to induce societal change by promoting ideas such as agricultural innovations, sanitary standards, or sustainability. Thus, major efforts of IO public communication can be attributed to a mission to implement ambitious policy programs by governing societal discourses in a variety of issue areas. Consequently, social media activities, too, may be expected to reflect such mandates.

Hypothesis 5: Social media adoption and use is more likely if their mandates include the direct implementation of policy programs vis-à-vis non-state audiences.

Hypothesis 6: The adoption and use of multiple channels is more likely if IO mandates include a diversity of issue areas.

Organisational capacities for communication: Another approach is to explain social media adoption by the distribution of resources in an organisational field. For example, social movements scholars have argued that globalisation critics have successfully tried to compensate for lacking organisational capacities and access to mass media organisations by focusing on social media tools (Bennett and Segerberg 2013). However, research on NGOs suggests that those with professional capacities for public communication find it easy to integrate social media activities in their professional routines. Consequently, public attention for social media campaigns tends to be skewed towards the already established voices instead empowering new ones (Thrall et al. 2014, cf. Margolis and Resnick 2000). This observation is instructive, given that many IOs have substantially enhanced and professionalised their organisational capacities for public communication over recent years. Hence, we may expect that well-organised and staffed communication departments find it comparatively attractive to establish their own social media channels, far and foremost, because they have the capacities to regularly feed such channels with content in terms of posting or, for example, responding to comments in time.

Hypothesis 7: Social media adoption and use is more likely if an IO has developed professional capacities for communication.

Potential reach of social media activities: Turning to external conditions, new technologies seem to have had a remarkable impact on the political opportunity structure in some less developed countries, because digital communication – via cell phones as well as social media – may substitute for a restricted access to analogue channels of individual or mass media communication (Hussain and Howard 2013). Thus, while some authors have argued that social media are part and parcel of a more general process of modernisation (Barberá and Zeitzoff 2017), wealth is not a necessary condition for the effectiveness of communication via social media. Nevertheless, if we assume organisations to use social media in order to effectively engage with other users, the benefit of digital communication might depend on public access to respective technologies and their use by relevant audiences. For this reason, authors interested in modelling social media adoption have thought to control for related variables, and, for example, shown that governmental leaders tend to use social media more intensively in societies with higher levels of internet penetration (Bulovsky 2019, 9). Similarly, IOs should be tempted to use social media the more they can expect targeted audiences within reach of such activities.

Hypothesis 8: Social media adoption and use is more likely if target audiences extensively use these technologies.

Diffusion of social media: *Adaption to a changing script?* A last way to understand the increasing use of social media by IOs is diffusion, that is, the interdependent adoption of "contagious" ideas or technologies within an interconnected group of organisations. For one, IOs should learn from peers they perceive as successful in using social media to more efficiently communicate with publics (in order to legitimise own procedures or implement policy programs). Additionally, social media use may increasingly become part of the institutional script of modern political organisation. Thus, IOs' adoption of social media could reflect organisational adaption to an upcoming "new normal" in the organisational field – partly independent from a strategic demand for intensifying communication vis-à-vis external publics. In both ways, similar processes of diffusion have been theorised and empirically illustrated in a number of areas, including economic policies (Simmons and Elkins 2004), LGBT rights (Ayoub 2015), and participatory arrangements within IOs (Sommerer and Tallberg 2019). However, with regard to social media activities, research on governmental leaders did not find significant evidence for a process of diffusion (Barberá and Zeitzoff 2017). Therefore, one should not prematurely treat clustered adoption of social media as conclusive evidence of diffusion, but test its causal significance vis-à-vis alternative factors.

Hypothesis 9: Social media adoption and use is more likely if successful competitors in the organisational field widely use these technologies.

Explanatory analysis

Data and Model Specification

To test the empirical validity of causal arguments I employ multivariate regression. The main dependent variable counts active social media presences on Facebook or Twitter per IO body covered in the list of 290 major IO bodies provided by the Transaccess project (Tallberg et al. 2013). This list includes all major bodies mentioned as such in the constitutional documents, organisational charts, or self-presentations. The main rational for drawing on such list of major bodies is that any causal analysis has to include "non-cases" for which the creation of social media presences could have been expected but did not occur. The list fulfils both conditions: first, it includes "non-cases" for which no page on Facebook or Twitter could be identified. Second, it excludes smaller bodies and those with only internal tasks (such as budgetary committees) for which own means for external communication seem rather unlikely per se (ibid., 59).

Some additional choices need justification: First, pooling counts from two competing social media platforms is justified by a high correlation of both kinds of observations ($r = .881$, $t = 111.58$, $p < .001$).[7] Importantly, robustness checks with separate models for Facebook pages and Twitter accounts yield very similar results (see Appendix). Second, counting social media presences results in a discrete variable that only includes integer values and substantially deviates from normality, with many zeros and decreasing density with higher values. This is a characteristic distribution for event-count data, which suggests that an analysis based on ordinary least squares would be problematic. What is more, the variance of these counts significantly exceeds the overall mean number of social media presences per IO body, which indicates overdispersion (Table 2.1). Note that such overdispersion makes intuitive sense, because the decisions of singly IO bodies to run multiple pages and accounts in a given year should be interdependent to some substantial degree. Nevertheless, it implies that the data might fit a negative binomial distribution significantly better than simple Poisson. Consequently, I employ negative binomial regression to test explanatory hypotheses.

Regarding explanatory variables, I draw on various sources to operationalise causal conditions of politicisation as well as alternative factors. Table 2.1 provides

TABLE 2.1 Descriptive statistics

Variable	Obs.	Mean	Var.	Min.	Max.
Social Media presences per IO body, N	3190	1.723	3.503	0	288
Scandal, dummy	3190	0.065	0.496	0	1
Scandal Coverage, logged	3190	0.085	0.627	0.000	3.871
Protest, dummy	3190	0.122	0.572	0	1
Protest Coverage, logged	3190	0.168	0.714	0.000	2.944
Transnational Access, index	3190	0.513	0.659	0.000	1.960
Democratic Membership, index	3190	5.071	1.924	−6.333	10.000
Implementation Mandate, index	3190	0.248	0.729	0	2
Multi-Issue Mandate, dummy	3190	0.310	0.680	0	1
Centralised Public Communication	3190	5.517	1.868	0	12
Internet Penetration in percent	3190	39.820	4.186	9.249	76.607
Social media presences of peers, mean N	3190	0.860	0.988	0.000	3.500
Budget > Euro 1 million, dummy	3190	0.934	0.497	0	1
Budget > Euro 10 million, dummy	3190	0.597	0.701	0	1
Administrative body, dummy	3190	0.172	0.615	0	1
Governmental body, dummy	3190	0.703	0.676	0	1

descriptive statistics for the following independent variables used in the next section.

Protest activities have been identified using Associated Press (AP) content as provided by LexisNexis. Relevant information is captured by two variables: (a) The dummy variable *Protests* indicates whether I found any evidence for societal protest activities in a given IO-year – a robust measure of politicisation over different levels of overall public attention for individual IOs. (b) The count variable *Absolute Coverage of Protest* equals the logged number of identified AP articles on protests per IO-year. I assume that this measure best captures absolute levels of public delegitimation of an IO by contentious political activities. The two protest variables are lagged in the analysis by one year to address concerns of reverse causality and selection.

IO scandals were identified using the *New York Times* (*NYT*) archive as the main source of information. Again, two variables were constructed: (a) the dummy variable *Scandals* indicates whether there was evidence for scandals of an IO in a given IO-year; (b) the count variable *Absolute Coverage of Scandals* equals the logged number of identified *NYT* articles on scandals per IO-year. Scandal variables enter the analysis lagged by one year as well.

TNA Access is a composite index from the Transaccess-dataset (Tallberg et al. 2014), which comprises information on four dimensions of access by transnational non-state actors: depth (level of involvement), range (range of non-state actors entitled to participate), permanence, and legal codification of arrangements for the year 2010 – the last year covered by Transaccess. I take the use of constant values to be unproblematic because there is minimal variation in original dataset for the years post 2000.

Democratic IO-Membership measures the degree to which member states of the respective IO show high levels of internal democracy and equals the one-year lagged mean score of democracy institutionalisation in a given IO membership. Information on IO membership from the most recent version 2.3 of the COW-2 International Organizations Dataset Version was updated for the year 2008 to 2017; next, the mean scores of democracy institutionalisation of all member states per IO were calculated using the most recent update of Polity IV data now ranging until 2017 (Marshall et al. 2016).

Implementation Mandate captures the degree to which mandates commit specific IO bodies to deal with local implementation of policy programs. The variable builds on information provided by Tallberg and colleagues (2013) for 2009, who coded the relevance of local implementation (ranging from "not relevant" to "highly relevant") for each of the major bodies of covered IOs using the description of tasks in the official documents and self-presentations. Again, the use of constant values is deemed unproblematic because there is minimal variation in this variable over time.

Multi-Issue Mandate counts the number of issue areas the respective unit is active in. This is including under the assumption that multi-issue IOs (as well as bodies) should have an additional incentive to set up multiple channels to better address issue-specific publics.

Centralised Public Communication is an index from the recent ComIO project (Ecker-Ehrhardt 2018c). It is based on a concept of centralisation of IO public communication as having two dimensions, namely (a) the codification of communication tasks assigned to the IO central administration (including those specifying target audiences as well as management tasks) and (b) the departmentalisation of assigned tasks into administrative units. The index combines both dimensions in a multiplicative index, which weights *codification* (the number of observed communication tasks assigned to IO central administration) by *departmentalisation* (the degree to which these tasks are matched by organisational capacities). It ranges from 0 to 12 and varies over years and IOs.

Additional controls include *Internet Penetration*, which is calculated with data provided by the most recent version of the World Development Indicators. It equals the mean percentage of internet users across member states. The variable *Peers' social media presences* capture the mean number of social media presences per IO body in the sample of the same issue area. I also control for variation in IO *budgets*. Empirically, social media presences can even be observed in case of EUROMET – the IO with the smallest annual budget of only €200,000 in 2010 but running a Twitter account since 2011. However, resource scarcity might nevertheless negatively affect IOs' ability to effectively run multiple sites much more than larger budgets. To account for this possibility, estimated models include two indicators, one for budgets exceeding €1 million and a second for those exceeding 10 million. Indicators are based on data provided by Tallberg and colleagues for 2010. Finally, two indicators – *Governmental body* and *Administrative body* – are included to capture variation over various types of IO bodies unaccounted for by other variables.

Results

Table 2.2 reports main results of a series of negative-binomial regression models with robust standard errors clustered by IO bodies to account for heteroscedasticity. All models share the number of social media presences per IO body and year as the dependent variable. Models test each of the politicisation variables separately and in combination, each controlling for alternative explanations. To further inform the interpretation of results, Table 2.3 reports marginal effects in terms of factor change coefficients.

Estimates first of all grant strong support for the recent turn of IO studies towards self-legitimation as an important driver of IO communication towards non-state publics. *Protest activities* that address a specific IO in one year increase this IOs' propensity for running multiple social media presences the next year. The estimated factor change for the first variable *Protest* indicates that, if we observe protest in a given year, the expected number of pages for the next year increases more than fourfold. Taking different degrees of public salience of protest into account, expected number of pages increase by an estimated factor of 1.5 per standard-deviation of protest coverage. Empirical cases that drive these results are, for example, NATO's repeated strengthening of its social media presence – both on Twitter as well as Facebook – after notable summits in Strasbourg (2009) and later Chicago (2012), which both received massive media coverage because thousands of peaceful protesters called an end to the war in Afghanistan as well as related symbolic events such as the returning of military medals by US veterans and violent public riots by anarchist groups. Of course, such correlation is not conclusive evidence of a causal relationship; however, it is remarkably in line with theoretically driven expectations.

Second, scandals do not seem to have the same relevance, as can be drawn from the estimates. Factor changes suggest a less substantial increase of expected number of presences by about 1.7 for the year after a scandal. However, scandals are comparatively rare events – we count only 21 instances where the reputation of covered IOs has publicly been called into question by scandalised behaviour of representatives. Hence, in these rare events, empirical correlations suggest substantial impact. To illustrate, most Facebook pages run by the Office of the President at the Worldbank have been launched during and right after "Rizagate," which spurred massive media coverage and led to the resignation of the then President Paul Wolfowitz within weeks.

Third, results strongly support the intuition that opening IOs for representatives of transnational civil society might foster IOs' demand for additional communication channels to address citizens directly. Expected number of pages changes by a factor of 1.5 per standard-deviation of *Transnational Access*.

TABLE 2.2 Negative binomial regression of number of social media presences per IO body and year

Model	1	2	3	4	5	6	7
Protest, dummy	1.502*** (0.305)					1.465*** (0.285)	
Protest Coverage, logged N		0.905*** (0.168)					0.856*** (0.146)
Scandal, dummy			1.037*** (0.162)			0.511*** (0.120)	
Scandal Coverage, logged N				0.614*** (0.095)			0.413*** (0.084)
Transnational Access, index					0.783* (0.385)	0.985** (0.344)	0.961** (0.353)
Democratic Membership, index	−0.042 (0.071)	−0.048 (0.072)	−0.073 (0.073)	−0.069 (0.073)	−0.114 (0.076)	−0.057 (0.074)	−0.055 (0.074)
Implementation Mandate, index	0.923*** (0.233)	0.942*** (0.236)	0.920*** (0.243)	0.924*** (0.242)	0.774** (0.285)	0.754** (0.261)	0.786** (0.267)
Multi-Issue Mandate, dummy	1.070** (0.329)	1.018** (0.339)	1.189*** (0.345)	1.152*** (0.348)	0.933** (0.355)	0.781* (0.304)	0.707* (0.316)
Centralised Public Communication, index	0.240*** (0.043)	0.230*** (0.044)	0.273*** (0.051)	0.271*** (0.051)	0.274*** (0.058)	0.193*** (0.050)	0.178*** (0.051)
Internet Users, percent	0.018 (0.012)	0.021# (0.012)	0.022# (0.012)	0.021# (0.012)	0.026* (0.013)	0.020 (0.012)	0.022# (0.012)

	(1)	(2)	(3)	(4)	(5)	(6)	(7)
Social media presences of peers, mean N	0.092	0.109	-0.073	-0.058	-0.073	0.119	0.155
	(0.112)	(0.117)	(0.130)	(0.130)	(0.142)	(0.104)	(0.106)
Budget > Euro 1 million, dummy	-0.159	-0.160	-0.086	-0.061	-0.246	-0.344	-0.318
	(0.628)	(0.643)	(0.648)	(0.648)	(0.677)	(0.648)	(0.672)
Budget > Euro 10 million, dummy	0.734	0.836	0.929	0.947	0.995	0.623	0.724
	(0.569)	(0.576)	(0.599)	(0.596)	(0.609)	(0.560)	(0.567)
Administrative body, dummy	1.321***	1.321***	1.285**	1.304**	1.510**	1.644***	1.661***
	(0.382)	(0.384)	(0.468)	(0.464)	(0.524)	(0.410)	(0.406)
Governmental body, dummy	-1.872***	-1.875***	-1.923***	-1.908***	-1.733**	-1.533***	-1.523***
	(0.440)	(0.443)	(0.523)	(0.515)	(0.531)	(0.420)	(0.416)
Constant	-3.889***	-3.940***	-3.932***	-3.939***	-4.177***	-4.187***	-4.246***
	(0.588)	(0.594)	(0.646)	(0.646)	(0.656)	(0.621)	(0.634)
Alpha (over-dispersion)	1.922**	1.975***	2.277***	2.271***	2.405***	1.722**	1.734**
Log Likelihood	-2369.679	-2374.488	-2421.224	-2419.533	-2430.473	-2331.012	-2330.155
N IO-Body-Years	3190	3190	3190	3190	3190	3190	3190
N IO-Bodies	290	290	290	290	290	290	290

Note: The table reports coefficients from negative-binomial regression models with robust standard errors clustered by IO bodies in parentheses. # $p<0.10$, * $p<0.05$, ** $p<0.01$, *** $p<0.001$

TABLE 2.3 Estimated substantive effects of explanatory variables

	Factor change in predicted number of social media presences		Estimates are based on
	over range of X	per SD increase in X	
Protest, dummy	4.326	1.615	Model 6
Protest Coverage, logged N	12.434	1.547	Model 7
Scandal, dummy	1.666	1.134	Model 6
Scandal Coverage, logged N	4.956	1.176	Model 7
Transnational Access, index	6.581	1.518	Model 7
Implementation Mandate, index	4.814	1.519	Model 7
Multi-Issue Mandate, dummy	2.029	1.387	Model 7
Centralised Public Communication, index	8.451	1.860	Model 7
Administrative body, dummy	5.217	1.867	Model 7
Governmental body, dummy	0.233	0.514	Model 7

Illustrative example of IO bodies that most comprehensively grant access to non-state actors include the Secretariats of the Organization of American States (OAS) and the Council of Europe (CoE) as well as the Andean Parliament and UN Environmental Programme. These bodies do all extensively use social media to approach non-state publics, which is in line with expectations.

Turning towards *alternative explanations*, a couple of indicators successfully account for additional variation in the dependent variable:

With regard to internal conditions of social media activities, more ambitious mandates positively relate to social media activities. The expected number of social media presences increases almost fivefold if IO bodies are tasked with the local implementation of programs compared to those that are not. Similarly, IO bodies that are tasked with multiple issue areas tend to have twice as many presences on Facebook and Twitter than those with an issue-specific mandate. This is substantial support for the idea that social media usage partly reflects operational mandates to govern societal discourses (Avant et al. 2010).

What is more, the development of organisational capacities facilitates social media activities substantially. Expected number of presences almost twofold per standard-deviation of *Centralised Public Communication* scale. At the lower end of the centralisation scale we see IOs that do not codify public communication as a major organisational task and, relatedly, have not established any office or department mainly concerned with public communication. That applies, for example, for the International Telecommunications Satellites Organization (ITSO), the Niger Basin Authority (ABN), or the South Asia Co-operative Environment Program (SACEP). Of these cases only SACEP uses social media at all. On the other end of the spectrum we find IOs with most capable public communication departments, such as the Asian Development Bank, the IMF, the International Regional Organization against Plant and Animal Diseases (OIRSA), and, for example, the International Criminal Court. All of these IOs have multiple social media presences, extensively using Twitter as well as Facebook across the board.

Interestingly, a couple of alternative explanations find no empirical support. Despite evidence that *democratic governments* tend to use social media more than their authoritarian counterparts (Bulovsky 2019), their membership in IOs does not correlate with increased usage of social media in global governance. Also, there is no indication that *Internet Penetration* or *"contagion" by peers* drives social media adoption by IOs. Both matches similar evidence for governmental leaders presented by Barberá and Zeitzoff (2017). What is more, estimates coefficients for *budget* indicators are statistically insignificant across models, suggesting that other variables sufficiently account for variation in organisational resources and complexity.

Finally, fixed effects for different kinds of IO bodies suggest important variation unaccounted for by other variables. As can be expected from the descriptive results presented above, administrative bodies show a much higher propensity to launch multiple presences on Facebook and Twitter, compared to other parts of IOs, most strikingly governmental bodies such as councils, assemblies, and committees gathering state delegates.

Note that results are fairly consistent across models presented in Table 2.2. However, I estimated additional models to check the *robustness* of these results. For example, Table 2.4 provides the results for models treating the number of Twitter accounts and Facebook pages separately. Also, the application of Event History Analysis by specifying Cox regression models has been tested. Notably, the results do not change significantly with alternative specifications.

Conclusion

To what extent do IOs adopt social media and why? The analysis of social media presences run by a stratified-random-sample of IOs suggest a remarkable interest in digital communication vis-à-vis non-state audiences. Even if most IOs start with a single social media presence for the entire organisation, most substantially diversified their presence on Facebook and Twitter over time. With regard to the causal conditions conducive to this process of "going digital," three major findings emerged from the quantitative analysis:

first, increased external contestation and the opening IO bodies for representatives of transnational civil society foster social media use. This is strong evidence that an impulse for self-legitimation drives IOs to open new channels of communication with non-state audiences. In this way, the findings add remarkable empirical evidence in support of recent calls to more systematically engage with self-legitimation as an organisational imperative of IOs (Dingwerth et al. 2015; Gronau and Schmidtke 2016).

Secondly, evidence suggests that internal factors such as mandates shape IO demands for social media, for example, by calling for direct implementation of multiple policy programmes on the ground. This result directly speaks to research on the ubiquitous role of IOs in global governance arrangement. States have pooled significant resources and competences in IOs to directly monitor the local spread of diseases, human rights violations, or compliance with peace

TABLE 2.4 Platform-specific regression models separating the observed number of Facebook and Twitter presences

Model	1	2	3	4	5	6
Dependent variable	N Facebook pages	N Facebook pages	N Twitter accounts	N Twitter accounts	N Twitter accounts	N Twitter accounts
Protest, dummy	1.547*** (0.315)		1.226*** (0.303)		1.246*** (0.295)	
Protest Coverage, logged N		0.894*** (0.160)		0.733*** (0.146)		0.710*** (0.101)
Scandal, dummy	0.471*** (0.132)		0.638*** (0.120)		0.467* (0.220)	
Scandal Coverage, logged N		0.398*** (0.090)		0.418*** (0.081)		0.316*** (0.085)
Transnational Access, index	1.018** (0.344)	0.987** (0.354)	0.882** (0.297)	0.884** (0.304)	0.900* (0.354)	0.908* (0.394)
Democratic Membership, index	−0.073 (0.076)	−0.071 (0.076)	−0.065 (0.060)	−0.065 (0.062)	−0.122 (0.076)	−0.122 (0.084)
Implementation Mandate, index	0.631* (0.279)	0.671* (0.286)	0.786*** (0.218)	0.828*** (0.225)	0.840** (0.255)	0.911*** (0.276)
Multi-Issue Mandate, dummy	0.927** (0.342)	0.831* (0.358)	0.623** (0.233)	0.575* (0.238)	0.626* (0.250)	0.554* (0.253)
Centralised Public Communication, index	0.176** (0.054)	0.160** (0.056)	0.240*** (0.038)	0.224*** (0.039)	0.280*** (0.034)	0.250*** (0.037)
Internet Users, percent	0.024# (0.013)	0.026* (0.013)	0.018# (0.010)	0.020# (0.011)	0.023# (0.012)	0.026* (0.013)

Social media presence of peers, mean N	0.064	0.093	0.208	0.253#	0.305*	0.361**
	(0.081)	(0.082)	(0.131)	(0.137)	(0.133)	(0.137)
Budget > Euro 1 million, dummy	−0.488	−0.449	−0.429	−0.428	−0.844	−0.844
	(0.642)	(0.660)	(0.586)	(0.604)	(0.622)	(0.642)
Budget > Euro 10 million, dummy	0.954#	1.080#	0.188	0.302	0.208	0.409
	(0.573)	(0.574)	(0.356)	(0.360)	(0.380)	(0.391)
Administrative body, dummy	1.849***	1.877***	1.379***	1.385***	1.346**	1.306**
	(0.435)	(0.428)	(0.368)	(0.367)	(0.460)	(0.454)
Governmental body, dummy	−1.444**	−1.435**	−1.837***	−1.852***	−1.934***	−1.957***
	(0.450)	(0.445)	(0.445)	(0.450)	(0.501)	(0.496)
Constant	−4.835***	−4.930***	−4.707***	−4.755***	−4.596***	−4.649***
	(0.696)	(0.704)	(0.629)	(0.643)	(0.717)	(0.732)
Alpha (over-dispersion)	1.722**	1.747**	0.810	0.802		
Log Likelihood	−1902.854	−1903.531	−1390.903	−1389.206	−1685.796	−1691.949
N IO-Body-Years	3190	3190	3190	3190	3190	3190
N IO-Bodies	290	290	290	290	290	290

Note: The table reports coefficients from negative-binomial regression models 1–4 replicating "full models" as reported in Table 2 (models 6 and 7), separated for counts of Facebook pages and Twitter accounts. Note that Alpha statistics for models 3 and 4 are insignificant, suggesting that simple Poisson regression might be sufficient. Consequently, additional Poisson regression models 5 and 6 are reported. Robust standard errors clustered by IO bodies are given in parentheses. # $p < 0.10$, * $p < 0.05$, ** $p < 0.01$, *** $p < 0.001$

agreements. They administer the delivery of humanitarian aid and local order in post-conflict societies (Karns and Mingst 2004; Avant et al. 2010; Oestreich 2012; Abbott et al. 2015). The massive enhancing of social media presences by IOs concerned with such tasks suggests that social media becomes to be seen as tools for core organisational goals.

Thirdly, the development of centralised capacities for communication – typically in the form of communication departments located at headquarter level of the administrative branch – substantially facilitates the adoption and use of social media. This finding resonates with research that has pointed to a notable "normalisation" of social media use, for example in the case of transnational human rights campaigning (Thrall et al. 2014). According to this research, social media was most easily accommodated by the stronger and more professional actors, which falsify earlier hopes that social media may compensate for a lack of resources and contribute for bringing about a level playing field in global governance (e.g., Deibert 2000; Bennett and Segerberg 2013). In this regard, social media use in the IO field strikingly matches a picture of public resonance clustered around the usual suspects in terms of professionalised public communication.

Implications for future studies are manifold. As stated in the introduction, enhanced capacities for direct communication provide opportunities for public information and therefore enhance public accountability by making IOs more transparent (Florini 2000; Buchanan and Keohane 2006; Grigorescu 2007). At the same time, social media may enable IOs to more effectively manage and manipulate societal perceptions of policy effectiveness and the democratic credentials of internal processes, for example, with regard to issues of stakeholder inclusiveness and empowerment (Ecker-Ehrhardt 2018b). However, the presented evidence remains radically deficient in this regard. What we need is more comprehensive analysis of dialogical qualities of social media use as well as communicated content – including possible selectivity of provided information on IO decision-making, policies, and impact.

Relatedly, public relation scholars have long pointed to the substantial variation by which the work of communication practitioners working inside public administrations or companies is connected to other parts of the same organisation (Grunig 1992). IO scholars have applied ideas of neo-institutionalism to argue that organisational "talk" vis-à-vis relevant publics is often stunningly "decoupled" from internal decision-making and outward policy action (Lipson 2007). Thus, in order to really understand IOs' use of social media we need more careful analysis of the modes of producing content. Who is in charge of running social media accounts? How much are social media activities connected to other practices of public communication? How much "decoupling" do we find with regard to the internal process of problem definition, policy formulation, decision-making, and implementation? To what extent do those responsible for social media pages have access to upper echelon of the organisation – so that, for example, direct interaction with citizens on social media can have an impact on central decision-making or implementation of these decisions on the ground?

Such questions can arguably be addressed with case study evidence, for example, based on process-tracing of internal workflows (Dimitrov 2014; Corrie 2015). However, complementary evidence of comparative studies would help to come up with sound general conclusions about the role of digital communication in the current (and future) trajectories of global governance.

Appendix

The sample: name of covered IOs (N = 49)

- African Civil Service Observatory (ACSO)
- African Union (AU)
- Andean Community of Nations (CAN)
- Arab Maghreb Union (AMU)
- Asia-Pacific Economic Cooperation (APEC)
- Asian Development Bank (ADB)
- Association of Southeast Asian Nations (ASEAN)
- Bank for International Settlements (BIS)
- Black Sea Economic Cooperation Zone (BSEC)
- Caribbean Community and Common Market (CARICOM)
- Caribbean Development Bank (CDB)
- Central European Initiative (CEI)
- Commonwealth (COMW)
- Comunidade dos Países de Língua Portuguesa (CPLP)
- Council of Europe (CoE)
- Economic and Monetary Community of Central-Africa (CEMAC)
- Economic Cooperation Organization (ECO)
- European Bank for Reconstruction and Development (EBRD)
- European Collaboration on Measurement Standards (EUROMET)
- European Free Trade Association (EFTA)
- Fund for the Development of the Indigenous Peoples of L. America (FI)
- Inter-Governmental Authority on Development (IGAD)
- International Regional Organization against Plant and Animal Diseases (OIRSA)
- International Bureau for the Protection of the Moselle against Pollution (IKSMS)
- International Coffee Organization (ICO)
- International Council for the Exploration of the Sea (ICES)
- International Criminal Court (ICC)
- International Mobile Satellite Organization (IMSO)
- International Monetary Fund (IMF)
- International Telecommunications Satellites Organization (ITSO)
- International Whaling Commission (IWC)
- Niger Basin Authority (ABN)
- Nordic Council (NC)

- North American Free Trade Agreement (NAFTA)
- North Atlantic Treaty Organization (NATO)
- North-East Atlantic Fisheries Commission (NEAFC)
- Northwest Atlantic Fisheries Organization (NAFO)
- Organization for Economic Cooperation and Development (OECD)
- Organization for Security and Defense and Cooperation in Europe (OSCE)
- Organization of American States (OAS)
- Organization of Arab Petroleum Exporting Countries (OAPEC)
- Organization of the Islamic Conference (OIC)
- Pacific Islands Forum (PIF)
- Shanghai Cooperation Organization (SCO)
- South Asia Co-operative Environment Program (SACEP)
- United Nations (UN)
- Wassenaar Arrangement (Wassenaar)
- World Bank Group (WB)
- World Trade Organization (WTO)

Notes

1 Essential research assistance by Lucas Wotzka, Philip Kreißel, and Sandra Meurer is gratefully acknowledged. Earlier versions were presented at workshops at Dalhousie University, Halifax; the ECPR Joint Sessions 2019, Mons; and the Pan-European Conference on International Relations 2019, Sofia. For helpful comments and suggestions, the author is particularly grateful to Susana Salgado, Thomas Sommerer, Ada Müller, Bernd Schlipphak, Hans Agné, Thomas Kreuder-Sonnen, Mathias Hofferberth, Corneliu Bjola, Ruben Zaiotti, Magdalena Müller, Tobias Lenz, Michal Parizek, Maja Granitz, and Nancy Groves.
2 See <https://www.facebook.com/comunidadandina> and <https://twitter.com/ASEAN>. Note that many of these presences entail more or less explicit hints to the main secretariat, for example, by the provided contact information (e.g., a telephone number directly leading to the CPLP Secretariat in Lisbon), the page's link reading "headquarter" (e.g., "@ebrdhq" in case of the EBRD main Facebook page or "@SG.Union.Maghreb.Arabe" for the respective page of the AMU).
3 <https://www.facebook.com/yourCCj; https://twitter.com/CaribbeanCourt>.
4 <https://www.facebook.com/European-Court-Of-Human-Rights-ECHR-1497 89481758705/>; <https://twitter.com/ECHR_Press>.
5 <https://www.facebook.com/panafricanparliament>; <https://twitter.com/AfrikParliament>.
6 <https://www.facebook.com/ParliamentaryAssembly>; <https://twitter.com/PACE_News>.
7 See Barberá and Zeitzoff (2017) for a similar approach of pooling social media data.

References

Abbott, Kenneth W., Philipp Genschel, Duncan Snidal, and Bernhard Zangl. *International Organizations as Orchestrators*. Cambridge: Cambridge University Press, 2015.
Aghi, Mira, and Neill McKee. *Involving People, Evolving Behaviour*. Penang and New York: Southbound and United Nations Children's Fund, 2000.

Alleyne, Mark D. *Global Lies? Propaganda, the UN, and World Order*. New York: Palgrave Macmillan, 2003.

Archer, Clive. *International Organizations*. London: Allen Press & Unwin, 1983.

Asia-Pacific Economic Cooperation. *APEC Secretariat's Communications and Public Affairs Strategic Plan, 2014–2016*. Singapore: Asia-Pacific Economic Cooperation, 2014.

Avant, Deborah D., Martha Finnemore, and Susan K. Sell. "Who Governs the Globe?." In *Who Governs the Globe?* edited by Deborah D. Avant, Martha Finnemore, and Susan K. Sell, 1–35. New York: Cambridge University Press, 2010.

Ayoub, Phillip M. "Contested Norms in New-Adopter States: International Determinants of LGBT Rights Legislation." *European Journal of International Relations* 21, no. 2 (2015): 293–322.

Barberá, Pablo, and Thomas Zeitzoff. "The New Public Address System: Why Do World Leaders Adopt Social Media?." *International Studies Quarterly* 62, no. 1 (2017): 121–30.

Barnett, Michael N., and Martha Finnemore. *Rules for the World. International Organizations in Global Politics*. Ithaca, London: Cornell University Press, 2004.

Bennett, W. Lance, and Alexandra Segerberg. *The Logic of Connective Action: Digital Media and the Personalization of Contentious Politics*. New York: Cambridge University Press, 2013.

Bennett, W., Victor W. Lance, David P. Pickard, Carl L. Iozzi, Taso Lagos Schroeder, and C. Evans Caswell. "Managing the Public Sphere: Journalistic Construction of the Great Globalization Debate." *Journal of Communication* 54, no. 3 (2004): 437–55.

Bexell, Magdalena, Jonas Tallberg, and Anders Uhlin. "Democracy in Global Governance: The Promises and Pitfalls of Transnational Actors." *Global Governance* 16, no. 1 (2010): 81–101.

Boin, Arjen, Paul 'tHart, and Allan McConnell. "Crisis Exploitation: Political and Policy Impacts of Framing Contests." *Journal of European Public Policy* 16, no. 1 (2009): 81–106.

Boomgaarden, Hajo G., Andreas R.T. Schuck, Matthijs Elenbaas, and Claes H. de Vreese. "Mapping EU Attitudes: Conceptual and Empirical Dimensions of Euroscepticism and EU Support." *European Union Politics* 12, no. 2 (2011): 241–66.

Bortree, Denise Sevick, and Trent Seltzer. "Dialogic Strategies and Outcomes: An Analysis of Environmental Advocacy Groups' Facebook Profiles." *Public Relations Review* 35, no. 3 (2009): 317–19.

Brändström, Annika, and Sanneke Kuipers. "From 'Normal Incidents' to Political Crises: Understanding the Selective Politicization of Policy Failures." *Government & Opposition* 38, no. 3 (2003): 279–305.

Brüggemann, Michael. *Europäische Öffentlichkeit durch Öffentlichkeitsarbeit? Die Informationspolitik der Europäischen Kommission*. Wiesbaden: VS Verlag für Sozialwissenschaften, 2008.

Bruns, Axel. *Blogs, Wikipedia, Second Life, and Beyond: From Production to Produsage*. New York: Peter Lang Publishing, 2008.

Buchanan, Allen, and Robert O. Keohane. "The Legitimacy of Global Governance Institutions." *Ethics & International Affairs* 20, no. 4 (2006): 405–37.

Bulovsky, Andrew. "Authoritarian Communication on Social Media: The Relationship Between Democracy and Leaders' Digital Communicative Practices." *International Communication Gazette* 81, no. 1 (2019): 20–45.

Cárdenas, Emilio J. "UN Financing: Some Reflections." *European Journal of International Law* 11, no. 1 (2000): 67–75.

Coldevin, Gary. "Participatory Communication and Adult Learning for Rural Development." *Journal of International Communication* 7, no. 2 (2001): 51–69.

Corrie, Karen L. "The International Criminal Court: Using Technology in Network Diplomacy." In *Digital Diplomacy*, edited by Corneliu Bjola, and Marcus Holmes, 159–77. New York: Routledge, 2015.

de Wilde, Pieter. *How Politicisation Affects European Integration: Contesting the EU Budget in the Netherlands, Denmark and Ireland.* Oslo: University of Oslo, 2011.

Defourny, Vincent. "Public Information in the UNESCO: Towards a Strategic Role." In *The Global Public Relations Handbook. Theory, Research, and Practice*, edited by Krishnamurthy Sriramesh, and Dejan Vercic, 425–40. Mahwah, NJ: Routledge, 2003.

Deibert, Ronald J. "International Plug'n play? Citizen Activism, the Internet, and Global Public Policy." *International Studies Perspectives* 1, no. 3 (2000): 255–72.

della Porta, Donatella. *The Global Justice Movement: Cross-National and Transnational Perspectives.* Boulder, CO: Paradigm Publications, 2007.

Dellmuth, Lisa Maria. "The Knowledge Gap in World Politics: Assessing the Sources of Citizen Awareness of the United Nations Security Council." *Review of International Studies* 42, no. 4 (2016): 673–700.

Dellmuth, Lisa Maria, and Jonas Tallberg. "The Social Legitimacy of International Organisations: Interest Representation, Institutional Performance, and Confidence Extrapolation in the United Nations." *Review of International Studies* 41, no. 3 (2015): 451–75.

Dimitrov, Roumen. "Bringing Communication up to Agency: UNESCO Reforms Its Visibility." *Public Relations Inquiry* 3, no. 3 (2014): 293–318.

Dingwerth, Klaus, Ina Lehmann, Ellen Reichel, Tobias Weise, and Antonia Witt. "Many Pipers, Many Tunes?. Die Legitimationskommunikation internationaler Organisationen in komplexen Umwelten." In *Internationale Organisationen: Autonomie Politisierung, interorganisationale Beziehungen und Wandel*, edited by Eugénia da Conceição-Heldt, Martin Koch, and Andrea Liese, 191–217. Baden-Baden: Nomos, 2015.

Dingwerth, Klaus, Antonia Witt, Ina Lehmann, Ellen Reichel, and Tobias Weise. *International Organizations Under Pressure: Legitimating Global Governance in Changing Times.* Oxford: Oxford University Press, 2019.

Ecker-Ehrhardt, Matthias. "Why Parties Politicise International Institutions: On Globalisation Backlash and Authority Contestation." *Review of International Political Economy* 21, no. 6 (2014): 1275–312.

Ecker-Ehrhardt, Matthias. "International Organizations 'Going Public'? an Event History Analysis of Public Communication Reforms 1950–2015." *International Studies Quarterly* 62, no. 4 (2018a): 723–36.

Ecker-Ehrhardt, Matthias. "IO Public Communication and Discursive Inclusion: How the un Reported the Arms Trade Treaty Process to a Global Audience." *Journal of International Relations & Development* (online first) (2018b): 1–29. doi:10.1057/s41268-018-0143-3.

Ecker-Ehrhardt, Matthias. "Self-Legitimation in the Face of Politicization: Why International Organizations Centralized Public Communication." *The Review of International Organizations* 13, no. 4 (2018c): 519–46.

Finnemore, Martha. "International Organizations as Teachers of Norms: The United Nations Educational, Scientific and Cultural Organization and Science Policy." *International Organization* 47, no. 4 (1993): 565–97.

Florini, Ann. *The Third Force: The Rise of Transnational Civil Society.* Washington, DC: Carnegie Endowment for International Peace, 2000.

Florini, Ann M., and Peter J. Simmons. "What the World Needs Now?" In *The Third Force: The Rise of Transnational Civil Society*, edited by Ann M. Florini, 1–15. Tokyo and

Washington, DC: Japan Center for International Change and Carnegie Endowment for International Peace, 2000.

Gilson, Julie. "Structuring Accountability: Civil Society and the Asia-Europe Meeting." In *Building Global Democracy*, edited by Jan A. Scholte, 206–24. Cambridge: Cambridge University Press, 2011.

Grigorescu, Alexandru. "Transparency of Intergovernmental Organizations: The Roles of Member States, International Bureaucracies and Nongovernmental Organizations." *International Studies Quarterly* 51, no. 3 (2007): 625–48.

Gronau, Jennifer, and Henning Schmidtke. "The Quest for Legitimacy in World Politics–International Institutions' Legitimation Strategies." *Review of International Studies* 42, no. 3 (2016): 535–57.

Grunig, James E. *Excellence in Public Relations and Communication Management*. Hillsdale, NJ: L. Erlbaum Associates, 1992.

Hussain, Muzammil M., and Philip N. Howard. "What Best Explains Successful Protest Cascades? ICTs and the Fuzzy Causes of the Arab Spring." *International Studies Review* 15, no. 1 (2013): 48–66.

Jacobson, Harold K. *Networks of Interdependence: International Organizations and the Global Political System*. New York: Random House, 1984.

Johnson, Tana. "Guilt by Association: The Link Between States' Influence and the Legitimacy of Intergovernmental Organizations." *The Review of International Organizations* 6, no. 1 (2011): 57–84.

Karns, Margaret P., and Karen A. Mingst. *International Organizations. The Politics and Processes of Global Governance*. Boulder, CO: Lynne Rienner, 2004.

Keck, Magret, and Kathryn Sikkink. *Activists Beyond Borders: Transnational Advocacy Networks in International Politics*. Ithaca, NY: Cornell University Press, 1998.

Koch, Martin. "Autonomization of IGOs." *International Political Sociology* 3, no. 4 (2009): 431–48.

Lehmann, Ingrid A. *Peacekeeping and Public Information: Caught in the Crossfire*. London and Portland, OR: F. Cass, 1999.

Lehmann, Ingrid A. *The Political and Cultural Dynamics of United Nations Media Scandals: From Waldheim to Annan. MEDIA@LSE Electronic Working Papers No. 22*. London: London School of Economics and Political Science, 2011.

Lipson, Michael. "Peacekeeping: Organized Hypocrisy?" *European Journal of International Relations* 13, no. 1 (2007): 5–34.

Loader, Brian D., and Dan Mercea. "Networking Democracy? Social Media Innovations and Participatory Politics." *Information, Communication & Society* 14, no. 6 (2011): 757–69.

Margolis, Michael, and David Resnick. 2000. *Politics as Usual*. Thousands Oaks, CA and London: Sage.

Marshall, M.G., K. Jaggers, and T.R. Gurr. *Polity IV Project: Political Regime Characteristics and Transitions, 1800–2015*. Vienna, VA: Center for Systemic Peace, 2016.

Mefalopulos, Paolo. *Development Communication Sourcebook: Broadening the Boundaries of Communication*. New York: World Bank Publications, 2008.

Meyer, Christoph O. "Does European Union Politics Become Mediatized? The Case of the European Commission." *Journal of European Public Policy* 16, no. 7 (2009): 1047–64.

Meyer, Jeffrey A., and Mark G. Califano. *Good Intentions Corrupted: The Oil-for-Food Scandal and the Threat to the UN*. New York: Public Affairs, 2006.

Moulin, Carolina, and Peter Nyers. 2007 "'We Live in a Country of UNHCR' – Refugee Protests and Global Political Society." *International Political Sociology* 1, no. 4: 356–72.

Nah, Seungahn, and Gregory D. Saxton. "Modeling the Adoption and Use of Social Media by Nonprofit Organizations." *New Media & Society* 15, no. 2 (2013): 294–313.

Nay, Olivier. "International Organisations and the Production of Hegemonic Knowledge: How the World Bank and the OECD Helped Invent the Fragile State Concept." *Third World Quarterly* 35, no. 2 (2014): 210–31.

Norris, Pippa. "Global Governance & Cosmopolitan Citizens." In *Governance in a Globalizing World*, edited by Joseph S. Nye, Jr., and John D. Donahue, 155–77. Washington, DC: Brookings Institution Press, 2000.

North Atlantic Treaty Organization. *NATO Strategic Communications Policy*. Brussels: North Atlantic Treaty Organization, 2009.

Nullmeier, Frank, Dominika Biegon, Martin Nonhoff, Henning Schmidtke, and Steffen Schneider. *Prekäre Legitimitäten: Rechtfertigung von Herrschaft in der postnationalen Konstellation*. Frankfurt a. M.: Campus, 2010.

O'Brien, Robert, Anne Marie Goetz, Jan A. Scholte, and Marc Williams. *Contesting Global Governance: Multilateral Economic Institutions and Global Social Movements*. Cambridge: Cambridge University Press, 2000.

Odell, John, and Barry Eichengreen. "The United States, the ITO, and the WTO: Exit Options, Agent Slack, and Presidential Leadership." In *The WTO as an International Organization*, edited by Anne O. Krueger, 181–206. Chicago, IL: Chicago University Press, 1998.

Odugbemi, Sina, and Taeku Lee. *Accountability Through Public Opinion: From Inertia to Public Action*. New York: World Bank Publications, 2011.

Oestreich, Joel E. *International Organizations as Self-Directed Actors: A Framework for Analysis*. Abingdon: Routledge, 2012.

Organization of American States. *Annual Report of the Secretary General 2005–2006*. Washington, DC: Organization of American States, 2006.

Risso, Linda. 2014. *Propaganda and Intelligence in the Cold War: The NATO Information Service*. Studies in Intelligence. Abingdon: Routledge.

Scholte, Jan A. *Building Global Democracy? Civil Society and Accountable Global Governance*. Cambridge: Cambridge University Press, 2011.

Servaes, Jan. "Harnessing the un System into a Common Approach on Communication for Development." *International Communication Gazette* 69, no. 6 (2007): 483–507.

Simmons, Beth A., and Zachary Elkins. "The Globalization of Liberalization: Policy Diffusion in the International Political Economy." *American Political Science Review* 98, no. 1 (2004): 171–89.

Smith, Courtney B. "The Politics of US–UN Reengagement: Achieving Gains in a Hostile Environment." *International Studies Perspectives* 5, no. 2 (2004): 197–215.

Sommerer, Thomas, and Jonas Tallberg. "Diffusion Across International Organizations: Connectivity and Convergence." *International Organization* 73, no. 2 (2019): 399–433.

Steffek, Jens, Claudia Kissling, and Patrizia Nanz. *Civil Society Participation in European and Global Governance. A Cure for the Democratic Deficit?* Houndmills: Palgrave Macmillan, 2008.

Suchman, Marc C. "Managing Legitimacy: Strategic and Institutional Approaches." *The Academy of Management Review* 20, no. 3 (1995): 571–610.

Tallberg, Jonas, Thomas Sommerer, Theresa Squatrito, and Christer Jönsson. *The Opening up of International Organizations: Transnational Access in Global Governance*. Cambridge: Cambridge University Press, 2013.

Tallberg, Jonas, Thomas Sommerer, Theresa Squatrito, and Christer Jönsson. "Explaining the Transnational Design of International Organizations." *International Organization* 68, no. 4 (2014): 741–74.

Tarrow, Sidney. "Transnational Politics: Contention and Institutions in International Politics." *Annual Review of Political Science* 4, no. 1 (2001): 1–20.

Thompson, John B. *Political Scandal: Power and Visibility in the Media Age.* Cambridge: Polity Press, 2000.

Thrall, A. Trevor, Dominik Stecula, and Diana Sweet. "May We Have Your Attention Please? Human-Rights NGOs and the Problem of Global Communication." *The International Journal of Press/Politics* 19, no. 2 (2014): 135–59.

Weber, Max. *Economy and Society: An Outline of Interpretive Sociology.* Berkeley, CA: University of California Press, 1978.

World Bank. *A Guide to the World Bank.* Washington, DC: World Bank, 2011.

Zürn, Michael, Martin Binder, and Matthias Ecker-Ehrhardt. "International Authority and Its Politicization." *International Theory* 4, no. 1 (2012): 69–106.

3

DIGITAL DIPLOMACY OR POLITICAL COMMUNICATION? EXPLORING SOCIAL MEDIA IN THE EU INSTITUTIONS FROM A CRITICAL DISCOURSE PERSPECTIVE[1]

Michał Krzyżanowski

Introduction

This chapter considers digital diplomacy – seen as "the use of social media for diplomatic purposes" (Bjola 2015, 4) – in the context of institutional constellation of the European Union. However, looking beyond the strictly institutional-communicative or international relations aspect, the chapter explores how the key EU institutions such as, very notably, its executive branch, i.e., the European Commission (EC), use social media not only as the channel of information sharing or diplomatic activity but also, or perhaps predominantly, as a channel of political communication. Exploring this aspect alongside the digital diplomacy considerations is particularly vital in the EU context which for a while now has been considered not only as a set of international organizations but more commonly as a unique arrangement of supranational political institutions (Majone 2005). In a similar vein, the EU institutional actions were often re-evaluated from the point of not only its wider "democratic deficit" (Majone 1998; Folesdal and Hix 2006; Nicolaidis 2010) but also, ever more increasingly, from the point of view of its pervasive "communication deficit" (Meyer 1999; Krzyżanowski 2012) which was often identified as one of the key reasons why the EU was unable to move beyond its intergovernmental roots towards a federal, supranational polity (Krzyżanowski and Oberhuber 2007; Krzyżanowski 2010).

While tackling the above challenges to EU institutions, the chapter looks specifically at how Twitter, a microblogging platform and social medium most commonly used for purposes of contemporary political communication, is used in the context of the institutions of the European Union (EU). The main interest of the chapter is in the in-depth analysis of how social/online media – using the example of Twitter – are used as a tool for communication in/by political institutions of the EU. More specifically, the chapter tackles such research questions as

(a) whether Twitter can help in changing patterns of politico-organisation communication in/of the EU and democratizing it by offering new ways of digital-diplomatic thinking and doing and (b) whether social/online media in general bring any new quality to the often-criticised EU political communication.

The chapter hypothesises that while, to some extent, bringing change or "modernisation" to EU political communication patterns, social/online media do, in fact, support sustaining, rather than eradicating, several of the deep-seated dispositions in EU communicative practices as political discourses. Hence, as this chapter aims to show, social/online media do not constitute any significant break in EU communication policies and practices, despite often being presented as such.

On the contrary, as the chapter shows, instead of bringing some new qualities, social media actually help in solidifying some, often controversial, patterns in EU political communication. This points to the enduring eminence of the so-called "linearities of organisational practice" (Krzyżanowski 2011) or to the indeed peculiar "autopoiesis" (Luhmann 1995; Muntigl, Weiss and Wodak 2000) of EU institutional organisms. Both the former and the latter remain, it seems, a driving force in EU political action and in communication thereof, arguably with the main interest being in preserving and sustaining EU institutions (and their logic, procedures, structures, etc.), rather than changing them into political beings, as well as subsequently opening them up to the wider European citizenry.

In general terms, the chapter looks at the social media communication practices where these are not actually used for purposes that are essentially "social" (or sometimes not even "political," see below). It focuses instead on wherever interactivity and social/online mediation are used for the purposes of gaining or sustaining political power, including via hegemonic discourses mediated cross-nationally through online contexts, as well as via elite (political-diplomatic but also journalist and other) networks and practices. Therefore, the analysis looks in detail at the discourse of spokespeople in the political-institutional context of the EU and treats the discursive practices of spokespeople in social media contexts as essentially politico-organisational, yet inherently hybrid in nature due to their targeting of both EU internal (i.e., institutional) actors and politicians, as well as looking at extra-EU actors including, very prominently, national politics in Europe, the (in most cases traditional) European mass media, and, probably at least, self-mediated European publics.

The chapter looks specifically at the social media presence of the EU as "created" by the EC's Spokesperson's Service, i.e., the main part of the European Commission responsible for not only the shape but also the content of the EC and the wider EU social/online media presence. The chapter offers a Critical Discourse Analysis of EU politico-organisational communication on Twitter by proposing a qualitative framework for Twitter (and other social media) analysis that relates interactive strategies to their discursive counterparts. It showcases a pathway of analysis which, on the one hand, explores how *social media behaviour* is indicative of different forms of political and otherwise understood networking, and is part of communicating the EU to its external environment. On the other hand, the focus on *social media discourse* allows an exploration of what kinds of key strategies are deployed in the EU's social media presence and how the use of those discursive strategies underlines some of the key tendencies indicated above (autopoiesis, closeness, etc.), while pointing to processes of recontextualisation (Bernstein 1990; Krzyżanowski 2016) of discursive elements across spatial and temporal scales. Relating both the above levels/areas of analysis is vital for not only showing the actual form/content of EU online and social media discourse, but also depicting how the relationship between "Twitter behaviour" and "Twitter discourse" is indicative of wider processes, e.g., the elitisation of EU communication in the process of building and sustaining networks with selected, in most cases elite, media, political actors, and audiences.

The European Union, external communication, and online/social media

Many classic works on the EU's external communication (see esp. Michailidou 2017) emphasise that the latter has traditionally been challenged by many shortcomings which, as such, questioned the de facto political character of the EU. Communication has surely never been at the forefront of EU interests and policies with the majority of the EU institutions – especially the intergovernmental Council of the EU, and to a lesser degree the EU's executive, i.e., the EC – traditionally operating a closed-door policy and contacting their external environment through official spokespeople. In this way, the EU has also, for a very long time, escaped the scholarly interest of e.g. (political) communication research (cf Schlesinger 1999 and 2003).

Also, although most of the European institutions have been around for several years, the majority of them have, until recently, looked only very reluctantly at the issue of external communication in general, and at communication between those institutions and the wider European public, media, etc., in particular. This has been the case for, inter alia, the widely-debated EU "organisational cultures" (Krzyżanowski 2011) which, as such, have extensively borrowed from other transnational (and in particular intergovernmental) milieus many of their organisational procedures. These included patterns and ways of shaping the institutions' internal and external communication and were, often not surprisingly, very often based on intra- and inter-institutional secrecy, rather than openness and transparency. It seems that, at a time when the EU was increasingly becoming a political supranational structure and required increased support and closer connections to the European citizenry (see, inter alia, Nicolaïdis 2010), its institutions hardly followed suit in opening up by means of (online) communication or strengthening a much-needed, coordinated, inter-institutional communication policy (Krzyżanowski 2012).

Accordingly, while most of the EU institutions have developed their own spokesperson services – probably most elaborate in the case of the EC, as analysed below – all of those services were focused on "informing about" the EU and its actions, rather than on "communicating between" those institutions and the European public. That situation did not change, even during the initial crises of the EU institutions in the late 1990s (e.g., the 1999 crisis of the Santer Commission), when a drive towards political communication rather than just top-down information would certainly have helped in eradicating some of the then key criticisms of the EU system (Meyer 1999; Anderson and McLeod 2004; Schneeberger and Sarikakis 2008).

A period of, unfortunately not enduring, change in EU external communication arrived in the early 2000s and was characterised by a profound institutional overhaul of, in particular, the EC (Anderson and McLeod 2004; Kassim 2008) and, later on, the development of an EU Communication Policy in the aftermath of the EU's so-called constitutional crisis in the years 2003–2007 (see esp. Krzyżanowski 2012). Especially in the latter period, the EU turned increasingly to new forms of communicating with its citizens and to some extent embraced the then available mode of online communication, including, most prominently, online fora (see Wodak and Wright 2006; Krzyżanowski and Oberhuber 2007). At this time, as part of its aforementioned policy, the EC also issued the famous document "Communicating about Europe via the Internet, Engaging the Citizens" (European Commission 2007) which, albeit quite vaguely, pleaded that the EU must increase its use of online affordances to communicate with European citizens in a much more concise and efficient manner.

However, still before the arrival of social media as a widespread political communication tool (see above), the EU started to gradually retreat from its wider thinking about online (political) communication, especially following some of its failures in the period after the 2008 economic crisis. Eventually, with the 2010 changes to the EC set-up, the aforementioned EU communication policy was largely abandoned (including the controversial removal of an EU Commissioner for Communication post) and returned de facto to the EC's Directorate General Communication, i.e., predominantly the EC Spokesperson's Service. Here, one could observe, in particular, a retreat to the classic approach to "information," rather than political or other "communication." However, as evidenced though the analysis presented below, some aspects of especially top-down political communication known from national politics (see above) – and in particular the formation of elitist networks between politicians, spokespeople, and journalists – could also be clearly observed in the EU's presence on social media which eventually developed in the second decade of the 2000s.

Yet, it would be a mistake to say that the European Union is not present in social and online media, especially as a topic of political debates. Research has shown, for example, that the move towards an online presence by the traditional mass media has accelerated many online debates about the EU (see esp. de Wilde, Michailidou, and Trenz 2013; Michailidou, Trenz, and de Wilde 2014; Barisione and Michailidou 2017), while at the same time often solidifying patterns of contestation of European ideas, as in national-political arenas.

Work that has focused explicitly on social media and/or Twitter (see esp. Michailidou 2017) emphasises this trend, yet it shows that while EU-related topics do occupy a significant chunk of online media debates at present, the EU as such is not a significant "influencer" of EU-specific debates, contrary to national public spheres where European ideas are still nested and contested (see also Krzyżanowski, Triandafyllidou, and Wodak 2009). Thus, the EU clearly trails, especially behind those national politicians and journalists who set the tone in debates on European matters. In a similar vein, the character of social media discourse about the EU and European politics has clearly diversified. While it is often strictly induced by EU-related events (e.g., EP Elections), or policies and actions (e.g., with regard to the recent "refugee crisis"), there is very limited input into those debates from EU institutional actors as such, and definitely almost none on Twitter and Facebook (Bosetta, Dutceac-Segesten, and Trenz 2017).

Of the EU institutions present on social/online media, probably the major one remains the European Parliament (EP), i.e., the only directly elected EU institution, chosen every five years by means of universal suffrage across all EU member states. Existent scholarship has shown, for example, that EP candidates have extensively deployed social media in their pre-election campaigns for several years now (Rodríguez and Garmendia Madariaga 2016). Similarly, social media have been key in the peculiar process of the "permanent" political campaigning of EP Members (Larsson 2015), indeed often in similar ways to the electoral social-media use known from national contexts (especially in the context of right-wing populist parties, see Krzyżanowski 2013). Other research has also shown that especially the coverage of EP elections in the national media (e.g., via televised debates and the like) has a direct influence on relevant political social media content as well as on the public's interest in the candidates, as expressed in interactions on, for example, Twitter (Nulty et al. 2016).

All of the above, however, point to the still isolated instances where the EU makes its way into social/online media reality. They show that the EU still does not have – or is not interested in – a strategy that, via its own communicative channels on social media, would allow either quantitative or qualitative increases in its presence in EU-related debates. Indeed, the above results from the EU's apparent lack of a clear understanding of its potential interlocutor "publics" (Tarta 2017) that could effectively be reached by European institutions and politics via social and online media channels.

Twitter "behaviour," Twitter "discourse," and EU spokespeople: analysis

Design of the study

The aim of the analysis below is to highlight similarities and differences between the Twitter practices of key members of the EC Spokesperson's Service in the previous (2009–2014) as well as the current (2015–2019) term of the European Commission.

Explored here from the point of view of its social media presence, the EC Spokesperson's Service is an integral part of the European Commission's Directorate General for Communication (DG COMM), i.e., the section of the EC responsible for "informing and communicating about the policies of the European Union with the public at large."[2] Although the remit of the Spokesperson's Service is narrower than that of the entire DG COMM – boiling down to contacts and communication with the media – it is widely known that the Service is the central source of both information about EU actions and politics in a wider sense, and EU's own social media discourse about EU politics and policies.[3]

The aim of the analysis below is to showcase key tendencies in the interactive and discursive behaviour of EC Spokespeople on Twitter, as well as to observe the dynamics of and change in their interactions/discourse. Those dynamics are grasped over two sample periods of one month each, observed in 2014 and 2015, in-between which the cohort of EC spokespeople underwent a very substantial change. Whereas in the period 2009–2014 – covered by the 2014 analysis – members of the Service were still mainly recruited from among skilful and long-serving EC (and wider EU) officials (thus catering for a large degree of uniformity of experience and skills in the Service), as of 2015, the group became much more hybridised to then include not only EC/EU officials but also many former journalists who previously covered EU affairs across EU countries.

The above change might, on the one hand, be considered a case of professionalisation of the service, especially since it follows the traditional pattern of media-to-spokespeople migration often encountered in political PR. On the other hand, however, it has certainly meant a change in and a break from many practices, perhaps especially as far as social media are concerned. For example, current members of the EC Spokesperson's Service widely use strongly personalised Twitter accounts (@NameSurname or similar, sometimes with the addition "EC"), while in the previous EC term several key spokespeople used standardised institutional-like account names (especially @ECSpokesNAME). This shows a tendency towards personalisation of the service as well as, very likely, also being a strategy whereby many new EC spokespeople – especially those recruited from outside EU institutions – could retain their "previous" identities as well as contacts and networks and continue using them while working for the EC.

The analysis below covers interactions and discourse in the Twitter activity of five key spokespeople in the 2009–2014 term of the European Commission (2014 analysis) and seven spokespeople in the 2015–2019 term (2015 analysis). The analysis is performed on, in total, a data set of 519 tweets/retweets, of which 316 were posted in 2014, and 203 in 2015. The relatively small/medium size of the data set is intended to enable in-depth analysis along both the aforementioned interaction- and discourse-oriented lines. The difference in the numbers of accounts stems from the lower degree of Twitter activity in the latter period.

In both cases, the analysis follows a sample period of 30 days and covers the days April 1–30 of, respectively, 2014 and 2015. The aforementioned change in the EC term took place in autumn 2014, i.e., between the two periods of investigation. The selection of the month of April as a period of analysis was not arbitrary, as this is traditionally a month of moderate (i.e., relatively usual) Twitter activity which includes both increased periods (especially in some unexpected situations) as well as "quieter" periods (especially around the Easter break). Using tweets in April also allows diversity in tweets. Due to the EU Calendar – and several key dates/anniversaries in early May (May-Day celebrations and Anniversary of 2004 EU Enlargement on May 1, Day of Europe on May 9, etc.), the month of April usually constitutes a run-up to many of those events and hence includes EU social media discourse that not only focuses on day-to-day activities and policy-related tweets, but also on wider discourses about Europe, including its history, future, global role, etc.

Pathways and categories of analysis

The analysis performed here falls into two areas (see Figure 3.1). The first area of analysis looks at the *interactive strategies* deployed in social media communication by members of the EC Spokesperson's Service. Here, the main interest is in

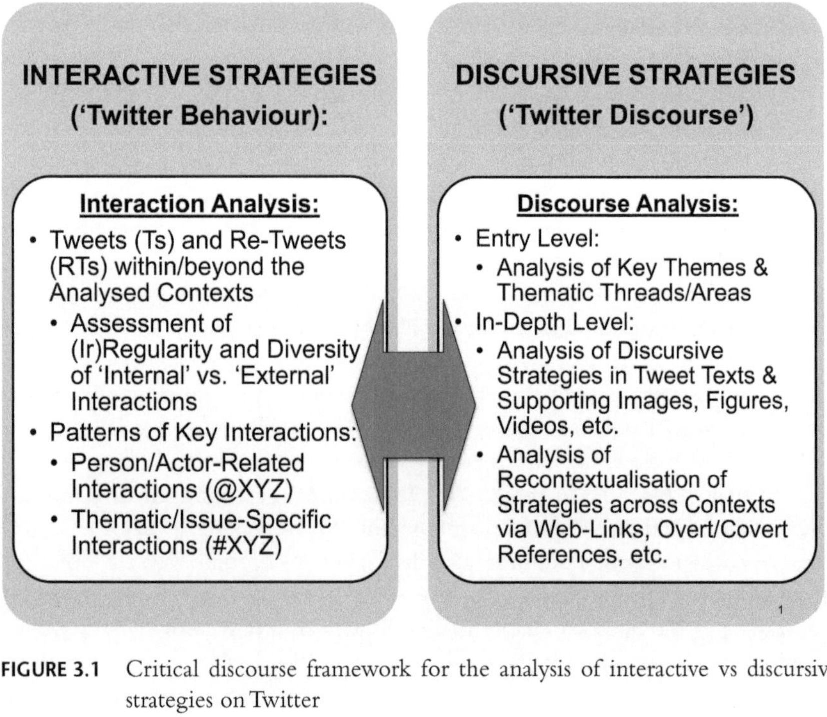

INTERACTIVE STRATEGIES
('Twitter Behaviour):

Interaction Analysis:
- Tweets (Ts) and Re-Tweets (RTs) within/beyond the Analysed Contexts
  - Assessment of (Ir)Regularity and Diversity of 'Internal' vs. 'External' Interactions
- Patterns of Key Interactions:
  - Person/Actor-Related Interactions (@XYZ)
  - Thematic/Issue-Specific Interactions (#XYZ)

DISCURSIVE STRATEGIES
('Twitter Discourse')

Discourse Analysis:
- Entry Level:
  - Analysis of Key Themes & Thematic Threads/Areas
- In-Depth Level:
  - Analysis of Discursive Strategies in Tweet Texts & Supporting Images, Figures, Videos, etc.
  - Analysis of Recontextualisation of Strategies across Contexts via Web-Links, Overt/Covert References, etc.

FIGURE 3.1 Critical discourse framework for the analysis of interactive vs discursive strategies on Twitter

both de facto performed interactivity (especially by means of re-tweets, or RTs, from other accounts) but also in the intended interactivity as displayed by both thematic mentions and interactions (by means of hashtags as well as weblinks included in the tweets) and personal mentions and interactions (by means of account references @Name).

The aim of the first area of the analysis is to display the extent to which the analysed Twitter presence is in fact self-constructed – including by means of one's own tweets, or Ts – by EU sources, or whether it relies on social media content produced by other actors, including those replicated by means of RTs from across non-EU (institutional) accounts. As far as the latter are concerned, the main interest is in the typology of sources and targets of interactions initiated on Twitter by members of the EC Spokesperson's Service. The analysis here aims to assess to what extent the social media input that the spokespeople rely on comes from EU-internal or EU-external sources and, if so, whether any relevant tendencies or regularities (or lack thereof) in online interactive "behaviour" can in fact be observed, especially as far as the variety of "externally" oriented and politically-driven interactions is concerned.

Meanwhile, the second area of analysis looks at *discursive strategies* and focuses explicitly on the Twitter discourse of key members of the EC Spokesperson's Service. Here, the examination of discourse follows the usual two-level analysis as deployed in, in particular, the discourse-historical analysis in Critical Discourse Studies (see esp. Krzyżanowski 2010). Hence, at first, the analysis focuses on general maps of themes (topics) in the analysed Twitter data and looks for the semantic meaning of Ts/RTs. It attempts to classify them as belonging to wider thematic areas/threads characteristic of the studied contexts (in the current case, EU institutions as well as non-EU contexts). On the other hand, the more in-depth discourse analysis pertains to following the key arguments and strategies deployed in the Twitter discourse in a pragmatic way, often wholly relying on the semantic aspects indicated above. Here, the key interest is in following patterns of construction of one's own ideas as well as the purposeful/ strategic *recontextualisation* (Bernstein 1990; Krzyżanowski 2016) of arguments and ideas from other discourses, be they originating within or outside EU institutions, and recontextualised both synchronically and diachronically.

Indeed, the recontextualising aspect lays the foundation of the second strand of the analysis. Here, drawing on existent literature and, in particular, on previous critical analyses of EU discourse, one can establish a set of prototypical tendencies that can then be tested to see if, and to what extent, they are present and deployed in the analysed Twitter material at hand. Among the key tendencies used as a point of reference, one should certainly mention, first and foremost: the ongoing struggle between political and democratic discussions about the EU on the one hand, and how it is economically driven, up to neoliberal framing, on the other (Krzyżanowski 2016), the EU's ever-prevalent tendency to discursively revisit and reconstruct its own identity (and history) including while fostering one's self-perception as a global leader in policy and humanitarian actions (see

Krzyżanowski 2015) or while arguing for the EU as the fulfilment of long-standing – and often pre-EU-institutional – visions of Europeanness (Krzyżanowski 2010).

Analysis of interactive strategies

An analysis of the EC Spokesperson's Service's interactive strategies on Twitter shows that within the two periods of investigation – i.e., throughout April 2014 and April 2015, respectively – there was a rather significant drop in the online activity of the analysed accounts. This, as indicated above, took place even despite the fact that the number of accounts covered by the analysis in the second period was much larger than in the first one.

While in April 2014 the overall number of analysed tweets and retweets (henceforth Ts and RTs) from the EC spokespeople accounts numbered 316, in 2015 the total was almost a third less and numbered, in total, 203 Ts/RTs. Despite that significant difference in the totals, the cumulative numbers of Ts and RTs, and the "own" Ts to RTs ratio, remained largely the same in both of the analysed periods, while oscillating at approximately 60% of all posts (with 189 RTs or 59.8% in 2014, and 125 RT posts or 61.5% in 2015).

In a similar vein, and again despite the significant cumulative differences in the total numbers of Ts and RTs, similar tendencies occurred in the level of interactivity assessed via the ratio of retweeting from "own" EU-originating (institutional) accounts vs non-EU ones. The percentage of RTs from EU vs non-EU Twitter accounts clearly turned in favour of the former with, on average, approximately 75% of all RTs of the analysed accounts coming from EU sources (specifically: 138 RTs or 73% in 2014, and 97 RTs or 77% in 2015).

A more qualitative look at the sources of RTs and of the wider interactive strategies in the EU spokespeople discourse reveals tendencies of both continuity and change (see Table 3.1). The continuity aspect is particularly visible within EU-internal sources, which practically did not change between the two focal periods of investigation. Accordingly, the main RT sources were the Twitter accounts of other EU (EC) Spokespeople and EU politicians, of whom the key ones were European Commission members (whose accounts, by the way, are often managed by the spokespeople responsible for particular Commissioners and portfolios). Other internal accounts included, very prominently, other European Commission Directorates General (DGs) which were the source of RTs especially whenever specific policies or areas of activity within the remit of those DGs were highlighted in debates. In a similar way, the accounts of specific European Commission Field Offices (present in each of the EU member states) were also used as sources of RTs. From other EU – but non-EC – sources, EU Spokespeople RTs mainly originated within the European Parliament (and specifically the accounts of its members, or MEPs), as well as within EU Agencies' accounts. Some RTs were, finally, also taken from generic institutional accounts

TABLE 3.1 Outline of sources for retweets within the analysed EU spokespeople accounts (April 2014 and 2015)

RT Sources	2014	2015
EU-Internal Sources	EC spokespeople	EC spokespeople
	EU politicians	EU politicians
	(especially EC members)	(especially EC members)
	EC DGs and services	EC DGs and services
	Field offices and reps	Field offices and reps
	EP members	EU agencies
	EU agencies	EP members
	Generic profiles	Generic profiles
	(@EU, @EU_Commission)	(@EU_Commission)
EU-External Sources	Journalists	Ext. organisations
	(especially ext. national	(e.g., EBF, German Marshall
	media)	Fund)
	EU member state politicians	Econ. consultancies
	Pro-EU think tanks and	Journalists
	NGOs	EU member state politicians
	(e.g., Euractiv)	Non-EU politicians
	Political parties	

(such as @EU, @EU_Commission), which are, however, run by the very same spokespeople that initiated the RTs.

Unlike EU-internal sources which remained largely the same within both of the periods of investigation, a rather significant change occurred in the array of external source accounts of EU Spokespeople's retweets. And so, in 2014, the main external sources were those of journalists, especially those known for their pro-EU opinions and working for large media organisations in key EU countries. Similarly, EU national media (e.g., @LesEchos or @LeFigaro in France) were still the main RT sources for EU spokespeople in 2014. The above were followed by the accounts of EU-friendly think tanks and NGOs or their representatives/leaders (e.g., @EurActiv), as well as by political parties in EU member states (e.g., @partisocialiste in France).

In 2015, on the other hand, the array of source accounts for the retweets of EU Spokespeople changed rather significantly. The main source, unlike the previous period of investigation, was now various international organisations (EBF, German Marshall Fund, or the like), as well as economic consultancies. This shows that with the arrival of several former journalists as EU spokespeople in 2015, their "use" for other journalists and media as sources significantly decreased, as well as giving more voice to non-EU institutional bodies. Indeed, journalists, who only came after the above as key RT sources, were only followed by EU member-state and third-country politicians' accounts (e.g., the Ukrainian President @poroshenko) as well as by the accounts of EU officials and politicians including, very prominently, Euro-Parliamentarians.

Analysis of key discursive strategies

An initial, theme-oriented look at EC Spokespeople discourse confirms that some rather significant changes occurred between the 2014 and 2015 periods of investigation, including the related change in the set-up of the spokespeople cohort. By the same token, it should be noted that, although quantitatively "smaller" than its 2014 counterpart, the 2015 discourse was much richer in terms of the variety of topics and issues debated on Twitter by EC Spokespeople (see Table 3.2)

In 2014, with the still strictly EU-internal set-up of key EU Spokespeople personnel, the thematic focus of Twitter discourse remained very strongly EU-internally oriented. It focused on imminent EU-specific events including, most prominently, the 2014 European Parliament elections (eventually held May 22–25, 2014), as well as on one symbolic event for the tenth anniversary of the 2004 EU Enlargement (on May 1). The event-specific discourse in 2014 also revolved around events related to the then ongoing actions between Euro-group and Greece aiming to end the latter's economic and fiscal crisis, then seen as gravely endangering the stability of the European Monetary Union.

In fact, the Euro-group and Greece theme remained the only one of the EU-internally oriented ones that became equally evident in the 2015 discourse where, however, the latter clearly started to give way to representations of events and EU activities related to the then dominating EU-wide "refugee crisis" (named throughout most of the EU Twitter discourse the "migration" crisis). Unlike the 2014 discourse, the 2015 one also included EU-policy-oriented debates: on matters such as the EU Capital Markets Union (clearly foregrounded by the then EU Commissioner for Financial Stability, Financial Services, and Capital Markets Union, Jonathan Hill, see below) and those related to EU anti-trust and competition policies and actions, and especially the Google Anti-Trust Case driven by Margrethe Vestager (EU Commissioner for Competition) and announced in mid-April 2015.

TABLE 3.2 Key hash-tagged themes of the analysed 2014 and 2015 EC spokespeople discourse

Themes(Types of Threads)	2014	2015
EU-Internal (Event-related)	EPElections 2014 10 years of 2004 EU Enlargement Euro-group and Greece	EU migration "crisis" Euro-group and Greece
EU-Internal (Policy-related)	N/A	Capital Markets Union Google and competition
EU-External (Event-related)	Ukraine Crisis	Ukraine crisis Nepal earthquake
EU-External (Policy-related)	N/A	European migration crisis EU–Africa relations

As far as EU-externally focused topics were concerned, in 2014, those were very limited and only focused on the then ongoing Ukraine Crisis in a rather strictly event-oriented manner. In fact, the Ukraine Crisis remained prominent in the EU-external discourse in 2015 as well, though in a strictly event-related manner, and it gave way to tweets concerning the Nepal earthquake that took place on April 25. Unlike in 2014, when there were no externally oriented policy-specific tweets, in 2015 there was already an ongoing, policy-driven discussion of the aforementioned EU migration crisis. Here, however, the topic was perceived from the point of view of non-EU actors and members. Of these, special attention was paid to African countries and regional alliances – e.g., the African Union – which also drove a separate topic focusing more closely on EU–Africa relations and related policies.

A more in-depth look at selected discursive strategies deployed in the EC spokespeople discourse in 2014 and 2015 shows, just as above, little continuity and a rather clear tendency to change.

In the 2014 discourse, the *strategy of personalisation/familiarisation* was dominant. It was deployed to give some familiarity and a less official tone to discourses about EU politics, especially at a time when the entire cohort of EC spokespeople was still recruited from among long-standing EU officials and functionaries. This strategy was, on the one hand, deployed to express various affinities and similarities in viewpoints. This was particularly visible in the RTs from media organisations which were retweeted along often nationally specific lines (with the German member of the Spokesperson's Service retweeting @spiegelonline, the French one @Le_Figaro, or the Polish one @gazeta_wyborcza etc.).

On the other hand, this strategy of personalisation/familiarisation was chiefly used to create commonality with the Twitter "audience," especially by presenting EU officials (including Commissioners and Spokespeople) not only from the point of view of their official roles and activities, but also as those who are close to EU demos, as people who not only work but also make jokes, have a social life, etc.

One of the (many) examples of when such a strategy was deployed was in early April 2014, when the then EU Commissioner for Home Affairs, Cecilia Malmström, sent a tweet "thanking" the press service for the so-called Brussels Press Review, i.e., an annual social event for journalists and the EU (it usually includes many sketches about EU politics mainly prepared by journalists and spokespeople). In a thread initiated by the Commissioner's account @MalmstromEU (see Example 1), a spokesperson – in this case @OliverBaillyEU – joined in to share his experiences and initiated a very peculiar exchange which, later on, was also joined by other Commission officials (in this case, @trishbrussels). In the exchange, in which replies across accounts were used, it was seen that spokespeople were not only "relaying" messages but were also close to and very familiar with EU politicians and officials, sharing not only their professional interests but also private/social views.

Example 1:

@MalmstromEU, 05/04/2014
Great Brussel press revue this year! Thanks for a good show with many laughs
@TeresaKuchler

@OliverBaillyEU, 05/04/2014:
@MalmstromEU My favourite was certainly "10 years a slave"
05/04/14

@OliverBaillyEU – RT from @MalmstromEU, 05/04/2014:
"@OlivierBaillyEU:@MalmstromEU My favourite was certainly
"10 years a slave":-)"Mine too!

@trishbrussels – Reply to @MalmstromEU, 05/04/2014
@MalmstromEU @OlivierBaillyEU Lisbon Treaty goes to the repair shop was a piece of
brilliance too.

Another strategy salient in the 2014 EC Spokespeople discourse was that of *thematic demarcation/colonisation*. It mainly boiled down to EC spokespeople (over)using various hashtags to show that EU policy is not limited to a few areas but has some wide and very significant meanings. Indeed, the use of many hashtags by the EC spokespeople seems too generic, yet it helped the officials to create an image of the EU as highly relevant not only for selected foci/issues but also for wider (tagged) spaces, events, etc. One example of the deployment of this strategy was in an RT by one of the spokespeople (@PiaAhrenkilde) from the account of the then EC Commissioner for Transport (@SimKallas, see Example 2). In the RT, practically only hashtags and other non-tagged keywords were used to demarcate/colonise as many areas/topics/spaces as possible, and thus emphasise the salience of EU policies on all those areas.

Example 2:

@PiaAhrenkilde – RT from @SiimKallasEU, 15/04/2014
MEPs vote 4 #safer, #greener #lorries, cutting fuel costs, emissions and road deaths.
#EUtransport #cyclists http://t.co/Ro1x2S53xB

Further to the above, the strategy of thematic demarcation/colonisation was also used extensively in EC spokespeople discourse to describe historical events, rather than only present actions/policies, as seen above. Interestingly, the thematic demarcation/colonisation of history extended well beyond the EU's lifespan and even embraced events such as, for example, the Prague Spring (see Example 3). This shows that the EU history-oriented discourse – indeed very strongly revived in 2014, i.e., at the time of the tenth anniversary of the "histori-cal" EU 2004 Enlargement – was constructed by EC spokespeople in a way that represented the EU as, in fact, extending beyond its institutional spatio-temporal range, as well as presenting the EU as a fulfilment of many civil ideas across Europe in the post-war period.

Example 3:

@ECspokesCezary, 29/04/2014
A. #Dubček Europe is a living organism linked together through common history and destiny and hopes for freedom and better living conditions

Further to such "quote"-based tweets, the history-oriented discourse also included many RTs from media organisations (e.g., @spiegelonline), and this helped to create a positive image of the EU as successful, or even "triumphant," in its policies and actions.[4]

Of the aforementioned 2014 strategies, the key – and only – one that contin-ued in the 2015 discourse was the *strategy of personalisation/familiarisation*. However, in the 2015 discourse, that strategy was no longer aiming, as before, to create an image of closeness or familiarity of EU officials and politicians – including spokespeople – to the European demos. On the contrary, it was now transformed into a rather clearly elite-driven strategy of political communication and was chiefly deployed to create and mediate the political image of key EU figures such as, very prominently, the EU Commissioners. The latter used both their own Twitter accounts (as was the case with the French commissioner @pierremosco-vici in Example 4, below; NB: note the very strong personalisation via use of I/my and other personal pronouns) and the channels of EC Spokespeople (in this case, @vannesamock) who, via their RTs, provided further dissemination of the Commissioners' politically self-centred communication. Interestingly, even if thematically operating within discourse on international affairs (e.g., the Greek Crisis), this strategy was mainly deployed to address the national audiences of countries from where the commissioners were recruited, along with the national media in those countries (in Example 4, below, French and French-language media such as @RFI or @ARTEfr).

Example 4:

@vanessamock - RT from @pierremoscovici, 12/04/15
Mes réponses dans l'émission @CarrefourEurope à écouter tout de suite sur @RFI http://m.rfi.fr

@vanessamock - RT from @pierremoscovici, 12/04/15
L'#Europe n'est pas faite pour punir, mais pour convaincre les pays d'avancer. Je veux une Europe des réussites @CarrefourEurope @RFI

@vanessamock - RT from @pierremoscovici, 28/04/15
*La @EU_Commission est là pour aider la #Grèce et les Grecs. Il n'y a pas de temps à
perdre @ARTEfr @ARTEjournal*

@vanessamock - RT from @pierremoscovici, 29/04/15
*The recovery in #Europe – the way forward: my introductory remarks today at the
@gmfus in #Washington #GMFEurope http://bit.ly/1CPRu7M*

Further to the above, the 2015 EC spokespeople discourse was also strongly
characterised by frequent use of the discursive strategy of *constructing the EU as
an international leader*. As part of this strategy, tweets – along with many other
genres of both online and offline politico-organisational communication – were
deployed to create an image of the EU as a responsible international actor and,
indeed, a leader of international activities in humanitarianism and other areas.
This image was particularly desirable at a time when the EU's reaction to a
variety of crises and events of a short-term (e.g., earthquakes and other disasters)
and long-term (e.g., European migration/refugee crisis) nature was in focus (see
Example 5). It constitutes a recontextualisation of a classic trait in EU identity
that shows the EU as a global leader, whether in humanitarian or other types of
"response" to international and global crises.

Example 5:

@Marg_Schinas, 19/04/15
*@EU_Commission statement on tragic developments in the Mediterranean. A joint respon-
sibility of EU MS & Institutions http://europa.eu/rapid/pressrelease_STATEMENT-15-4
800_en.htm*

@Mina_Andreeva, 26/04/15
#NepalEarthquake: EU mobilises all emergency response means http://europa.eu/!yw67Ny

However, the problem with the above strategy was that, as such, it was part of
presenting a general, or macro-level, voice of the EC (including via the Head and
Deputy Head of the Spokesperson's Service, as above). At the same time, individual EU Commissioners – and their relevant spokespeople – continued their
communication on their portfolio/policy-specific topics and issues. This often led
to rather unfortunate – and highly insensitive – coincidences whereby tweets about
important human and natural disasters were immediately followed, in sequence,
by those, for example, related to economic policy (such as the Capital Markets
Union promoted by the then EU Commissioner Jonathan Hill, see Tables 3.3 and
3.4). This proved to be not only politically and image-wise insensitive but tortured
the cliché that, no matter what the topic, the EU's economic – and indeed neoliberal – considerations tend to resurface across the board and at the least desirable
times.

TABLE 3.3 Immediate sequence of EC spokespeople tweets about the Mediterranean migrant boat tragedy/Capital Markets Union, 04/19/2015

Date	Account	RT/Source Account	Tweet
04/19/2015	@NatashaBertaud		@EU_Commission statement on #Mediterranean tragedy: @JunckerEU @TimmermansEU @Avramopoulos @FedericaMog http://europa.eu/rapid/press-release_STATEMENT-1 5-4800_en.htm …
04/19/2015	@Mina_Andreeva	@EU_Commission	Deeply chagrined by the tragic developments in the #Mediterranean today, but also over the past days&weeks. Statement http://europa.eu/!pG97FU
04/19/2015	@MargSchinas		@EU_Commission statement on tragic developments in the Mediterranean. A joint responsibility of EU MS & Institutions http://europa.eu/rapid/press-release_STATEMENT-15-4800_en.htm …
04/19/2015	@NatashaBertaud	@JunckerEU	The @EU_Commission is deeply chagrined by the tragic developments in the Mediterranean. Our actions must be bold http://europa.eu/rapid/press-release_STATEMENT-15-4800_en.htm …
04/19/2015	@NatashaBertaud		Statement by Commissioner @Avramopoulos and Spanish Minister of the Interior, Jorge Fernández Díaz http://europa.eu/rapid/press-release_STATEMENT-15-4801_en.htm …
04/19/2015	@vanessamock	@EU_Commission	Live chat w/@JHillEU on #CapitalMarketsUnion Monday 20/4 15.30CET Get alerted when it starts: http://ou.ly/LKoO1
04/19/2015	@vanessamock	@JHillEU	#CapitalMarketsUnion: breaking down barriers to completing the single market. Full speech #newsmaker @reuters http://europa.eu/rapid/press-release_SPEECH-15-4796_en.htm …

TABLE 3.4 Immediate sequence of EC spokespeople tweets about the Nepal earthquake and Capital Markets Union, 04/25–04/27/2015

Date	Account	RT/Source Account	Tweet
04/25/2015	@MargSchinas		*Statement on the #earthquake in #Asia. @FedericaMog @StylianidesEU @MimicaEU http://eur opa.eu/rapid/press-release_STATEMENT-15-4857_en.htm …*
04/26/2015	@Mina_Andreeva		*#NepalEarthquake: EU mobilises all emergency response means http://europa.eu/!yw67Ny*
04/27/2015	@vanessamock	@JHillEU	*#CapitalMarketsUnion can play pivotal role in boosting financial integration & in enhancing financial stability @EU_Commission*
04/27/2015	@vanessamock	@JHillEU	*By helping to create a more diversified & resilient European financial system, we can reinforce financial stability @EU_Finance*
04/27/2015	@vanessamock	@JHillEU	*Read my full speech at joint @EU_Commission & @ecb conference http://europa.eu/rapid/press-r elease_SPEECH-15-4861_en.htm …*
04/27/2015	@vanessamock	@EU_Finance	*Follow our joint conference with @ecb live here: http://ow.ly/M9yFH . Now keynote address by @JHillEU*

Conclusion

The above analysis indicates that the EU strives to be present on Twitter in a variety of ways and that EC Spokespeople are the main driving force behind creating as well as sustaining the EU's social media profile. As the analysis shows, this presence boils down to a variety of topics and issues and aims to foster an overall image of the EU as not only a good and skilful communicator but also as a responsible, international actor. It also promotes – albeit with often mixed results – an image of EU officials and politicians as familiar with and close to the European demos, and thereby aims to foster an image of the EU as an open, democratic, politico-institutional actor.

However, as the analysis also explicitly shows, EU social/online media communication, as exemplified by EC spokespeople's use of Twitter, suffers from two types of challenges. On the one hand, as shown by both the interactive and the discourse-oriented analyses above, despite using "new" channels such as Twitter, the EU still largely replicates many facets of its previous (or pre-social-media) politico-organisational communication. This boils down to re-using some of the key discursive traits of, inter alia, speaking about the EU as an international leader/actor or viewing it as a fulfilment of Europe's history (see Krzyżanowski 2010, 2015), treating the EU as a new kind of normative or soft power (Diez 2005; Manners and Diez 2007), or foregrounding economic (neoliberal) ideas over social and political considerations (Krzyżanowski 2016).

By the same token, even while on Twitter, EU communication seems very elitist and largely *autopoietic* (Luhmann 1995; Muntigl, Weiss, and Wodak 2000; Krzyżanowski 2010). It hence remains rather strictly closed within the EU politico-institutional realm (be it of the EC, as such, or of other EU institutions), with the main "external" input being drawn from wider elite networks of, in particular, national European media and journalists (and only to a limited extent including the pan-European non-governmental sector, though strictly limited to EU-friendly organisations, see above). This, as has been indicated above, comes on top of the still evident lack of desire to connect to the wider European citizenry (especially by means of social media interactions which clearly create such an opportunity) and with the clear intention of operating with elite networks that help to sustain the ongoing autopoiesis, rather than seek effective democratisation of EU politico-organisational communication.

On the other hand, while still sustaining the said problematic deep-seated dispositions of its communication and discourse, the use of Twitter by the EU – in our case especially the EC – falls prey to challenges of using social/online media as elements of organisational as well as political communication. The widely deployed and, as evidenced, gradually transforming personalisation/familiarisation strategy is a good example here. It shows how the use of social media gradually contributes to the replacement of collective (organisational as well as wider democratic) concerns via the very strong individualisation of communication (Bennett and Entman 1999), as also seen in the wider field of mediated "digital" politics (Vaccari 2013). In this context, the very strong focus on the construction of individual political personas (such as mediatisation-savvy EU Commissioners) – and indeed their own images, careers, and interests – replaces the otherwise desired construction of familiarity with (EU) politics as part of familiarising the wider public with not only the "frontstage" but also the "backstage" of everyday politics (Wodak 2009). To be sure, this comes alongside other typical tendencies in the public/political use of social media, such as those whereby highly performative and superfluous "few to many" communication (Berglez 2016) prevails, thus ignoring communication for political or democratic meanings and instead forging self-presentation as well as the self-preservation of elite-driven networks.

By the same token, as indicated above, the Twitter-based communication of the EU also tends to be, just like in many other political contexts, very accidental and often cuts across a largely desired coordinated approach which would allow politico-institutional actors such as the EU to speak in one strong and largely coordinated voice that would be both recognisable to and resonant with the wider European public (Krzyżanowski and Oberhuber 2007). Instead of that, as shown, the EC spokespeople discourse remains largely uncoordinated and often creates the image of being a demand-driven jack of all trades trying to colonise as many topics and have a say on as many events as possible.

The above points to the fact that, even if modernised somewhat by the use of Twitter and other social/online media, EU politico-organisational communication still falls short of playing a vital role in effectively politicizing EU institutions. Even if it is deploying social/online media, the EU is still not fully able to open its key institutions up to the wider EU public and, by breaking out from elite networks, to forge a public dialogue and increase its political legitimacy through an array of communicative practices that would help to decrease Eurosceptic moods and attitudes. This, it is claimed, would be of direct relevance to effectively communicating how the EU responds to current developments including how, as a politico-institutional organism, it faces multiple crises and challenges, including the recent fierce wave of right-wing populism and Euroscepticism (including in the context of Brexit) that undermines the very foundations of the EU-ropean project (Wodak and Krzyżanowski 2017). The EU's political and institutional communication must hence become less accidental and more coordinated, reflexive and strategic – all in order to be able to prove the salience of European politics for Europe's society as well as to thereby emphasise the EU's role as one of the key guardians of European liberal democracy.

Notes

1 This chapter is a modified version of the article "Social Media in/and the Politics of the European Union: Politico-Organizational Communication, Institutional Cultures and Self-inflicted Elitism" published in *Journal of Language and Politics* 17(2), 2018, and reused with permission of John Benjamins Publishing Company.

2 See   http://ec.europa.eu/dgs/communication/about/index_en.htm   and   https://
   ec.europa.eu/info/sites/info/files/organisation-chart-dg-comm_en_14.pdf,   last
   accessed 12/28/2017.
3 As such, the EC Spokesperson's Service is organised in a rather strict hierarchical
   way. It is headed by an EC Chief Spokesperson (who is also a Deputy Director
   General at the wider DG COMM), supported by two Deputy Chief Spokespersons
   as well as two Coordinating Spokespersons, including one with a remit for the
   Activities of the EC President. The aforementioned group of key spokespeople
   is then further supported by an array of Spokespersons specialising within specific policy areas of the EC and who, at the same time, work closely with the EU
   Commissioners in charge of those policy areas (for details, see: http://ec.europa
   .eu/dgs/communication/about/contact_us/ec_spokespersons/index_en.htm,   last
   accessed 02/08/2017).
4 See   http://www.spiegel.de/forum/wirtschaft/zehn-jahre-eu-osterweiterung-de
   r-triumph-des-sanften-imperiums-thread-125127-1.html   of   30/04/2014   (last
   accessed 11/30/2017).

References

Anderson, Peter J., and Aileen Macleod. "The Great Non-Communicator? The Mass
   Communication Deficit of the European Parliament and Its Press Directorate." *Journal
   of Common Market Studies* 42, no. 5 (2004): 897–917.
Barisione, Mauro, and Asimina Michailidou, eds. *Social Media and European Politics*.
   Basingstoke: Palgrave Macmillan, 2017.
Bennett, W. Lance and Robert M. Entman (1999). *Mediated Politics*. Cambridge:
   Cambridge University Press.
Berglez, Peter. "Few-to-Many Communication: Public Figures' Self-Promotion on
   Twitter Through 'Joint Performances' in Small Networked Constellations." *Annales:
   Series Historia et Sociologia* 26, no. 1 (2016): 171–84.
Bernstein, Basil. *Strategies of Pedagogic Discourse*. London: Routledge, 1990.
Bjola, Corneliu. "Introduction – Making Sense of Digital Diplomacy." In *Digital
   Diplomacy – Theory and Practice*, edited by Corneliu Bjiola, and Marcus Holmes, 1–10.
   London: Routledge, 2015.
Bosetta, Michael, Anamaria Dutceac-Segesten, and Hans-Jörg Trenz. "Engaging
   with European Politics Through Twitter and Facebook: Participation Beyond the
   National?." In *Social Media and European Politics*, edited by Mauro Barisione et al.,
   53–75. Basingstoke: Palgrave Macmillan, 2017.
de Wilde, Pieter, Asimina Michailidou, and Hans-Jörg Trenz. *Contesting Europe: Exploring
   Euroscepticism in Online Media Coverage*. Colchester: ECPR Press, 2013.
Diez, Thomas. "Constructing the Self and Changing Others: Reconsidering 'Normative
   Power Europe'." *Millennium: Journal of International Studies* 33, no. 3 (2005): 613–36.
European Commission. *Communication to the Commissions: Communicating About Europe
   via the Internet, Engaging the Citizens*. (SEC-2007-1742). Brussels: The European
   Commission, 2007.
Follesdal, Andreas, and Simon Hix. "Why There Is a Democratic Deficit in the EU:
   A Response to Majone and Moravcsik." *Journal of Common Market Studies* 44, no. 3
   (2006): 533–62.
Kassim, Hussein. "'Mission impossible', but Mission Accomplished: The Kinnock
   Reforms and the European Commission." *Journal of European Public Policy* 15, no. 5
   (2008): 648–68.

Krzyżanowski, Michał. *The Discursive Construction of European Identities. A Multilevel Approach to Discourse and Identity in the Transforming European Union.* Frankfurt am Main: Peter Lang Publishing, 2010.

Krzyżanowski, Michał. "Political Communication, Institutional Cultures, and Linearities of Organisational Practice: A Discourse-Ethnographic Approach to Institutional Change in the European Union." *Critical Discourse Studies* 8, no. 4 (2011): 281–96.

Krzyżanowski, Michał. "(Mis)Communicating Europe? On Deficiencies and Challenges in Political and Institutional Communication in the European Union." In *Intercultural (Mis)Communication Past and Present*, edited by Barbara Kryk-Kastovsky, 185–213. Frankfurt am Main: Peter Lang Publishing, 2012.

Krzyżanowski, Michał. "From Anti-Immigration and Nationalist Revisionism to Islamophobia: Continuities and Shifts in Recent Discourses and Patterns of Political Communication of the Freedom Party of Austria (FPÖ)." In *Rightwing Populism in Europe: Politics and Discourse*, edited by Ruth Wodak et al., 135–48. London: Bloomsbury Publishing Academic, 2013.

Krzyżanowski, Michał. "International Leadership Re-/Constructed? On the Ambivalence and Heterogeneity of Identity Discourses in European Union Policy on Climate Change." *Journal of Language & Politics* 14, no. 1 (2015): 110–33.

Krzyżanowski, Michał. "Recontextualisations of Neoliberalism and the Increasingly Conceptual Nature of Discourse: Challenges for Critical Discourse Studies." *Discourse & Society* 27, no. 3 (2016): 308–21.

Krzyżanowski, Michał, and Florian Oberhuber. *(Un)Doing Europe: Discourses and Practices of Negotiating the EU Constitution.* Brussels: PIE – Peter Lang, 2007.

Krzyżanowski, Michał, Anna Triandafyllidou, and Ruth Wodak. "Europe, Media, Crisis and the European Public Sphere: Conclusions." In *The European Public Sphere and the Media: Europe in Crisis*, edited by Anna Triandafyllidou et al., 261–68. Basingstoke: Palgrave Macmillan, 2009.

Larsson, Anders-Olof. "The EU Parliament on Twitter – Assessing the Permanent Online Practices of Parliamentarians." *Journal of Information Technology & Politics* 12, no. 2 (2015): 149–66.

Luhmann, Niklas. *Social Systems.* Palo Alto, CA: Stanford University Press, 1995.

Majone, Giandomenico. *Dilemmas of European Integration. The Ambiguities and Pitfalls of Integration by Stealth.* Oxford: Oxford University Press, 2005.

Majone, Giandomenico, and G. Majone "Europe's "Democratic Deficit": The Question of Standards." *European Law Journal* 4, no. 1 (1998): 5–28.

Manners, Ian, and Thomas Diez. "Reflecting on Normative Power Europe." In *Power in World Politics*, edited by Felix Berenskoetter, and M. J. Williams, 173–88. New York: Routledge, 2007.

Meyer, Christoph. "Political Legitimacy and the Invisibility of Politics: Exploring the European Union's Communication Deficit." *Journal of Common Market Studies* 37, no. 4 (1999): 617–39.

Michailidou, Asimina. "Twitter, Public Engagement and the Eurocrisis: More than an Echo Chamber?" In *Social Media and European Politics*, edited by Mauro Barisione et al., 241–66. Basingstoke: Palgrave Macmillan, 2017.

Michailidou, Asimina, Hans-Jörg Trenz, and Pieter de Wilde. *The Internet and European Integration.* Opladen: Barbara Budrich Publishers, 2014.

Muntigl, Peter, Gilbert Weiss, and Ruth Wodak. *European Union Discourses on Unemployment.* Amsterdam: John Benjamins, 2000.

Nicolaïdis, Calypso. "The JCMS Annual Review Lecture – Sustainable Integration: Towards EU 2.0?." *Journal of Common Market Studies* 48 (Annual Review) (2010): 21–54.

Nulty, Paul, Y. Theocharis, S.A. Popa, O. Parnet, and K. Benoit. "Social Media and Political Communication in the 2014 Elections to the European Parliament." *Electoral Studies* 44 (2016): 429–44.

Rodríguez, Javier Lorenzo, and Amuitz Garmendia Madariaga. "Going Public Against Institutional Constraints? Analyzing the Online Presence Intensity of 2014 European Parliament Election Candidates." *European Union Politics* 17, no. 2 (2016): 303–23.

Schlesinger, Philip. "Changing Spaces of Political Communication: The Case of the European Union." *Political Communication* 16, no. 3 (1999): 263 –79.

Schlesinger, Philip. "The Babel of Europe? An Essay on Networks and Communicative Spaces." *ARENA Working Paper* 22/03 (2003).

Schneeberger, Agnes-Inge, and Katherine Sarikakis. "Editorial – Media and Communication in Europe: Babel Revisited." *Journal of Contemporary European Research* 4, no. 4 (2008): 269–72.

Tarta, Ancuţa-Gabriela. "A Framework for Evaluating European Social Media Publics: The Case of the European Parliament's Facebook Page." In *Social Media and European Politics*, edited by Mauro Barisione et al., 143–65. Basingstoke: Palgrave Macmillan, 2017.

Vaccari, Cristian. *Digital Politics in Western Democracies*. Baltimore, MD: The Johns Hopkins University Press, 2013.

Wodak, Ruth. *The Discourse of Politics in Action: Politics as Usual*. Basingstoke: Palgrave Macmillan, 2009.

Wodak, Ruth, and Scott Wright. "The European Union in Cyberspace. Multilingual Democratic Participation in a Virtual Public Sphere?" *Journal of Language & Politics* 5, no. 2 (2006): 251–75.

Wodak, Ruth and Michał Krzyżanowski. Eds. *Right Wing Populism in Europe and the USA*. Amsterdam: John Benjamins (Special Issue *Journal of Language and Politics* 16:4).

4

IS THERE A PLACE FOR A CROWDSOURCING IN MULTILATERAL DIPLOMACY? SEARCHING FOR A NEW MUSEUM DEFINITION

ICOM vs the world of $_m$useu$_m$ professionals

Natalia Grincheva

Introduction

The discourse on the public and cultural diplomacy 2.0 is not new. For at least a decade, many diplomacy scholars have discussed, debated, and explored through empirical evidence interesting cases of public involvement in shaping informational flows in the global media environment (Seib 2012; Bjola and Holmes 2015; Manor 2019). In the age of digital interactivity, the old principles of diplomacy based on a "top-down branding approach, which treats people as targets rather than participants in an exchange of views" have become irrelevant (Leadbeater 2010). More than a decade ago, American public diplomacy expert Nancy Snow (2008) asserted "global publics will not allow themselves just to be talked to but are demanding fuller participation in dialogue and feedback through the help of Web 2.0 communication technologies and new media" (8).

These global public expectations and demands transformed government-led broadcasting and promotional campaigns into more complex and sophisticated exercises in public engagement. On the state level, many governments around the world now actively utilise digital tools and social networks to engage audiences across borders in global conversations and negotiations (Fletcher 2016; Manor 2019). However, it remains questionable whether the global public has been really admitted to take part in international conversations to constitute global democratic governance. This democracy in global governance is understood as an "inclusion of manifold voices through participation of civil society that represent different and previously excluded groups" (Kalm et al. 2019, 500).

Van Langenhove (2010) argued that in the 21st century we might witness the emergence of Multilateralism 2.0, which promises to provide an "increased room for nongovernmental actors at all levels" and might even offer an "ad hoc order in which no single institution or organisation is the centre" anymore (267).

For example, some scholars explored such innovative practices as crowdsourcing as new tools to "address governance issues, strengthen communities, empower marginalized groups, and foster civic participation" (Bott et al. 2011, 1). Coined by American politician Jeff Howe (2006), crowdsourcing refers to the outsourcing of tasks to a network of people. While it is not new for governments to invite citizens for assistance in the delivery of their services (Dutil 2015), the advances in information technology have significantly increased the capacity of broader publics to share their knowledge and expertise in ways that can advance global democracy (Spiliotopoulou et al. 2014, 547).

The use of crowdsourcing is argued by some to enhance the inclusiveness of decision-making efforts and even increase their transparency (Lehdonvirta and Bright 2015). "Greater inclusiveness may yield more input, better ideas, and a greater sense of ownership over the outcomes resulting from participation" (Gellers 2016, 419). However, while theoretically Multilateralism 2.0 has been reckoned by some as "the most revolutionary aspect" of contemporary global diplomacy, it still remains "the most difficult one to organize" (Van Langenhove 2010, 267). Furthermore, as some scholars stress, while democratic global governance is in principle possible, its democratic potential is usually "hampered by current practices" (Kalm et al. 2019, 500). Specifically, shortcomings inherent to the processes of global democratic governance, that are more desirable rather than realistic, continue to inspire debate (Gellers 2016, 417).

For example, even though crowdsourcing is believed to enhance inclusiveness (Spiliotopoulou et al. 2014), this inclusiveness comes with "more noise in the system without the guarantee that marginalized voices will emerge from the shadows" (Gellers 2016, 420). More importantly, it remains unclear if crowdsourcing as a platform for participation can provide a robust avenue for making quality decisions that can result in efficient global policies (Radu et al. 2015, 364). Such practices, for instance, as "aggregation and filtering" of public input can significantly skew final outcomes in decision-making processes (Prpie et al. 2015, 79).

This chapter specifically explores the practice of crowdsourcing in global governance as a tool of multilateral diplomacy to interrogate its exact role and place in decision-making processes. Though crowdsourcing provides a platform for a global public engagement that helps IOs demonstrate their democratic aspirations, it remains questionable if the democratic input, produced through crowdsourcing, can be effectively integrated in global policy making. The chapter examines how and why inefficient strategies to properly manage crowdsourcing input can compromise IOs' accountability, foster global contestation of their decisions, and lead to loss of public trust.

Specifically, the chapter investigates the case of the multilateral cultural diplomacy of the International Commission of Museums (ICOM). This is a non-governmental international organisation under formal relations with the United Nations Educational, Scientific, and Cultural Organization (UNESCO) and holding its consultative status with the United Nations Economic and Social

Council. First established in 1946, ICOM has built its global reputation as a leader in the world's museum sector. It strives to harness the collective knowledge of its thirty thematic International Committees, over a hundred of National Committees and six Regional Alliances. Attempting to provide the forum for debate about global museum issues, ICOM takes a strong diplomatic role in advocating on behalf of museums on the global stage.

ICOM works to provide museums with guidelines, policies, tools, and best practices to support and enable them to better serve the societies they exist in. In this sense, ICOM actively exercises multilateral diplomacy and aims for global cultural engagement for "the enlightenment of many policymakers, and the development of many professional networks working on culture and international development issues" (Memis 2009, 298). Conducive to cultural diplomacy stewardship and the cooperative engagement of the professional museum community, ICOM strives to tackle cultural engagement challenges and promotes "creativity, innovation, and systematization in this field of inquiry and practice" (Memis 2009, 298). As former ICOM Vice President, Bernice L. Murphy (2004), stressed, while serving the professional international museum world, "ICOM has a much greater potential to realise" (3). The global diplomatic ambition of ICOM is to address and serve international society "as a cultural leader" or "as an effective public advocate" for achieving democratic sustainable development of cultural communities across borders.

Since its inception, ICOM has passed through several stages of democratisation by making its global governance structure more transparent and inclusive for international engagement. While in 1946 ICOM National Committees were mostly represented by the largest museums in Europe, by 1974 the organisation became a global membership organisation with its members' electoral influence in its governance and activities (Murphy 2004). From only 700 members in the 1970s, ICOM has grown into a 35,000 members' community, representing more than 20,000 museums from 136 countries, with the list of engaged territories continuing to expand. Following global trends in contemporary diplomacy to "advocate for group actions" by multiple stakeholders "to reflect on cross-cutting issues," ICOM implemented an unprecedented campaign in 2019 demonstrating "synergetic approaches to cultural engagement interventions" (Memis 2009, 298).

The case in point is the online global crowdsourcing campaign delivered by ICOM's Standing Committee for Museum Definition, Prospects, and Potentials (MDPP) in 2019. It aimed to collect public contributions to re-define the museum agency in the 21st century so that it can better reflect the rapid and dynamic changes in contemporary museology. As ICOM's President Suay Aksoy explained, this campaign became "one of the most democratic processes in the history of ICOM" (Gould 2019). Despite its inclusiveness, openness, and democratic aspirations, the campaign resulted in a failure to adopt a new proposed definition of the museum during the ICOM Extraordinary General Conference in Kyoto in 2019, "the biggest and most important conference of museums in the world" (ICOM 2019a). The decision to postpone the vote, taken on September 7, 2019 in Kyoto by more than 70% of the participants, served "a severe blow to the NGO's leadership" (Noce 2019). What had gone wrong? This chapter aims to address this question by exploring if and how exactly the crowdsourcing input informed and shaped the MDPP Committee's decisions in proposing the new definition for the global museum community.

Before the chapter unfolds the analysis, it is worthwhile, though, to step back to explain the background story of the historical development of the museum definition, which is heavily charged with colonial European legacies. Going back to the times of the Renaissance, one can trace the development of the first European museums that emerged from collections of strange objects arriving from the New World. Most of the collections in the 16th century were housed in the "cabinets of curiosity," called "studiolo" in Italian; "cabinet de curiosites" in French; and "Wunderkammer," or chamber of wonders, in German (Olmi 1985, 7). "Everyone thinks they know what a 'museum' is, but the boundaries of that definition are constantly evolving. The last century has seen the purpose and values of the museum largely transformed to the point where, it could be argued, collections – once so central to museums – are considered of secondary importance today" (Brown and Mairesse 2018, 525).

In 1946, ICOM defined the museum as a *collection*; in 1951, the museum agency turned into an *establishment*, finally becoming a *permanent institution* only in 1961. The latest version was adopted in Vienna in 2007 and defined the museum as the "a *non-profit, permanent institution* in the service of society and its development, open to the public, which acquires, conserves, researches, communicates and exhibits the tangible and intangible heritage of humanity and its environment for the purposes of education, study, and enjoyment" (ICOM 2007, emphasis added). In July 2019, upon completion of its global crowdsourcing exercise and "following the processes of active listening, collecting and collating alternative definitions through its standing committee on Museum Definition," ICOM proposed a new definition:

> Museums are democratizing, inclusive and polyphonic *spaces for critical dialogue* about the pasts and the futures. Acknowledging and addressing the conflicts and challenges of the present, they hold artifacts and specimens in trust for society, safeguard diverse memories for future generations and guarantee equal rights and equal access to heritage for all people. Museums are not for profit. They are participatory and transparent, and work in active partnership with and for diverse communities to collect, preserve, research, interpret, exhibit, and enhance understandings of the world, aiming to contribute to human dignity and social justice, global equality and planetary wellbeing.
>
> *(ICOM 2019b, emphasis added).*

The new definition was met with significant opposition in the world of museum professionals. In August 2019, 24 national ICOM branches, including French,

Italian, Spanish, German, Canadian, and Russian, submitted a petition, requesting ICOM to postpone the vote on the proposed definition (Gould 2019). Despite the crowdsourcing exercise, it was debated in the media that "ICOM has sparked controversy over its decision to select a definition, which was not submitted as part of the public campaign" (Hatfield 2019). In the international media, the MDPP Standing Committee was widely accused of ignoring public voices and delivering an "ideological text," "that would have little legal value" and that was launched without required consultations with key constituents (Noce 2019). This chapter will explore whether that was indeed the case, given ICOM's two-year, multi-layered processes of creating a new definition that culminated with the Kyoto 25th Extraordinary General Assembly.

To address this question the study employs a mixed methodology that includes multiple qualitative approaches. First, the chapter draws on media discourse analysis of the public debates concerning the new definition, focusing mostly on the international Anglophone media and on the blog posts written by museum professionals. Second, it applies content analysis to the 268 definitions submitted by the public to the ICOM official online platform (ICOM 2019d). It is important to note that this meticulous content analysis resulted in rich and illuminating insights on contemporary museology, which, for space reasons, aren't fully given here and would be valuable to publish in a separate piece. This chapter, therefore, focuses on the most relevant part of this analysis that is mainly used to explore the role of crowdsourcing and its direct inputs in the processes of global policy making.

Finally, the chapter takes readers behind the scenes of the work of the ICOM MDPP Standing Committee by integrating two sources of institutional analysis. On the one hand, it draws on the desk research of numerous open access reports and statements (ICOM 2018a–b; 2019a–d; 2020), published by ICOM to document its work on the museum definition. On the other hand, this chapter features insights from the MDPP Committee Chair, Jette Sandahl, interviewed specifically for this research in February 2020. Sandahl is a Danish Museum curator, with an impressive museum career earned through her dedicated service to the Museum of World Cultures in Gothenburg, Te Papa Museum in New Zealand, and the Copenhagen City Museum. To understand better the failures of global digital diplomacy, the chapter draws on a focused semi-structured interview with Sandahl to gain insight from her experience in leading the ICOM campaign of public engagement.

This analysis unfolds in two parts. The first section, "Radically democratic," positions the case study within the current debates on the role and place of public engagement in global multilateral governance by specifically looking at issues of public trust and institutional accountability. It reviews current scholarship on international organisations and their practices in adopting more democratic approaches in international policy making, identifying key challenges and obstacles they bring to IOs' decision-making processes. This literature helps develop a framework that can explain the role of the ICOM crowdsourcing campaign in the system of global governance. Building on this framework, the following section titled "Pursuing a 'common good'" seeks to explain the negative out-come of the first ICOM's attempt to exercise "transnational democracy." On the one hand, it investigates competing policies and agendas that surrounded the ICOM decision-making processes in revising the old definition. On the other hand, it reveals how the failure to listen and understand global voices can lead to detrimental results compromising institutional accountability. The chapter interrogates the role and place of digital technologies of public engage-ment in facilitating democratic systems of global governance and argues that Multilateralism 2.0 still remains a desirable vision rather than reality.

"Radically democratic": Transparency at the cost of accountability

As Sandahl pointed out in one of her media interviews, since the appointment of the MDPP Committee in 2017, the whole process of developing the new defi-nition has become "radically democratic" (de Wildt 2019). It consisted of sev-eral stages of membership and public engagement and was guided by open and transparent communication efforts that included publications of several foun-dational documents on the ICOM website (ICOM 2018b), a Special Issue in the *Museum International Journal* featuring articles written by several committee members (Sandahl 2019), international round tables organised through National ICOM committees across countries in 2018, and even a crowdsourcing cam-paign (ICOM 2019c).

According to Sandahl (2020), even the appointment of the MDPP Standing Committee, which consisted of a diverse and international team of museum experts, was a step forward in democratising the process of making revisions to the museum definition. The museum definition has traditionally been a part of the ICOM statutes and its revision "is a formally regulated process. It is some-thing that takes a lot of focus and there is a formal process around this proce-dure" (Sandahl 2020). However, in 2017 the ICOM Executive decided to open the procedures and embrace new democratising opportunities. While "we were quite formally appointed as a committee" the Chair explained, "we are civil servants, our main role is to analyze, review, prepare documentation for discus-sion sessions, but we are not the part of the decision making process" (Sandahl 2020).

The creation of such expert groups or international committees to investigate a specific global issue and provide recommendations is a growing practice among international organisations (Pouliot and Therien 2018). As explained by Lapeyre (2004), these groups usually serve as a "transmission belt" for the introduction of new ideas and fresh perspectives in the process of global governance (1). They aim to provide an important stimulus to global policy making by facilitating "the political debate beyond the bureaucratic or intergovernmental spheres to include individuals whose expertise renders them seemingly impartial" (Pouliot and Therien 2018, 168). Furthermore, as Lapeyre (2004) stressed, these committees are expected to deliver a work process that is "open, visible and participatory," receiving "the broadest range of views on the key issues it was addressing" (60). Indeed, the work of the MDPP Committee included two important phases, both new, and both designed to involve the broader international community of museum professionals in the process of redefining the museum in the new century to reflect on social, cultural, and political changes.

Firstly, MDPP invited National ICOM Committees across countries and continents to take part in Roundtable sessions. They aimed to determine whether a change of the existing museum definition was necessary through focused discussions with participants on current museum issues, challenges, and opportunities (ICOM 2018a). In 2018, the Roundtables working groups received responses from 37 sessions from different countries, including Costa Rica, Kenya, New Zeeland, the USA, Singapore, and Austria, with a total of just under 900 participants. Transcribed and translated into English, they resulted in 320 closely analysed responses that revealed "strong trends and concerns" in the international professional sector of museums and pushed the process of redefining the museum further to next stages (Bonilla-Merchav 2019, 164).

A member of the MDPP Standing Committee, Bonilla-Merchav (2019), suggested that Roundtables offered "a democratic platform where voices from around the world could express themselves" (162). This format was "new and very experimental, not anything that is common in big international organizations, like ICOM," and Sandahl (2020) confirmed. "They were open for everyone … they provided much more flat, non-hegemonic working methods" (Sandahl 2020). Most importantly, they revealed a greater need not only to continue the search for a new museum definition, but also to employ new digital tools that would allow ICOM to make the process more automated, and even more transparent and open. As a result, in January 2019 ICOM opened an online platform on its official website to collect museum definitions from the public (ICOM 2019c). It was open to everyone without restrictions, even to non-ICOM members, who were asked to submit text contributions in the language of their choice.

By April 2019, the MDPP Standing Committee collected 268 definitions from 73 countries across continents written in 23 languages, including Arabic, Chinese, Farsi, Hungarian, Ukrainian, and Hebrew. As Sandahl (2020) assessed, such a result indicated a high level of public participation "that is unlike anything that ICOM has had before. We have got contributions from places where there is barely an ICOM National Committee …, places where the ICOM does not necessarily usually hear voices from." Notably, while there was a close monitoring of the crowdsourcing process, none of the definitions submitted online was censored away. "I think that we greatly exaggerate the fear of receiving inappropriate feedback," Sandahl (2020) shared. The crowdsourcing exercise proved that online participants were highly motivated, interested, and engaged museum professionals who took the challenge with great enthusiasm and commitment.

"Definitely the process was different," the Chair stressed, pointing out at the new media possibilities that offered ICOM "tools that have not been available for previous discussions":

> What we had on the ICOM platform for collecting museum definitions from the public is new. And it is also new for big international organizations to have that kind of public hearing process with members …. There are huge democratizing potentials in the open public platforms for discourse and conversations, like we had for collecting museum definitions.
>
> *(Sandahl 2020)*

As the quote illustrates, the new digital technologies allowed ICOM to open up the discussion on a global scale. Most importantly, they allowed the organisation to enhance the democratic dimension of its public engagement approach and to place it at the core of its campaign. In this regard, the disappointing result of not being able to develop a global consensus on the new proposed definition constitutes a critical puzzle that requires explanation. Current scholarship on global governance, international organisations, and transnational democracy provides important insights and analytical approaches to explain this situation.

While the trend toward stronger public engagement has the potential to "increase the level of participation of civil society in global governance" (Van Langenhove 2010, 267), global governance is believed to be a real challenge for democracy (Lamy 2010). In order for the multilateral governance to improve its practices to establish truly democratic processes in global decision making, IOs have to incorporate principles of "horizontal accountability" (Hoffmann-Lange 2012). Accountability is defined as the establishment of a process through which an actor can exercise punishments or grant rewards to another actor (the accountable party) in response to its actions or mis-actions (Gent et al. 2015). Accountability requires a strong level of transparency in the decision-making processes as well as the power to exercise rewards or punishments (Grant and Keohane 2005). Consequently, horizontal accountability entails an increased IO transparency towards the public and greater participation of civil society in the adoption and implementation of IO policies (Grigorescu 2008). A failure to neglect or poorly handle at least one of these important components can compromise institutional accountability and lead to public distrust. It seems that the MDPP Committee faced significant challenges in addressing both these critical issues.

First, as Bauhr and Nasiritori (2012) pointed out, "if IO decision-making processes are perceived as unfair, unpredictable and ineffective, *transparent* IO decision-making processes may be ineffective at best and counterproductive at worst" (10). Indeed, MDPP's two-years-long process of creating a new museum definition radically restructured the traditional decision-making procedures without necessarily making them more efficient. In fact, it diminished the role of internal stakeholders, such as ICOM National Committees, in the decision-making process. It is important to acknowledge that the basic rules and structures that shape key IOs operations are primarily based on productive interactions and efficient cooperation between major players or representatives of member states (Yi-Chong and Weller 2015). Their input in the decision-making process is important as they are entitled to "legitimize the actions and operation of the international organization" to "pursue collective interests" by representing their national communities in international arenas and mobilising support from their states and civil societies (Yi-Chong and Weller 2015, 11).

Decision-making processes that neglect these traditional players may significantly compromise institutional accountability. They usually result in a loss of trust in IOs from its member states while growing criticism of their decisions. In this case, the National Committees' global mobilisation through direct petitions to ICOM and the unfolding public debates contesting the proposed definition actually manifested "institutional social counter-powers." It "has evolved in order to compensate for the erosion of confidence," expressing "distrust against power-holders, pressuring them to stay committed to the common good" (Kalm et al. 2019, 504). These activities are known in the scholarship on democratic governance as "denunciation," they aim at exposure, centre on the norms of transparency, and often involve the act of "naming and blaming" (Rosanvallon 2008).

Furthermore, as Ecker-Ehrhardt (2018) observed, a centralised public communication usually results in a significant loss of control for members "over how internal negotiations are communicated back home to national constituencies" that limits the extent to which they are able to effectively shape domestic perceptions (520). Indeed, after losing their powers over the final decision making via the process of public engagement, ICOM National Committees contested the new museum definition proposed by ICOM. They accused the organisation in launching the definition "without consultation of the national committees" and even argued that the definition poorly articulated global views of a larger museum community (Noce 2019). Addressing this criticism, Sandahl (2020) concurred with the idea that the Kyoto heated debate and the decision to postpone the vote was the result of the lack of time given to the National Committees to think through and discuss the new definition:

> I think it would have been good if we had quite a bit longer time between the proposal and the Kyoto debate, so people have had more time to meet with their National Committees to discuss new changes. Only a few committees managed to do that and, in most cases, only Executive Boards had the time to discuss it.
>
> *(Sandahl 2020)*

By moving to take a decision on the new definition too soon, ICOM not only undermined the decision-making powers of the National Committees, but also minimised their important roles in communicating with their direct constituencies and communities. However, the lack of time, as Sandahl suggested, was not the key reason of such a negative outcome leading to compromising institutional accountability.

The second component of horizontal accountability, such as the direct involvement of the public in the decision-making processes, in fact, was also missing in the MDPP campaign, despite the promising potentials of crowdsourcing to make the process more open and inclusive. As Bauhr and Nasiritori (2012) stressed, even decision-making processes that are designed for enhancing "transparency" in the global governance are usually blamed "for lack of impartiality, fairness and effectiveness in IO decision-making." "IO disclosure policies coupled with inadequate support for a well-governed internal system can result in greater misuse and corruption within the system," reducing public accountability (10). A stronger level of public participation, enabled by crowdsourcing, does not automatically lead to more productive deliberations (Aitamurto 2012), nor can it necessarily produce "reasonable, well-informed opinions" to fairly represent the diversity or the majority of viewpoints across participants (Chambers 2003, 309). In fact, methods employed by IOs to manage, analyse, and integrate the public input in the decision-making processes are important tools that can either help organisations to achieve desirable results in global democratic governance or compromise their accountability.

In the case of ICOM, the disappointing outcomes of the museum definition campaign points to a lack of "a well-governed internal system" that could have helped the organisation better handle "transnational democracy" and manage public input more efficiently, without compromising its institutional accountability. This efficiency is understood as an organisational ability "to solve collective problems and to meet the expectations of the governed citizens" (Mayntz 2010, 10). ICOM's first exercise in democratic crowdsourcing governance revealed the lack of efficient institutional strategies and policies to gauge global public response in a way that could have delivered meaningful problem solving.

According to the global survey conducted by Macnamara and Zerfass in 2012, 80% of international organisations do not have well-developed institutional policies for the strategic use of social media and digital means of global communications. Furthermore, in most cases the majority of organisations have not developed Key Performance Indicators along with measurement methods and procedures to understand the online public and strategically integrate its input into their organisational communication and decision-making process. Finally, Macnamara and Zerfass (2012) revealed that the majority of international organisations do not properly conduct content analysis of online public contributions shared through social media to "identify the issues and topics being discussed" and assess the sentiment towards these issues (12).

As disappointing as it could be, this situation seems to be still relevant, evidenced in the 2019 ICOM crowdsourcing campaign that was the first and maybe the last of its kind in the work of the Standing Committee on the ICOM statutes. In fact, the Committee's approach towards the analysis of the museum definitions submitted through its official portal reveals a complex nexus between the democratic input and authoritative institutional output in global governance. Specifically, Sandahl (2020) shared that the analysis of public contributions of museum definitions was strictly guided by eight predefined parameters, explicitly outlined in the 2018 Report of the MDPP Standing Committee, submitted to the Executive Board after finishing the Roundtable phase of the process.

"We had 8 parameters in place that were the guidelines for how we sorted through the whole body of definitions that we got," Sandahl (2020) shared, "they were the sieve through which we sifted through all public contributions."

> Some definitions were really good, let's say on four of them [parameters], then we tried to add from one or two others which were really strong in other criteria. In the end, we created hybrids, where we brought together different definitions, because there was not any ... (or there have might been a couple) that pretty much expressed all of it, or met all eight parameters ...

The process had at least three or four layers of "sifting public contributions," on each stage reducing them to smaller groups and creating new hybrids. Finally, the Committee chose five definitions to present to the ICOM Executive Board, who then selected one for discussion in Kyoto at the Extraordinary General Assembly (Sandahl 2020). Not surprisingly, such a strong authoritative curatorial approach to explore global public voices, as in many similar cases, significantly undermined the integrity of the Committee's work on creating the museum definition based on horizontal democratic principles.

In fact, while online global contributions greatly inform IOs' international panels' thinking, their participants usually admit that it is "impossible to do them all justice, and to address all the issues they raise" (Ramos-Horta 2015, 4). Strong selective approaches applied to the analysis of public contributions do "impose certain political priorities and opinions over others," skewing final results in favour of institutional agenda (Pouliot and Therien 2018, 169). Pouliot and Therien (2018) indicate that while global political deliberations exercised by IOs can enlarge the voice of non-state actors, these "practices also encourage cooptation, non-transparency, and normative homogeneity" (171). Specifically, the scholars argue that a common dialectic of inclusion and exclusion in these practices marginalise important viewpoints and tend to stress existing inequalities between the Global North and South (Pouliot and Therien 2018, 171). This inevitably leads to the contestation of the results of such "transnational democracy" campaigns challenging the organisational accountability. The following section provides a convincing illustration of these observations to further explore the role and place of crowdsourcing in the digital infrastructure of global governance.

Pursuing "common good": balancing between the Global North and Global South

In many cases, IOs' legitimacy and accountability rest on their "autonomy" or "neutrality" (Barnett and Finnemore 2004). "As a general principle, then, an independent actor has interests that are neutral or impartial with respect to other political actors," especially to specific state actors or regional alliances (Haftel and Thompson 2006, 256). IOs that are driven by universalist values and concerned about "the common good" represent democratic ideals of global governance. This "common good" is usually linked to "universalist principles of equal rights and obligations no matter for example race, class or gender" (Kalm et al. 2019, 510).

A pursuit of the "common good," though, is a direct and logical response of IOs to address a challenge of diversity of interests or, in other words, local, regional, and global clashes of interests in search for effective solutions. As a result, IOs tend to articulate their vision that can

> transcend all such difference, that predicts positive outcomes for all competitors, that formulates its mantra in terms that none can readily falsify, and that enables all parties to global governance to justify their universal prescriptions in seemingly clear and compelling language(s).
>
> *(Halliday 2018, 951)*

For example, the ICOM's greatest commitment and organisational value is "recognizing and promoting cultural diversity," that was explicitly articulated as the main vision of the MDPP work on revising the museum definition (ICOM 2018b). While being quite utopian, the "common good" vision is argued to appeal to and attract global publics (Mallard and Lakoff 2011). The question is, though, how to sustain, express, and even represent this commitment for a "common good" to "act as guardians of a transnational public interest" (Steffek 2015, 278). In recent decades, a rapid raise of digital media established the presence and increased the visibility of previously marginalised actors, like economically disadvantaged communities, women, people of colour, or transgender groups.

In this regard, the trend in international organisations has been one emphasising the "promotion as reinforcing Othering" (Kunz and Maisenbacher 2015). The current IR scholarship argues that digital technologies not only expose this marginalisation, but more importantly, enable the growing emancipation and consequently visibility of "those on the margins" (Jackson 2019, 526; Lindsay 2013). In the struggle for de-colonisation, it has become a common place among IOs, such as UNESCO, to acknowledge and promote ideas and viewpoints coming from the Global South, exactly with the aim to reach institutional "neutrality" in establishing transnational democracy (Singh 2018). This seemed to be the case in the work of the MDPP Committee as well, which drew on public discourse originally stemming from the Global South to push forward new "decolonisation" agenda for museums, a move that was highly contested from the very beginning.

Specifically, the 2018 MDPP Report pointed out that creating a new definition was needed for "historicizing and contextualizing it [the museum], on denaturalizing and de-colonizing it, and on anchoring the discussion of museums and the futures of museums in a larger framework of general societal trends and issues of the 21st century" (ICOM 2018b, 5). In particular, the challenge for the Committee was to "to counter the systemic European and Western dominance in the development of its strategies and policies" and to ensure "a real global representation" (ICOM 2018b, 4). Jette Sandahl (2020) emphasised: "I don't think that there is anything at the moment where the Global North–Global South divide is not present. I think it's a subtext to pretty much everything we do and say." In the processes of revising the old definition, the MDPP Committee aimed "to provide ... guidance in the conflicts between what is currently often called the Global South and Global North and make 'de-colonisation' ... a mutual and shared need and commitment" (ICOM 2018b).

It seems, that this strong vision really affected the work of the Committee. It led to a quite biased reading of the global public contributions, which, in fact, conveyed much less concern about the inequalities between the Global South and North. Particularly, this "divide" set the context for re-defining the museum from "a permanent non-for-profit *institution*" (ICOM 2007) to a "democratizing, inclusive and polyphonic *space*" (ICOM 2019b). This radical imbalance between the traditional conservation purpose of museums and their social functions can, in fact, be conceptualised through a tense historical relationship between the Global South and Global North, specifically through their differences in understanding the museum's role and place in society.

Brown and Mairesse (2018) stressed that the 2007 ICOM Definition "was still largely European in origin and from a time of colonial expansion" (526). However, in the recent decades, multiple entities across regions no longer fulfil all of the requirements in the definition, but, in fact, claim their museum status. Especially in Latin America, the development of new experimental museums significantly challenged the canon of contemporary museology, by interrogating whether a museum was still a permanent institution or a more inclusive organisation, or even a form of a political resistance and social activism (Brown and Mairesse 2018). In Santiago de Chile in 1972, the "Round Table on the role of museums in relation to the social and economic needs of modern day Latin America" brought together museologists from Central and South America, rural development specialists, and representatives from UNESCO and ICOM. As a result, the "Declaration of Santiago de Chile" (1972), published by UNESCO, asserted the idea that a museum should be "at the service of society and its development," a phrase found in the UNESCO Declaration of 1972, that remains in the ICOM museum definition until now (Brown and Mairesse 2018).

Since the 1970s, Latin New Museology inspired "decolonisation" working practices of museums in many countries, including Brazil, Mexico, Canada, China, and Japan. In many cases, museums in these countries had already functioned in contexts outside the confines of the ICOM museum definition (Brown and Mairesse 2018). However, the idea of the "ecomuseum," that emerged in the second part of the 20th century, a "fluid and open concept" of new museology, has mainly remained excluded "from the ICOM definition, and even from the Oxford English Dictionary" (Brown and Mairesse 2018, 529). Despite a high level of activism in Latin America to reinforce the value of a museum as predominantly a social actor to address the problem of "colonialism, imperialism, nationalism and elitism" (Brown and Mairesse 2018), the concept has been contested for its utopian outlook (Hudson 1975). For example, in 1970s, Jean Chatelain, Director of the Musees de France severely criticised the idea of ecomuseums. He stressed that "a museum without collections is not a museum" (Debary 2002, 40). By contrast, an ecomuseum is not a collection or even an institution, rather it "is an invention. It is something that is invented by people … to answer local questions" (Brown and Mairesse 2018, 530).

Sandahl (2020) revealed that this debate on the key museum roles and functions was, indeed, quite old, and various unsuccessful attempts to change the museum definition in favour of its social democratising agenda go back at least five decades:

> In fact, I worked with somebody back in the 1970s on changing the museum definition who also tried to propose these changes and it was very contentious then. There were museum people and directors who thought that it was a really inappropriate politicization of the sector and it had nothing to do with museums. This was just politics. So, that resistance was there already in the 1970s, and I feel that now we have the same voices.

Sandahl was quite accurate when she referred to the "same voices." The proposed definition sparked global protests and led to heated debates contesting the radical changes suggested by the MDPP Committee. Many ICOM members, including National Committees from European countries, opposed the new definition, expressing a great concern about how their governments and legislation systems, in which an old museum definition has been embedded, would deal with such significant changes (Nelson 2019).

For example, Museology Professor François Mairesse stressed that, "It would be hard for most French museums – starting with the Louvre – to correspond to this definition" (Gould 2019). CEO of ICOM Germany, Klaus Staubermann, also challenged the implications of the absence in the proposed definition of such keywords as "institution" and "education": "Both these words are very important, because their presence has a crucial effect on legislation in the German states" (Solly 2019). Juliette Raoul-Duval, who chairs ICOM France, denounced the new definition as an "ideological" manifesto, and even Hugues de Varine, a former director of ICOM and an early proponent of the "new museology" movement in the 1970s, found the definition to be too vague (Small 2019). Such proposed characteristics of museums as "democratising" and "polyphonic," some professionals argued, "would sit rather uneasily next to jurisdiction systems in many countries" (Gould 2019). Others also indicated that the proposed definition undermined the institutional status of museums that could negatively "influence government funding and public support for exhibits" (Johnston 2019).

By contrast, though, it was pointed out in the media that museum professionals in emerging economies contested the previous museum definition as it was "too narrow to encompass the work they are doing to grow their sectors – they may not have 'permanent institutions' but they are adapting 'spaces.'" In this sense, the new proposed definition offered "crucial validation for their efforts and gave extra weight to their advocacy" (Nelson 2019). Executive Director of Portughese Organisation Acesso Cultura, Maria Vlachou, accused the previous definition of its poor ability to serve the museum field, because the museum core functions "to acquire, conserve and research" is "not an aim, a purpose in itself, but rather a tool, in order to fulfil the purposes mentioned by the new definition" (Debono 2019). The report produced by MINOM, the ICOM-affiliated international organisation Museum Movement of New Museology, though, rightfully pointed at the "complex reality of contemporary museology." On the one hand, there are "museums that continue to reproduce and value colonial processes" and, on the other hand, there are those "that affirm themselves as decolonial experiences" (MINOM 2019).

Before the 2019 Kyoto Assembly, MINOM called ICOM to postpone the voting in order to enhance the current proposal, stressing that even though the new definition was "well-intentioned, [it] does not help the universe of normative museology and much less the museal processes and the museums" (MINOM 2019). In fact, this middle-ground reasoning can excellently illustrate a wide range of opinions that were not only well expressed in the press of the day but were also conveyed in public contributions through the ICOM crowdsourcing platform. Notably, this much-expected polarisation of opinions between museum professionals from the Global North and Global South was not present in definitions submitted by online participants.

First, it is important to note that there was a quite fair distribution of voices representing countries from both regions, 149 definitions from the Global North (with the majority from Spain, United States, and Germany) and 119 from the Global South (with the majority from Brazil, Mexico, and Colombia) (see Figure 4.1). In this sense, the crowdsourcing, indeed, allowed for a more inclusive global public engagement. The key question, though, is whether the voices of the international contributors have been really heard and acknowledged.

Second, the keywords' density (frequency) analysis specifically indicated that key terms used in the old and new definitions amounted equally in public contributions from both regions with slight differences that are discussed below. Table 4.1 shows the keyword frequency across the Global North and South, thus

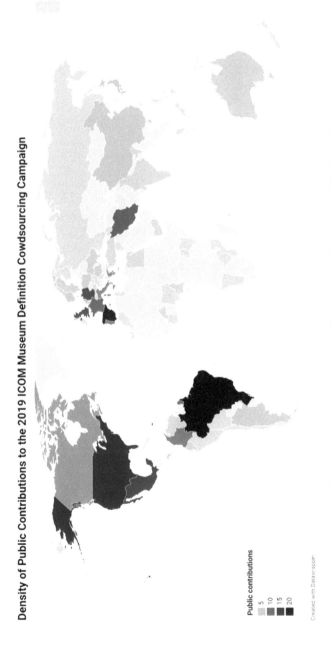

Density of Public Contributions to the 2019 ICOM Museum Definition Cowdsourcing Campaign

Public contributions

5
10
15
20

Created with Datawrapper

FIGURE 4.1   Density of public contributions submitted to the ICOM platform (created by the author)

TABLE 4.1 Keyword frequency in texts of museum definitions submitted to the ICOM platform

Type	Keyword	Global South	Global North
Current definition	Institution/Institute *(used without "not")*	70	73
	Permanent	18	29
	Place	23	44
	Education	32	38
New definition	Space	43	32
	Democracy/atising/atic	10	4
	Inclusive	12	13
	Polyphonic	0	1

demonstrating that the terminology of the current ICOM museum definition still prevails in the global public understanding of the museum, while new key terms with a strong "decolonising" agenda remain in the minority. For instance, the term "institution" appeared (in the positive sense) almost an equal amount of times in publicly proposed definitions submitted from the Global North and South. Moreover, this number is almost twice as large as the frequency of the word "space" (see Table 4.1) in definitions from both North and South "hemispheres." Notably, "democratising," "inclusive," and "polyphonic" keywords did not appear very frequently in the online definitions submitted by the global public, specifically in comparison with the word "education" that had a strong density in public contributions across regions.

Interestingly, though, contributions defining the museum as a "space," rather than a physical "place" or an "permanent institution," were more representative of voices coming from the Global South. Specifically, a focused content analysis revealed that contributors from the Global South most frequently avoided the traditional terminology of museum definition and, in some cases, even stressed, that a museum is not necessarily a permanent institution. Table 4.2 lists some quotes from definitions that came from the Global South. On the one hand, these quotes highlight the diversity of countries represented in the crowdsourcing campaign, while on the other hand, they offer interesting examples of how a museum is understood in these countries.

Reflecting on the analysis of public contributions, Sandahl (2020) noted that, "there were really beautiful definitions from Latin America. The Latin languages can capture processes, their nouns contain the process." She further revealed that, "the definition that was chosen by the Executive Board [among five versions proposed by the MDPP] has very strong Latin derivatives, that came very much from Spanish, Portuguese, Latin American contributions. In comparison, other four definitions, were rather Anglophones." This quote rather explicitly

TABLE 4.2   Quotes from museum definitions contributed by participants from the Global
South

Country	Quote
Cuba	"an iterative *creation* between reality and the subject"
Ecuador	"a timeless *portal*"
Egypt	"the *process* of fusion the gaps between civilisations"
El Salvador	"living *culture*, visibilised heritage and the identity"
Iran	"inclusive cultural *houses*"
Kuwait	"an integrated *system* that works as a house of history and culture"
Mauritius	"is *not necessary an institution* but a place where knowledge and history are disseminated"
Mozambique	"*a non-institution of permanent character*, with or without juridical personality"
Nigeria	"a *network* of places where the tangible and intangible cultural heritage of communities has been deposited and preserved"
Yemen	"*no longer an institution* to preserve and display monuments"
Brazil	"are *processes* and must be at the service of society and its development"
China	"a social *phenomenon*"
Colombia	"is a *Cultural Horizon* where human life forms converge with nature and the universe"

indicates that the definition selected by ICOM favoured contributions from the
Global South, in line with its "decolonisation" agenda, a result of "a couple of
years of intensive analysis of the histories and paradigms, which have shaped
museums" (ICOM 2019d).

In many cases, IOs are criticised for their lack of accountability exactly
because they cannot realistically meet their democratic aspirations "to speak
on behalf of a given population" and "articulate the needs and desires of that
population accurately" (Pallas 2013). One of the main reasons of this is a "(mis)
use of their power and agency … to set development and advocacy agendas"
(Pallas and Guidero 2016, 618). As Pallas and Guidero (2016) explain, some
IOs "have significant agency, but use that agency to satisfy organizational
interests" (618). Moreover, their mission and vision in specific activities or
programs "may be chosen with little regard for external input" with no direct
"responsiveness to affected populations" (ibid.). Specifically, IOs' executive
boards with their "invisible hand" very often tend to promote their "own
agenda and interests, and shaping the decision making of IOs with [their]
expertise, executive mandates, entrepreneurship, and discourse" (Yi-Chong
and Weller 2015, 4).

The formal ties between ICOM and UNESCO have always strongly shaped
museum definition in direct link with the evolution of international law after
the Second World War. For example, in 2007, in reaction to the UNESCO
"Convention for the Safeguarding of the Intangible Cultural Heritage 2003,"
the ICOM museum definition added the concept of intangible cultural heritage,

"significantly expanding the sphere of operation of the museum as an institution traditionally associated with material culture" (Simansons 2020). As Simansons (2020) observes, quite logically the 2019 museum definition was shaped by ICOM commitments to address issues of sustainable global development, explicitly stated in the 2015 UN General Assembly Resolution, "The 2030 Agenda" (UN 2015).

Furthermore, in the past several years, ICOM invested significant efforts to "strengthen its partnerships with high-level intergovernmental organisations to promote the value of museums in contemporary society" (ICOM 2018a). For example, in 2018 it joined forces with the Organisation for Economic Cooperation and Development (OECD) to promote and reinforce the role of museums in local development. In 2019 in collaboration with the OECD, the ICOM Secretariat developed a Guide for Local Governments, Communities and Museums, that offered a road map for state and non-state actors to pursue an economic and social development agenda of museums to achieve a more sustainable future of local communities, especially in emerging economies (ICOM 2019e). This agenda significantly shaped the work of the MDPP Committee who applied strong selective approaches in the analysis of global online submissions. For example, key parameters used for creating a new museum definition, outlined in the 2018 MDPP Report, included acknowledging and addressing global, social, and environmental problems and expressing commitment and responsibility towards sustainable development of museum communities (ICOM 2018b). As a result, the definition specifically articulated the ambition of ICOM to define museums as "democratising spaces" that "contribute to human dignity and social justice, global equality and planetary wellbeing (ICOM 2019b).

The clash of preferences between the larger institutional global agenda and the majority of opinions expressed through public crowdsourcing input produced a disappointing outcome and instigated heated debates at the General Assembly. Sandahl (2020) admitted: "But then, the interesting thing was that in Kyoto, this alternative new definition was not backed up by Latin American countries. And that was for me a surprise!" While, according to the MDPP Committee Chair, Latin America "was so dominant, so eloquent" in the "raw material" of submitted definitions, in fact, Brazil along with other Latin American countries expressed a sharp opposition to the proposed definition, evidenced in both online debates and at the Kyoto Conference.

Sandahl (2020) concluded that "there was no clear relationship between where these definitions came from and which countries would support the new proposed definition." She added, "For example, they [representatives from Latin America] were upset that the word 'education' is not in there [in the new definition]. A very strong critique on this issue was from Brazil. There was a strong resistance on that" (Sandahl 2020). It thus appears that the MDPP Committee created the proposed definition by drawing on ICOM's predefined priorities and vision rather than by actively "listening" to the online voices. Otherwise, it is difficult to explain why the word "education," one of the most frequently used in public contributions, would not be included in the definition.

Indeed, the proposed definition instigated a polarisation of opinions between those who strongly opposed it and those who saw its values to the sector and to larger communities. However, the polarisation line did not go along the perceived divide between the Global South and North. Instead, as Sandahl (2020) herself pointed out, the proposed definition strongly resonated with those countries, where what it "has expressed, is already an established practice," and "a way to catch up with existing practices." "Of course, you would see the Global South, but also you would see countries like the US, Canada, Australia, New Zealand who were very supportive." Furthermore, there is "a solid community of Northern Europe in support of the new definition: Iceland, Norway, Sweden, Finland, Denmark." She further clarified that these "are the regions where the indigenous populations have changed the concept of museum or museology very strongly" (Sandahl 2020). The final decision in Kyoto to postpone the vote clearly indicated that these voices were still in the minority and the new proposed definition in fact did not reflect the vision and voices of the global public.

Unbiased reading of the online public contributions, collected by ICOM from 73 countries, without such a strong commitment to the institutional agenda, could have helped the MDPP Committee acknowledge the majority preference and avoid such a detrimental effect on organisational accountability. The final section reflects further on this example of unsuccessful decision-making processes delivered around the crowdsourcing campaign, while outlining the key learning points from this case.

Conclusion

At the 2019 Extraordinary General Assembly, the ICOM Director General, Peter Keller, addressed the global museum community, admitting that "the Secretariat have been deeply affected by the emotional reaction this proposal has provoked." In his speech he emphasised:

> The strength of our network lies in its diversity, and its ability to overcome any linguistic, cultural and ideological barriers to ensure that the values of our museums are upheld and evolve to remain relevant in the world we live in today. The diversity of reflections on the new proposal to define our museums illustrates the need for ongoing cross-cultural debate and exchange on the future of our sector, independently of the decision that you, as our committees, will be taking. We therefore call on all ICOM committees to express their opinion on the new museum definition proposal, to respect the democratic process according to ICOM's statutes, and to respect the opinion of others.
>
> *(Keller 2019)*

While in his address the ICOM Director stressed the organisational values of diversity and democracy, the next stages in the process of revising the museum definition seem to be a return to more traditional, more closed, approaches of working through the National Committees. Sandahl (2020) confirmed that "the next stage will be more structured through the Committees rather than in a very direct relationship between ICOM and individuals, and some individuals who might not be even ICOM members, as we had in the first process." The Executive Board has appointed a new Standing Committee MDPP2 with assigned responsibilities to collect results of discussions, surveys, and workshops conducted by the National Committees as a preliminary input for the ICOM June 2020 Meeting, where a new process and methods for the definition's revisions will be adopted (ICOM 2020). This meeting will mainly provide a platform for a more extensive discussion to negotiate a new definition through a "convergence of different viewpoints." A new vote for a revised museum definition is expected then to take place in the next year of ICOM's 75th anniversary, in June 2021 (ICOM 2020).

Challenged by a direct question as to whether ICOM will organise a new crowdsourcing campaign in the second round of the museum definition process, Sandahl (2020) stated that, while she personally believed that public contributions were "really meaningful, useful and needed," "we don't know yet how to go about this." She further explained that the main challenge for ICOM now is "to shift from a critical mode to a creative mode … and it is difficult to make this transition" (Sandahl 2020). It seems that the institutional approach to address this challenge is mostly based on restructuring the work of the MDPP2 Committee to regain the institutional control over the whole process and to rebuild its accountability.

Macnamara and Zerfass (2012) indicated that a perceived "loss of control" over organisational image building and policy-making processes is understood by the majority of international organisations as the main obstacle and risk in delivering input-oriented, online, public engagement campaigns (13). Furthermore, "the need for self-legitimation is assumed to increase with greater public contestation in the form of contentious activism addressing international organizations" (Ecker-Ehrhardt 2018, 521). These observations explain the outcome from the first round of the MDPP committee's work on the museum definition, which was highly contested in the global public space. However, as this chapter illustrates, the public input-oriented approaches and the crowdsourcing exercise itself were not the main reasons for global contestations and protests against the new proposed definition, challenging ICOM's accountability. As Bauhr and Nasiritori (2012) point out, the adversarial relationship between IOs, the media, and key stakeholders could be a direct result from a "poor quality decision-making combined with transparency" (13).

In fact, online public contributions supplied the MDPP Standing Committee with rich material. If properly analysed and understood, it could have signalled to the Standing Committee that the global museum community was not ready for radical "decolonising" changes which assigned museums new responsibilities to "contribute to human dignity and social justice, global equality and planetary wellbeing" (ICOM 2019b). It is important to acknowledge, though, that this attempt to do so was a timely and important milestone in the evolution of the museum agency from a private collection of material artefacts into an active social and cultural agent with global visions and commitments. It instigated public debates across continents and brought important issues to the surface to question the status quo of contemporary museums. In fact, it was a bold move for the MDPP Committee to assert a new vision of the museum's role in the society in the current context, where the majority of stakeholders still believe that museums "are not spaces with the mission of favouring democracy and cultural citizenship, nor are they inclusive, nor polyphonic, and much less do they favour a critical dialogue about the past and the future" (MINOM 2019).

This case provides evidence in support of the argument that Multilateralism 2.0 is still an aim and a desirable model of global governance rather than an established practice, especially in such international organisations as ICOM. The attempt to enhance the democratic profile of ICOM governance through public participation proved this time unsuccessful. It revealed a lack of strategic institutional policies and procedures to properly incorporate the public input into the decision-making process. The failure to understand and acknowledge the diversity of views of its main constituencies resulted in public contestations of ICOM's accountability, pushing the organisation back to traditional working methods. It would be interesting to explore at later stages if ICOM will accept the challenge to repeat its attempts in building platforms for digital transnational democracy. It would be even more fascinating to further investigate whether ICOM will seek not only to facilitate global public deliberations but, more importantly, to make them a meaningful part of its global diplomatic outreach.

References

Aitamurto, T. *Crowdsourcing for Democracy: New Era in Policy-Making.* Helsinki: Committee for the Future, Parliament of Finland, 2012.

Barnett, M., and M. Finnemore. *Rules for the World.* Ithaca, NY: Cornell University Press, 2004.

Bauhr, M., and N. Nasiritori. "Resisting Transparency: Corruption, Legitimacy, and the Quality of Global Environmental Policies." *Global Environmental Politics* 12, no. 4 (2012): 9–29.

Bjola, C., and M. Holmes. *Digital Diplomacy: Theory and Practice.* London; New York: Routledge New Diplomacy Studies, 2015.

Bonilla-Merchav, L. "Letting Our Voices Be Heard: MDPP Roundtables on the Future of Museums." *Museum International* 71, no. 1–2 (2019): 160–9.

Bott, M., B. S. Gigler, and G. Young. *The Role of Crowdsourcing for Better Governance in Fragile State Contexts.* Washington, DC: World Bank Publications, 2011.

Brown, K., and F. Mairesse. "The Definition of the Museum Through Its Social Role." *Curator: the Museum Journal* 61, no. 4 (2018): 525–39.

Chambers, S. "Deliberative Democratic Theory." *Annual Review of Political Science* 6, no. 1 (2003): 307–26.

de Wildt, A. "The Backbone of the Museum?" *Amsterdam Museum @Work*. 2019, accessed February 26, 2020. https://bit.ly/2IfPvoX.

Debary, O. *La fin du Creusot ou L'art D'accomoder les Restes*. Paris: Editions du C.T.H.S., 2002.

Debono, S. "A Risky Controversy or a Potential Convergence?" 2019, accessed February 26, 2020 https://bit.ly/2TF2xBo.

Dutil, P. "Crowdsourcing as a New Instrument in the Government's Arsenal: Explorations and Considerations." *Canadian Public Administration* 58, no. 3 (2015): 363–83.

Ecker-Ehrhardt, M. "Self-Legitimation in the Face of Politicization: Why International Organizations Centralized Public Communication." *The Review of International Organizations* 13, no. 4 (2018): 519–46.

Fletcher, T. *Naked Diplomacy: Power and Statecraft in the Digital Age*. New York: William Collins, 2016.

Gellers, J. "Crowdsourcing Global Governance: Sustainable Development Goals, Civil Society, and the Pursuit of Democratic Legitimacy." *International Environmental Agreements: Politics, Law & Economics* 16, no. 3 (2016): 415–32.

Gent, S.E., J.C. Mark, E. Crescenzi, J. Menninga, and R. Lindsay. "The Reputation Trap of NGO Accountability." *International Theory* 7, no. 3 (2015): 426–63.

Gould, E. "ICOM Postpones Vote on New 'Museum' Definition." *Institute of Art & Law*, 2019, accessed February 26, 2020. https://bit.ly/3ajCsie.

Grant,R. W., and R. Keohane. "Accountability and Abuses of Power in World Politics." *American Political Science Review* 99, no. 1 (2005): 29–43.

Grigorescu, A. "Horizontal Accountability in Intergovernmental Organizations." *Ethics & International Affairs* 22, no. 3 (2008): 285–308.

Haftel, Y., and A. Thompson. "The Independence of International Organizations: Concept and Applications." *Journal of Conflict Resolution* 50, no. 2 (2006): 253–75.

Halliday, T. "Plausible Folk Theories: Throwing Veils of Plausibility over Zones of Ignorance in Global Governance." *The British Journal of Sociology* 69, no. 4 (2018): 936–61.

Hatfield, B. "The Definition of a Museum Revealed." *Art Law & More* (20 Aug 2019), accessed February 26, 2020 https://bit.ly/2A8W4Ju.

Hoffmann-Lange, U. "Vertical and Horizontal Accountability of Global Elites: Some Theoretical Reflections and a Preliminary Research Agenda." *Historical Social Research* 37, no. 1 (2012): 130–45.

Howe, J. *Crowdsourcing: Why the Power of the Crowd Is Driving the Future of Business*. New York: Crown Publishing Group, 2006.

Hudson, K. *A Social History of Museums*. London: Macmillan, 1975.

ICOM. "Article 3 Statutes." 2007, accessed February 26, 2020. https://bit.ly/2PNLwUN.

ICOM. "Annual Report." 2018a, accessed February 26, 2020. https://bit.ly/2ISlAmM.

ICOM. "Report of the Standing Committee for Museum Definition, Prospects and Potentials." 2018b, accessed February 26, 2020. https://bit.ly/2TDrCwB.

ICOM. "ICOM Kyoto 2019." *The 25th ICOM General Conference*, 2019a, accessed February 26, 2020. https://bit.ly/2xabF9Q.

ICOM. "ICOM Announces the Alternative Museum Definition That Will Be Subject to a Vote." 2019b, accessed February 26, 2020. https://bit.ly/2TlwMhQ.

ICOM. "Culture and Local Development: Maximising the Impact." 2019e, accessed February 26, 2020. https://bit.ly/2CkodhT.

ICOM. "Plenary. The Museum Definition: The Backbone of ICOM." 2019d, accessed February 26, 2020. https://bit.ly/39oiwuu.

ICOM. "Museum Definition Brief." 2020, accessed February 26, 2020. https://bit.ly/39SxVnd.

Jackson, S. "A Turning IR Landscape in a Shifting Media Ecology: The State of IR Literature on New Media." *International Studies Review* 21, no. 3 (2019): 518–34.

Johnston, E. "At Meeting in Kyoto, Global Body Debates How to Define and Protect Museums." *The Japan Times*, September 9, 2019.

Kalm,S., L. Strömbom, and A. Uhlin. "Civil Society Democratising Global Governance? Potentials and Limitations of "CounterDemocracy." *Global Society* 33, no. 4 (2019): 499–519.

Keller, P. "Reopening the Discussion About #museumdefinition." 2019, accessed February 26, 2020. https://bit.ly/2PPaJhE.

Kunz, R., and J. Maisenbacher. "Women in the Neighbourhood: Reinstating the European Union's Civilising Mission on the Back of Gender Equality Promotion?" *European Journal of International Studies* 1, no. 23 (2015): 122–44.

Lamy, P. "Global Governance Is a Challenge for Democracy (but an EU Opportunity)." *Europe's World* 14, no. 1 (2010): 48–52.

Lapeyre, F. *The Outcome and Impact of the Main International Commissions on Development Issues*. Working Paper 30, World Commission on the Social Dimension of Globalization. Geneva: International Labour Office, 2004.

Leadbeater, C. *Cloud Culture: The Future of Global Cultural Relations*. London: British Council, 2010.

Lehdonvirta, V., and J. Bright. "Crowdsourcing for Public Policy and Government." *Policy & Internet* 7, no. 3 (2015): 263–7.

Lindsay, J. "Stuxnet and the Limits of Cyber Warfare." *Security Studies* 22, no. 3 (2013): 365–404.

Mallard, G. and A. Lakoff. "How Claims to Know the Future Are Used to Understand the Present: Techniques of Prospection in the Field of National Security", in C. Camic, N. Gross and M. Lamont (eds), *Social Knowledge in the Making*, Chicago: University of Chicago Press, 339–77, 2011.

Mayntz, R. *Legitimacy and Compliance in Transnational Governance. Cologne.* MPIF. G Working Paper 10/5, 2010.

Memis, S. "Fostering a Cultural Diplomacy Policy Dialogue: The Quest for Stewardship and Cooperative Engagement." *The Journal of Arts Management, Law, & Society* 39, no. 4 (2009): 297–304.

MINOM. "Position Paper on the Proposal for a New Museum Definition." 2019, accessed February 26, 2020. https://bit.ly/32P4Iqf.

Murphy, B. "The Definition of the Museum." *ICOM News* 3, no. 2 (2004), accessed February 26, 2020. https://bit.ly/382NVTd.

Nelson, T. "Why ICOM Postponed the Vote on its New Museum Definition." *Museums Association*, 2019, accessed February 26, 2020. https://bit.ly/2wpf3gK.

Noce, V. "Vote on ICOM's New Museum Definition Postponed." *The Art Newspaper*, September 9, 2019.

Olmi, G. "Science-Honor-Metaphor: Italian Cabinets of the Sixteenth and Seventeenth Centuries." In *The Origins of Museums: The Cabinet of Curiosities in Sixteenth and Seventeenth Century Europe*, edited by Oliver Impey and Arthur MacGregor. Oxford: Clarendon Press. Brown, 1985.

Pallas, C. *Transnational Civil Society and the World Bank: Investigating Civil Society's Potential to Democratize Global Governance*. Basingstoke, UK: Palgrave McMillan, 2013.

Pallas, C., and A. Guidero. "Reforming NGO Accountability: Supply vs. Demand-Driven Models." *International Studies Review* 18 (2016): 614–34.

Pouliot, V., and T. Therien. "Global Governance in Practice." *Global Policy* 9, no. 2 (2018): 163–72.

Prpie, J., P.P. Shukla, J.H. Kietzmann, and I.P. McCarthy. "How to Work a Crowd: Developing Crowd Capital Through Crowdsourcing." *Business Horizons* 58, no. 1 (2015): 77–85.

Radu, R., N. Zingales, and E. Calandro. "Crowdsourcing ideas as an emerging form of multistakeholder participation in internet governance." *Policy and Internet* 7, no. 3 (2015): 362–82.

Ramos-Horta, J. *Statement of the Chair of the High-Level Independent Panel on Peace Operations Addressed to the Secretary-General.* New York: United Nations, A/70/95–S/2015/446.

Rosanvallon, R. *Counter-Democracy: Politics in an Age of Distrust.* Cambridge: Cambridge University Press, 2008.

Sandahl, J., ed. "Special Issue: The Backbone of Museums." *Museum International* 71, no. 1–2 (2019).

Sandahl, J. (2020). "Interview Taken by Grincheva, N. on February 24."

Seib, P. *Real-Time Diplomacy.* Palgrave Macmillan, 2012.

Simansons, R. "Creative Museum Opinion on the Alternative ICOM Museum Definition." *News: Creative-Museum,* 2020, accessed February 26, 2020. https://bit .ly/2w9dgMW.

Singh, J. "UNESCO: Scientific Humanism and Its Impact on Multilateral Diplomacy." *Global Policy* 9, no. 53 (2018): 53–9.

Small, Z. "A New Definition of "Museum" Sparks International Debate." *Hyperallergic,* 2019, accessed February 26, 2020. https://bit.ly/3aqQ773.

Snow, N. "Rethinking Public Diplomacy." In Snow, N. and Taylor, P. *Routledge Handbook of Public Diplomacy.* New York: Routledge (2008): 1–9.

Solly, M. "The Term 'Museum' May Be Getting Redefined." *Smithsonian Magazine,* 2019, accessed February 26, 2020. https://bit.ly/2uWOSh0.

Spiliotopoulou, L., Y. Charalabidis, E. Loukis, and V. Diamantopoulou. "A Framework for Advanced Social Media Exploitation in Government for Crowdsourcing." *Transforming Government: People, Process & Policy* 8, no. 4 (2014): 545–68.

Steffek, J. "The Output Legitimacy of International Organizations and the Global Public Interest." *International Theory* 7, no. 2 (2015): 263–93.

UN. "Transforming our world: the 2030 Agenda for Sustainable Development." 2015. accessed February 26, 2020. https://bit.ly/2U9BtL6.

Van Langenhove, L. "The Transformation of Multilateralism Mode1.0 to Mode 2.0." *Global Policy* 1, no. 3 (2010): 263–70.

Yi-Chong, X., and P. Weller. *The Politics of International Organizations: Views from Insiders.* London: Routledge, 2015.

PART II

International organisations and autonomy

5

THE UNITED NATIONS IN THE DIGITAL AGE

Harnessing the power of new digital information and communication technologies

Caroline Bouchard

Introduction

International organisations such as the United Nations are created to foster cooperation and to harmonise the relations and the actions of states in the attainment of common goals. As Hocking and Smith (2014, 287) have stressed, the "political process, at the world level … is essentially a process of communication between actors with an interest." With globalisation, this process of communication in international organisations has experienced significant changes. Patterns of relationship between international actors have changed with new powers and non-state actors emerging on the international sphere (Bouchard et al. 2013). Multilateral diplomatic interactions and dynamics have also been shaped by the emergence of new digital information and communication technologies (ICTs) (see Copeland 2013; Bjola and Holmes 2015; Hocking and Melissen 2015; Bjola, 2017; Manor 2017; Pamment 2017; Bjola, Cassidy, and Manor 2019) As Hocking and Melissen (2015, 11) argue, "the tools of the digital age create new issues and routines [for international actors], and simultaneously redefine existing ones."

This chapter investigates the influence of the new digital communication environment on the United Nations. It examines how and to what extent the introduction and adoption of new digital information and communication technologies (ICTs) by UN actors have affected processes in this international organisation. It explores how the UN "went digital."

Digital ICTs can be broadly defined as a combination of digital hardware, software, media and delivery systems (UNESCO 1999). They can range from "email to the smartphone and social networking sites" (Manor 2016, 3). Social media platforms which include "social network sites, video-sharing sites, blogging and microblogging platforms, and related tools that allow participants to create and share their own content" (boyd 2014, 6 cited in Fuchs 2017, 38) and are designed to "support in-depth social interaction, community formation, collaborative opportunities and collaborative work" (Hunsinger and Senft 2014, 1 cited in Fuchs 2017, 38), are new digital ICTs that have significantly contributed to the emergence of the new digital communication environment. However, it is important to stress that new digital ICTs include but are not limited to social media platforms. We consider new digital ICTs as digital technologies that differ from older forms of ICTs. In fact, with new digital ICTs, "mediated content and interaction become socially diversified (rather than directed primarily at the masses), channels are technologically convergent (rather than distinct systems), [and] mediated communication processes are interactive (rather than one-to-many, with separate producers and receiver roles)" (Lievrouw and Livingstone 2006, 7).

This chapter aims to offer insight on how these new digital ICTs have affected UN processes, more precisely those related to communication and information sharing. UN processes can be understood as "the entire policy process as defined by the international legal framework of [the United Nations] in which Member States, the international secretariat and various other actors participate" (see Reinalda and Verbeek 2007, 14). Studying UN processes "can contribute to a better understanding and assessment of [the organisation's] impact" (Smith 2006, 9)and can help us identify "the forces and influences that can move the organisation" (ibid.). By questioning how and to what extent UN processes have been affected by the introduction of new digital communication tools, we wish to further our understanding of the inner workings of the United Nations in the digital age.

The first section of this chapter gives an overview of the United Nations in the digital era. The chapter then introduces a conceptual framework to study the introduction and adoption of new digital ICTs by UN actors in communication and information sharing processes. The framework combines tools drawn from three types of scholarship: studies on UN processes (Smith 2002 and 2006), research on new media and their associated social contexts (Lievrouw and Livingstone 2006a), and work on the diffusion of innovations theory (Rogers 2003). By doing so, we aim to contribute to academic efforts in IR which have integrated research done by communication scholars IR (see Mowlana 1997; Gilboa 2001; Seib 2012; Melissen and de Keleunaar 2017).

The UN is a complex, multifaceted system made up of six main organs (including the General Assembly, the Security Council), multiple funds, programmes, entities and specialised agencies. To narrow the scope of this chapter, we have chosen to adopt a case study approach and focus on one UN entity: the UN Secretariat and more specifically its Department of Global Communications (DGC), previously known as the Department of Public Information (DPI). The Department of Global Communications' mission is to communicate the work of the United Nations to both internal and external audiences and to develop strategies for internal communication. It has thus been at the centre of discussions within the UN on how the organisation should adapt to the new digital environment.

The last section of the chapter presents results from our case study The analysis relies on two qualitative methods: documentary analysis and elite interviewing The use of qualitative methods is particularly advantageous as it allows us to explore experiences, practices, and attitudes (Yin 2014 and Devine 2002) of UN actors in the new digital environment.

Documents analysed for this study include communication guidelines, strategies as well as annual reports of activities produced by various UN entities. These "primary sources" – mostly intended for internal or restricted circulation (Burnham et al. 2004) – help provide specific details and information about the organisation's workings. In addition, they can point to information about communication processes within the organisation (Yin 2014).

A dozen semi-structured elite interviews were also conducted with UN practitioners working in the UN Secretariat. Elite interviewing allows us to gather information from experts – individuals who took part in or witnessed the events being studied or who have direct knowledge of the phenomenon (Leech 2002). It is also an effective way to collect information about the internal workings of an organisation (Burnham et al. 2004). To our knowledge, limited research has been conducted on this specific group of UN actors.Yet, UN practitioners (international civil servants) play a crucial role in the organisation. They can be advocates for change. They can introduce new initiatives anddiscuss them formally and informally with UN Member States. They also , design and implement programmes based on general decisions adopted by the organisation (see Weiss 2012). Using evidence from multiple sources (documents and interviews with UN experts) helps us achieve a more comprehensive account (Hakim 2000) of the UN in the digital age.

The United Nations in the digital age

Scholars have stressed the important role of communication technologies in International Relations and diplomacy (see Mowlana 1997; Potter 2002; Gilboa 2005; Seib 2012; Hocking and Melissen 2015). For instance, the telegraph, the telephone, and personal computers all disrupted and redefined the practice of IR when they were first introduced. Similarly, digital ICTs have had transformative effects on diplomacy practises (see Bjola, 2015; Hocking and Melissen 2015 ; Manor 2017; Pamment 2017; Bjola, Cassidy and Manor 2019). Social media platforms, for instance, "change the timeframes for diplomatic relationships, offering a transformational potential with regards to agenda setting and the framing of issues" (Pamment 2017, 3). They also bring a real-time dimension to diplomacy, encouraging faster, but also, in some cases, less precise communication (Seib 2012; Hocking and Melissen 2015). To help them manoeuvre in this new communication environment, international actors have been encouraged to develop their "digital skills" (Pamment 2017) and have adapted their practices. Diplomats have always had to develop new skills to integrate new technologies in their work. However, the case of new digital ICTs appears to differ from other forms of communication technologies. Whereas, in the past, diplomats were usually using new communication technologies before the general public, with new digital ICTs, they have had to catch up and keep up with technological standards set by the wider social and technological context (Hocking and Melissen 2015).

In the United Nations system, the increasing use of social media by international actors have led to changes both in the ways UN actors interact within the organisation and how the organisation communicates with external audiences (ONU 2015). Multilateral diplomacy in the UN has thus also "gone digital." The United Nations has increasingly been using social media platforms since the mid-2000s. The organisation has been active on Facebook since early 2007. A Twitter account @UN was also created in 2008 to be the official account of the organisation. In 2010, a Social Media Team was created within the then Department of Public Information (now the Department of Global Communications) to coordinate UN activities on social media platforms and manage the UN's various social media accounts. As of 2019, the United Nations had multiple Facebook pages (13), Twitter accounts (23), and YouTube channels (4) available. It also held accounts on Pinterest, Tumblr, Snapchat, Instagram, LinkedIn, Medium, Weibo, WeChat, and Vkontakte. The organisation has created a dedicated webpage – *The UN on Social Media* – which displays all its social media presence (https://www.un.org/en/sections/about-website/un-social-media/). UN content on digital platforms was available in the UN's six official languages: Arabic, Chinese, English, French, Russian, and Spanish as well as Hindi, Kiswahili, and Portuguese.

The integration of digital platforms "including social networking tools such as Facebook, Twitter, Tumblr, Flickr and YouTube is considered an increasingly important component of the [organisation]'s communication strategies" (United Nations 2015). These platforms are seen by the organisation as a way to develop a closer and more personal relationship with individuals around the world (ONU 2015) as they provide "the opportunity for people and organizations to quickly and easily publish their own material, make comments and/or engage with others" (United Nations DPI 2011, 1).

The expanding activities of the UN and its entities on social media have generated growing interest. In fact, back in 2013, the United Nations Children's Fund (UNICEF) was named the second most effective international organisation on Twitter (in terms of tweets retweeted) by a public relations firm (Burson-Marsteller 2013). In 2017, in another report by the same PR firm, the United Nations was named the most followed international organisation and with three other UN entities (UNICEF, UNESCO, and UN Refugee Agency) also in the top ten (Burson-Marsteller 2013).

While social media platforms have been integrated into the work done by several UN entities, a comprehensive approach of the organisation towards the new digital environment appears to have taken some time to develop. In May

2012, UN Secretary-General Ban Ki-moon announced the launch of "The Foundation for a Digital United Nations" which main goal would be "to provide advice and resources that [would] enable the United Nations to harness the power of information and communications technology" (UN 2012:1). At the time, the Secretary-General declared that information and communication technologies were a high priority for the organisation. However, to our knowledge, no clear initiative has emerged from this initiative. In fact, the Foundation has left little trace.

In January 2015, the UN organised its first "UN Social Media Day." The event was organised by the then UN Department of Public Information (DPI) jointly with the governments of Canada, New Zealand, the Netherlands, Switzerland, and the Digital Diplomacy Coalition (DDC) to "provide participants with new knowledge and inspiration, as well as acting as a working guide to the exciting – and sometimes challenging – social media environment" (United Nations 2015). It was estimated, at the time, that more than 80% of UN Member States were already active on social media (ONU 2015).

The "UN Social Media Day" included panels on digital diplomacy with high-ranking UN diplomats from Canada, Fiji, and Pakistan; on social media platforms with experts from LinkedIn, Twitter, and Tumblr; and social media trends with experts in journalism, marketing, and advertising. A series of short presentations also included speakers from the International Committee of the Red Cross, Wikipedia, and All Out (a global movement campaigning for LGBT rights). Designed to encourage all UN actors to use social media tools by providing knowledge and guidance, the "UN Social Media Day" generated great interest, but it did not lead to the definition of a clear UN approach to social media. In fact, due to limited budget and timing issues, the United Nations has yet to organise another "UN Social Media Day."[1]

Since the appointment of António Guterres as the new UN's Secretary-General in 2017, a number of initiatives have been launched that specifically focus on new technologies. One significant initiative was the establishment in July 2018 of the High Level Panel on Digital Cooperation. Composed of 20 experts from diverse academic and professional backgrounds in fields related to technology and policy, the panel was to "[r]aise awareness about the transformative impact of digital technologies" and "[r]ecommend ways for effective and inclusive systems of digital cooperation among all relevant actors in the digital space." (UN Secretary-General's High Level Panel on Digital Cooperation, Terms of Reference 2018). The High Level Panel signalled the new Secretary-General's intention to position the UN as a key player in player in the area of I digital cooperation. The panel, however, did not discuss how the organisation itself should adapt to new digital environment. This would be addressed with the publication of the "UN Secretary-General's Strategy on New Technologies in September 2018. Presented as the "first-ever internal United Nations system strategy on the topic" (United Nations Secretary-General 2018), the document covers a wide range of issues related to the integration of new technologies.

The strategy defines how the UN as an organisation should adapt to development of new technologies. It aims to describe how the UN system will support the use of new technologies to achieve the organisation's mandates, especially the achievement of the 2030 Sustainable Development Agenda (United Nations Secretary-General 2018). New technology in this strategy refers to digital ICTs including social media as well as other developing technologies including robotics, material sciences and biotechnology. While recognising, the "risks and benefits of new technology," the Secretary-General commits to strengthening "UN capacity to engage with new technologies: by training staff, increasing our knowledge and staying current with major technological advancements" (United Nations Secretary-General 2018, 3).

While the strategy does not specifically address the question of the integration of digital tools in UN processes, it does indicate the organisation's will to reflect on the use and impacts of new technologies on its work. Yet, in the word of one observer, digital ICTs, and more particularly there is growing evidence that the use of digital technologies, including social media platforms, has already affected "all aspects of UN work" (see Wikina 2015). To explore how and to what extent digital ICTs have influenced the UN's activities, this chapter uses a conceptual framework drawing from both IR literature and communication studies.

Studying the integration and impacts of new digital ICTs in UN processes

To study the UN in the digital age, this chapter draws conceptual tools from research done on UN internal dynamics (Smith 2002, 2006), communication studies on new media and their associated social contexts (Lievrouw and Livingstone 2006a), and research on the diffusion of innovations theory (Rogers 2003).

Smith's (2002 and 2006) research on the UN and Lievrouw and Livingstone's (2006) work on new media offer useful conceptual tools to study the use of new digital ICTs in UN processes, more particularly those involving communication and information sharing activities.

Factors influencing UN processes of communication

C.B. Smith's (2002 and 2006) work on UN internal dynamics offers several valuable conceptual tools to identify and study factors which influence UN processes of communication. Drawing upon the literature on international organisations, the literature on the UN and organisational sociology, Smith has identified several factors which come into play in UN processes. We argue that three factors identify by Smith are particularly relevant to studying UN processes of communication as they are linked to communication and information sharing activities: 1) rules of procedure; 2) strategic interactions; and 3) informal networking.

Specific *"rules of procedure"* have developed within the UN system (Smith 2006). These "structural" or "institutional" factors. shape interactions between UN actors and thus can influence how communication activities are conducted within the UN system. It is important to question whether changes in the rules or new rules of procedure have been introduced with the increasing use of new digital ICTs.

Strategic interactions are another factor which can affect UN processes. These interactions include both the actions and choices made by UN actors and the influence of "the larger social context" (Smith 2002, 124). Strategic interactions are influenced by the strategies chosen by actors to attain their goals and the role they wish to play in formal UN processes (Smith 2002; see also Cox and Jacobson 1973). Choices made by the actors are thus considered important in strategic interactions. Smith stresses that the environment in which an international organisation operates can also have an impact on strategic interactions as "each actor within the organisation has linkages to the outside environment and ... these linkages have an impact on the power and resources an actor has within the organisation" (Smith 2002, 124–5). The influence the new digital communication environment on these strategic interactions should thus be studied.

Informal networking isanother important factor in UN processes, but takes place behind the scenes at the UN. Smith argues, "the public and private side of UN diplomacy are two interwoven processes; you cannot assess the impact of one of these without considering both" (2002, 130). Informal networking can be influenced by informal contacts, working relationships developed over time and specific attributes of actors. Informal contacts happen outside formal UN meetings. They can facilitate UN processes by providing opportunities for UN actors to communicate, share information, strategise, exchange ideas, or clarify their positions (Smith 2002). Working relationships are "long-term patterns of interaction that can emerge when participants have worked together across a wide range of specific issues" (Smith 2002, 130–1). Smith (2006) and several other studies (Weiss 2012; Reinalda and Verbeek 2007) have also stressed that personal attributes of actors (personality, leadership and negotiating skills, knowledge competencies, etc.) can directly influence informal networking as actors must "sell" policies to other actors and gain their support (Smith 2006).

New digital ICTs: artefacts and practices

To have a better understanding of the UN in the digital age, we argue that the role of digital ICTs in all of these three categories of factors should be examined. We agree with Archetti (2012) that the role of digital ICTs in the UN's work "cannot be explained only through the impact of technology on communication practice," but must also be "about the appropriation of technological tools" by the organisation and individuals within the organisation (Archetti 2012, 185–6). To study the integration of digita ICTs in the UN's work, we use conceptual tools drawn from studies by Lievrouw and Livingstone (2006) on new media and their associated social contexts. These two authors argue that new (digital) media (or ICTs) should not only be studied in terms of technical features, content, or channels but that their associated social contexts – social, political, and economic factors – should also be taken into account.

Lievrouw and Livingstone's approach suggests that the study of new media should integrate three main components: the artefacts and devices that enable communication, the communication activities and practices in which individuals use the devices, and the social arrangements or organisations developing around the devices and practices (Lievrouw and Livingstone 2006b: 23). These three components are useful in our study as they help us question whether and in what ways, "particular configurations of artefacts and practices" (Lievrouw and Livingstone 2006b, 2) associated with new digital ITCs which are used in UN processes of communication are different from those related to older forms of technologies

Combining conceptual tools from Smith's work on UN processes with Lievrouw and Livingstone's research on new media allows us to examine the digital artefacts used by UN actors in UN processes. It also helps us examine the activities in which UN practitioners used new digital ICTs.

However, to gain insight into how the United Nations took a digital turn, we argue that it is also important to understand how these digital tools were introduced and by which UN actors. One should also consider the overall consequences of the introduction and adoption of new digital ICTs. To do this, this chapter draws from communication studies on the diffusion of innovations (Rogers 2003, 2003).

The diffusion of innovations theory (Rogers 2003) focuses on the introduction of a new (technological) innovation in a social system, the rate of its adoption, and the success of its spread. It focuses on the role of key actors, particularly opinion leaders and change agents, who influence the diffusion process. It also pays attention to the overall effects created by the diffusion of the innovation within the system. This theoretical approach allows us to study how digital ICTs were introduced and adopted in the UN system. It helps us question the role of UN actors in the diffusion of digital ICTs in the organisation and examine some of the effects created by the use of new digital ICTs by actors in UN processes of communication.

An innovation is defined by Rogers (2003, 12) as "an idea, practice, or object that is perceived as new by an individual or other unit of adoption." According to diffusion studies, successful diffusion and adoption of an innovation usually follows an S-shaped (cumulative) curve. Relatively few individuals adopt the innovation in the early phases of diffusion. Adoption then accelerates until it reaches a threshold or ceiling (Lievrouw 2006). At this stage, diffusion "increases at a slower rate as fewer and fewer remaining individuals adopt the innovation" (Rogers 2003, 272). The diffusion approach is useful to study both the "planned and the spontaneous spread" (Rogers 2003: 6) of a new digital tool within a system. Rogers' approach helps us identify actors who were involved in the introduction and adoption of digital ICTs in the UN system. It also allows us to examine some of the consequences of the introduction and adoption of innovations in UN processes.

Adopters and change agents

Rogers identifies several categories of actors who play a significant role in this diffusion process. Two of these categories – adopters and change agents – will allow us to investigate which UN actors were the first to use new digital ICTs and influence the early phase of diffusion of new digital ICTs in the UN.

Adopters are actors who make the decision to adopt the innovation. Rogers defines several types of "adopters" (innovators, early adopters, early majority, later majority, and laggards). Two of these categories of adopters are particularly relevant to our study: innovators and early adopters. Innovators play a significant role in the diffusion process as they are gate-keepers: these actors are responsible for the introduction of an innovation in the system by importing it from outside its boundaries. Early adopters are members within the system with the "highest degree of opinion leadership." Early adopters as opinion leaders can "provide information and advice about innovations to many other individuals in the system" (Rogers 2003, 26). According to Rogers (2003, 283), "potential adopters look to early adopters for advice and information about an innovation." Early adopters "serve as role models for many other members of a social system." They help decrease uncertainty about the adoption of an innovation. As opinion leaders, they can "lead in the spread of new ideas or they can head an active opposition" (Rogers 2003, 27). Early adopters thus play an influential role in the diffusion of new ideas within a system.

Rogers (2003) identifies change agents as another type of actors who can influence the diffusion process. Usually from outside the system, change agents play a role in "facilitating the flows of innovation" between those who have the (external) expertise regarding an innovation and the "clients" within the system (Rogers 2003, 368). Change agents can influence the decision to adopt or slow down the diffusion of an innovation within a system (Rogers 2003, 27). Change agents often consider early adopters as allies, "local missionar[ies] for speeding up the diffusion process" (Rogers 2003, 283). Thinking in terms of adopters and change agents can help us identify UN actors who play a role in influencing the decisions to adopt (or not) and make full use (or not) of new digital ICTs in UN processes. In the context of the UN, we would argue that change agents can come both from inside or outside the UN system and the main client would be the organisation itself. Change agents would therefore be sensitive to the needs of organisation.

Impacts of diffusion

According to Rogers (2003), the diffusion of an innovation within a system can create all sorts of consequences. The diffusion can have both functional effects (desirable consequences) and dysfunctional effects (undesirable effects) to a social system or to individuals within a system. Furthermore, it can create direct consequences – changes that occur in direct response to adoption digital ICTs – which in turn produced other indirect impacts within the organisation. The diffusion process can also have both anticipated and unanticipated effects. Anticipated effects would usually be welcomed within the system as they are changes that are "recognized and intended by the members of the social system" (Rogers 2003, 448). However, an innovation, such as digital ICTs, can also produce changes which are neither recognised nor intended by UN actors (unanticipated consequences). Questioning the various effects of the diffusion of new digital ICTs helps us to further understand how the UN is affected by the new digital communication environment.

How the UN went digital: the case of the UN Secretariat's Department of Global Communications

To examine how new digital ICTs have been introduced and adopted in the UN system and to what extent they have affected UN processes, we adopt a case study strategy and focus on one UN entity: the Department of Global Communications (DGC), previously known as the Department of Public Information (DPI).

Part of the UN Secretariat, the DPI was created in 1946 to "promote to the greatest possible extent an informed understanding of the work and purposes of the United Nations among the people of the world" (UN GA Resolution 13(1)). Member States of the newly established United Nations believed that the organisation could not "achieve its purposes for which it has been created unless the peoples of the world [were] fully informed of its aims and its activities" (UN GA Resolution 13(1)). While its structures and specific responsibilities have evolved through the years (see Alleyne 2003), the main mandate of the Department remains to communicate the work of the UN to the world. It is also responsible for the formulation and implementation of the organisation's internal and external communication strategies.

The Department is also in charge of the global network of United Nations Information Centres (UNICs) located in more than 60 countries. The name change of the Department from "Public Information" to "Global Communications" in January 2019 was meant to demonstrate the continuing commitment of the organisation that "a culture of communications and transparency should permeate all levels of the Organization as a means of fully informing the peoples of the world of the aims and activities of United Nations" (United Nations 2019a). The Department of Global Communication has been at the centre of discussions within the UN system on how the organisation should adapt to the new digital environment. The creation of the Social Media Team in 2010 in the Strategic Communications Division is considered by many a significant a turning point in the organisation's approach to new digital ICTs.

The Department of Global Communications is one of the departments of the UN Secretariat. The Secretariat is headed by the UN Secretary-General and is responsible for the day-to-day work of the organisation. The Department of Global Communications is led by an Under-Secretary-General and staffed with international civil servants (UN practitioners). The work of the Department of Global Communications is overseen by the Committee of Information, a subsidiary body of the General Assembly which deals with question relating to public information (see Alleyne 2003). Now composed of 116 UN Member States, this Committee provides the department guidance on its policies, programmes, and activities (https://www.un.org/en/ga/coi/).

The Department of Global Communications is composed of three divisions: the Strategic Communications Division, the News and Media Division, and the Outreach Division. The Strategic Communications Division (SCD) is in charge of delivering communications strategies and global campaigns to support the work of the UN.. It has been described as a key player in making sure that the organisation "harnesses communications to achieve its goals." The News and Media Division (NMD) produces news stories about the UN's activities and priorities in different formats and develops partnerships with journalists and media organisations. The mission of the Outreach Division (OD) is to build support for the work of the United Nations by engaging with a wide range of actors including civil society, academia, media, the entertainment industry, as well as students and educators (see https://www.un.org/en/sections/departments/department-global-communications/). As we will see in the next sections, all three divisions of DGC were involved in the diffusion and adoption of new digital ICTs.

Evidence shows that new digital ICTs, particularly social media platforms, have led to the redefinition of the UN's external communications strategies, but the impacts of the diffusion of new digital ICTs have been also been visible in internal communication processes. New artefacts and practices (Lievrouw and Livingstone 2006b) have been introduced in UN process and have shaped rules of procedure, strategic interactions, and informal networking (Smith 2002, 2006) within the UN system.

Rules of procedure

One of the first visible changes related to the use of digital ICTs within the organisation were linked to the redefinition of *rules of procedure* in communication and information sharing practices in the UN secretariat. Since the growing use of the internet in the late 1990s, UN actors had developed new communication practises. As Alleyne (2003) stresses, by the turn of the millennium, "every single significant actor in international relations, especially the UN offices, programs and agencies [was] expected to have a presence on the World Wide Web and did so" (Alleyne 2003, 34). In 2005, a new intranet system called iSeek was introduced. Primarily an internal communication tool, the new system aimed to "bring disparate parts of the organization together" (Stoddart 2007, 184). It aimed to inform UN staff "about the UN's common objectives and where they fit into the overall picture, linking headquarters with regional offices and field missions" and "establish one intranet for one UN worldwide, with consistent layout, standard technology, providing relevant and consistent messages to reach staff everywhere" (Stoddart 2007, 184). The introduction of iSeek intended to initiate "a new way of working and interacting internally" with UN staff using the system to share and post stories, information, and news (Stoddart 2007, 189).

iSeek is still presented today by the organisation as the "primary internal communications and knowledge-sharing tool of the UN Secretariat, connecting staff members all over the world" (https://iseek-external.un.org/) and managed by the Outreach Division of the DGC. Recent efforts have been made by the iSeek team to "raise awareness among staff members of new initiatives and developments in different departments of the Secretariat" (UN General Assembly 2019, 30) and to promote the platform as an internal communication tool that brings together practitioners from various parts of the organisation. iSeek does appear to be an important tool for UN practitioners to find useful information about, for example, UN meetings and conferences, the description of each UN department or human resources issues.[2]

Interestingly, iSeek and other digital tools have also played a critical role in a time of crisis. Following the earthquake in Haiti in 2010, efficient internal communication within the UN system was considered crucial as the United Nations had just lost 102 of its staff (https://www.un.org/en/memorial/haiti/). The Outreach Division of the DPI was particularly active on this front. It circulated information on the situation on the ground including statements by the Secretary-General to staff via iSeek and launched a new webpage with links to information on Haiti coming from all around the UN system and civil society. Furthermore, it contributed to the creation of digital tools such as a dedicated e-mail account and an eRoom space to help UN staff deal with grief and the loss of their colleagues (UN General Assembly 2010b).

iSeek, however, does not appear to be the main platform privileged by all UN practitioners for daily interactions with other actors of the UN system.[3] For some observers, most of daily internal communications activities between UN practitioners occur through "plain old emails."[4] While iSeek is still being promoted within the organisation as the primary internal communication tool, there is evidence to show that UN practitioners are also increasingly using new "external" digital artefacts to communicate and share information with colleagues in the UN system and thus introducing new "rules of procedure." Some UN practitioners prefer communicating via the messaging platform Slack.[5] Others find online platforms for video and audio conferences such as Webex and BlueJeans useful tools to organise meetings and seminars.[6] The messaging app WhatsApp is used for communicating and coordinating with UN colleagues particularly in the context of a conference, a specific event, or a special UN session.[7] UN practitioners have also been using Trello, project management boards (https://trello.com/unitednationssocialmedia), to coordinate and plan activities and campaigns and create editorial calendars to share content for communication campaigns.[8] In its own report of activities for 2018, the Department of Global Communications also acknowledged the use of these external digital tools. It highlighted that "digital collaboration tools such as WebEx and Skype for Business" had been used to conduct as training resources and briefings for United Nations information centre staff around the world (UN General Assembly 2018a).

The limited use of iSeek and the use of external tools might be explained by the fact that it could not be easily used for communication and information sharing between UN practitioners and other UN actors including diplomats from UN Member States. Indeed, as of 2019, iSeek did not integrate the UN Member States' e-deleGATE portal into its platform (UN General Assembly 2019, 30). The e-deleGATE portal (delegate.un.int) is managed by the Department for General Assembly and Conference Management and centralises digital services and information for delegates from UN permanent missions. According to the Committee of Information, the integration of e-deleGATE into iSeek would allow UN practitioners to have a "more efficient and effective sharing of information with Member States" (UN General Assembly 2019a, 30). It will be interesting to see if the integration of these two platforms happens in the future and if this has any incidence on the *rules of procedure* of the organisation.

Strategic interactions

The introduction of new artefacts and practices linked to digital ICTs has also been witnessed in *strategic interactions*. When it was first introduced, social media were seen by the department as an innovative approach to reach individuals around the world, especially younger audiences (UN General Assembly 2009a and 2009b). Social media platforms are now considered a significant component of the UN's communication strategies with all external audiences. While social media platforms are seen a useful tool to counter misinformation about the UN and to support fundraising activities,[9] social media and other new digital ICTs appear to have been mostly used by the Department of Global Communications to communicate about priority topics which had been put on the UN agenda by the UN Secretariat.[10] One UN practitioner stressed that UN actors are encouraged to view the use of social media as a strategy to "stay on message" and "amplify other [UN actors]'s messages."[11]

The first communication campaign by the department that integrated new digital media alongside traditional media focused on nuclear disarmament. It was launched in June 2009 with the slogan "WMD-We Must Disarm" and ended with the International Day of Peace on September 21, 2009. Social media was mainly used to attract visitors to the United Nations International Day of Peace website. Twitter and Facebook accounts were employed by the Department to promote the "We Must Disarm" campaign. Twitter was also used by the Department to show public support for the campaign to delegates from the Member States as "Messages sent out over Twitter were also screened in the General Assembly

Hall just before the general debate in September" (UN General Assembly 2010a, 5–6).

In recent years, the "main" campaign for the Department of Global Communications, particularly the Strategic Communications Division and the Social Media Team, has been to support the 2030 Agenda for Sustainable Development and the 17 Sustainable Development Goals (SDGs). New digital ICTs have played a significant role in the promotion of the SDGs. The UN website on the Sustainable Development Goals was redesigned in 2018 to offer information in the six official languages of the organisation. Dedicated social media accounts (@GlobalGoalsUN) and a mobile application account were created to promote the Sustainable Development Goals (Department of Public Information 2018). Furthermore, in recent years, the Strategic Communications Division and the Social Media Team have made specific efforts to link all communication campaign to the SDGs campaign. The SDGs campaign is in fact considered a long-term campaign as well as an umbrella campaign – encompassing several communication campaigns on key sustainable development issues.

The communication campaign to promote the 70th anniversary of the Universal Declaration of Human Rights in 2018 is another interesting example. The Strategic Communication Division with the Office of the High Commissioner for Human Rights specifically designed this campaign around new digital ICTs.[12] Digital tools were considered as "major components of the campaign" seen as useful tools to "reach people around the world" to "promote, engage and reflect" on the work of the United Nations.[13] A new website for the campaign was launched in November 2017 (http://www.standup4humanrights .org) as well as specific hashtags (#StandUp4HumanRights #RightsOutLoud) for social media campaigns with the help of the Social Media Team.

New digital ICTs, especially social media platforms have also become important tools to circulate information about the work being done by the UN, especially in times of humanitarian crisis. Following the earthquake in Haiti in January 2010, social media platforms were used by the then Department of Public Information in collaboration with the UN Department of Peacekeeping Operations to inform UN staff and the public about the situation on the ground (UN General Assembly 2010a).

In *strategic interactions*, the choice of using one digital ICT over another by UN practitioners is guided by both the nature of the digital platform and the nature of the UN event or work that is being promoted.[14] Twitter, Facebook, and Instagram are the three most used digital platforms on a daily basis by the Social Media Team,[15] with Twitter being the most used platform. Instagram posts often show the "behind the scenes" and "lighter side" of the organisation.[16] Snapchat is typically used "for special moments like the nomination of a new Secretary-General or side events at a conference."[17]

In the context of *strategic interactions*, the Department of Global Communications has also developed a relationship with digital platforms to develop new communication initiatives. In 2017, the department launched a campaign to encourage users of social media platforms to get active on climate change. The campaign was developed in collaboration with Facebook and used advances in artificial intelligence. The campaign focused on an interactive and responsive chat bot on the main United Nations Facebook page called ActNow.bot. Based on its inter-action with the user, the chat bot recommends daily actions that can be taken to reduce the users' carbon footprints (UN General Assembly 2018a). In the con-text of this campaign, the UN stressed that its partnership with the private sector plays a crucial role in its efforts to raise awareness and combat climate change (https://www.un.org/en/actnow/partners.shtml).

Informal networking

There is also evidence to suggest that new digital ICTs have been involved, but to a lesser extent, in fostering *informal networking* – which take place outside the UN's formal framework – between UN actors. They are specifically used by UN practitioners of the department to engage with two other actors involved in the UN system: UN Member States and civil society.

According to one interviewee, UN practitioners use social media platforms such as Twitter to highlight the work they do at the UN, but also to promote their partnership with other UN departments and offices as well as joint efforts with UN diplomats of Member States. In fact, social media, and more specifi-cally Twitter, are popular communication tools used by UN practitioners to publicly recognise the initiatives of diplomats who support specific UN cam-paigns and create relationship with new delegates from Member States.[18]

New digital ICTs are also used by UN practitioners to create stronger links with civil society. Since 2016, for example, the Department of Global Communications has been setting up a "media zone" at the sidelines of key UN meetings to foster collaboration with civil society on Sustainable Development Goals issues. The media zone includes among other activities live broadcasts of panel discussions and interviews on digital platforms as well as conversations using the hashtag #SDGLive on social media (UN General Assembly 2018a). Civil society can be a crucial ally for the promotion of the work of the United Nations. Digital tools have allowed creating additional spaces of dialogue between UN practitioners and members of civil society.

Our analysis of the use of new digital ICTs in UN processes has shown that new digital ICTs have been increasingly used to attempt to bring closer together various parts of the organisation, including in times in crisis. They have played a significant role in strategies put in place for attaining the organisation's main objectives. New digital ICTs have allowed the organisation to explain and pro-mote its objectives and work. Digital tools have also encouraged a more open and closer dialogue with Member States, civil society, and the general public.

To better understand how the integration of new digital ICTs has happened in the United Nations, the next sections will examine the role played by actors involved in the diffusion – the introduction and adoption – of digital tools.

Impacts from the diffusion of digital ICTs will also be discussed. This will help us assess in what ways new digital tools have affected the activities of the Department of Global Communication, and more broadly the UN's work.

Adopters and change agents

As we mentioned above, Rogers (2003) identifies two categories of actors who play important roles in the diffusion of innovations within a system: adopters and change agents.

Our analysis suggests that two kinds of adopters – innovators and early adopters – of new digital ICTs were working in various divisions of the Department of Global Communications. The creation of the Social Media Team in 2010 provided an organisational structure for a small group of innovators to work together within the Department of Global Communications. The team was first composed of a small number (only three practitioners in 2016) of UN information officers who had developed knowledge on the use of digital platforms. Some of these individuals also had previous experiences working with the UN's intranet iSeek[19] (see also Wikina 2015).

At the time of the Social Media Team in 2010, various individuals within other divisions of DPI were also innovators as they had already introduced social media platforms in the professional work. These innovators included practitioners in the News and Media Division.[20] For instance, in 2010, practitioners in the organisation's radio station, United Nations Radio, became early adopters when they created Twitter accounts for all language units (Arabic, Chinese, English, French, Russian, and Spanish as well as in Hindi, Kiswahili, and Portuguese). Facebook pages in English, French, Russian, and Spanish were also launched (UN General Assembly 2010a, 3).

Members of the Social Media Team became early adopters in the UN system as they served as role models and provided "information and advice about innovations to many other individuals in the system" (Rogers 2003, 26). The Social Media Team was specifically put in place with a view to design a digital strategy for the organisation and coordinate social media activities of the various entities of the UN system. Monthly coordination meetings with the Social Media Team and other UN entities were also organised by the then Department of Public Information to discuss issues associated with digital media and share best practices.[21]

Interestingly, early adopters in the then Department of Public Information also tried to slow down and even limit the diffusion of digital ICTs in the wider UN system. According to one observer, UN officials were asked by the DPI to "think twice about opening accounts on social media"[22] and to thoroughly reflect on the challenges and risks of using digital media strategies. DPI also published Social Media Guidelines for UN staff in order to avoid "unnecessary errors that might harm the organization's reputation." The guidelines stressed that the UN's social media accounts should be managed by "active users of the tool so as to better understand the rules and etiquette of the communication medium" (DPI 2011, 1). Enhancing coherence, consolidating resources, and avoiding duplication have been key arguments put forward to justify limiting the number of social media accounts (UN General Assembly 2018a).

Evidence suggests that the diffusion of new digital ICTs such as social media platforms in the UN system often depends on innovators or early adopters being in top positions: "all has to do with how much the Head of a specific department or agency has accepted the role of social media and has asked the question, 'who needs it and why do we need it?'"[23]

The Secretary-General, the individual at the top of the United Nations Secretariat, has played a key role in the diffusion of new digital tools within the UN system. As mentioned above, Ban Ki-moon, when he was Secretary-General, pushed for the organisation to integrate digital initiatives. He also appears to have been an early adopter: "Ban Ki-moon was very tuned into digital media and was himself willing to use social media."[24] The Social Media Team was created during his tenure. Ban Ki-Moon, however, contrary to his successor, did not devise a clear strategy for the integration of new technologies in the organisation.

Since his appointment as Secretary-General, António Guterres has launched several initiatives focusing on new technologies. These initiatives gave a clear signal that he favours the diffusion of new technologies in general in the UN system. In his 2018 "Strategy on New Technologies," the Secretary-General encourages all UN staff members to "understand how new technologies are impacting their area of work, and they must be provided with the space to explore and test how technology can be leveraged to better deliver on respective mandates" (United Nations Secretary-General 2018, 6). He also commits to asking "UN leadership to encourage initiatives at all levels and with all staff designed to deepen our understanding of new technologies and their impact on individual and entity wide mandates" (ibid.13). The Secretary-General has, however, also emphasised the need for UN to "be humble in recognizing the limits of our own knowledge and potential impact" and to continue to learn about these new technologies (ibid.15).

It is worth noting that the Secretary-General does not appear to have been an innovator or an early adopter of new digital ICTs. Prior to his election at the head of the organisation, he did not have a social media presence. His personal Twitter account (@AntonioGuterres) was only activated on January 1, 2017 when he took office. Guterres also appears to have a cautious and youth-oriented approach to new digital ICTs. Guterres writes his own posts on Twitter,[25] which is in tune with his insistence of having "a personal voice" on social media platforms.[26] He has also particularly championed the use of digital ICTs to reach younger audiences.[27] These two elements were highlighted when the Secretary-General joined Instagram in May 2019 (@antoniogutteres): the platform which is "very popular with young audiences" would allow Guterres to "share a personal, inside look into his work and the priorities of the Organization." His first post on the platform was characterised as "both personal and authentic" (UN News 2019).

While the Secretary-General and the UN Secretariat have encouraged practitioners to use social media platforms, they also issued in February 2019 "Guidelines for the Personal Use of Social Media." The document states that "UN staff have an important role to play as the face of the Organization, including on social media." UN practitioners should use social media to promote the work of the organisation. However, they should also be mindful "of the value of tact, discretion, care and good judgment when using personal social media" as "staff members' activity on personal social media, even when unrelated to official duties, may reflect on the Organization and may expose the United Nations to reputational risk" (United Nations Secretariat 2019, 1). Similar to DPI Guidelines, the UN Secretariat seems to have privileged a careful approach to the diffusion and use of social media platforms by insisting the UN practitioners: "Think before posting and use common sense" (. ibid. 2).

According to Rogers (2003), change agents also influence the decision to adopt or slow down the diffusion of an innovation within a system. We argue that UN Member States acted as change agents in the integration of new digital ICTs. In contrast to adopters, change agents are actors that come from "outside" the system. Member States can be considered to come from outside the system we are studying as they are not active in the UN Secretariat.

Through the Committee of Information, UN Member States clearly expressed their position on the diffusion of digital ICTs:

> [w]hile delegations [of Member States] voiced strong support for the Department [of Global Communication]'s strengthening of its new and social media capacity, many [Member States] urged the Department to continue to devote resources to traditional media such as print, television and radio.
>
> *(UN General Assembly 2019b, 11)*

To justify this position, Member States have pointed to the issue of the digital divide. Member States have argued that inequality of access between states persist in terms of digital ICTs. Technical skills' limitations and high costs also remain important challenges to accessing new digital tools in some parts of the world. Member States have urged the DGC not to prioritise the diffusion of new digital ICTs over traditional media but "to be inclusive in its approach and to use a mix of new and traditional media in disseminating the principles and activities of the United Nations to the global public" (UN General Assembly 2019, 11).

Impacts of new digital ICTs in the UN system

Within the Department of Global Communications and the wider UN system, the diffusion of digital ICTs has produced various direct desirable and anticipated effects. As we have seen above in our analysis of UN process and digital ICTs, digital tools have brought closer together various parts of the organisation. They have encouraged a more open and closer engagement with Member States, civil society, and the general public. They have also allowed the organisation to explain and promote its objectives and work.

Nevertheless, the introduction and adoption of digital ICTs have also produced several unanticipated and indirect effects. Some of the impacts have also revealed themselves as being undesirable for the UN system and have created significant concerns for UN practitioners. One of these impacts was the blurring lines between internal and external communication and the potential repercussions for the reputation of the organisation. This appears to have been one of the main reasons behind the establishment of social media guidelines and directives by various UN entities.

When it issued its guidelines in 2011, the then Department of Public Information stressed that guidelines were important to help UN staff use social media platforms – both in professional and personal communications – in an effective manner, and also to "protect the privacy of individuals, including colleagues, depicted in social media materials (videos, photos, etc.)" as well as to avoid the UN's misrepresentation on social media (United Nations Department of Public Information 2011, 1). DPI recognised that the use of social media platforms brought clear benefits such as "enabling direct and real-time interactivity with UN audience," but it also argued that social media tools create challenges as "the distinction between internal and external communication, and professional and personal communication" is often blurred (United Nations Department of Public Information 2011, 1).

Another department of the UN Secretariat, the Department of Management and its Office of Human Resources, has also warned staff that they "should also be careful in [their] use of social media and social networks" (United Nations 2014, 101). Practitioners should use discretion when using these platforms as postings could be interpreted as statements or commitments made by the United Nations. They also insisted that, in internal communications, "it is important not to rely solely on digital formats – face-to-face time is critical." (ibid., 162).

The "Guidelines for the Personal Use of Social Media" issued by the UN Secretariat in 2019 pointed to the same concerns: it called on UN practitioners to make sure

> "that the expression of their personal views and convictions on social media does not adversely affect their official duties, reflect poorly on their status as international civil servants or call into question their duty of loyalty, impartiality and responsibility to the Organization".
>
> *(United Nations Secretariat 2019, 1)*

The Secretariat recognised the UN staff members' "right to freedom of expression through their own personal social media accounts" but stressed that, as international civil servants, they "should be mindful at all times that their conduct on social media must be consistent with the [UN] principles" (UN Secretariat 2019, 1).

The guidelines also mention issues of privacy and security. They encouraged UN staff to check and manage their accounts' privacy setting and to make sure that information posted was not sensitive, privileged, and/or confidential. These directives might have been introduced to partly respond to a news story in September 2018 that revealed that that sensitive information and material were made available online on several UN Trello boards (Lee 2018). At the time, a UN spokesperson said that the UN, following the incidents, had "reached out to all staff reminding them of the risks of using a third-party platform to share content and to take the necessary precautions to ensure no sensitive content is public" (cited in Lee 2018). The use of "external" digital tools by UN actors has thus also created additional challenges for the organisation.

Another significant consequence of the diffusion of digital ICTS is the increasing number of tasks the Social Media Team is now asked to perform. Since its creation in 2010, the team has had to face growing demands from various UN actors both in terms of its coordination activities and the management of the UN official accounts. In its early years, the Social Media Team had remained quite small (composed of only three practitioners in 2016). However, in recent years, the team has been expanding and, in 2019, was composed of around 20 practitioners.[28]

One of the main objectives of the reshaping of the Social Media Team was the inclusion of more multilingual staff to help manage its activities. These changes have been introduced in response to criticism that most of the content produced by the UN on social media was in English as well as increasing pressures from Member States for the UN to produce multilingual content on digital platforms.[29]

Mainstreaming multilingualism has been an important issue in the UN system, particularly in the UN Secretariat. In 2016, the UN General Assembly requested that the Secretary-General "exert all efforts to ensure that publications and other information services of the Secretariat, including the United Nations website, the United Nations News Service and United Nations social media accounts, contain comprehensive, balanced, objective and equitable information in all official languages" (UN Resolution, 71/101, 5). As mentioned before, while an English version of the UN official Twitter account was created in 2008, it took several years before official UN accounts were established in other UN official languages. The Spanish version was only created in 2010, the French version in 2011, and the Russian and Arabic versions in 2012.

Member States have been critical of the Department of Global Communications initiatives in this area. They have repeatedly reaffirmed the need to achieve full parity among the six official languages on all UN Websites and on social media and criticised the disparity between the English and non-English languages regarding digital content creation including the use of hashtags for social media campaigns (UN General Assembly 2019b, 30). They have also called for "the equitable distribution among all official languages of financial and human resources within the Department of Global Communications allocated to the United Nations website and social media, with full respect for the needs and the specificities of all six official languages." (ibid.). This last issue points to another impact of the diffusion of new digital ICTs: stretching resources and funding.

Adding more staff in the Social Media Team to contribute to the mainstreaming multilingualism also requires more funding. With resources being limited in the UN Secretariat, the remodelling of the Social Media Team to enhance its multilingualism has created important adjustments and lively discussions in the whole of Department of Public Information and the other DPI entities.[30]

Indeed, the Department of Global Communications – as the rest of the UN Secretariat – has limited financial resources. In fact, the Secretary-General's request in the 2018–2019 budget for 18 additional posts to help the Department of Global Communications achieve its mandate, including producing digital content in all six official languages, was not approved by the General Assembly. This problem is not new: limited or even diminishing resources has always been a problem for this department as well as getting UN Member States to invest in its activities (see Alleyne 2003).

However, the new digital environment and the diffusion of ICTs in the UN have created extra challenges for this department. As Member States have been reluctant to invest more resources in this specific area, any initiatives introduced to respond to the consequences of the diffusion of digital ICTs have had to be made using "existing resources."[31] The enlarged Social Media Team was only made possible by a movement of UN practitioners from the News and Media Division to the Strategic Communication Division.[32]

Finally, there has been an emphasis made by many UN actors including the Secretary-General regarding the importance of UN staff getting more training related to the use of digital ICTs and other new technologies to achieve greater efficiency. However, resources have also been limited for these types of activities.[33] With new technologies constantly emerging, it will be interesting to see if in the future the question of training becomes a significant issue in the UN system.

Conclusion

In recent years, the United Nations has taken a digital turn. This chapter has shown that new digital ICTs have been increasingly used in UN processes linked to communication and information sharing activities. It has also highlighted that specific UN actors have played a role in the diffusion of new technologies in the UN system. Lastly, it showed that the diffusion of digital ICTs in the organisation has created both anticipated and unanticipated effects as well as positive and negative effects.

With new technologies and digital tools continually emerging, we would argue that the United Nations and international organisations should take the time reflect on how the introduction and adoption of new technological tools affect its processes of communication. It is important to ask how the new tools will shape internal communication between actors in the organisation. The organisations should question the use of "internal" and "external" tools and their respective advantages and disadvantages. They should also reflect on how these new technologies can help them best attain their objectives, but also think about how they can help them foster crucial informal relationships with other international actors. The role played by specific actors in the organisation for the successful integration of new technologies should also be considered. International organisations should also be attentive to unanticipated and undesirable effects created by the use of new technologies.

This chapter aimed to contribute to a better understanding of the UN in the digital age. New digital ICTs have created new opportunities for the organisation to further engage with other international actors and global audiences and to explain its work and its importance in the international system. However, the new digital environment has also created several challenges for the United Nations and especially for its Department of Global Communications. Increasing demands and limited resources have been recurrent concerns over the years for this department. Several other questions will also need to be addressed in the future to make the UN a truly efficient "digital" international organisation, one navigating confidentially in the digital era. These issues include, inter alia, multilingualism, the digital divide and the organisation's relationships with different partners including social media platforms and the private sectors.

In an ever-increasing digital world, finding the most efficient ways to communicate what it does to the global public will continue to be an important question for the organisation. In the words of the Department of Global Communications: "at a time when multilateralism, the very foundation of the United Nations, [is] being questioned, the Organization want[s] and need[s] to be understood. For the United Nations communications to succeed, they must be clear and they must engage audiences in ways they underst[and], on platforms they [use] and in languages they comprehend" (UN General Assembly 2019b, 10).

Notes

1 Interview with UN practitioner, New York, 12/09/2016.
2 Interview with UN practitioner, New York, 07/19/2018.
3 Interview with UN practitioner, New York, 07/19/2018.
4 Interview with UN practitioner, New York, 07/16/2018.
5 Interview with UN practitioner, New York, 12/09/2017.
6 Interview with UN practitioner, New York, 12/08/2017.
7 Interview with UN practitioner, New York, 07/16/2018.
8 Interview with UN practitioner, New York, 12/09/2017.
9 Interview with UN practitioner, New York, 07/18/2018.
10 Interview with UN practitioner, New York, 07/17/2018.

11 Interview with UN practitioner, New York, 12/09/2016.
12 Interview with UN practitioner, New York, 12/08/2017.
13 Interview with UN practitioner, New York, 12/08/2017.
14 Interview with UN practitioner, New York, 12/13/2016.
15 Interview with UN practitioner, New York, 07/17/2018.
16 Interview with UN practitioner, New York, 07/17/2018.
17 Interview with UN practitioner, New York, 12/13/2016.
18 Interview with UN practitioner, New York, 12/09/2016.
19 Interview with UN practitioner, New York, 12/09/2016.
20 Interview with UN practitioner, New York, 12/08/2017.
21 Interview with UN practitioner, New York, 12/09/2016.
22 Interview with UN practitioner, New York, 12/09/2016.
23 Interview with UN practitioner, New York, 12/08/2016.
24 Interview with UN practitioner, New York, 12/09/2016.
25 Interview with UN practitioner, New York, 07/17/2018.
26 Interview with UN practitioner, New York, 07/17/2018.
27 Interview with UN practitioner, New York, 07/18/2018.
28 Interview with UN practitioner, New York, 07/18/2018.
29 Interview with UN practitioner, New York, 12/08/2017.
30 Interview with UN practitioner, New York, 12/08/2017.
31 Interview with UN practitioner, New York, 07/18/2018.
32 Interestingly, in 2019, the Social Media Team appears to have been integrated in the Digital and Promotion Branch of the News and Media Division – see The Social Media Section https://www.un.org/en/sections/departments/department-global-communications/news-media/index.html
33 Interview with UN practitioner, New York, 07/19/2018.

References

Alleyne, Mark D. *Global Lies? Propaganda, the UN and World Order*. Houndmills, Basingstoke, Hampshire: Palgrave Macmillan, 2003.

Archetti, Cristina. "The Impact of New Media on Diplomatic Practice: An Evolutionary Model of Change." *The Hague Journal of Diplomacy* 7, no. 2 (2012) : 181–206.

Bjola, Corneliu. "Introduction – Making Sense of Digital Diplomacy." In *Diplomacy – Theory and Practice*, edited by Corneliu Bjola, and Martin Holmes, 1–9. London and New York: Routledge, 2015

Bjola, Corneliu. *Adapting Diplomacy to the Digital Age: Managing the Organisational Culture of Ministries of Foreign Affairs*, Working Chapter Project "Diplomacy in the 21st Century." Berlin: Stiftung Wissenschaft und Politik (SWP)/ German Institute for International and Security Affairs, 2017.

Bjola, Corneliu, Jennifer Cassidy, and Ilan Manor. "Public Diplomacy in the Digital Age." In *Public Diplomacy in the Digital Age*, edited by J. Melissen and J.Wang, 83-101. Leiden, Nederland: Brill, 2019.

Bjola, Corneliu, and Martin Holmes, eds. *Digital Diplomacy – Theory and Practice*. London and New York: Routledge, 2015.

Bouchard, Caroline, John Peterson, and Nathalie Tocci, eds. *Multilateralism in the21st Century: Europe's Quest for Effectiveness*. London: Routledge, 2013.

boyd, danah. *It's Complicated : The Social Lives of Networked Teens*. New Haven and London: Yale University Press, 2014.

Burnham, Peter, Karin Gilland, Wyn Grant, and Zig Layton-Henry. *Research Methods in Politics*. Houndmills, Basingstoke: Palgrave Macmillan, 2004.

Burson-Marsteller. *Twiplomacy 2013 – How International Organisations Use Twitter.* 2013, accessed December 15, 2017. http://twiplomacy.com/.

Copeland, Daryl. "Digital Technology." In *The Oxford Handbook of Modern Diplomacy,* edited by A. Cooper, J. Heine, and R. Thakur, 453–70. Oxford: Oxford University Press, 2013.

Devine, Fiona. "Qualitative Methods." In *Theory and Methods in Political Science.* 2nd ed., edited by David Marsh and Gerry Stoker, 197–215. New York: Palgrave Macmillan, 2002.

Fuchs, Christian. *Social Media: A Critical Introduction.* 2nd ed. London: Sage Publications, 2017.

Gilboa, Eytan. "Diplomacy in the Media Age: Three Models of Uses and Effects." *Diplomacy & Statecraft* 12, no. 2 (2001): 1–28.

Gilboa, Eytan. "The CNN Effect: The Search for a Communication Theory of International Relations." *Political Communication* 22, no. 1 (2005): 27–44.

Hakim, Catherine. *Research Design.* 2nd ed. London: Routledge, 2000.

Hocking, Brian, and Melissen, Jan. *Diplomacy in the Digital Age.* Clingendael Report. The Hague: Clingendael Institute, 2015.

Hocking, Brian, and Michael Smith. *World Politics – An Introduction to International Relations.* 2nd ed. London and New York: Routledge, 2014.

Hunsinger, Jeremy and Theresa Senft, eds. *The Social Media Handbook.* New York: Routledge, 2014.

Lievrouw, Leah A., and Sonia Livingstone. *The Handbook of New Media Updated Student Version.* London: Sage, 2006a.

Lievrouw, Leah A., and Sonia Livingstone. "Introduction to the First Edition (2002) – the Social Shaping and Consequences of ICTs." In *The Handbook of New Media Updated Student Version,* edited by L. A. Lievrouw, and S. Livingstone, 15–32. London: Sage, 2006b.

Lee, Micah. "United Nations Accidentally Exposed Passwords and Sensitive Information to the Whole Internet." *The Intercept,* September 24, 2018, accessed December 9, 2018.

Leech, Beth L. "Interview Methods in Political Science." *Political Science and Politics* 35, no. 4 (2002): 663–88.

Lievrouw Leah, A. "New Media Design and Development – Diffusion of Innovations v Social Shaping of Technology." In *The Handbook of New Media Updated Student Version,* edited by L. A. Lievrouw, and S. Livingstone, 246–65. London: Sage, 2006.

Lievrouw Leah, A., and Sonia Livingstone. "Introduction to the Updated StudentEdition. " In *The Handbook of New Media – Updated Student Version,* edited by L.A. Lievrouw, and S. Livingstone, 1–14. London: Sage, 2006c.

Manor, Ilan. "Are We There *Yet*: Have MFAs Realized the Potential of Digital Diplomacy?" *Brill Research Perspectives in Diplomacy & Foreign Policy* 1, no. 2 (2016): 1–110.

Manor, Ilan. "The Digitalization of Diplomacy: Towards Clarification of a Fractured Terminology." Working Chapter. *Exploring Digital Diplomacy,* 2017, accessed October 27, 2017. https://digdipblog.files.wordpress.com/2017/08/the-digitalization-of-diplomacy-working-chapter-number-1.pdf.

Melissen, Jan, and Emilie V. de Keulenaar. "Critical Digital Diplomacy as a Global Challenge: The South Korean Experience." *Global Policy* 8, no. 3 (2017): 294–301.

Mowlana, Hamid. *Global Information and World Communication.* London: Sage, 1997.

ONU. *Journée des médias sociaux à l'ONU : la « diplomatie numérique » à l'honneur.* New York: Centre d'actualités de l'ONU, 2015.

Pamment, James. *Report – New Diplomacy*, WP 1531, Wednesday, March 15–Friday, March 17, 2017. Steyning : Foreign Commonwealth Office. Wilton Park, 2017.

Potter, Evan H., ed. *Cyber-Diplomacy: Managing Foreign Policy in the Twenty First Century*. Montreal-Kingston: McGill-Queen's University Press, 2002.

Reinalda, Bob, and Bertjan Verbeek, eds. *Decision Making Within International Organisations*. London: Routledge, 2007.

Rogers, Everett M. *Diffusion of Innovations*. 5th ed. New York: Free Press, 2003.

Seib, Philip. *Real-Time Diplomacy – Politics and Power in the Social Media Era*. New York: Palgrave Macmillan, 2012.

Smith, Courtney B. "Three Perspectives on Global Consensus Building: A Framework for Analysis." *International Journal of Organizational Theory & Behavior* 5, no. 1&2 (2002): 115–44.

Smith, Courtney B. *Politics and Process at the United Nations*. Boulder, CO: Lynne Rienner, 2006.

Stoddart, Linda. "Organisational Culture and Knowledge Sharing at the United Nations: Using an Intranet to Create a Sense of Community." *Knowledge & Process Management* 14, no. 3 (2007) : 182–9.

UNESCO. *World Communication and Information Report 1999–2000*.Geneva: UNESCO Publishing, 1999.

United Nations. The Office of Human Resources Department of Management. *The Essential Guidebook for United Nations Secretariat Staff*. New York: United Nations, 2014.

United Nations. *UN Social Media Day: Schedule and More*, United Nations Blog. New York: United Nations, January 26, 2015.

United Nations Department of Public Information. *Social Media Guidelines*. New York : DPI, 2011. June 2011, DPI/2573.

UN General Assembly. *Activities of the Department of Public Information: Strategic Communications Services. Report of the Secretary-General*. New York: United Nations, 2009a.

UN General Assembly. *Report of the Committee on Information*. New York: United Nations, 2009b.

UN General Assembly. *Activities of the Department of Public Information: Strategic Communications Services. Report of the Secretary-General*. New York: United Nations, 2010a.

UN General Assembly. *Activities of the Department of Public Information: Outreach. Report of the Secretary-General*. New York: United Nations, 2010b.

UN General Assembly. *Report of the Committee on Information*. New York: United Nations, 2017.

UN General Assembly. *Activities of the Department of Public Information: Strategic Communications Services. Report of the Secretary-General*. New York: United Nations, 2018a.

UN General Assembly. *Activities of the Department of Public Information: Strategic Communications Services. Report of the Secretary-General*. New York: United Nations, 2019a.

UN General Assembly. *Report of the Committee on Information*. New York: United Nations, 2019b.

UN News. *From His Room with a View, UN Chief Takes to Instagram with an Eye on Hope and a Brighter Future*. New York: United Nations, May 9, 2019.

United Nations Secretariat. *Guidelines for the Personnal Use of Social Media*. New York: United Nations, 2019.

United Nations Secretary-General. *Secretary-General's Video Message for Launch of "The Foundation for a Digital United Nations."* New York: United Nations May 31, 2012.

United Nations Secretary-General. *UN Secretary-General's- Strategy on New Technologies.* New York: United Nations, September 2018.

United Nations Secretary-General. *Guidelines for the Personal Use of Social Media.* New York: United Nations, February 2019.

Weiss, Thomas. *What's Wrong with the United Nations and How to Fix It.* 2nd ed. Cambridge: Polity Press, 2012.

Wikina, Ebenezar. "#SocialUN: My Stroll With Nancy Groves, United Nations Social Media Team Leader." *The Huffingtong Post – The Blog,* December 10, 2015.

Yin, Robert K. *Case Study Research – Design and Methods.* 3rd ed. Thousand Oaks, CA: Sage, 2014.

6

CLOCK, CLOUD, AND CONTESTATION

The digital journey of the Commonwealth Secretariat

Nabeel Goheer

Introduction

Our world is in the midst of major shifts at the systemic level as we continue to move from an industrial to an information age.[1] This transition is an interesting time. Our lives are being affected and increasingly lived in cyber time and space. The information age is instant, interactive, and omnipresent. Its dominant dynamic is emergent. Its effects are exponential. Both time and space have to be understood differently in this age. The digital age is characteristically different from the previous one, which means that it requires new ways of organisation and doing business.

The hallmark of the industrial age was "industry" itself. Industries worked mechanically like a CLOCK. They were Complicated, Linear, Ordered, Closed, and Kinetic. They were designed to process inputs into outputs in confined spaces in a planned manner. Industry became the symbol of development, modernity, and wealth in that age. Everything else around it took shape accordingly. As such, organisations were designed like machines. Management processes were put in place to maximise the efficiency of outputs. Governments worked with the help of bureaucratic machineries wherein each ministry, department, and agency performed like a CLOCK within their remit.

Intergovernmental organisations (IGOs) were established during the height of the industrial age. They are called intergovernmental because governments formed, controlled, governed, and made use of them. As a result, they emulated the mechanical structures of governments. By design, they became the slowest moving CLOCKS. Whereas national bureaucracies, which were designed for and within one country, at least had a uniform gear train, IGOs were formed by cobbling together an assortment of cogwheels and chains from across different government systems. These supranational organisations therefore became super bureaucracies that were even more complicated than those at the national level. As a result of this design, the IGO CLOCK ticks slowly and changes infrequently as it depends upon many mechanics.

The information age is radically different from its predecessor. It exists virtually rather than physically. It hives in cyber space. It is organised around information and works like a CLOUD. It is not linear, complicated, or inert like an industrial process. Its relational and interactive nature makes it "Complex." It facilitates the flow of information, communication, products, and services across "Large" distances instantly. It has been relatively "Open," with hardly any boundaries or borders. Its evolving and emergent nature makes it "Unpredictable."[2] It is "Dynamic" because of its enormous potential to facilitate the flow of social intelligence and collaborative energy at an unprecedented speed and scale.

The CLOUD way of life is different from the CLOCK way. It is shared and not siloed. It is open for interpretation rather than categorised or confined. It constantly evolves. It has a shapeshifting nature. It moves with unprecedented speed. These CLOUD characteristics necessitate a different organisational design. They require faster, flexible, and fleetfooted responses. Organisations that are failing to anticipate this changed context and to adapt to this fundamental shift have either died already or are withering away. IGOs are not an exception to this new reality (Goheer 2018d).

Most of today's IGOs were designed after the Second World War when the world was relatively predictable and worked like a CLOCK. It was politically bipolar. The rules of the game were negotiated and set during this period. International conventions, diplomatic protocols, and standard operating procedures for bureaucratic action and interaction kept the CLOCK ticking. The dawn of the digital century, however, has brought with it a new deal. It has empowered diverse actors and created new channels of communication for influencing policies and decisions. Governments and their IGOs can feel the pressure. The handlers of the CLOCK world are perplexed. They are accustomed to operating like a machine, which works either by precedent or the "Rules of Business." The CLOUD world does not run by compliance. Bureaucracies, both governmental and intergovernmental, are baffled when they have to deal with constant change, disruption, and wicked problems. But this is the name of the game in the digital century (Goheer 2011).

The CLOUD world has created a huge new space for action and interaction (called the digital universe in this volume). Its effects on international organisations and diplomatic discipline have been the focus of a number of recent studies (Bjola and Holmes 2015; Abbot et al. 2015; Manor 2019; UN 2019). This world has reshaped the context in which IGOs operate. Failure to recognise, understand, act, and interact with this context can result in their descent into irrelevance and eventual extinction. Adapting to it, however, opens up new opportunities for connecting, cooperating, and co-creating value. It offers many opportunities to enhance their limited authority, orchestration, pooling power, and social legitimacy (Hooghe and Marks 2015; Bauer, Knill, and Eckhard 2017; Zürn, Binder, and Ecker-Ehrhardt 2012).

The CLOUD world is still unfolding and has not (yet) fully replaced the CLOCK world. So, in this transitional time, the two worlds coexist. IGOs consequently operate in a hybridity, which is shaped by a blend of these two intertwined worlds. They exist on a continuum. At the CLOCK extreme is the closed and hierarchical bureaucracy. At the CLOUD extreme is the open and interactive network of vibrant relationships.

This chapter tells a tale of two stories of one IGO – the Commonwealth Secretariat – that has experimented with shades of hybridity and that continues to adapt to the CLOUD world through digital transformation. The Commonwealth came into being in 1949 with eight member states. Its Secretariat was established in London in 1965 to run the intergovernmental business of the political association. Since its original founding, the organisation has grown significantly. Presently, it has 54 member (states) from across the globe and represents 2.4 billion people – more than 60% are young.

In order to research and write this tale, the author employed a combination of ethnographic observation and a case study. The case study was constituted of an empirical inquiry in which the author investigated a phenomenon (here, the transformation experience of the Commonwealth Secretariat) within its real-life context (Feagin, Orum, and Sjoberg 1991). The ethnographic component of the project is based on the author's experience of being "positioned" at the Secretariat from December 2010 until the present.[3] Ethnography is an established mode of inquiry that is supported by different theoretical perspectives in sociology, anthropology, and critical management (Ferguson 1994; Escobar 1994; Arce and Long 2000; Gould and Marcussen 2004).

More specifically, this chapter is situated within a broader field of ethnographic work that utilizes "organisational ethnography" in order to develop understandings of organisations and their processes of organising (Ciuk, Koning, and Kostera 2018). Organisational ethnography relies on in-depth participant observation in order to gain valuable insights on the culture and workings of an organisation from the inside. This mixed methods research design has enabled the production of a thick description, which is an interpretive analysis that is context-rich, robust, and rooted in the construction of social reality (Geertz 1973; Thompson 2001).

Adopting ICT – the story of CLOCK work

The first story began in 1999, when leaders met in Durban for the Commonwealth Heads of Government Meeting (CHOGM). Given that ICTs and globalisation were already changing the world, they discussed the potential impacts of these dynamics on the Commonwealth. Leaders decided to establish a High Level Group (HLG) to review the role of the Commonwealth, and to advise on how it could best respond to the challenges of the new century (The Commonwealth

1999). This decision (called "mandate" in IGO-speak) triggered the typical CLOCK response by the organisation.

Following the leaders' decision, an intergovernmental expert group on Information Technology was constituted by the Commonwealth in September 2000. The group was asked to examine the constraints that were preventing the wider adoption of ICT in developing countries. Their terms of reference included proposing a Commonwealth mechanism that could promote the wider use of ICTs. The group presented a report in June 2001 highlighting the issues that needed to be addressed and suggested a Plan of Action for the Commonwealth (Mansell and Couldry 2001). They also drew up a Commonwealth Action Plan on Digital Divide (CAPDD).

The report and CAPDD were considered by the CHOGM in Abuja in 2003, at which point leaders decided to constitute a coordination committee under the chairmanship of the Secretary-General to take the Plan of Action forward. The coordination committee submitted a report to the Malta CHOGM in 2005, which issued a declaration endorsing an Action Plan for the Commonwealth and the establishment of a Special Fund (Commonwealth Secretariat 2005). The Action Plan and Fund were finally in place after seven years of CLOCK work.

In 2006, CPADD was rebranded and formally launched as the *Commonwealth Connects* programme. A strategy was drafted and a steering committee was established. Several sub-committees of the steering committee were constituted. A Deputy Secretary-General was designated as the focal person for this purpose. Administrative arrangements for the working of the Special Fund were put in place by designating a department at the Secretariat. The bureaucratic machine was officially in motion. It was establishing mechanical structures, adhering to the established path of corporate guidelines, conducting meetings, and churning out reports. The only problem was that it was not producing results. As of 2008, two years after its creation, the programme had only been able to finance 11 small projects with a total amount of £2,30,000. The CLOCK was ticking, but very slowly.

The programme was supposed to be a vehicle for making the organisation fit for the 21st century. A lot had happened in nine years in terms of the bureaucratic process but nothing much in terms of results. At the Port of Spain CHOGM in 2009, Commonwealth leaders again emphasised the role of ICT in social and economic transformation (CHOGM 2009a, paragraphs 104–5). It was evident, however, that the organisation was moving slowly on this front. In their statement, the Commonwealth leaders asked the Secretary-General to constitute (yet another) Eminent Persons Group (EPG) to strengthen the Commonwealth as a Network, by bringing its institutions closer together, establishing strategic partnerships and consolidating its governance "to remain relevant to its times and people in future" (CHOGM 2009b, paragraphs 13–16). This parallel track was established to speed up the CLOCK and to make it more efficient.

The requested EPG was established in 2010, headed by a former prime minister. The group presented recommendations to the Perth CHOGM in 2011.

The EPG report had no less than 106 recommendations to modernise the organisation, however there was no mention of ICT. During the CHOGM, the Commonwealth Secretariat made an attempt to influence the leaders by presenting an idea for the establishment of a grand portal to connect Commonwealth communities of practice. But this proposal did not gain traction. Leaders did not want to sanction an idea that had not worked for a decade. After exhaustive discussions by the senior officials, foreign ministers, and prime ministers, consensus was eventually reached on "reform of the Commonwealth to ensure that it is a more effective institution, responsive to members' needs, and capable of tackling the significant global challenges of the 21st century" (CHOGM 2011b, paragraph 1).

The EPG had started as a parallel track with its own separate trajectory of ideas. The steering committee of the *Commonwealth Connects* continued on with its usual business of holding regular meetings. In its 20th meeting in 2010, the committee decided to commission an impact assessment of the programme. The study found that the few projects that had been financed by the programme (such as a radio programme on micro enterprise development and a training of trainers for organic farming) were only tangentially related to the broader ICT agenda (Narotra and Tabone 2011).

In 2011, the Department for International Development (DFID) of the UK carried out a multilateral aid review of its funding to IGOs. The Commonwealth Secretariat was a part of that review and ranked the lowest as a "C" grade IGO. The report noted weak strategic oversight, unsatisfactory resource management, and lack of cost and value consciousness as the main elements of its bad performance. The reviewers observed that they were "uncertain" about the likelihood of positive change in the organisation (DFID 2011).

The Commonwealth Secretariat responded to the DFID management review and vowed to modernise its systems and processes (Commonwealth Secretariat 2011). Meanwhile, the *Commonwealth Connects* programme continued its usual CLOCK operations. It carried on ticking, but it was not working. On January 27, 2014, the steering committee of the programme decided to bring it to an end because of its dismal results. From its start in 2000 until its termination, the programme had only raised and spent approximately £1 million without demonstrating much success in achieving its objectives. In the wake of its dissolution, the steering committee requested an ex post evaluation of the programme. The Secretariat, accordingly, commissioned an independent evaluation.

The terms of reference for evaluation indicate that the Secretariat was mandated to help its developing member countries use ICT to support equitable growth, good governance, and the empowerment of individuals. The programme was aimed at reducing the digital divide within and amongst Commonwealth countries by providing strategic leadership in building linkages between developed and developing countries of the Commonwealth, fostering partnerships, helping develop national ICT strategies, building capacity, and supporting pan-Commonwealth ICT initiatives (Commonwealth Secretariat 2014).

The evaluation found that the programme was badly and bureaucratically managed. It had failed to recognise the paradigm shift that the rise of ICT had caused, had not set a strategic direction, could not keep up with developments in this fast-moving field, and was unable to raise funds.[4] Moreover, it was a poor decision to create a "special operating vehicle" under the Office of the Secretary-General through the creation of a parallel structure to the institutional frameworks. This decision decoupled the programme from the overall policy, strategic, and delivery frameworks. The study concluded that the focus on ICT by Commonwealth leaders made eminent sense, but that serious flaws in its governance, financing, management, and operating procedures resulted in the closure of the programme in 2014 (Commonwealth Secretariat 2015b). One significant finding of the report was that the Secretariat bureaucracy was unable to deal effectively with the ICT-related issues.

Seven years of CLOCK work (from 1999 to 2005) produced a mandate, an action plan, and a dedicated fund to finance projects. As it continued for another nine years (from 2006 to 2014), CLOCK work added new bureaucratic structures, a lot of processes, plenty of meetings, and a few projects but no benefits or results. The programme evaluation made it evident that CLOCK machinery was not fit for purpose – at this point, it was barely ticking and hard to tune. The ICT age in 2015 was already in full swing. The breakneck digital CLOUD world required entirely new ways of thinking, organising, and working.

What next?

The debacle of *Commonwealth Connects* and its evaluation was the catalyst for a new internal debate. Should the Commonwealth as an IGO be engaged in delivering ICT programmes? Is ICT a typical development programme or an entirely new paradigm? Is the Commonwealth fit for (digital) purpose? A Commonwealth conference in Maputo in July 2015 placed the idea of a "Smart Commonwealth" on the agenda. Participants discussed the seismic shifts that were being created by the ICT age and the fundamental changes that were coming to the world of work, life, and leisure. They agreed that the Commonwealth as an association as well as its member states would have to adapt quickly.

The Commonwealth's younger population was more ICT savvy than the older generations. To remain relevant to both populations, the participants realized that it was imperative to open up and think outside the CLOCK structure. The association had to think afresh, utilise digital opportunities to connect, collaborate, and cocreate a common future. This required a radical shift in thinking, a new organisational design, and innovative ways of doing business. The organisation was creaking under the weight of its own bureaucratic burden. The issues it faced were protean, fast moving, and shapeshifting, which required swift and coordinated actions. It had to change to keep up with its times (Goheer 2015a).

The Maputo conference was a technical meeting. Its delegates wanted the association to revive itself, though they did not have much political influence. Moreover, the Secretariat had toyed with ICT transformation for more than a decade without much success. Thus, member states were not confident that the Secretariat, or any other organisation in the Commonwealth, was ready to advance this complex agenda in an effective manner.[5] The issues of relevance, efficiency, effectiveness, and visibility repeatedly emerged in intergovernmental discussions, such as in the Malta "CHOGM Communique" (2015), the reports of the Commonwealth High Level Group on Arrangements and the Summary and Decisions of the Board of Governors meetings of the Commonwealth Secretariat (2014–2016). The youth, comprising 60% of population, were increasingly alienated from the association. Many did not even care whether it existed or not (House of Commons Foreign Affairs Committee 2013).

A presentation by the Commonwealth Secretariat at the "Global Strategy Innovation Summit" in London highlighted the issues that were making the organisation irrelevant and invisible. Its slow-moving diplomatic design,[6] top-heavy management structure, silo-based working, and inability to adapt to the demands of an interconnected and interactive world were at the heart of its failures. Its distance from the digital world was pushing it into insignificance. The organisation was urged to redesign, rethink and reinvent itself as a network, be inclusive, become agile, embrace interoperability, and create space for collaborative action (Goheer 2015b). It was not possible, however, for a CLOCK as a machine to achieve the necessary agility or to foster effective collaboration. A flexible business model was needed to provide solutions to contemporary problems.

Transformation (adapting to the CLOUD world) was a tall order. The Secretariat's bureaucracy was risk averse. It was used to receiving financial contributions from members, which worked like winding the crown of the CLOCK. But the situation became worrying with DFID's "C" rating. Members had started slashing Secretariat funding from 2010/11 onwards. By 2015/16, Commonwealth Fund for Technical Cooperation (CFTC) contributions had gone down by 42%.[7] The senior management group of the Secretariat discussed this alarming situation in its annual retreat. The then Deputy Secretary-General of Corporate Affairs alluded to the dire situation and said that the "Secretariat stood on a burning platform" (Commonwealth Secretariat 2015a). The organisation was slipping into a state of limbo.

Getting ready

The second story starts when a new Secretary-General began her tenure. She joined on April 1, 2016, and one of her first orders of business was the commissioning of an independent review of the Secretariat. The reviewers identified rigid bureaucratic culture, top-heavy structure, excessive process orientation, and lack of innovation as the main challenges to effective functioning and delivery

(KYA Global 2016). A selected part of the review report was made public. There was a discordant response to this report among members states: some members supported it, others did not like the way this review was commissioned, and another group wanted the report done differently. As the history of IGO reform shows, tinkering with the CLOCK has never been an easy task.

The Secretary-General decided to proceed with the structural overhaul of the bureaucracy. Seven programme divisions were consolidated into three delivery clusters called directorates. They were empowered to make decisions in their respective areas of operation. A number of administrative and procedural structures were dismantled. This delayering resulted in freezing the management rung of the Deputy Secretaries-General.[8] A post called the Assistant Secretary-General (ASG) was created to deputise the Secretary-General, advance the reform process, leverage partnerships and innovation, and put the organisation on a learning and digitalisation path.

A lot of thinking and reflection helped set the reform plan. The adaptation journey benefitted a great deal from the earlier research, analyses, and deliberations. This included CHOGM discussions and decisions (CHOGM 1999, 2002, 2005, 2009a, 2011b, 2013), evaluation reports (Commonwealth Secretariat 2014, 2015a, 2015b), EPG recommendations (The Commonwealth 2011), the KYA global review (2016), and UK parliament debates on the future of the Commonwealth. The treatises on this subject written by Prof Tim Shaw and Lord David Howell were also immensely useful resources (Shaw 2007; Howell 2011).

It was evident that the Secretariat was inward looking and stuck in CLOCK work. The CLOUD world was an interconnected system. The Secretariat had to connect and catch up with this world, as systems cannot be separated from their context (Senge et al. 1999). It had to become tactile, bionic, and interoperable to deal with contemporary challenges. The delivery of results was bound to getting rid of bureaucracy, shedding the superman mentality, and replacing ineffective structures with smart teams (McChrystal et al. 2015). It had to be ready to respond to nonlinear and emergent challenges (Taleb 2007). Learning to go beyond its own silos and delivering in response to contextual challenges were the keys to become fit for purpose (Scharmer and Kaufer 2013).[9]

A new Strategic Plan was written that was in line with the external context.[10] A Delivery Plan was developed with a set of smart management practices. In this way, systems for partnerships, innovation, and continuous learning were established. Member states wanted the reform to run parallel with the normal delivery of Secretariat operations. It was a difficult task that was equivalent to refuelling a plane mid-air. Despite this difficulty, six months down the line things were looking up.

The foreign ministers appreciated the reforming and rising Commonwealth in their annual meeting in September 2017 in New York. They were pleased with the Secretariat's leaner and more flexible structure, development of new Strategic and Delivery Plans, and its social media strategy. The organisation was on its way to becoming more agile, transparent, collaborative, and social media savvy. In just one year, the Commonwealth's profile had experienced substantial growth, with the number of Twitter followers growing by an average of 55% each month and the number of Facebook followers improving by an average of 40% each month year-on-year (The Commonwealth 2017). Pleased with these indicators of success, the ministers asked the Secretary-General to deepen and broaden the reform process. The Secretariat did set the sails for its digital journey.

Adapting to digital – the story of CLOUD work

The challenges, demands, and expectations of the wider Commonwealth stakeholders were being increasingly shaped by the CLOUD world. They wanted increased access and transparency, and expected nimble responses. This necessitated novel and faster ways of creating value (Denning 2018). The Secretariat had to reinvent its way of doing business in order to become a diamond in the 21st century rather than be remembered as a dinosaur (Goheer 2019a). Thinking and doing digital was the best way to turn the CLOUD challenges into opportunities.

The new journey started with structural changes. The new Department of Innovation and Partnerships, which was staffed with a small team, was intended to create an enabling environment and to facilitate this work across the organisation. The Information Technology department that used to provide corporate and programme services was upgraded as a strategic unit. It was renamed as Digital and tasked with the additional responsibility of assisting the organisation in its digital transformation journey. The innovation, partnerships, and digital teams were placed under the supervision of the ASG.

Work started on evaluating the organisation through a digital lens and redesigning it on digital footing. A strategy called "4D*P" was developed to set the direction of travel for digitalisation, which included five facets. 4D represented the four domains of digital transformation and action – data, display, delivery, and discovery. P was the partnerships vector that was to cut across all four domains (Goheer 2017). The digitalisation process was initiated as the ultimate frugal exercise in promoting innovation across the Secretariat. That is, a digital turnaround was to be accomplished by maximising the use of existing resources; building on ongoing work where possible; and using the imagination, ideas, and ingenuity of the Commonwealth network.

It was important to prepare internally for the incoming changes before beginning to deliver services externally. Tech-refresh was done in order to modernise internal IT networks. Two-step authentication was put in place to strengthen security. Small states offices in New York and Geneva were digitally connected and integrated with the Secretariat. Marlborough House meeting rooms were upgraded to conduct virtual meetings.[11] Cloud-based computing replaced local servers. Twenty-three terabytes of personal and organisational data can now be accessed by the Secretariat staff anywhere in the world. New IT tools and applications have enabled remote working, including joint document development, system access, virtual meetings, and the delivery of various products and services to member states.

Data was chosen to be the first priority for digitalisation. It had both internal (organisational) and external (country and Commonwealth) dimensions. The Commonwealth had produced immense amounts of data in the past six decades. Most of it from the last two decades was already in the digital form. It was, however, locked in silos across the organisation. The first step was to map, collate, organise, and classify it. The library was best suited for this purpose. It was professionally organised but remained hidden in the basement of the building, and was hardly used or visited. The library and archives (L&A) already contained a treasure trove of information – hundreds of thousands of ministerial meeting records, books, journals, archives, and reference materials.

The L&A were reorganised and rebranded as the "Knowledge Centre." More than 60,000 records were made available on an online searchable catalogue, including confidential materials that were declassified. An I-library was established that provided access to 826 e-books, 9,244 book chapters, and 246 working papers. The OECD provided a technology platform for this purpose. An image bank containing 6,750 historical images was made public, and an electronic record management system was acquired to initiate the digital archiving of electronic materials. Furthermore, the electronic document sharing platform was reorganised. By November 2019, it had 33,000 shared files containing documents from the CHOGMs, High Level Ministerial Meetings, and Board Meetings (Commonwealth Secretariat 2019).

The second task of internal data organisation was "data systems integration." The Secretariat was a classic silo-based IGO – it had small and disparate data systems that belonged to different departments. The annual planning and budgeting software belonged to the Strategic Planning section. A project planning system called ARTEMIS sat with the Evaluation section. Annual and historical expenditure data was recorded in a system called CODA. It was under the ownership of the Finance section. Employee data records were stored in a separate system in Human Resources called "HR self-service." A country project information system for member states called "Extranet" was run and managed by the office of a former Deputy Secretary-General. The external communication records were with the Secretary-General's Office.

The Programme Management Information System (PMIS) brought it all together. The antiquated software for planning and budgeting and extranet were abandoned. ARTEMIS, which was a tailor-made system, became the base for PMIS. A new software helped CODA expenditure tally with the programme budget. New modules for planning, budgeting, monitoring, and reporting were developed. PMIS connected the small and disparate systems and reduced data fragmentation. The entry of programming, operational, and expenditure data on one system meant that there was automatic triangulation, which enhanced data integrity. It helped individuals, teams, and directorates monitor their own performance. The modular system made the Secretariat joined-up and interoperable.

PMIS enhanced the Secretariat's transparency, visibility, and outreach. All project expenditures of CFTC above the level of £500 are now available online. Information on ongoing projects is posted on the International Aid Transparency Initiative (IATI) web portal.

The third step was general data management. The Secretariat did not have a data governance framework. The political data was mostly unstructured in the form of sensitive narratives, records, and reports. The corporate data was better organised as it was based upon actual numbers from audited financial statements, management accounts, and reports of internal and external auditors. PMIS enabled collaborative planning, budgeting, delivery, monitoring, and management for existing and future programmes. It did not, however, contain the historical data that was still locked in the Secretariat silos and servers. The political teams and professionals wanted access to their own and historical data while travelling for work. For this reason, a decision was made to switch from a server to a cloud-based operating system. This move ensured the global availability of historical data as well as access to personal, team, and organisational files and folders.

The external dimension of data management was much more challenging. Firstly, the Commonwealth, like other IGOs, did not have its own country datasets. It relied on the national datasets of member states. The Secretariat used to hire consultants to collate data country by country. It required a lot of effort and coordination. Secondly, other IGOs have dedicated statistical departments, which collect and collate data as per their own priorities and specialised areas of operations.[12] The Secretariat had neither such a department nor a focused area of technical operation. It had a wide variety of mandates as it operated in diverse spheres like a mini United Nations. It did not have the field offices or resources to collect, collate and analyse data itself. Thirdly, international datasets were organised at subnational, national, regional, and international levels. The Commonwealth is spread across all geographical regions of the world, but not all members of any particular region are members of the Commonwealth. An innovative approach was therefore needed to create Commonwealth datasets.

The first Commonwealth Trade Review was done internally by the Secretariat and presented to the Malta CHOGM (The Commonwealth 2015). It assessed the association's collective trade potential for the first time. The study contributed to the development of an understanding of intra-Commonwealth trends and effects. It provided a solid foundation for further analysis and forecasting. The review used the UNCTAD trade and investment datasets. After the review, those datasets were saved on the Secretariat's server. The utility of statistics from other IGOs gave rise to the idea of establishing a data portal. In order to facilitate this project, partnerships were established and secondary data from other IGOs was secured in 2017 and 2018. An algorithm was written to extract the data of 54 countries from these datasets, which were then organised and standardised as per the Commonwealth requirements. Data from the library and PMIS was also added to this data portal. Data analysis and visualisation tools were acquired. With all of the tools in place, once in-house expertise was developed, a Commonwealth data analytics service was finally established in 2019.

Another important development on the data front was the signing of a collaboration agreement with Bloomberg. The Commonwealth struck a deal with Bloomberg philanthropies in April 2018, in which the latter agreed to provide free Bloomberg terminal and data services to the Commonwealth Secretariat for three years. They also helped establish a training room at Marlborough House[13] with state-of-the-art communication and e-meeting facilities. This partnership provided instant access to financial and private sector data, enhanced the Secretariat's data analytical capacity, and enriched its understanding of the environmental, social, and governance (ESG) aspects of private sector operations. A Commonwealth climate scope was added to the suite of Commonwealth data services. It provided snapshots of clean energy policy and finance as well as future scenarios for Commonwealth countries.

Digitalising delivery was the second strand of the digitalisation strategy. The Secretariat's primary business is to provide services to its member states. It worked like a bureaucratic machine where governments requested its services, each request was processed internally, and the service was eventually provided after being approved by the relevant authority. Digital service delivery was to cut bureaucracy and provide these services online. This strategy was intended to leverage the internet, create an online interface, increase access, develop applications, and drive down the cost of delivery. The ICT infrastructure was in place and the requisite internal systems and structures were established.

The first step of digital delivery was to reimagine the existing services. The Secretariat worked as a consultant from whom members could request short-term and long-term experts in diverse areas such as development, democracy, and the strengthening of public institutions. From 1971 to 2016, the Secretariat had provided £250 million worth of technical services. Requests were received from member states by various departments, which were then processed internally (through planning, budgeting, approvals, selection, and contracting) before experts were dispatched. A Technical Assistance Unit within the Secretariat coordinated this service with programme departments along with the Finance and Human Resource departments.

As part of the digital scheme of delivery, all Commonwealth experts were contacted afresh with requests to update their contact information, expertise, and willingness to share details as per the General Data Protection Regulation (GDPR) requirements. Consequently, a cleaned-up and updated database of approximately 4,000 consultants is now available directly to Commonwealth member states. This updated information does not sit in departmental silos anymore, and TAU has been disestablished. Member states do not have to write letters and emails, or call different departments, to request these services. Instead, they can dip into the database directly, select consultants of their choice, and work with them.

A majority of Commonwealth countries carry high public debt burdens, and the Secretariat has been providing assistance in this area since 1983. It has a debt management system; builds institutional capacity to raise, record, and report debt; and helps members develop policies to reform debt portfolios. The Commonwealth Secretariat Debt Recording and Management System (CS-DRMS) was originally a local server-based system. Millions of pounds were being spent on capacity building, training, and the provision of advisory services. This was the case because the relevant experts from the Secretariat had to travel periodically to countries to set up the system, update it as and when required, and troubleshoot when it had functional issues.

A new and improved cloud-based version of the platform called *Meridian* was developed and launched in June 2019. It is a holistic system with a variety of new features such as improved data integrity and cost-risk analysis. It has a smooth interface with the International Monetary Fund (IMF), The World Bank, and the Society for Worldwide Interbank Financial Telecommunication (SWIFT). In addition, it has dashboards for tracking debt against legislation and sustainability. The system is currently being used to manage the debts of 63 countries[14] with a total amount of $2.6 trillion USD. The cloud-based *Meridian* has significantly reduced the need for overseas travel. An issues log helps Secretariat staff provide instant technical, advisory, and troubleshooting support remotely from their offices.

The Rule of Law programme used to build local capacity and strengthen justice institutions. These in-country services have increasingly been replaced with online services and support. An online Office for Civil and Criminal Justice Reform (OCCJR) has now been established. It is a repository of information on good legislation practice from across the Commonwealth. OCCJR contains model laws, standards, templates, legal insights, and access to legal networks across the Commonwealth. The programme has worked with a technology company to develop a block-chain-based application. It also includes a secure messaging system to help law enforcement and prosecutors in different Commonwealth countries cooperate more effectively on criminal investigations. The mobile-based application has been made available to the Commonwealth Network of Contact Persons (CNCP).[15]

Over 230 million women and girls across the Commonwealth do not have access to an official identity. Because mobile phones can help bridge the gap, the Commonwealth has partnered with the Global System for Mobile Communication Association (GSMA) to address this issue ("Commonwealth Digital Identity Initiative" 2020). Through the Commonwealth Digital Identity Initiative, the GSMA Digital Identity programme is partnering with the World Bank Identification for Development (ID4D) programme and Caribou Digital to help make progress in providing a digitally enabled identity for every woman and girl in the Commonwealth by 2030. This project includes researching the unique barriers that women and girls face when accessing or using identity systems, delivering projects that test new approaches to overcoming these barriers, and providing advocacy support to countries to bridge the gap on inclusive digital identity systems.

Further, providing training and assisting with capacity building have been pivotal Commonwealth services to developing member states. An evaluation of Commonwealth training programmes in 2010 recommended the use of new technologies and online meetings and exchanges for this purpose (The Commonwealth 2010). To that end, an online training platform was launched by the Commonwealth Secretariat in late 2019. The Commonwealth Blue Charter working groups are sharing information and coordinating activities on their own microsite. A disaster-risk finance portal will be launched at the Kigali CHOGM in June 2020 to provide online information and services. Video conferencing is fast replacing face-to-face meetings.[16]

Display was the third strand of the strategy. It was important to discard the archaic image of the association and replace it with a new look. The Commonwealth of Nations was established in 1949, though had started as the British Commonwealth in 1886. Some of its vocabulary, structures, ways of doing business, and communication practices still contained vestiges of its colonial roots. It was an old CLOCK whose colonial image continued to haunt contemporary discussions and its future (Murphy 2018). This was because no serious and concerted effort had yet been made to overhaul its branding and business. Advances in digital technology had created opportunities to revitalize its creased face. The vast expanse of cyber space presented new possibilities for interaction and displaying a new image and its collective power.

The organisational effort started with the getting rid of old, redundant, and static displays. The exterior and interior of the headquarters were redesigned with the new reality in mind. The glory of the past was digitised and enhanced with pictures of young people engaging in exciting activities. TV screens that showed inspiring programmes and projects were installed. Old technologies such as overhead scanners, projectors, and static screens with wheels were chucked out and replaced with large flat-screen displays in the meeting rooms. A dynamic display that combined Commonwealth history with real time information about financial markets was added to the assemblage by placing a Bloomberg media wall at the reception area of Marlborough House.

The printing press was another relic of the previous century. Though it had provided valuable services in the past, using paper was simply not the best practice in the digital century. The Commonwealth, through the Langkawi Declaration in 1989, had placed environmental degradation on the global agenda. To follow through on this agenda, it could not continue to use paper as the primary means of communication. The printing services were gradually phased out and replaced with electronic information and display systems. The printing shop was closed down in 2019. It signalled the change of direction to smarter and sustainable ways of doing work. "Online" was the channel of choice in the CLOUD world.

Facebook, Twitter, Flickr, and Instagram accounts were created to establish new connections with the stakeholders – especially young people and women.

They facilitated new spaces for dynamic dialogue as the interactive design of social media enabled a continuous flow of content from the Secretariat as well as feedback from the users. This feedback was instrumental in understanding the public sentiment, gauging their needs, and adjusting Commonwealth services and delivery accordingly. Having direct contact with people strengthened the Commonwealth network relationship beyond its intergovernmental remit, which resulted in broadening public engagement and outreach. One of the best outcomes of the utilisation of social media was that the Commonwealth was able to enhance the social legitimacy of the organisation.

The Commonwealth Innovation Hub was launched at the London CHOGM (Ministry of Public Telecommunications 2018). It is an online portal which brings together the ideas and innovations of 54 countries, 90 Commonwealth organisations,[17] and 2.4 billion people. The display section is devoted to showcasing the collective power of the system. It has an innovation newsletter and a digital digest which both contain stories of replicable success. The Commonwealth Innovation Index ranks countries according to the World Intellectual Property Rights Organisation (WIPO) methodology in order to create healthy competition across member states. The (Sustainable Development Goals) SDG's tracker depicts the association's progress towards achieving these global goals.

The innovation platform is fast becoming a digital arena of collaboration and cocreation. Thousands of innovators have already shared their ideas, inventions, projects, and programmes with others. The SDG awards, innovation competitions, and ecosystem workshops are bringing people, professionals, and places together to think and act collaboratively. The continuous data feed on technology, climate change, and sustainability has made the platform a source of credible information on these contemporary topics for students, researchers, and journalists. Furthermore, this portal is being seen as an opportunity for small, developing, landlocked, and island states to use technology and innovation to make significant strides in their journey towards sustainable development.

Discovery was the fourth stage of digitalisation. This dimension was conceived as an "innovation lab" of the Secretariat. This development was aimed at exploring new horizons and testing novel ideas as well as looking at ways of incubating, accelerating, and disseminating information about innovations within the Commonwealth. A digital space has been created on the Commonwealth Innovation Hub that will house these ideas and information.

The Commonwealth Blue Charter was agreed upon at the London CHOGM in April 2018.[18] In December 2018, the Commonwealth and Nekton signed a partnerships agreement to boost actions under this Charter (Nekton 2020). The Nekton Indian Ocean Mission has already started and will run from 2019 to 2022 to collect deep sea data in two Commonwealth member states – the Seychelles and Maldives. The expedition ship, a floating research station, is equipped with cutting-edge subsea technologies, including a submersible that is capable of descending hundreds of metres into the ocean. Some of the world's top scientists are on board to test the health of the ocean. They will be collecting data from those depths of the sea that have never been explored before (Nekton Indian Ocean Mission 2020). This data will be publicly available through the Octopus database and will be used for research and analysis, as well as to track the health and wealth of the world's oceans.

High resolution satellite imagery is proving extremely useful for understanding the effects of climate change (Conniff 2017). Remote sensing data combined with ground information provides a composite picture that can be used for better mitigation of and adaptation to changes in the climate. The Commonwealth Secretariat has joined forces with a consortium of organisations[19] who specialise in the use of satellite imagery. The Common Sensing project aims to improve resilience to the effects of climate change in three Commonwealth countries in the Pacific – Fiji, the Solomon Islands, and Vanuatu. The project will contribute to sustainable development and disaster risk reduction for these countries, which are particularly vulnerable to climate change (UNITAR 2020). The project will leverage satellite data to provide access to vital information regarding disaster and climate risks. The information will be readily available to member states through both a web portal and a mobile application, and will be used for projects related to better disaster planning, food security, and other environmentally oriented initiatives.

The Secretariat is benefitting from its informal partnership with the Global Fishing Watch (GFW). GFW promotes ocean sustainability through greater transparency. Forty-seven of 54 Commonwealth member states have coastlines, 32 of which are classified as small states. Illegal fishing has been a perennial problem for these small states in particular because they do not have the capacity to monitor their territorial waters themselves. GFW is an open data platform that collects and analyses data from vessel tracking systems (such as the global positioning system, universal shipborne automatic identification system, and maritime mobile service identities). The assemblage of data from these systems results in an online map and downloadable data on GFW's platform that can be used to track 60,000 commercial fishing boats and patterns of their activity. This service will help small member states of the Commonwealth reduce illegal fishing in their territorial waters.

A number of other ongoing projects include the development of toolkits on frugal innovation, FinTech and Gov Tech. These toolkits will provide step-by-step guidance on policies as well as identify the institutional and technological arrangements that are needed to build such ecosystems. A Commonwealth Guide on best practice in cybersecurity in elections was developed and tested in 2019, and launched on March 4, 2020. Another project with the UN Technology Bank will map and enhance the scientific, technological, and digital capacities of the least developed countries. A letter of agreement has been signed with the Global Innovation Fund to establish a £25 million facility to incubate and accelerate social innovation projects in Commonwealth countries. Another project on understanding the effects of virtual, augmented, mixed, and extended reality on diplomacy has been initiated in collaboration with the Oxford Digital Diplomacy Research Group.

Partnerships was the fifth component of the Commonwealth reform project, and was to cut across all four dimensions. Although collaboration was supposed to be the Commonwealth way of doing business, unfortunately it was neither practiced nor institutionalised. The Commonwealth bureaucrats responsible for specific areas of operation worked in silos. These conditions began to change with the introduction of three significant documents that were developed through interactive planning and consultative processes: The Commonwealth Charter that was agreed upon in 2012, the global SDGs that were adopted in 2015, and the Secretariat's Strategic Plan that was approved in 2017. In particular, the Strategic Plan identified partnerships and innovation as the cross-cutting themes for delivery. All three documents emphasised that collaborative action was integral to the organisation's ability to deal with the complex, interdependent, and dynamic issues of the fast-changing world.

An annual Delivery Plan was developed for the first time, which provided a detailed joint action of teams to deliver the results contained in the Strategic Plan. A partnerships strategy approved by the Executive Committee of the Board of Governors in 2018 kickstarted this much-needed process. A partnerships team facilitated collaboration both within the Secretariat team and across the Commonwealth countries, organisation, professional bodies, and people. Since 2016, more than 40 strategic and delivery partnerships have been established with member states, Commonwealth associations, international organisations, regional mechanisms, and the private sector.

Thriving in the CLOUD world

Adapting to the CLOUD world has proved to be the right direction of travel. The Government of the United Kingdom's DFID reassessed the organisation in 2018 and revised its organisational rating from "C" to "A+." The report noted that the organisation had improved its capability, capacity, resourcing, and impact (DFID 2018). It had become more systematic, open, and transparent. The Secretariat even won an international anti-corruption award for its exemplary work in 2018 (CAACC 2018). KPMG, the internal auditor, had earlier given the Secretariat's strategic and business planning processes a good assurance rating. In 2019 and 2020, they further provided good assurance on the budget setting process and the management of the Commonwealth Fund for Technical Cooperation (KPMG 2019; KPMG 2020).

At a dinner speech to the editorial Board of the Roundtable (the Commonwealth Journal of International Affairs), the Secretariat elaborated on the strategic aspects of the CLOUD reform that had contributed to a turnaround (Goheer 2018b). It had become an attractive and thriving network of the 21st century (Goheer 2018c). The Gambia, which had left the organisation in 2013, re-joined on Feb 8, 2018. The Secretary-General of the Gulf Cooperation Council (GCC) visited the Secretariat in 2018 to learn about its journey of transformation. The GCC had been mulling over the need to reform and rebuild trust for some time (Stratfor 2017). A case study on the digital transformation of the Commonwealth was presented at Oxford University in 2019 (Goheer 2019b). What these anecdotes illustrate is that the Commonwealth's successful process of reform had become a model and inspiration for others to follow.

Professor Amartya Sen, a Nobel laureate, commended the Secretariat's preventive diplomacy work, in particular its sharp focus on pursuing dialogue and civil paths to peace in a turbulent and unpredictable world (Sen 2018). The UN Secretary-General expressed his appreciation for the network multilateralism that was practiced by the Commonwealth in a High Level Dialogue with leaders of IGOs in June 2018 (UN 2018). A training programme on the UN system's leadership framework and the Commonwealth way of reform was subsequently developed. It was delivered jointly by the Commonwealth Secretariat and UN System Staff College (UNSSC) at the Commonwealth Office in Geneva. The conceptual frameworks of CLOCK and CLOUD were first introduced in that training.

The Secretariat is now positioned at the centre of a network-based Commonwealth system. It is facilitating intergovernmental clusters of activity (including cyber cooperation, trade connectivity, and ocean action). Requisite arrangements are in place to help member states convene, consult, and cooperate virtually. The Commonwealth Secretariat ICT and Innovation Day on July 29, 2019 was livestreamed across the globe. Member states were invited to learn about the digital capabilities that the Secretariat had attained in the last two years. Subsequently, the CHOGM working groups from 54 member states met remotely in March 2020 – the first time in the history of the Commonwealth.

It goes without saying that the Secretariat's way of redesigning the IGO as a network to deal with the complexity, largeness, openness, unpredictability, and dynamism of the digital world is working. Its vibrancy has brought another country back into the association. Maldives re-joined the Commonwealth on Feb 1, 2020 as its 54th member. Zimbabwe has also applied to return. The Secretariat has six more indications of interest for membership. These countries are waiting in the wings for the membership process to be initiated. This is happening at a challenging time for IGOs. Nationalism is on the rise. Multilateralism is threatened by its equation with infringements on sovereignty. At this testing time, even the treaty based IGOs are in trouble (Chatham House 2019).

Contestations

The Commonwealth Secretariat's transformation journey was not an easy one. It began with a long, drawn-out battle against the internal bureaucracy. The bureaucratic CLOCK has long been known as an iron cage, which is hard to mend (Weber 1930).[20] Going to war with bureaucracy is no mean feat. It takes guts (Hamel and Zanini 2018). Hierarchies were, however, broken. Smart delivery teams of cross divisional professionals were put in place. Partnerships were promoted. Space for innovation was created for the newly formed clusters. Both actions and interactions were prioritised over process and compliance. The resulting change in power dynamics at the Secretariat resulted in contestation between the CLOCK-type bureaucracy and CLOUD-type professionals.

Another contestation arose amongst the member state CLOCKs. As discussed at the beginning, the IGO CLOCK is made up of a variety of sovereign CLOCKs. The sovereign mechanics (diplomats) are always jostling amongst themselves to influence the policies and structures of IGOs. Every state, especially the powerful ones, tries to make the IGO CLOCK tick in a way that benefits them the most. The indication of reform starts a race, which intensifies with time. The members of the association use different influencing strategies and power tactics. The large and powerful members would use funding as a strategy, while small and vulnerable huddle together to counter this influence. This political contestation either results in a stalemate or in negotiated settlements. The Secretariat, like any other IGO, had to tread on this path very carefully to negotiate solutions that would be amenable to all parties. Otherwise, the battle of CLOCKs would have slowed or stalled its journey towards digital destination.

Tensions between the CLOCK shareholders and CLOUD stakeholders rise during any IGO reform process. The CLOUD group is an early adopter and comes forward with the power of transnational networks and social media. Unlike sovereign states, they are not confined within national boundaries, driven by foreign policy interests, or organised as bureaucracies. The IGOs would like to move closer to these networks, but member states resent this interest because it will mean relinquishing some of their governing power, which will ultimately reduce their leverage on the IGOs. This creates another contestation. The Secretariat drew up a partnerships strategy that was approved by the member states and that opened up collaborative arrangements with the CLOUD group. As a result, the Secretariat began to build a new ecosystem of powerful partners (Goheer 2018d). This network multilateralism facilitated the flow of cooperation across diverse systems. New interoperable ways of working were found which gave rise to "systemic symbiosis," a mutually rewarding web of relations that helped the Secretariat move forward (Goheer 2019d).

Another contestation is related to the core business of IGOs, which has evolved in the digital age. IGOs are primarily the avenues for multilateral diplomacy. The conventional CLOCK diplomacy is closed door, secretive, and limited to diplomats (bureaucrats of foreign ministries). Social media, however, have empowered other actors to participate in or influence the diplomatic processes in unprecedented ways. The digital form of diplomacy is inherently different from conventional diplomacy. It is open, transparent, and public (Goheer 2019c). Both CLOCK and CLOUD forms of diplomacy coexist and compete, which creates this contestation. IGOs like the Secretariat have to strike a fine balance between the two to retain their relevance as well as their social legitimacy.

And the last but certainly not the least of the contestations manifests itself at the cutting edge of the digital age. This is where the limits of CLOCK-only actions (both governmental and intergovernmental) are being tested. New technologies such as artificial intelligence, block-chain, remote sensing and extended reality are rapidly changing the operational landscape. The CLOCK action is slow and cannot adapt to these changes fast enough. Similarly, emergent issues such as the spread of COVID-19 require a multi-stakeholder response. IGOs, as the agents of governments, are increasingly experiencing difficulties in attempting to navigate these issues through a CLOCK lens. The Commonwealth Secretariat is watching and experimenting in this space by bringing fresh CLOUD perspectives into the game.

The Secretariat is now a visible and sociable player in the international system. Though its first story of digital adoption was rather disappointing, the second one is more promising. It is adapting to the CLOUD world by opening up, connecting, collaborating, and co-creating solutions. The Commonwealth is moving forward in a hybrid environment and a contested multilateral space. This journey of reform continues.

Notes

1 Also known as the computer age, digital age, or the new media age.
2 This is precisely the reason disruption is the new normal in the information age.
3 Director of Strategic Planning and Evaluation from December 2010 to September 2017 and Assistant Secretary-General from October 2017 onwards until the writing of this chapter.
4 This happened at a time when the Secretariat was flushed with funds. It was underspending every year at the tune of approximately £4 million. Board papers and minutes of successive board meetings reflect concerns on underspending.
5 There are 90 organisations in the Commonwealth. The Commonwealth of Learning is another IGO (https://www.col.org/ accessed March 5, 2020) which is a specialized agency based in Vancouver and doing great work in the area of distance and digital learning, but its mandate is very limited. The Commonwealth Telecommunication Organisation (https://www.cto.int/ accessed March 5, 2020) is another Commonwealth associated organisation with limited mandate and capacity to advance this intergovernmental agenda. Furthermore, both organisations do not have the full membership of the Commonwealth.
6 Discussions to agree on a four-year Strategic Plan took two years, three months, and 11 days.
7 It decreased from £30.68 in 2010/11 to £17.79 in 2015/16.
8 There used to be three Deputy Secretaries-General responsible for political, developmental, and corporate affairs, respectively.
9 The full story of systemic and network reform is not part of this tale. This chapter focuses mainly on the ICT and digital aspect of the Commonwealth Secretariat journey.
10 An alignment with SDGs reduced the intergovernmental negotiation time. The new plan was agreed upon in three months as SDGs were the globally agreed goals. An agreement on the previous Strategic Plan had taken two years, three months, and 11 days of negotiations.
11 Four-hundred e-meetings were conducted in the last quarter of 2019, which saved money and reduced the Commonwealth's carbon footprint.
12 The International Labour Organisation, for example, had datasets related to the world of work, WHO about health, UNCTAD about trade, and WIPO about innovation and intellectual property
13 Headquarters of the Commonwealth in London.

14 It is being used by the federal and state governments. A few non-Commonwealth countries are also using this system in exchange for a license, service, and maintenance fee.

15 CNCP was established in 2005 to facilitate international cooperation in criminal cases between Commonwealth member states, including on mutual legal assistance and extradition, and to provide relevant legal and practical information.

16 At the time of writing this paper in March 2020, the entire Secretariat is now working remotely due to the restrictions imposed by COVID-19.

17 The Commonwealth system has three intergovernmental, nine quasi-governmental, and 78 professional and civil society organisations.

18 The Blue Charter is an agreement reached by all Commonwealth government at London CHOGM in 2018. It is about active cooperation to solve ocean-related problems and meet commitments of sustainable ocean development.

19 The consortium consists of United Nations Institute for Training and Research, Satellite Applications Catapult, DevEx, Radiant.Earth, University of Portsmouth, UK Met Office, and Sensonomic.

20 Weber called it *stahlhartes Gehäuse* which literally translates into "housing hard as steel."

References

Abbott, K.W., P. Genschel, D.Snidal, and B. Zangl. *International Organizations as Orchestrators*. Cambridge: Cambridge University Press, 2015.

Arce, A., and N. Long, eds. *Anthropology, Development and Modernities: Exploring Discourses, Counter-Tendencies and Violence*. New York: Routledge, 2000.

Bauer, M., C. Knill, and S. Eckhard. *International Bureaucracy: Challenges and Lessons for Public Administration Research*. London: Palgrave Macmillan, 2017.

Bjola, C., and M. Holmes. *Digital Diplomacy: Theory and Practice*. London: Routledge, 2015.

CAACC (Commonwealth Africa Anti-Corruption Centre). "Commonwealth and CAACC Adviser Wins Global Anti-Corruption Excellence Award." 2018, accessed March 16, 2020 http://www.thecaacc.org/commonwealth-and-caacc-adviser-wins-global-anti-corruption-excellence-award.

Chatham House. "Ideas for Modernizing the Rules-Based International Order." *Chatham House Expert Perspectives*, June 2019.

CHOGM (The Commonwealth Heads of Government Meeting). "Durban Communique." , South Africa, 1999.

CHOGM (The Commonwealth Heads of Government Meeting). "Coolum Communique " Australia, 2002.

CHOGM (The Commonwealth Heads of Government Meeting). "Valletta Communique", Malta, 2005.

CHOGM (The Commonwealth Heads of Government Meeting). "Port of Spain Communique." Trinidad and Tobago, 2009a.

CHOGM (The Commonwealth Heads of Government Meeting). "Affirmation of Commonwealth Values and Principles." Port of Spain, Trinidad and Tobago 2009b.

CHOGM (The Commonwealth Heads of Government Meeting). "Deliberations." Perth, Australia, 2011a.

CHOGM (The Commonwealth Heads of Government Meeting). "Perth Communique." Australia, 2011b.

CHOGM (The Commonwealth Heads of Government Meeting). "Deliberations." Colombo, Sri Lanka, 2013.

CHOGM (The Commonwealth Heads of Government Meeting). "Valletta Communique", Malta 2015.

Ciuk, S., J. Koning, and M. Kostera. "Organizational Ethnographies." In *The SAGE Handbook of Qualitative Business and Management Research Methods: History and Traditions*, edited by Catherine Cassell, Ann L Cunliffe, and Gina Grandy, 270–85. London: SAGE Publications Ltd, 2018.

"Commonwealth Digital Identity Initiative." *Mobile for Development*, 2020, accessed March 24, 2020. https://www.gsma.com/mobilefordevelopment/commonwealthi nitiative/.

"Commonwealth Innovation Ecosystem for Africa Launched in Seychelles." *Commonwealth Innovation Ecosystem for Africa Launched in Seychelles – Seychelles Nation*, 2020, accessed March 25, 2020. http://www.nation.sc/articles/560/commonwealth -innovation-ecosystem-for-africa-launched-in-seychelles.

Commonwealth Secretariat. "Networking the Commonwealth for Development: The Commonwealth, ICTs and Development." *A Report presented at the CHOGM Coordinating Committee*. London: Commonwealth Action Programme for the Digital Divide for the Commonwealth Secretary General, Commonwealth Secretariat, 2005.

Commonwealth Secretariat. "DFID Multilateral Aid Review – Commonwealth Secretariat Response." 2011, accessed March 5, 2020 https://assets.publishing.serv ice.gov.uk/government/uploads/system/uploads/attachment_data/file/214115/CO MSEC-response.pdf.

Commonwealth Secretariat. "Terms of Reference for the Evaluation of Commonwealth Connects Programme." 2014. https://thecommonwealth.org/sites/default/files/do cuments/vacancies/terms-of-service/termsofreference_7.pdf.

Commonwealth Secretariat. "Minutes of Annual SMG Retreat Meeting." June 11, 2015a.

Commonwealth Secretariat. "Evaluation of the Commonwealth Connects Programme." Evaluation Series No. 101, 2015b.

Commonwealth Secretariat. "Huddle Quarterly Review Report." November, 2019.

Commonwealth Secretariat. "Commonwealth Secretariat Accounts and Internal Reports." *Commonwealth Secretariat Accounts and Internal Reports | The Commonwealth*, accessed March 12, 2020. https://thecommonwealth.org/about-us/accounts-intern al-reports.

Conniff, R. "Eyes on Nature: How Satellite Imagery Is Transforming Conservation Science." *Yale Environment 360*, June 22, 2017. https://e360.yale.edu/features/eyes-on -nature-how-satellite-imagery-is-transforming-conservation-science.

Denning, S. *The Age of Agile How Smart Companies Are Transforming the Way Work Gets Done*. New York: AMACOM Book Company, 2018.

DFID (UK Department for International Development). "Multilateral Aid Review – Commonwealth Secretariat." 2011.

DFID (UK Department for International Development). "Implementing Agenda 2030: Increasing the impact of Commonwealth Organisations 2017–2019." *Internal Review Report*, 2018.

Escobar, A.. "Welcome to Cyberia – Notes on the Anthropology of Cyberculture." *Current Anthropology* 35, no. 3 (1994): 211–321.

Feagin, J.R., A.M. Orum, and G. Sjoberg. *A Case for the Case Study*. Chapel Hill: The University of North Carolina Press, 1991.

Ferguson, J. *The Anti-Politics Machine: "Development", Depoliticization, and Bureaucratic Power in Lesotho*. Minneapolis, MN: University of Minnesota Press, 1994.

Geertz, C.. *The Interpretation of Cultures*. New York: Basic Books, 1973.

Goheer, N. *"Facing Exponential Times."* *Keynote speech presented at the South America Business Forum*, Buenos Aires, Argentina, 2011, accessed February 8, 2020. https://alchetron .com/South-American-Business-Forum.

Goheer, N. "A Smart Commonwealth." *Presented at the Commonwealth Telecommunication Organisation Conference*, Maputo, Mozambique, 2015a.

Goheer, N. "Strategy Innovation Through Partnerships." *Presented at the Global Strategy Innovation Summit*, December 2015b, accessed February 8, 2020. https://channels.the innovationenterprise.com/presentations/strategy-innovation-through-partnership4.

Goheer, N. "Turning Commonwealth into an Innovation Hub." Presented internally to senior management, 2017.

Goheer, N. "Embarking on a Digital Journey with 4Ds and P." Commonwealth Secretariat Internal Document, 2018a.

Goheer, N. "A Rising and Innovating Commonwealth." *Speech Delivered at the Roundtable Editorial Board Dinner at the Royal Overseas League Club in London*, March 26, 2018b.

Goheer, N. "The Relevance of Intergovernmental Organisations to African States: The Role of the Commonwealth." *Speech Delivered at Chatham House*, April 12, 2018c.

Goheer, N. "Network Multilateralism in the CLOUD Age." *LinkedIn*, October 14, 2018d, accessed March 5, 2020. https://www.linkedin.com/pulse/network-multil ateralism-cloud-world-nabeel-goheer-phd/.

Goheer, N. "The Commonwealth: Discovery of a Diamond or Dinosaur." *Lecture Delivered at Oxford and Cambridge Club*, 71 Pall Mall, London, 2019a. 31 January 2020.

Goheer, N. "Digital Transformation of the Commonwealth." *Talk Given at Queen Elizabeth House*, University of Oxford, March 7, 2019b. Accessed March 15, 2020. https://talks.ox.ac.uk/talks/id/8161cde5-6fac-42c4-8b46-35f56560cf48/.

Goheer, N. "Diplomacy in the Digital Age." *Talk Given at the SOAS Diplomatic Society*, April 17, 2019c.

Goheer, N. "Interoperability and IGOs." *Presentation given at the Systems Innovation Conference in London*, September 7–8, 2019d.

Gould, J., and H. Marcussen, eds. "Ethnographies of Aid – Exploring Development Texts and Encounters." *Occasional Paper Series No. 24*. International Development Studies, Roskilde University, 2004.

Hamel, G., and M. Zanini. ""Busting Bureaucracy." 2018, accessed March 29, 2020. http://www.garyhamel.com/blog/busting-bureaucracy.

Hooghe, L., and G. Marks. "Delegation and Pooling in International Organizations. " *The Review of International Organizations* 10, no. 3 (2015): 305–28.

House of Commons Foreign Affairs Committee. "The Role and Future of the Commonwealth: Fourth Report of Session 2012–13." November 15, 2013.

Howell, D. *Old Links and New Ties: Power and Persuasion in the Age of Networks*. New York: I.B. Taurus & Company, 2011.

KPMG. "Budget Setting." *Internal Audit Report of the Commonwealth Secretariat*, 2019.

KPMG. "Commonwealth Fund for Technical Cooperation." *Draft Internal Audit Report of the Commonwealth Secretariat*, 2020.

KYA Global. "Review Report on the Commonwealth Secretariat." 2016.

Manor, I. *The Digitalization of Public Diplomacy*. Basingstoke, UK: Palgrave Macmillan, 2019.

Mansell, R., and N. Couldry. "A Commonwealth Action Programme for the Digital Divide." *Report of the Commonwealth Expert Group on Information Technology to the Commonwealth High Level Review Group*, June 20, 2001.

McChrystal, S.A., C. Fussell, T. Collins, and D. Silverman. *Team of Teams: New Rules for Engagement for a Complex World*. London: Penguin Books, 2015.

Ministry of Public Telecommunications for the Republic of Guyana. "Commonwealth Launches Digital Innovation Hub." April 19, 2018. https://mopt.gov.gy/news/related -news/commonwealth-launches-digital-innovation-hub/.

Murphy, P. *The Empire's New Clothes: The Myth of the Commonwealth.* Oxford: Oxford University Press, 2018.

Narotra, J.P., and J.V. Tabone. "Review of the Connects Projects." *Report Presented to the Steering Committee,* April 2011.

Nekton. "Strategic Partners." 2020. https://nektonmission.org/partners/strategic-partn ers.

"Nekton Indian Ocean Mission." *The Commonwealth,* 2020, accessed March 8. https:// www.thecommonwealth.io/innovation-projects/nekton-indian-ocean-mission/.

Scharmer, O., and K. Kaufer. *Leading from the Emerging Future.* Berrett-Koehler Publishers Inc, 2013.

Sen, A. "Promotion of Respect and Understanding by the Commonwealth in a Volatile World." *Concluding Statement Given at a workshop held at Nuffield College.* University of Oxford, June 7–8, 2018.

Senge, P., A. Kleiner, C. Roberts, R. Ross, G. Roth, and B. Smith. *The Dance of Change: The Challenges of Sustaining Momentum in Learning Organizations.* New York: Doubleday Publishing, 1999.

Shaw, T. M. *Commonwealth: Inter- and Non-State Contributions to Global Governance.* London: Routledge, 2007.

Stratfor. "A Return to Reform in the Gulf Cooperation Council." January 23, 2017, accessed March 15, 2020. https://worldview.stratfor.com/article/return-reform-gulf -cooperation-council.

Taleb, Nassim Nicholas. *The Black Swan: The Impact of the Highly Improbable,* New York: Random House, 2007.

The Commonwealth. "The Durban Communique." *Report Presented at the Commonwealth Heads of Government Meeting,* Durban, South Africa, November 12–15, 1999.

The Commonwealth. "Evaluation of Commonwealth Secretariat Training Programmes 2003/4-2008/9." Centre for International Development and Training, University of Wolverhampton, UK, 2010.

The Commonwealth. "Commonwealth of the People: Time for Urgent Reform." *A Report of EPG to Commonwealth Heads of Government,* 2011.

The Commonwealth. "The Commonwealth in the Unfolding Global Trade Landscape: Prospects, Priorities, Perspectives." 2015.

The Commonwealth. "Review and Renewal of Commonwealth Media Development Fund." 2016a.

The Commonwealth. "Meta Evaluation – A Synthesis of Evaluation Studies from 2005 to 2016." Evaluation Series No.104, December 2016b.

The Commonwealth. "Summary and Decisions of the Commonwealth Foreign Affairs Ministers Meeting." New York, September 2017.

Thompson, W.B. "Policy Making Through Thick and Thin: Thick Description as a Methodology for Communications and Democracy." *Policy Sciences* 34, no. 1 (2001): 63–77.

UNITAR, 2020, accessed March 8, 2020. https://www.unitar.org/about/news-storie s/news/commonsensing-building-climate-resilience-small-island-developing-st ates.

United Nations. "Personal Records from the Proceedings of un Secretary-General's High-Level Interactive Dialogue with Heads of Regional and Other Organisations." *Held at Greentree Estate, New York,* June 12–13, 2018.

United Nations. "The Age of Digital Interdependence: Report of the Secretary-General's High-Level Panel on Digital Cooperation." New York: UN Secretariat, 2019.

Weber, M. *The Protestant Ethic and the Spirit of Capitalism.* London: Unwin Hyman, 1930.

Zürn, M., M. Binder, and M. Ecker-Ehrhardt. "International Authority and Its Politicization." *International Theory* 4, no. 1 (2012): 69–106.

PART III

International organisation and legitimacy

7

TWEETING TO SAVE SUCCEEDING GENERATIONS FROM THE SCOURGE OF WAR? THE UN, TWITTER, AND COMMUNICATIVE ACTION

Matthias Hofferberth

Introduction[1]

The international order of global governance as we know it, with the UN at its core and a strong commitment to multilateralism, has recently come under severe stress. In fact, events and developments such as the election of Donald J. Trump and other right-wing leaders around the world, Brexit, the rise of new, non-democratic powers, and overall renewed emphasis on national over global solutions, have been interpreted not only as challenges but as profound crises of and for global governance (Hooghe et al. 2019; Zürn 2018). Practitioners and scholars, still believing in global governance, thus have repeatedly called for reforming the United Nations (UN) and the global order which it represents (Moore and Pubantz 2017; Acharya 2016; Commission on Global Security, Justice & Governance 2015). Crucial for such reform efforts, it has been argued, is to increase the legitimacy of the order provided. Since there is no direct democratic control on the global level, "going public" and "cultivating support" from different constituencies by committing to and communicating efforts to increase accountability, participation, and performance has thus become a new imperative for any global governor (Ecker-Ehrhardt 2018; Tallberg et al. 2018).

With the introduction of social media as a new form of public engagement, global governors have a new tool at their disposal to directly relate to their audience to influence the tone of deliberation and increase their legitimacy (Duncombe 2017; Bruns and Highfield 2016).[2] This is particularly important for the UN because ever since its creation, its role and impact in world politics has been debated. In these unsettled debates, different images, from instrument of the powerful to collective agency for the weak, have been evoked to describe what this unique organisation does and what it stands for, leaving us with rather different images, assessments, and interpretations (Weiss et al. 2010; Archer

1983; Claude 1956). Against this background, the UN, through social media and "corporate branding," is now actively engaged in forming and sustaining its own image(s). More specifically, the UN has expanded its social media presence significantly within the last couple of years and is currently exploring new avenues of engaging its global public.[3] In other words, the UN is clearly committed to project its own image(s) and thus establish and increase its legitimacy against public perception of its many shortcomings (Weiss 2009). In this communicative action, the UN presents, and opens for debate, its ideas, reasons, and narratives as to what kind of organisation it is and what it should be (Figure 7.1).

Drawing on recent literature on IOs and legitimacy (Tallberg and Zürn 2019; Tallberg et al. 2018; Dingwerth et al. 2014; Keohane 2011) as well as certain aspects of Habermas' Theory of Communicative Action (Habermas 1981a, 1981b) and its IR applications (Müller 2004; Risse 2000, 2004), I contend that social media, if committed to the dissemination and exchange of reason and arguments, holds the potential to improve global public deliberation and thus can contribute to a more legitimate form of global governance by the UN. More specifically, if oriented towards establishing consensus through "better arguments" (Habermas 1981a, 328), tweets of what the UN does and what it stands for carries the potential to improve UN governance and further its mission and mandate. Following Barbera and Zeitzoff (2018) as well as Seib (2012, 2016), political communication through social media thus can be a constitutive outlet that influences what the public thinks and feels about an otherwise abstract and distanced organisation. Engaged in critical discourses with their global public,

United Nations ✔
@UN

Official account of the United Nations. #ClimateAction #GlobalGoals #StandUp4HumanRights

◎ New York, NY ⊘ un.org ◎ Born October 24, 1945 ▦ Joined March 2008

1,183 Following   **12.5M** Followers

FIGURE 7.1   Current profile image of the main @UN Twitter handle

the UN's micro-blogging presence on Twitter can be understood as an opportunity to initiate and maintain deliberation and thereby bestow legitimacy to its actions. Through the effective use of social media in general and Twitter in particular, one can thus envision a more engaged and informed global public which, while holding the UN accountable, has a clear understanding of the values and beliefs this unique organisation represents as it critically engages with its reasons and justifications for policy-making. Put simply, UN social media *is* UN politics and can strengthen the very impact of this global organisation (Nahon 2016).

On the other hand, social media and its impact can remain limited in many ways. Whether it is sharing only trivial information and thereby not engaging in discussion or in fact trying to deceive the public by presenting a deliberately manipulated image, sceptics have pointed out that social media mainly serves the strategic end of self-presentation and, in the case of the UN, blue-washes the organisation and its actions. Merely offering a streamlined but otherwise not representative self-image to its stakeholders, the impact of social media framed as communicative action in a Habermasian sense thus assumingly remains limited or, even worse, can be used by incumbent elites to purposefully manipulate the public (Chadwick 2013; Morozov 2011). With the potential of communicative action in social media thus undecided, following Murthy (2012, 1061–2), the chapter studies and assesses the *UN Twittersphere* as a case study of the broader potential of IOs using (or misusing) social media. To reconstruct whether and how the UN engages its audience through Twitter, I introduce the theoretical framework in two steps. First, I discuss how social media plays a role as IOs legitimate their action. Second, using a communicative action framework, I theorise the potential of Twitter to stimulate public discourse and increase the legitimacy of the UN. In the third section, I introduce the notion of the *UN Twittersphere* in full detail and discuss conditions under which tweets reflect communicative action. This section also includes the coding scheme developed to explore and map the nature, content, direction, and UN images expressed in tweets. The fourth section then discusses the results in regards to whether the *UN Twittersphere* provides and nourishes an engaged public discourse on the UN or not. The conclusion summarises findings and discusses how social media research can provide an additional angle on international organisations.

International Organisations, Legitimacy, and Social Media

Just like other global governors, IOs are "subjects of ongoing legitimation" within their broader social environments and depend on acceptance and recognition from stakeholders (Deephouse and Suchman 2008, 54). Even more so, arguably, in the absence of direct democratic control and diverse stakeholder expectations, "cultivating support" from their constituencies – including nation states as primary stakeholders (i.e., principals) but also broader public and civil society actors as well as those who are affected by IO decisions (Dingwerth et al. 2014, 168–70) – is the sine qua non for ongoing IO existence and operations in world politics. In other words, IOs have to constantly reach out to their environment and different groups within to justify their existence and seek legitimacy as they compete in organisational turf-battles over respective areas of responsibility and mandate. Drawn from successful rule as well as the justification thereof through engaging with one's constituencies, legitimacy can be thought of as an organisational resource for IOs to further extend overall authority to develop new rules and norms (Gronau and Schmidtke 2016, 539–42). As Tallberg and Zürn (2019, 3) argue, organisational legitimacy rests in the "beliefs of audiences that an IO's authority is appropriately exercised" while legitimation reflects efforts by the organisation to direct "process[es] of justification and contestation intended to shape such beliefs." Thus, organisational legitimacy equally stems from words as it does from deeds: while organisational legitimacy *substantially* depends on congruency between prevailing norms of one's constituencies and one's action, it can also be established and sustained *procedurally* through responding to and addressing concerns of different stakeholders.

As a consequence of these two dimensions of legitimacy and the overall lack thereof in global governance, IOs have adapted their communication strategies to signal responsiveness (Dingwerth et al. 2014, 180–5; see also Ecker-Ehrhardt 2018). Practiced as "public diplomacy" and "information policy," establishing legitimacy procedurally through responding to stakeholder expectations, in fact, has become critically important for IOs (Nye 2010). Attempts intended to reach broad(er) audiences become "observable when international institutions" representatives engage in proactive communication, in which they justify institutional identity and purpose on the basis of social norms" (Gronau and Schmidtke 2016, 541). Arguably, such "going public" has become just as relevant as substantial action and perceived appropriateness thereof in the IOs' quest for legitimacy. Evidently, (a) IOs have become more strategic about it and (b) scholars of international organisations discovered this as a newly emerging research agenda (Ecker-Ehrhardt 2018, 2–4; see also Hurd 2018).

In the most recent iteration of "going public," IOs comprehensively embraced social media as a direct means of reaching out to their constituencies. While still in a rather early, and thus to some extent experimental stage, almost all IOs today have a social media presence to connect to their constituencies (Twiplomacy 2018).[4] More specifically, for the self-legitimation of IOs, social media has been recognised as "a positive force in supporting their communication with constituents" (Ross and Bürger 2014, 48). Research on social media in IR in general, and on IOs in particular, however, is still in its infant stage. [5] Put differently, "social media adoption in organizations is outpacing [our] empirical understanding of the use of these technologies and our theories about why they may alter various organizational processes" in a rather dramatic fashion (Treem and Leonardi 2016, 144). Drawing from work on social media and non-profit organisations (Smith and Gallicano 2015; Lovejoy et al. 2012; Macnamara and Zerfass 2012) as well as research on political communication, elections campaigns, and global conferences (Hopke and Hestres 2018; Thelwall and Cugelman 2017; Usherwood and Wright 2017; Gervais 2015; Ross and Bürger 2014), three mutually related, reinforcing characteristics of this particular form of communication have been discussed in the literature:

- Social media is *instantaneous and direct*. It establishes an immediate connection between the author and its audience without any delay or filter, providing instant reaction time. There is virtually no limit such as airtime or paper space to communicate through social media, and new content can always be produced in the blink of a tweet.
- Social media is *interactive and dynamic*. Widely adopted, it represents egalitarian, horizontally organised communication. While the author produces content, the audience decides whom to follow or unfollow. As such, social media relinquishes control as it involves the co-creation rather than the simple delivery of meaning.
- Social media is *efficient and impactful*. Given its low costs and the potential to reach broad if not global audiences, social media significantly expands the ability of any organisation to influence public relations and increase visibility.

While all three characteristics broadly apply to all social media, Twitter features particularly high connectivity, sociality, and impact (or at least the potential thereof). Indeed, Twitter with its brevity, conciseness, and immediacy further "amplifies" the characteristics and effects of social media (Murthy 2012). Tweets have become "common means of sharing opinions and updates for individuals as well as for business, governments and nongovernmental organizations" and as such serve as important indicators of self-legitimation discourses (Denskus and Esser 2013, 405). Instant message updates, hashtags and retweets, the ability to directly address other users and add hyperlinks, the embedding of other media (images, videos, etc.), as well as the restrictive character limitation taken together explain why this micro-blogging application, in particular, became so successful. In fact, as the largest micro-blogging site and the seventh most popular website globally, Twitter has become the "most used social media application in official public relations, advertising, and marketing campaigns" (Lovejoy et al. 2012, 313; see also Usherwood and Wright 2017). The UN follows this trend closely as it is very dedicated to the cultivation of its own *Twittersphere* with its agencies, programmes, and senior officials active on Twitter every day.[6]

Theorising the *UN Twittersphere*: tweeting as communicative action

Concerned with social structure, individual motivation, and language, Habermas in his *Theory of Communicative Action* developed a typology of different modes of social interaction (Habermas 1981a, 1996). In this ideal-type scheme, *instrumental action* oriented towards and driven by consequences as well as individual interests (i.e., action motivated by *Zweckrationalität*) is juxtaposed to *communicative action* oriented towards and driven by reaching consensus and establishing social understandings (i.e., action motivated by *Wertrationalität*) (Heath 2001, 12–14). Whereas the former compels actors to engage in strategic bargaining, rhetorical action, and potentially deception to maximise one's interest, the latter pre-supposes that actors depend on social context and constitutive arguing in order to seek reasoned consensus and stabilise it. Developing these different types, Habermas rejected individualist notions of action based on independent and isolated actors by stressing the importance of language and social discourse in the determination of such actors and their interests in the first place (Joas and Knöbl 2009, 234–5). Emphasising in particular the fundamentally social nature of actors and their interests, Habermas thought of communicative action "whenever the actions of the agents involved are coordinated not through egocentric calculations of success but through acts of reaching understanding" (Habermas 1981a, 285–6). In other words, since never fixed, communicative action is action not driven by interest. Rather, against the indeterminateness of social situations, actors rely on communicative action to establish intersubjective meaning and thereby maintain their agency (Risse 2000, 10–1).

While initially framed as an analytical ideal-type distinction, Habermas' approach was quickly read in normative terms as it reflected different qualities of communicative engagements. In this vein, communicative action firstly depends on the amount and quality of publicly shared reasons for action. Against these reasons, any "agent can be held accountable for her conduct in a way that an agent acting from strictly instrumental motives cannot" (Heath 2001, 14). Secondly, communicative action only works if actors are willing to argue as well as be persuaded. As Müller (2004, 397) put it, communicative action rests on the "presumption that both speaker and listener enter the communication with a readiness to submit to the better argument." Taken together, actors engage in communicative action when they justify their decisions, seek understanding and build consensus, as well as confirm norms, develop and stabilise their social identities, and "learn" their interests. Communicative action thus resonates with the hope to eventually transcend public discourses to a higher order of justification, reasoning, and understanding. Such new discourses would make the public more engaged and thereby provide more accountability and ultimately better decision-making (Taylor 1991, 23; see also Habermas 1981a, 397–9).

Reading communicative action in its normative dimension, one can contend that (a) actors should work towards informed discourses as they provide justifications for action and that (b) these actors prefer deliberative action (as in arguing) in these discourses over strategic action (as in bargaining). Taken together, these commitments reflect social progress (Owen 2002, 172–86). These ideas have been applied to global contexts otherwise characterised by the absence of rules and hierarchies. Here, commitment to communicative action can "increase the deliberative quality of decision-making" as it engages new stakeholders, fosters transparency, and provides reasons for actors to realign or even redefine their interest (Risse 2004, 311). Such deliberations are best advanced among equal actors able to empathise. Sharing a "common lifeworld," their interaction is aimed at reasoned consensus based on the "force of the better argument" but otherwise void of coercive power, manipulation, and threats (Habermas 1981b, 119–52). Arguably, such conditions are rare within world politics. However, given its potential to effectively and quickly disseminate ideas, however much reduced and potentially distorted in its limited characters, Twitter at least in theory provides new public spheres and an outlet to provide reasoning and justification. Granted, these spheres are "more complex, dynamic, and multifaceted" than Habermas originally anticipated but Twitter still "allows for connections and overlaps between a multitude of [these] coexisting public spheres" (Bruns and Highfield 2016, 58). Within and between those spheres, everyone can assess and evaluate reasons and justifications and thereby generate social action, whether it is through retweeting or through real-world engagements. In other words, the *UN Twittersphere* represents another outlet in which communicative action *can* take place, as tweets express either reasons for action and the desire to engage in real debate or they adhere to a strategic script of presenting the organisation in a positive light (Denskus and Esser 2013, 410–1). They can either connect to concerns, norms, and beliefs shared between the UN and its audience or, in non-empathic ways, remain unrelated and distanced. Either way, I understand tweets as expressive self-presentations advanced in social contexts to be assessed in terms of their claims:

> [E]xpressive self-presentations have, like assertions or constative speech acts, the character of meaningful expressions, understandable in their context, which are connected with criticizable validity claims. Their reference is to norms and subjective experience rather than facts. The agent makes the claim that his behavior is right in relation to a normative context recognized as legitimate.
>
> *(Habermas 1981a, 15)*[7]

Twitter, in its most basic features, facilitates social interaction and enables the exchange of ideas and collaboration. In other words, it features the potential of bottom-up deliberation and collaborative development of political goals and better arguments (Murthy 2012). Allowing users to directly share their concerns and political views, Twitter can reframe old and initiate new discourses. In the words of Seib (2016, 128–33), it holds the potential to sustain narratives which give answers to what an organisation represents. From the UN's perspective, Twitter thus offers the possibility to break its own news and communicate its visions directly as the organisation relates to constituencies and stakeholders in their own words. In the process thereof, the organisation can share its narrative and determine what it stands for. This is important since the UN is a highly pluralistic organisation with many different voices (Anderson 2018, 22). As a consequence, UN individuals and specialised agencies would meet established media on a more equal playing field: while it has never been easy to send concise messages from an organisation as diverse and complex as the UN, more voices and stories could be shared through Twitter than through traditional media (Crossette 2007, 282–3). Taken together, Twitter holds the potential to foster communicative action as it provides the UN with new opportunities to engage its audience in public discourse and increase the quality of governance through deliberation. Expressing willingness to open its actions up for debate, UN tweets can become a catalyst towards reaching consensus and ultimately contribute towards a more positive image of the organisation and support for its policies. In other words, tweets can help advance users from merely "interacting with the interface physically to becoming cognitively immersed in the content offered … and then onto proactively spreading the outcomes of this involvement (Smith and Gallicano 2015, 82).

However, tweets can also easily fall short of the tall order of communicative action. For example, if not sent with the intention to engage in debate *and* the willingness to be persuaded, tweets can shut down public discourse. More specifically, Twitter can be used just as another outlet for organisational showcasing and to disseminate redundant or otherwise limited "facts." As such, there would be few deliberative and democratising effects but rather "death by rampant, excessive, and over-stimulating information" (Murthy 2012, 1063–4). In Habermas' words, just as they could reflect arguing and reasoning, tweets could as well flow from an instrumental logic. This logic would rest on (a) the unwillingness to consider the audience as equal in deliberation and share reasons for action, (b) the inability to emphatically connect to the different "lifeworlds" of its audience(s), and (c) the reluctance to learn from the "better argument" and adapt interests and identity through interaction. More practically, it would express itself in a PR-streamlined use, presenting the UN as all but the most efficient and legitimate organisation of world politics.

Considering both sides, Twitter can be just as much one-way communication as other media if the UN communicates *to* instead of *with* its audience (Ross and Bürger 2014, 44–5). As such, the *UN Twittersphere* potentially transforms engagement and public interest into "point-and-click politics" which are otherwise ineffective in creating social progress. In other words, it remains to be seen whether the *UN Twittersphere* really reflects commitment to communicative action or not (Morozov 2011, 193–5). In other words, representing an "interactive framework" with instant communication and providing "the means whereby a debating space in which many voices can talk to each other is enabled, *finally realizing Habermas' vision,* quite how many of those voices are heard, by whom and with what consequences is currently unknown" (Ross and Bürger 2014, 50–1, emphasis added). To answer these questions, the next section introduces the *UN Twittersphere* in detail and discusses how to approach it in methodological terms.

Reconstructing and assessing the *UN Twittersphere*

With the "digital revolution percolat[ing] down to the political classes" (Ross and Bürger 2014, 46–7), social media has changed the ways IOs interact with their audience(s). The UN in particular began to use Twitter in 2009 and today reaches almost 12 million followers just through its main handle.[8] Institutionally, the UN Department for Public Information, according to its own website, "help[s] manage the United Nations" relationship with major social media platforms including Facebook, Instagram, LinkedIn, Snapchat, Twitter, WeChat, and Weibo; develop policies and procedures for the use of social media platforms by the UN; and provide social media guidance and support to UN officials and Member States."[9] However, in practice, the Department does not control but rather works with individual agencies and senior staff members (Bouchard, this volume). Accordingly, the "UN's Twitter presence is not accurately reported or integrated into its official communication strategy [given that] its affiliate and special agencies are widely represented" through separate and independent accounts (Anderson 2018, 42). For example, there are only a few Twitter handles tagged as "official" and those do not include the UN GA President, UN Women or, among others, certain specialised agencies. As such, the *UN Twittersphere* is just as "erratic and episodic" as the UN and its already established "multifaceted information system[s]" (Crossette 2007, 275–9).

Against this background, the *UN Twittersphere* is more than the actual @UN handle or the rather short list of official accounts. More specifically, given the complex structure of the UN as such (Weiss et al. 2010), different actors and agencies populate the *UN Twittersphere*, which thus reflects multiple and potentially conflicting commitments as it speaks to different discourses. Just like its geographical representations in New York, Geneva, Vienna, Nairobi, and elsewhere, the virtual space of the *UN* expands beyond any single group of actors but rather includes UN committees; different agencies within the UN; UN staff members; permanent missions; other state representations and their individual staff; as well as non-governmental organisations in consultative status, their senior staff, and other UN Special Ambassadors and celebrity supporters. Two dimensions are relevant to structure this diverse collection of voices in analytical terms. First, handles either represent institutions or individual positions. For example, @UN, @UNDPPA (Department of Political and Peacebuilding Affairs), @UNPeacekeeping, as well as the General Assembly and ECOSOC presidents (@UN_PGA and @UNECOSOC) are permanent features of the UN and its *Twittersphere*. As such, we can expect them to speak directly on behalf of the UN and/or their respective UN agency as they relate to the overall organisation in an official capacity. At the same time, we can think of exposed individuals and senior staff in the UN such as the directors and administrators of specific programmes. While still serving the UN, they do so in their individual capacity as they rotate in and out of office. Such a list includes, among others, the Secretary-General (@antonioguterres) and the Deputy Secretary-General

(@AminaJMohammed) but also, to name a few more, Phumzile Mlambo as Executive Director of UN Women, Jayathma Wickramanay as UN Youth Envoy, and Nancy Groves as UN Social Media Team Leader.[10]

Second, echoing the notion of three "different UNs" (Weiss et al. 2009, 125–9), the *UN Twittersphere* equally features an intergovernmental, an institutional, and a non-governmental dimension. More specifically, some handles represent agencies and individuals *working for* the UN, whereas others represent agencies and individuals *working towards* the UN. In other words, we distinguish handles that are authorised to tweet on behalf of the UN from those that tweet to the UN. For example, in addition to what has been discussed above, tweets can come from permanent state missions (such as @AfghanmissionUN or @USUN) or from the respective head delegates and ambassadors leading those missions (such as @MahmoudSaikal or @nikkihaley serving until the end of 2018). Both represent intergovernmental dynamics and advance national interests within the *UN Twittersphere* as they tweet and respond to the organisation with an agenda in mind. Finally, non-state organisations recognised under the consultative status through ECOSOC as well as their representative leaders and directors also contribute to the *UN Twittersphere*. Table 7.1 combines these two dimensions and lists selected examples.[11]

Given the many different voices within the *UN Twittersphere*, the next methodological step was to determine key agencies and individuals for each dimension (i.e., *who* is tweeting). Given the chapter's focus on how the UN uses Twitter, both institutional and individual handles within the UN had to be considered. At the same time, given that these serve as critical resonance bodies of the communicative engagement of the UN, intergovernmental agencies (i.e., Permanent Missions) and individuals (i.e., Permanent Representatives) speaking and acting on behalf of their sovereign Member States were included as well. Finally, given the further importance of non-state actors within the UN, handles from selected NGOs and their directors were also included. Following Denskus and Esser (2013) to narrow down data by focusing on specific events and conferences in real-world diplomacy, tweets during the 73rd UN Session were collected. Also known as the "UN season," these sessions typically start in September and last for a few weeks. As to the particular one in 2018, is started on September 18th and ended on October 5th. Put simply, this is when "things happen" in New

TABLE 7.1 Twitter handle ideal types and selected examples

	Institutional	*Individual*
For the UN	@UN	@antonioguterres
	@UNPeacekeeping	@jayathmadw
Towards the UN (state actors)	@AfghanmissionUN	@MahmoudSaikal
	@USUN	@nikkihaley
Towards the UN (non-state actors)	@UNWatch	@HillelNeuer
	@UNGlobal_Witness	@EmmaWatson

York, at least in terms of regular rather than emergency meetings (Moore and Pubantz 2017, 119–24). Granted, while there is a lot of "noise" to be expected for this particular time, with the General Assembly but also all other UN agencies involved and multiple high-level plenary meetings with heads of state occurring in conjunction, this selection, as a snapshot, offers a representative and rather recent insight into the *UN Twittersphere*.[12]

Table 7.2 lists all Twitter handles whose tweets, if sent in English, Spanish, German, or French, were collected and analysed during this time period. Among the institutional UN handles, the main UN account as well as those of the General Assembly and ECOSOC Presidents, the Departments of General Assembly and Conference Management, Political and Peacebuilding Affairs and Economic and Social Affairs as well as UN News Centre were collected. Trying to match institutional and individual handles, representatives, and directors of each UN agency followed were considered next. Unfortunately, only Secretary-General Antonio Guterres, Deputy Secretary-General Amina J. Mohammed, and Under-Secretary-General for Global Communications Alison Smale were active on Twitter during this time period.[13] As to state actors, all permanent Security Council members were followed. This included the Permanent Missions of all of the P5 as well as Karen Pierce (UK) and Nikki Haley (USA).[14] Finally, for non-state actors, relevant civil society organisations with special consultative status with access "not only to ECOSOC, but also to its many subsidiary bodies, the various human rights mechanisms of the United Nations, ad-hoc processes on small arms, and special events organized by the President of the General Assembly" were considered.[15] Among those, NGOs serving explicitly as "watch-dogs" for the UN were selected, including the United Nations Association of the United States of America (UNA-USA), and UN Watch. Correspondingly, their leading individuals Chris

TABLE 7.2 Twitter handles followed during 73rd UN session (2018)

	Institutional	*Individual*
For the UN	@UN	@antonioguterres
	@UN_PGA	@AminaJMohammed
	@UNECOSOC	@alsion_smale
	@UN_Spokesperson	
	@UNDGACM_EN	
	@UNDPPA	
	@UNDESA	
Towards the UN	@Chinamission2un	@FDelattre
(state actors)	@Franceonu	@NebenziaUN
	RussiaUN	@KarenPierceUN
	@UKUN_NewYork	@nikkihaley
	@USUN	
Towards the UN	@UNAUSA	@HillelNeuer
(non-state actors)	@UNWatch	

Whatley, Executive Director of UNA-USA, and Hillel C. Neuer, Executive Director of UN Watch, were also considered (Tables 7.3 to 7.9).[16]

In practical terms, tweets were collected using Twitter's application programming interface (API). This allowed the project to collect and analyse tweets in real-time, even if the respective user deleted them at a later point in time.[17] In methodological terms, I applied a qualitative content analysis in order to make sense of the large amount of data (Schreier 2012). Individual tweets were interpreted as "artefacts of social communication" and considered in terms of their words, meaning, and framing (Berg and Lune 2012, 353). Given the focus on assessing the quality of communicative action, tweets were coded based on their *content* (i.e., *what* is tweeted), *purpose* (i.e., *why* is tweeted), *direction* (i.e., *who* is

TABLE 7.3 Coding frame – categories and dimensions

Categories	*Dimensions*
Content of Tweet	Security
	Development & Economy
	Human Rights
	Environment & Health
	UN & UN Structure
Purpose of Tweet	Call for Action
	Discussion Statement
	Information Dissemination
Direction of Tweet	Towards Global Audience
	Towards States & World Leaders
	Towards the UN
	Towards other IOs
	Towards Non-State Actors
UN Image in Tweet	Positive
	Neutral
	Negative
	Not Addressed

TABLE 7.4 Institutional handles from UN – 73rd UN session (2018)

UN Institutions	*Twitter Handle*	*Total Tweets*
United Nations	@UN	536
UN General Assembly President	@UN_PGA	138
UN ECOSOC President	@UNECOSOC	23
UN Spokesperson	@UN_Spokesperson	205
UN Department for General Assembly and Conference Management	@UNDGACM_EN	112
UN Department of Political and Peacebuilding Affairs	@UNDPPA	40
UN Department of Economic and Social Affairs	@UNDESA	98

TABLE 7.5 Individual handles from UN – 73rd UN session (2018)

UN Individual	Position / Title	Twitter Handle	Total Tweets
Antonio Guterres	UN Secretary-General	@antonioguterres	64
Amina J. Mohammed	UN Deputy Secretary-General	@AminaJMohammed	63
Maria Fernanda Espinosa	President of the General Assembly	@mfespinosaEC	33
Alison Smale	Under-Secretary-General for Global Communications	@alison_smale	14
Jeffrey D. Feltman	Under-Secretary-General for Political Affairs	N/A	0
Rosemary A. DiCarlo	Under-Secretary of Political and Peacebuilding Affairs	N/A	0
Catherine Pollard	Under-Secretary for General Assembly Affairs and Conference Management	N/A	0

TABLE 7.6 Institutional handles towards UN (states) – 73rd UN session (2018)

Permanent Mission	Twitter Handle	Total Tweets
China	@Chinamission2un	18
France	@Franceonu	282
Russia	@RussiaUN	137
United Kingdom	@UKUN	375
USA	@USUN	74

TABLE 7.7 Individual handles towards UN (states) – 73rd UN session (2018)

Permanent Representative	Country Mission	Twitter Handle	Total Tweets
Ma Zhaoxu	China	N/A	0
Francois Delattres	France	@FDelattre	0
Vassily A. Nebenzia	Russia	@NebenziaUN	0
Karen Pierce	United Kingdom	@KarenPierceUN	49
Nikki Haley	USA	@nikkihalley	101

TABLE 7.8 Institutional handles towards UN (non-state) – 73rd UN session (2018)

Permanent Mission	Twitter Handle	Total Tweets
United Nations Association USA	@UNAUSA	83
UN Watch	@UNWatch	66

TABLE 7.9 Individual handles towards UN (non-states) – 73rd UN session (2018)

Permanent Representative	NGO	Title/Position	Twitter Handle	Total Tweets
Chris Whatley	UNA-USA	Executive Director	N/A	0
Hillel C. Neuer	UN Watch	Executive Director	@HillelNeuer	171

tweeted at), and the *UN image* (i.e., *how* is the UN represented) they conveyed. This initial coding scheme and its dimensions were devised based on an inductive sampling of a smaller number of tweets from different handles representing both institutional and individual tweets within and towards the UN. Further dimensions were then refined and ultimately applied in mass coding of all tweets collected for the time period mentioned above. As such, the coding reflects a data-driven but also theory-guided approach, generated through multiple iterations of going back and forth between data and theory but also focused on the quality of communicative action in the *UN Twittersphere* (Schreier 2012, 146–66). Table 7.3 lists the categories and dimensions of coding in detail applied to all tweets collected while the following paragraphs outline each dimension in more detail and provide arguments and conditions as to when the normative standards of communicative action are reached.

As to the *content of tweets*, the coding framework captures the larger issue areas the UN is committed to (Moore and Pubantz 2017). Tweets were thus coded whether their focus was on security, economy, human rights, environment and health, or the UN and its own structure.[18] With these dimensions, the coding was able to capture and reflect debates and topical differences within and between different handles. To assess the quality of communicative action and public engagement in this dimension, the overall distribution of tweets among different topics was considered. In addition to checking for a balanced representation of the full mandate of the UN, I also considered how much topics covered between the different groups of handles corresponded. While full consensus cannot be the yardstick, at least some basic agreement on what needs to be discussed is required to establish communicative action and ultimately consensus. In other words, if UN agencies developed their own "pet projects" irrespective of stakeholder concerns or, vice versa, if state and non-state actors pursued their own agendas, lifeworlds would drift apart and persuasion couldn't happen. In order to reflect mutual commitment to communicative action, tweets from different stakeholders must overall paint a consistent picture of what the UN deals with. Thus, the more thematic overlap between different stakeholders, the more the *UN Twittersphere* represents a shared public sphere of reasoning and meets the normative standards of communicative action.

Second, the *purpose of tweets* dimension was coded based on whether a tweet represented a call for action, a discussion statement, or information dissemination (Lovejoy et al. 2012). These dimensions assess whether tweets engage users in debate or shut down discourse. To qualify as a call for action, tweets needed to express an immediate notion to act.[19] Discussion statements, on the other hand, featured arguments that the audience could relate to and either confirm or contest.[20] Finally, information dissemination included announcements, events, and publications, as well as recognising new directors, new programmes, or something similar. This is particularly important and engaging since social media is an "information based" activity and used to receive current news (Smith and Gallicano 2015, 84–5). Given the shortness of tweets, each tweet was coded with only one dimension – a tweet either represented (more of) a discussion statement or (more of) an information announcement. In terms of assessment, an engaging *UN Twittersphere* should arguably feature a mix of different purposes. Just as mobilisation, debate, and information are crucial for ongoing communicative action. That said, despite the importance of information, calls for action and discussion potentially engage the audience more since both are value-driven and potentially speak directly to the beliefs and interests of the audience. This is specifically true if information disseminated remains trivial and limited in its depth and quality, or simply does not transcend the discourse from bargaining to arguing. Consequentially, against a balanced distribution, more tweets coded as mobilisation and discussion reflect a *UN Twittersphere* meeting the normative standards of communicative action (Anderson 2018, 33–4).

Third, in terms of *direction of tweets*, the coding scheme reflected intended audiences and whether or not specific entities were explicitly addressed. As such, the default code represented an unspecified "global public" – if no one was addressed explicitly, it was concluded that the tweet was meant for everyone. Following Karns et al. (2015, 8–20), further dimensions included Member States and world leaders, the UN itself, other international organisations, and NGOs, civil society, or towards business actors.[21] With potentially multiple addressees at once, tweets in this dimension could be double-coded (i.e., addressing states, civil society, and business actors alike). In terms of assessment again, arguably, the more a tweet specifies its audience, the more engaging it becomes. In other words, if there is a designated audience, rapport can be established and arguments can be exchanged (Risse 2004, 294–300). In other words, while one can expect that tweets are sent out without specific recipients, addressing those explicitly strengthens the overall potential for communicative action. Moreover, direct communication further strengthens the "shared lifeworld." Consequentially, against a balanced distribution, the more that audiences are explicitly identified, the more the *UN Twittersphere* meets the normative standards of communicative action.

As to the fourth and final category, the overall *UN image* conveyed in each tweet was coded. This included a range from positive and affirmative to neutral and balanced to negative and critical as well as a code for not addressing or mentioning the UN at all. Affirmative tweets include appreciations and argumentative efforts to strengthen the UN whereas negative tweets include challenges towards and explicit reservations about the UN and its mandate.[22] While positive images recognise the UN and as such establish legitimacy, there is a thin line not to be crossed which would entail entering the realm of PR streamlining and corporate branding in this dimension. More specifically, I considered a balanced assessment of the UN as such as a solid foundation for communicative action whereas narratives of excellence and greatness of the UN were perceived as potentially limiting discourses through blatant overstatements. To further assess this dimension, I considered whether the self-image of the UN and those of other stakeholders matched (i.e., do we overall have the same distribution of positive, neutral, and negative images?). Consequentially, the more the UN presents itself in a balanced fashion and the more this echoes stakeholders' assessments, the more the *UN Twittersphere* meets the normative standards of communicative action.

Results and discussion

Given the many different actors populating the *UN Twittersphere*, I first discuss tweets sent *for* the UN (i.e., from institutions and individuals *within* the UN) to then compare this with those tweeting *at* the UN (i.e., state and non-state actors relevant to the UN). I will further compare institutional to individual handles as I look at the different dimensions respectively. In terms of content, what really stands out for institutional tweets is that they are strongly self-referential as they intensively share information on the UN, its structure, and its proceedings. More specifically, more than half of all tweets speak about the UN and not about the topics the UN speaks about. Between the other topics, there is a reasonably even distribution with human rights and environmental topics slightly tweeted more than others. Interestingly, among individual handles, the UN receives less attention as preferences for certain topics can be identified (i.e., Antonio Guterres tweets more frequently about the environment and human rights whereas Amina Mohammed refers more often to development), which can be read as championing certain topics. Further comparing institutional and individual handles, security seems to be slightly less relevant for the Secretary-General, Deputy Secretary-General, and Under-Secretary-General of Global Communications, at least when measured in references made in tweets (see Figure 7.2).

Considering the purpose of tweets, the vast majority of institutional tweeting reflects rather generic information statements. Commonplace statements such that the UN is now in session or images of handshakes between diplomats and their meetings (without substantial reflection on what the meeting is about) are shared most consistently. Only about 20% of all tweets coded reflected discussion statements, in which the UN indicates a willingness to either initiate or respond to public debate. Even more so, very few direct calls for action or any other forms of mobilisation could be found. In other words, institutional handles, for the most part, remain reserved and non-committal.[23] Individual handles on the other hand, present a different picture, at least in regards to the amount of discussion statements which constitute slightly more than half of all tweets from these handles. UN individuals, potentially freer from institutional pressure, are

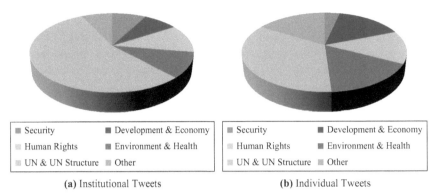

■ Security	■ Development & Economy
■ Human Rights	■ Environment & Health
■ UN & UN Structure	■ Other

(a) Institutional Tweets   **(b)** Individual Tweets

FIGURE 7.2   Content of UN tweets during 73rd session (n = 1,293)

seemingly more willing to raise hot button issues and engage in debate on those. At the same time, there is still a certain reluctance to translate discussion into mobilisation as even the individual handles restrain themselves from requesting direct action. Notably, they are also strongly committed to sharing information (42%) (see Figure 7.3).

The generic nature of why the UN tweets is echoed in terms of whom it tweets to. Obviously, given that this is constitutive for the medium, this comes as no major surprise. Nevertheless, a vast majority of 95% of all tweets not directed at any particular actor indicates non-commitment, as the UN does not use this tool to directly relate to other actors. Among those few instances where an actor or a group of actors is directly identified, it is nation states and their leaders. These tweets, arguably, present stronger cases of outreach as state actors are held responsible and reminded about their organisational obligations. These dynamics, however, we do not find with non-state actors as almost no tweets in the sample address NGOs, business actors, or other international organisations. This is true for both UN institutions and individuals, who are only slightly more likely

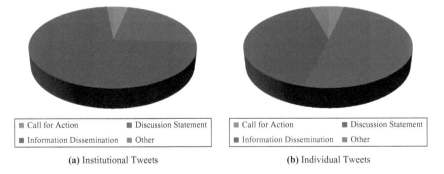

(a) Institutional Tweets   **(b)** Individual Tweets

FIGURE 7.3   Purpose of UN tweets during 73rd session (n = 1,293)

to address nation states directly but overall seem to be equally non-committal in terms of who they address. Overall the different UNs designated in research elsewhere (Weiss et al. 2009) are neither addressed nor engaged through the UN, which seems to use Twitter mostly as an echo chamber of its own. Assuming that designated addressees and clear direction are important for any discourse, the *UN Twittersphere* in this regard, even when considering the specific nature of the medium, falls short (see Figure 7.4).

Finally, in terms of UN images (i.e., self-assessment), the overall image conveyed is neutral. In fact, 75% of all tweets project the organisation in neutral terms, whereas the remaining tweets either paint a more positive picture or, interestingly, do not mention the UN at all. This is again true for both institutional and individual handles. In other words, among the 1,293 tweets coded from the UN, there are only two tweets that express concern about the institution as such. With virtually no reference to any shortcomings or weaknesses, the UN image conveyed is one based on neutral statements with moderately advanced indications of its potential for greater good under certain conditions (e.g., when supported by Member States and speaking with one voice) (see Figure 7.5).

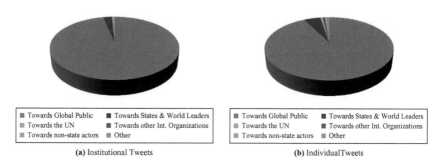

(a) Institutional Tweets   (b) Individual Tweets

FIGURE 7.4 Direction of UN tweets during 73rd session (n = 1,293)

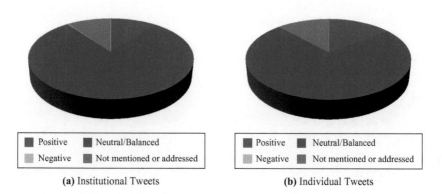

(a) Institutional Tweets   (b) Individual Tweets

FIGURE 7.5 Image of UN in UN tweets during 73rd session (n = 1,293)

Comparing these results to those tweeting *at* the UN (i.e., state and non-state institutions and individual representatives), some differences emerge. In terms of content, state and non-state actors in their institutional as well as individual representation refer to the UN less frequently. This is particularly true for individual handles where only one-quarter of all tweets directly speak about the UN. Overall, the organisation as such is more frequently mentioned as it relates to particular topics rather than the other way around. Among those topics, environment and health issues are almost not tweeted about at all. Rather, the more traditional UN responsibilities of development, security, and human rights are covered at greater length. Furthermore, among individual tweets, issues of human rights and security are far more likely to be tweeted while environment and health once again are not covered in the same amount of detail. Taken together, comparing state and non-state handles with UN handles, the topics tweeted about do not correspond. In other words, the *UN Twittersphere* does not seem to represent a cohesive public sphere in which relevant actors care about similar issues but rather breaks down into different spheres as different actors try to gain "airspace" for their own concerns and topics (see Figure 7.6).[24]

As to the purpose of tweets, both state and non-state institutions are more likely to share controversial statements and hence initiate debate. While still limited in terms of mobilisation and with only a few direct calls for action, at least there seems to be an understanding of the importance of discussing political topics critically and of opening oneself up to the global audience in this regard. In that regard, state institutions seem to have a very different understanding of what Twitter provides or at least are using this to send a different message. More specifically, for them it is essential to "deliver their own nations' narrative and countering those that are contrary to their nations' interests" (Seib 2016, 131). However, and quite notably, taking a closer look at the individual handles and comparing the missions with their leaders, permanent representatives focus as much on information-sharing as did the UN handles. In other words, the individual representatives are far more reluctant to engage in debate and seem to follow a more cautious script of diplomacy with few personal reflections and

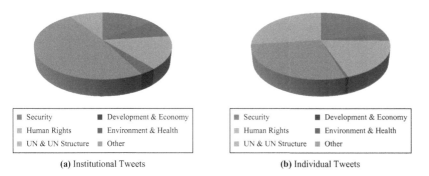

■ Security	■ Development & Economy
■ Human Rights	■ Environment & Health
■ UN & UN Structure	■ Other

(a) Institutional Tweets

■ Security	■ Development & Economy
■ Human Rights	■ Environment & Health
■ UN & UN Structure	■ Other

(b) Individual Tweets

FIGURE 7.6 Content of state and non-state tweets during 73rd session (n = 1,356)

opinions included. In fact, UN individuals voted into office by state representatives seem to be speaking more freely then the ambassadors. This indicates that individuals are much more cautious in their use of social media than institutions and that foreign services feature stronger protocols and hierarchies than the UN (see Figure 7.7).[25]

In terms of directing one's tweets, the results from state and non-state handles echo those of the UN handles. Again, the audience in both institutional and individual handles, for the most part, remains undefined as tweets are not addressed in any particular way. As such, state and non-state actors use Twitter just as the UN, as a generic message board in international diplomacy. In other words, the *UN Twittersphere* remains limited in its engagement as actors involved do not address each other directly or hold each other accountable. This is surprising to the extent that one could have expected at least that state actors use Twitter to directly engage other permanent missions in "twiplomacy" as an alternative or at least supplement for traditional outreach. If anything, such outreach marginally manifests in the individual tweeting when Nikki Haley and Karen Pierce in a few tweets address other members of the Security Council or conflict parties elsewhere. Overall, however, direct outreach remains scarce as state and non-state actors leave their audience(s) undefined. Just as with purposes, directing tweets is driven by caution and by the intention to not become the target of any particular campaign by not targeting anyone else. While reasonable from an institutional perspective, it remains disappointing from a communicative action perspective (Figure 7.8).

Finally, in terms of the UN image conveyed through their tweets, the institutional accounts of both state and non-state actors remain rather neutral again, with only a few negative references balanced out by a similar small number of positive remarks. This is true for all missions (including China and Russia) and UNA-USA, which echoes the neutral image of the UN handles.[26] On the individual level, on the contrary, we find a significant amount of tweets criticising the UN or simply not addressing it at all. Here, the image of the UN shared diverges significantly from the self-image expressed in the UN tweets as the individuals express strong criticism of the UN. Interestingly, if you recall the

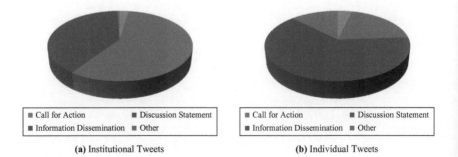

(a) Institutional Tweets　　　　　　　(b) Individual Tweets

FIGURE 7.7 Purpose of state and non-state tweets during 73rd session (n = 1,356)

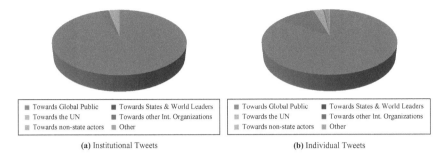

(a) Institutional Tweets   **(b)** Individual Tweets

FIGURE 7.8   Direction of state and non-state tweets during 73rd session (n = 1,356)

purpose of their tweets, this critical image is mostly shared through information and not turned into a discussion of the UN. In other words, individual state and non-state actors simply present the UN in a negative fashion but also remain unwilling to engage in public discussion. Thus, while they differ from the UN handles in overall assessment, their assessment to them is based on "facts." In other words, their criticism, just as the rosy picture shared by the UN itself, is not part of any public deliberation or subject to change (Figure 7.9).

In light of the normative standards following from Habermas' *Communicative Action*, granted that those are rather high, the *UN Twittersphere* seems not to exhaust its full potential to engage. More drastically, both the UN handles as well as state and non-state handles do not reflect the ideal type of communicative reasoning. Rather, the UN itself apparently follows an instrumental PR logic while other actors are not willing to debate or contest this approach. More specifically, what really stands out for the UN is that the organisation is only communicating *to* rather than communicating *with* the global public. Lecturing and self-referencing rather than debating, the UN handles treat their audience(s) as passive consumers instead of informed citizens interested in debate. Almost mimicking

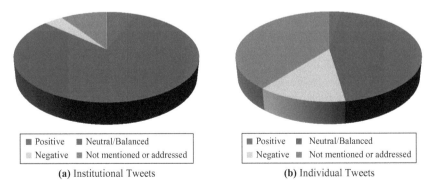

(a) Institutional Tweets   **(b)** Individual Tweets

FIGURE 7.9   Image of UN in state and non-state tweets during 73rd session (n = 1,356)

traditional media and thus not fully understanding the unique nature of social media (yet), one-way messages are *broadcast* rather than *shared* to initiate dialogue. As to state and non-state actors, while quite intensively using the new medium, reluctance remains as they "may neither understand nor believe that social media is the cure-all for organizational communication efforts" (Lovejoy et al. 2012, 316). Not connecting the two, missed opportunities to engage broader global audiences – whether through the climate crisis that Antonio Guterres cares about or through an honest and open debate about the role of the UN and future multilateralism – can be found in abundance.

As such, between those who tweet *for* the UN and those who tweet *at* the UN, a mismatch between the topics they tweet about remains. Given that information provides the foundation for any discourse, overall a clear imbalance between information dissemination and discussion (and the obvious lack of any mobilisation or generating support) remains, specifically since most of the information shared remains vague or generic. This genericity is echoed through the mutual non-specification of any particular audience. While Twitter quite obviously creates more than one public and public spheres are much more diverse than Habermas anticipated (Bruns and Highfield 2016; see also Fraser 1992), there is a loss of communicative engagement as they remain blatantly vague and unspecified again. Finally, considering the UN image, a dimension in which, despite all self-references, there is little recognition of the limitations of the organisation, the UN uses Twitter, it seems, mostly to generate a brand while state actors feel they are limited by diplomatic protocol. Overall, there is little creative use of the Twittersphere to capitalise on the advantages this new medium offers. In the bigger picture, the *UN Twittersphere* must be read as a missed opportunity. The concluding section will place this interpretation into the larger context of IOs, legitimacy, and the alleged crisis of global governance.

Conclusion and further research

Against the criticism of lacking legitimacy and accountability, the UN and other IOs over the last decade have committed themselves more heavily to "public diplomacy" and began to more directly engage with their stakeholders (Ecker-Ehrhardt 2018; Nye 2010). Against these developments, this research started with the assumption that social media in this quest for legitimacy could play a crucial role since it has the potential to project one's own messages directly to a global audience with little cost and no delay or filtering. Drawing on Habermas and his communicative action theory, the chapter sought to assess the UN's use of Twitter to publicly communicate as an organisation. Better understanding the use as well as the potential of social media seem important since the UN has indeed rather comprehensively embraced new forms of communication while IR scholars are only slowly catching up, at least compared to other fields (Bouchard, this volume). Often disregarded as either just an "echo chamber" for established political opinion or confined to private users, the role of Twitter in particular in public communication in world politics has not been fully considered yet as vast amounts of data – whether tweets from the president, from other high-ranked individuals, or from other international organisations and their representatives – wait to be explored (Murthy 2011). In an attempt not to test but rather apply Habermas' theory to provide insights into the *UN Twittersphere* and assess the quality of communicative action and public engagement within, the chapter discussed how institutions and individuals within as well as towards the UN use Twitter and thereby ascribe meaning to this unique organisation. More than 2.500 tweets from 22 different handles collected during the 73rd UN Session in 2018 were coded. Representing just a small sample of the UN *Twittersphere*, results obviously remain limited. As a snapshot, though, two preliminary conclusions stand out which deserve further discussion.

First, communication through social media and Twitter is still new for the UN, seems to be used only reluctantly, and thus remains limited when measured in terms of communicative action. Compared to other established forms of outreach, the *UN Twittersphere* is significantly less organised and coordinated, despite pull from the organisation to mainstream its different handles. It is also used more cautiously with less commitment. In this context, the fact that neither institutional nor individual UN handles are willing to express even the mildest form of self-criticism or indicate willingness to engage in deliberation is revealing. Thus, as it stands, Twitter does not constitute a tool of discursive engagement but rather serves as an organisational "echo chamber" of validation and promotion. Unlike, for example, the momentum created by #metoo or #FridaysForFuture, the *UN Twittersphere* falls short to sustain any kind of campaigns, potentially due to limited resources or because individual actors involved do not care about it. While Twitter serves as a constitutive element in individual identity construction – "I tweet, therefore I am" (Murthy 2012) – and in that regard offers authentic communication, organisational use by the UN, at least for now, remains distanced and arguably less impactful. In fact, the *UN Twittersphere* might diminish the legitimacy of the UN as such. After all, with global audiences listening, the impact of social media narratives remains highly conditional on the way they are presented and translated into real-world policies:

> For a narrative to be effective, it must have substance behind it. Mere glibness will not suffice and even respected world leaders will be held accountable if their promises are not backed up by solid policy.
>
> *(Seib 2016, 131–2)*

Second, while the *UN Twittersphere* remains limited when considered as communicative action, it nevertheless continues to grow as more and more institutions and individuals become involved. Assumingly, while not fully convinced by the medium or confident to use it, different handles still seem to feel compelled to be active in the first place. The fact that the UN Secretary-General only joined Twitter when he joined office is a case in point. Furthermore, the frequency of tweeting as well as the tone differ dramatically as some agencies such as the Department for Political Affairs or the ECOSOC President tweet rather seldom and only to the extent seemingly necessary. Even @antonioguterres and the UN Social Media team behind him tweet only occasionally with an average of 1.27 tweets per day since in office.[27] Equally important, even in relative terms to Twitter character limits, his tweets remain rather sober and terse while @UN often tweets in rather strong terms, creating a mismatch that stands out when one retweets the other. All of this reflects that while recognising the importance of social media, the willingness and capacity to embrace and use new media meaningfully differs among and between different accounts of the UN. Sad as it is, there might be a reason why the UN has less followers than individual politicians or celebrities.

As to further research, with the *UN Twittersphere* database now established, comparative projects over longer time periods as well as in light of particular crises could be advanced to see how the conclusions of this chapter hold over time in with other data. For example, a detailed follow-up study could look into the WHO's use of Twitter during CoViD-19. Further research could also utilise social network analysis, considering in particular the amount of retweeting to map out who is connected within the *UN Twittersphere*. This could, on the one hand, show connections between UN agencies to address issues of organisational dynamics, or, on the other hand, consider connections between different missions and ambassadors. Such a map of virtual exchange could be related and compared to what is going on in the real UN. This could further be complemented by an analysis on voting behaviour and public opinion to see whether social media indeed influences outcomes at and perception of the UN. All in all, given that the UN continues to expand its social media presence, scholars interested in this organisation have a lot of ground to cover. While tweeting alone will save no succeeding generation from the scourge of war, the UN will tweet about future wars and we thus need to understand the potential of this new form of communication to our best knowledge. Hopefully, such recognition will help push the *UN Twittersphere* forward to become more meaningful and impactful in the ongoing quest towards organisational legitimacy.

Notes

1 I would like to thank Julia Juarez, Javier Roman, Sara-Madeleine Torres, and Veronica Vazquez who provided research assistance for this project and coded the majority of tweets in the analysis as well as Ben Shirani for developing the API for collecting and coding.

2 Following Treem and Leonardi (2016, 145–6), I think of social media as those outlets in which the user, individual or institutional, is responsible for the generation of content and its exchange with others. Among others, social media thus includes blogs, wikis, social networking services, and social tagging, with Facebook, Twitter, Tumblr, Instagram, and YouTube arguably being the most popular sites.

3 With 72,500 total tweets and almost 12 million followers, the UN's primary Twitter account (@UN – see Figure 7.1) makes it one of the most active and most followed

international organisations, http://twiplomacy.com/organisation/un/un, last retrieved January 15, 2020. In addition to Twitter, there are four UN channels on YouTube, 13 official UN appearances on Facebook, and smaller presences on Flickr, Google+, Pinterest, Tumblr, Instagram, LinkedIn, Snapchat, and Medium. See http://www.un.org/en/sections/about-website/un-social-media/index.html for a full list.

4 The main UN Twitter account (@UN) was created in March 2008 just two years after Twitter was launched. At the same time, with important handles such as the ones of the General Assembly and the ECOSOC President (see discussion below) not starting to tweet until 2012, the use of social media within the UN, just like "traditional media" represents an ongoing process of trial and error and organisational learning (Crossette 2007).

5 Arguably, toddler stage might describe the field more accurately with "IR scholars … increasingly recognizing the importance of social media in world politics" but lacking coherent frameworks let alone producing consensus in high-ranked IR journals (Duncombe 2017, 549).

6 See https://www.similarweb.com/top-websites for a detailed ranking of social media websites and the Tables for numbers on UN Twitter handles.

7 Joas and Knöbl (2009, 234–5) expand on this argument and describe communicative action as different from strategic action based on "the fact that it suspends the validity of predetermined goals, because it resolves around honest discussion with other people, which cannot and must not be aimed at achieving a fixed goal."

8 See https://twitter.com/un, last retrieved January 15, 2020. How many of these are fake accounts or automated bots is beyond the scope of this paper.

9 See http://www.un.org/en/sections/departments/department-global-communications/news-media/index.html, last retrieved January 15, 2020.

10 The distinction between institutional and individual is helpful beyond the *UN Twittersphere* since it captures, for example, also the dynamics between @POTUS and @realDonaldTrump with the institutional account, featuring 22.5 million followers, being passed on from his predecessor and his individual handle sitting at almost 49 million followers. Thelwall and Cugelman (2017, 654) use a similar framework as they distinguish between "corporate" and "personal" accounts.

11 Despite the trend that nation states invest more into their social media presence (Barbera and Zeitzoff 2018), it is interesting to note that not every permanent mission nor every head delegate to the UN has their own account (yet). Furthermore, these distinctions are obviously ideal-types and thus gradual as well as relative. For example, a strong ECOSOC President tweeting from his institutional handle could represent his own individual views while an individual Executive Director, who strictly follows institutional protocol while using her individual handle, could echo official UN views. As a practical rule of thumb to distinguish between institutional and individual handles, I used the simple proxy of whether or not an identifiable individual was in charge of a handle (i.e., whether the handle featured an individual's name or not), assuming that this would allow them to fill their Twitter presence in different ways and potentially offer different content.

12 See http://sdg.iisd.org/events/73rd-session-of-the-un-general-assembly/, last retrieved January 15, 2020, for further information. During those three weeks, the 56 handles outlined below sent out a total of 5,353 tweets.

13 See https://www.un.org/sg/en/content/senior-management-group, last retrieved January 20, 2020. Rosemary A. DiCarlo, Under-Secretary of Political and Peacebuilding Affairs, Jeffrey D. Feltman, Under-Secretary-General for Political Affairs, and Catherine Pollard, Under-Secretary-General for General Assembly and Conference Management were not active on Twitter by the time of research.

14 The other Permanent Representatives are either not on Twitter (China) or did not tweet throughout the 73rd UN Session last year (France and Russia). For a broader debate on dynamics between permanent and non-permanent Security Council

members and why one should consider permanent members in particular, see Hurd (2002).

15 See https://research.un.org/en/ngo, last retrieved January 20, 2020.
16 See Tables 7.4–7.9 for an overview of all Twitter handles considered including the total number of tweets for each handle. This selection of handles obviously reflects only certain parts of the *UN Twittersphere* and does not include direct responses of a broader audience. However, I contend that the quality of communicative action in and through the *UN Twittersphere* can at least be approximated by looking at the three faces of the UN outlined above. In other words, I am interested in whether and how the UN and other actors involved engage in communicative action rather than determining whether they succeed and reach their audience(s). Further research might thus focus on whether and how different audiences respond and how this in turn influences the quality of communicative action.
17 In contrast to other social media platforms, Twitter provides rather comprehensive access to its data through its API. The now established and ongoing collection of UN tweets allows future research in light of special events or emergency meetings in the future and I am happy to share tweet data upon request.
18 During mass coding, we noticed that many tweets reflected at least two different topics. In these instances, the primary focus was coded (i.e., a tweet arguing for development through gender equality was coded as economic). Arguably, however, the choice to connect certain topics and their particular combinations reveals deeper logics of reasoning and thus should be revisited as an issue in further research.
19 Examples from the sampling included calls for ceasefires, preventing climate change, or supporting refugees.
20 Simply put, anything that reflected an expressed opinion on the topic at hand fell under this code. As such, I included the sharing of "facts" in this dimension as long as (a) the facts are contested and (b) the author presented them in an argumentative fashion. For example, a tweet that stated that torture during interrogations is illegal, immoral, and ineffective was coded as a discussion statement. The same tweet would have been coded as a call for action if the author had added that "all Member States are called upon to stop using torture during interrogations."
21 This does not represent a comprehensive list of actors in global governance necessarily but reflects the most commonly advanced substantial answers to the question of who governs the world. For a more advanced theoretical discussion on agency in global governance see Hofferberth (2019) and Franke and Roos (2010).
22 As such, well-intended and benevolent criticism based on the assumption, that the UN has the potential to meet its ambitious goals, was coded as a positive image whereas finite criticism not seeing a role for the UN to play in a world of nation states was coded as negative.
23 This echoes the results from the Twiplomacy report on user engagement throughout the same time period, see https://twiplomacy.com/blog/following-unga-2018-looking-engagement-followers/ for more details.
24 Given that we only coded tweets from permanent Security Council Member States, the focus on security is not surprising. At the same time, each of these states is also active in a wide range of other UN bodies and hence other topics should be discussed in the missions as well. If anything, this is an indication that in external communication, "hard issues" to prove UN relevance remain salient.
25 Note that from the P5 ambassadors, only Nikki Haley (USA) and Karen Pierce (UK) tweeted during the time period considered and hence this result remains rather limited and potentially anecdotal. That said, however, is it still nevertheless interesting that in particular these two UN representatives tread lightly on political issues in their own social media, given that the represent powerful and democratic countries and are otherwise, at least in the case of the USA, quite vocal about the UN.
26 Looking at the different handles separately, only UN Watch does not fit into this pattern since it is significantly more critical of the UN.

27 As of January 30, 2019, Antonio Guterres has been in office for 1,124 days and sent only a total of 1,422 tweets. Not necessarily the best role model, @realDonaldTrump exceeded that number within the last two months alone.

References

Acharya, Amitav. *Why Govern? Rethinking Demand and Progress in Global Governance.* Cambridge: Cambridge University Press, 2016.

Anderson, Emily. "Micro-Policy Discourse and Girls' Education in the #Post-2015 Agenda." *International Perspectives on Education & Society* 35 (2018): 21–45.

Archer, Clive. *International Organizations.* London: Routledge, 1983.

Barbera, Pablo, and Thomas Zeitzoff. "The New Public Address System. Why Do World Leaders Adopt Social Media?" *International Studies Quarterly* 62, no. 1 (2018): 121–30.

Berg, Bruce L., and Howard Lune. *Qualitative Methods for the Social Sciences.* New York: Pearson Longman, 2012.

Bruns, Axel, and Tim Highfield. "Is Habermas on Twitter? Social Media and the Public Sphere." In *The Routledge Companion to Social Media and Politics*, edited by A. Bruns, S56–73. New York: Routledge, 2016. In *The Routledge Companion to Social Media and Politics*, edited by Axel Bruns, Gunn Enli, Eli Skogerbo, Anders Olof Larson and Christian Christense. New York: Routledge.

Chadwick, Andrew. *The Hybrid Media System. Politics and Power.* Oxford: Oxford University Press, 2013.

Claude, Inis L. *Swords into Plowshares. The Problems and Progress of International Organizations.* New York: Random House, 1956.

Commission on Global Security, Justice & Governance. 2015. "Confronting the Crisis of Global Governance." In edited by The Hague Institute for Global Justice and the Stimson Center. https://www.stimson.org/wp-content/files/file-attachments/Commission_on_Global_Security_Justice%20_Governance_0.pdf

Crossette, Barbara. "Media." In *The Oxford Handbook on the United Nations*, edited by Thomas G. Weiss, and Sam Daws, 275–84. Oxford: Oxford University Press, 2007.

Deephouse, David L., and Mark Suchman. "Legitimacy in Organizational Institutionalism." In *The SAGE Handbook of Organizational Institutionalism*, edited by Royston Greenwood, Christine Oliver, Suddaby Roy, and Kerstin Sahlin, 49–77. London: Sage Publications, 2008.

Denskus, Tobias, and Daniel E. Esser. "Social Media and Global Development Rituals. A Content Analysis of Blogs and Tweets on the 2010 MDG Summit." *Third World Quarterly* 34, no. 3 (2013): 405–22.

Dingwerth, Klaus, Ina Lehmann, Ellen Reichel, Tobias Weise, and Antonia Witt. 2014. "Many Pipers, Many Tunes? Die Legitimationskommunikation internationaler Organisationen in komplexen Umwelten." *Politische Vierteljahreszeitschrift Sonderheft* 49: 165–90.

Duncombe, Constance. "Twitter and Transformative Diplomacy. Social Media and Iran-Us Relations." *International Affairs* 93, no. 3 (2017): 545–62.

Ecker-Ehrhardt, Matthias. "International Organizations "Going Public"? an Event History Analysis of Public Communications Reforms 1950–2015." *International Studies Quarterly* 62, no. 4 (2018): 723–36.

Franke, Ulrich, and Ulrich Roos. "Actor, Structure, Process: Transcending the State Personhood Debate by Means of a Pragmatist Ontological Model for International Relations Theory." *Review of International Studies* 36, no. 4 (2010): 1057–77.

Fraser, Nancy. "Rethinking the Public Sphere: A Contribution to the Critique of Actually Existing Democracy." In *Habermas and the Public Sphere*, edited by Craig Calhoun, 109–42. Cambridge: MIT Press, 1992.

Gervais, Bryan. "Tweeting to Victory? Social Media Use and Election 2014." In *The Roads to Congress 2014*, edited by Sean D. Foreman, and Robert Dewhirst, 59–72. London: Lexington Books, 2015.

Gronau, Jennifer, and Henning Schmidtke. "The Quest for Legitimacy in World Politics. International Institutions' Legitimation Strategies." *Review of International Studies* 42, no. 3 (2016): 535–57.

Habermas, Jürgen. The Theory of Communicative Action. Volume 1: Reason and the Rationalization of Society . Boston, MA: Beacon Press, 1981a.

Habermas, Jürgen. The Theory of Communicative Action. Volume 2: Lifeworld and System: A Critique of Functionalist Reason. Boston, MA: Beacon Press, 1981b.

Habermas, Jürgen. *Between Facts and Norms. Contributions to a Discourse Theory of Law and Democracy*. Cambridge: MIT Press, 1996.

Heath, Joseph. *Communicative Action and Rational Choice*. Cambridge, MA: MIT Press, 2001.

Hofferberth, Matthias. "Get Your Act(Ors) Together! Theorizing Agency in Global Governance." *International Studies Review* 21, no. 1 (2019): 127–45.

Hooghe, Liesbet, Tobias Lenz, and Gary Marks. "Contested World Order: The Delegitimation of International Governance." *The Review of International Organizations* 14, no. 4 (2019): 731–43.

Hopke, Jill E., and Luis E. Hestres. "Visualizing the Paris Climate Talks on Twitter: Media and Climate Stakeholder Visual Social Media During COP21." *Social Media + Society* 4, no. 3 (2018): 1–15.

Hurd, Ian. "Legitimacy, Power, and the Symbolic Life of the UN Security Council." *Global Governance* 8, no. 1 (2002): 35–51.

Hurd, Ian. "Legitimacy and Contestation in Global Governance: Revisiting the Folk Theory of International Institutions." *The Review of International Organizations* 14, no. 4 (2018): 717–29.

Joas, Hans, and Wolfgang Knöbl. *Social Theory. Twenty Introductory Lectures*. Cambridge: Cambridge University Press, 2009.

Karns, Margaret P., Karen A. Mingst, and Kendall W. Stiles. *International Organizations. The Politics and Processes of Global Governance*. Boulder: Lynne Rienner Publishers, 2015.

Keohane, Robert O. "Global Governance and Legitimacy." *Review of International Political Economy* 18, no. 1 (2011): 99–109.

Lovejoy, Kristen, Richard D. Waters, and Gregory D. Saxton. "Engaging Stakeholders Through Twitter; How Nonprofit Organizations Are Getting More out of 140 Characters or Less." *Public Relations Review* 38, no. 2 (2012): 313–8.

Macnamara, Jim, and Ansgar Zerfass. "Social Media Communication in Organizations: The Challenges of Balancing Openness, Strategy, and Management." *International Journal of Strategic Communication* 6, no. 4 (2012): 287–308.

Moore, John Allphin Jr., and Jerry Pubantz. *The New United Nations. International Organization in the Twenty-First Century*. New York: Routledge, 2017.

Morozov, Evgeny. *The Net Delusion. The Dark Side of Internet Freedom*. New York: Public Affairs, 2011.

Müller, Harald. "Arguing, Bargaining and All That: Communicative Action, Rationalist Theory and the Logic of Appropriateness in International Relations." *European Journal of International Relations* 10, no. 3 (2004): 395–435.

Murthy, Dhiraj. "Twitter: Microphone for the Masses?" *Media, Culture & Society* 33, no. 5 (2011): 779–89.

Murthy, Dhiraj. "Towards a Sociological Understanding of Social Media: Theorizing Twitter." *Sociology* 46, no. 6 (2012): 1059–73.

Nahon, Karine. "Where There Is Social Media There Is Politics." In *The Routledge Companion to Social Media and Politics*, edited by Axel Bruns, Gunn Enli, Eli Skogerbo, Anders Olof Larson, and Christian Christense, 39–55. New York: Routledge, 2016.

Nye, Joseph T. "The New Public Diplomacy." 2010. https://www.project-syndicate.org/commentary/the-new-public-diplomacy?barrier=accesspaylog

Owen, David S. *Between Reason and History. Habermas and the Idea of Progress.* Albany: SUNY Press, 2002.

Risse, Thomas. "Let's Argue!": Communicative Action in World Politics." *International Organization* 54, no. 1 (2000): 1–39.

Risse, Thomas. "Global Governance and Communicative Action." *Government & Opposition* 39, no. 2 (2004): 288–313.

Ross, Karen, and Tobias Bürger. "Face to Face(Book): Social Media, Political Campaigning and the Unbearable Lightness of Being There." *Political Science* 66, no. 1 (2014): 46–62.

Schreier, Magrit. *Qualitative Content Analysis in Practice.* Thousand Oaks, CA: Sage Publications Ltd, 2012.

Seib, Philip. *Real-Time Diplomacy. Politics and Power in the Social Media Era.* Houndsmills: Palgrave Macmillan, 2012.

Seib, Philip. *The Future of Diplomacy.* Cambridge: Polity Press, 2016.

Smith, Brian G., and Tiffany Derville Gallicano. "Terms of Engagement: Analyzing Public Engagement with Organizations Through Social Media." *Computers in Human Behavior* 53 (2015): 82–90.

Tallberg, Jonas, Karin Bäckstrand, and Jan Aart Scholte. *Legitimacy in Global Governance. Sources, Processes, and Consequences.* Oxford: Oxford University Press, 2018.

Tallberg, Jonas, and Michael Zürn. "The Legitimacy and Legitimation of International Organizations. Introduction and Framework." *The Review of International Organizations* 14, no. 4 (2019): 581–606.

Taylor, Charles. "Language and Society." In *Communicative Action. Essays on Jürgen Habermas's the Theory of Communicative Action*, edited by Alex Honneth, and Hans Joas, 23–35. Cambridge, MA: MIT Press, 1991.

Thelwall, Mike, and Brian Cugelman. "Monitoring Twitter Strategies to DISCover Resonating Topics: The Case of UNDP." *El Profesional de la Informacion* 26, no. 4 (2017): 649–61.

Treem, Jeffrey W., and Paul M. Leonardi. "Social Media Use in Organizations. Exploring the Affordances of Visibility, Editability, Persistence, and Association." *Annals of the International Communication Association* 36, no. 1 (2016): 143–89.

Twiplomacy. *Twiplomacy Study 2018*, 2018. https://twiplomacy.com/blog/twiplomacy-study-2018/

Usherwood, Simon, and Katharine A. Wright. "Sticks and Stones: Comparing Twitter Campaigning Strategies in the European Union Referendum." *British Journal of Politics & International Relations* 19, no. 2 (2017): 371–88.

Weiss, Thomas G. *What's Wrong with the United Nations and How to Fix It.* Cambridge: Polity Press, 2009.

Weiss, Thomas G., Tatiana Carayannis, and Richard Jolly. "The Third United Nations." *Global Governance* 15, no. 1 (2009): 123–42.

Weiss, Thomas G., David P. Forsythe, Roger A. Coate, and Kelly-Kate Pease. *The United Nations and Changing World Politics.* Philadelphia, PA: Westview Press, 2010.

Zürn, Michael. "Contested Global Governance." *Global Policy* 9, no. 1 (2018): 138–45.

8

RECONCEPTUALISING AND MEASURING ONLINE PRESTIGE IN IOs

Towards a theory of prestige mobility

Ilan Manor

Introduction

Recent years have seen growing academic interest in digital diplomacy, or the use of digital technologies by diplomats, embassies, and ministries of foreign affairs (MFAs). Scholars have asserted that digital technologies enable MFAs to overcome the limitations of traditional, offline diplomacy. Such is the case with virtual embassies that transcend national borders (Pamment 2012), the use of smartphone applications to deliver consular aid during crises (Manor 2019), and the employment of web forums to strengthen ties with distant Diasporas (Murti and Zaharna 2014). This chapter seeks to examine the relationship between online and offline prestige and to investigate whether digital diplomacy creates conditions in which states may offset prestige deficits. Previous studies have conceptualised prestige as a diplomatic institution's centrality to a network of its peers (Alger and Brams 1967; Kinne 2014; Small and Singer 1973). Following suit, this chapter examines nations' centrality in Twitter networks of diplomatic institutions.

Notably, online diplomacy does not mirror offline diplomacy. Following another nation on Twitter is not akin to opening an embassy in a foreign capital, an act that constitutes official diplomatic relations between two states. Indeed, enemy states, who do not officially recognise one another, tend to follow one another online. The Israeli MFA, for instance, follows the official Twitter accounts of Bahrain, Iraq, Kuwait, Morocco, Oman, and Saudi Arabia. Moreover, the cost of following one's counterpart online is far more economical than establishing a brick and mortar embassy.

Scholars have also begun to explore the relationship between online and offline diplomacy. For instance, studies have found that digital communications can help manage a state's offline image and increase its Soft Power resources

(Metzgar 2012). Other times, states use digital platforms to demonstrate their adherence with accepted norms and values thus creating a receptive environment for their foreign policy goals (Manor 2017; Natarajan 2014). This chapter contributes to the aforementioned literature by elucidating the relationship between online and offline prestige. It does so by examining whether digital activities can help states overcome offline prestige deficits. Moreover, the chapter demonstrates that the emergence of digital diplomacy offers scholars the ability to reconceptualise and even measure traditional concepts such as prestige.

Following the work of Manor and Pamment (2019) the chapter begins by reconceptualising and redefining online prestige as consisting of three elements: *Presence*, or the online interest a diplomatic institution generates among its peers; *Centrality*, or a diplomatic institution's status as a hub of information among its peers; and *Reputation*, or the perceived attractiveness and "goodness" of a state among its peers. Next, the chapter uses a sample of MFAs and UN Missions to identify those factors that contribute to both online and offline prestige. This is achieved through the employment of network analyses and statistical modelling. Both of these demonstrate that online prestige does not mirror offline prestige. Rather, online prestige rests on Hard Power resources (e.g., GDP Per Capita), digital savviness (following peers and sharing information), and perceived goodness. The results of this chapter indicate that digital diplomacy enables a state to perform an act of prestige mobility and boost its standing among its peers. The chapter focuses on UN venues as these have been shown to level the playing field of diplomacy, often dominated by nations with abundant Hard Power resources.

Finally, the chapter argues that prestige mobility can boost the legitimacy of IOs, including but not limited to the UN. Recent geopolitical processes such as the election of Donald Trump, the rise of populism in Europe and the United Kingdom's decision to exit the European Union have all challenged the legitimacy of IOs as national interests surpass those of the international community. In Eastern Europe, the UK, and the USA, IOs have been labelled as financial liabilities at best, and a threat to national sovereignty at worst. Yet prestige mobility indirectly strengthens IOs as peripheral states may challenge dominant powers. In other words, prestige mobility exhibits that IOs create a more levelled diplomatic playing field in which peripheral states can shape the global agenda.

Literature review

The emergence of digital diplomacy

The past decade has seen the mass adoption of digital technologies by MFAs. The emergence of digital diplomacy is a truly global phenomenon with MFAs from the Global South being as active as their Western peers online (Kampf, Manor, and Segev 2015). Non-Western MFAs have also been early adopters of digital technologies with the Kenyan MFA being the first in the world to evacuate its citizens from a foreign country using Twitter (Manor 2019). Diplomats now often use digital technologies to overcome the limitations of traditional diplomacy. Such was the case in 2008 when Sweden launched the first global embassy on the virtual world of Second Life (Pamment 2012). The embassy was meant to serve as a culture institute hosting gallery openings, film festivals, and lectures, while exposing global publics to Swedish culture.

Diplomats have also used digital technologies to overcome lack of diplomatic representation. Such was the case when the USA launched a virtual embassy to Iran (Metzgar 2012) or when the Palestinian government launched a Facebook embassy to Israel (Manor and Holmes 2018). In both cases, digital technologies enabled diplomats to interact with audiences beyond their reach as the USA and Iran have no formal ties while Palestine has no official diplomatic representation in Israel. Additionally, digital technologies have been employed to converse with critical online publics. Following President Obama's 2009 "New Beginning" address to the Muslim world, the State Department's Digital Outreach Team interacted with Muslim internet users, reiterating America's commitment to peacefully resolve crises with Muslim states (Khatib, Dutton, and Thelwall 2012).

While MFAs have adopted a host of digital technologies, ranging from web forums to internet chat rooms, smartphone applications, big data analytics, and messaging applications (Bjola, Cassidy and Manor 2019; Seib 2012; Seib 2016; Seo and Kinsey 2013), most focus their activities on social media platforms such as Facebook, Twitter, and LinkedIn (Bjola and Holmes 2015; Crilley, Gillespie, and Willis 2019; Spry 2018). It is currently estimated that 90% of UN Member States have established some form of social media presence (Manor and Segev 2020). Of these, Twitter is the most dominant featuring some 800 accounts managed by heads of state and governments. With this mass migration to Twitter, questions of relative influence, power, and even prestige have come to the fore as evident in rankings of these accounts' connectivity, audience size, and rates of engagement (Twiplomacy Study, Soft Power 30).

Importantly, MFAs and embassies migrated to social media to follow their peers. By following its peers on Twitter, an embassy or MFA can anticipate other nations' policy shifts or identify their policy priorities. Moreover, an MFA may assess possible objections to its own policy agenda. Recent studies suggest that MFAs and embassies increasingly follow one another on Twitter (Manor and Pamment 2019). For instance, the Polish ministry closely followed the Russian MFA on Twitter to monitor the possible escalation of the Crimean Crisis; the Lithuanian MFA has established listening units tasked with monitoring the Twitter accounts of neighbouring states while Israeli diplomats routinely monitor press statements published by their peers (Cassidy and Manor 2016; Manor 2019).

To summarise, studies suggest that digital diplomacy can be viewed as complementing and extending a nation's offline physical presence, while providing new opportunities for public engagement (Hocking et al. 2012; Neumann 2012). However, most studies have focused on the MFA or governmental level rather than that of the embassy. Yet embassies are often the most eager and innovative users of social media as they have lost their role as crucial intermediaries between capitals (Archetti 2012). In the age of emails, smartphones and constant global summits, world leaders and MFA policy makers can easily converse with one another, leading embassies to focus more on digital outreach. In addition, studies have yet to investigate the use of social media by UN Missions. This a substantial gap given that IOs such as the UN offer niche venues in which all states play an important role. As a former Israeli Ambassador to Geneva stated in an interview, "In Geneva every nation counts as one vote. A good Ambassador will be as engaged with his European peers as with his African ones."

Most importantly, studies to date have struggled to identify methodologies and conceptualisations that can support the assertion that digital technologies help overcome offline limitations or reconfigure power relations. One way of doing so is by examining networks of diplomatic institutions while analysing differences between online and offline prestige. This chapter analyses both offline and online networks of diplomatic institutions, specifically networks of UN Missions on Twitter. As such, it attempts to explore whether nations may overcome prestige deficits and perform an act of upward prestige mobility, or whether some nations suffer prestige deficits, thus performing an act of downward prestige mobility. This investigation is necessary if scholars are to separate hype from reality and effectively demonstrate that social media can aid nations overcome the limitations of offline diplomacy.

This chapter draws on classical studies that have conceptualised prestige based on measurements of the bilateral, brick and mortar embassy system. Yet the chapter also adapts these to the realm of social media by analysing the Twitter Networks of 67 MFAs and 33 Missions to the UN in New York (NY) and Geneva. First, the chapter reports on an analysis conducted in 2019 based on data gathered from Twitter in 2015. Next, the chapter offers a 2020 analysis of the UN networks, which investigates how these networks have evolved over a five-year period, while identifying additional factors that can contribute to prestige mobility including digital savviness. Firstly, however, the chapter reviews previous conceptualisations and measurements of prestige.

Defining and measuring prestige

To date, only a handful of studies have attempted to define, or calculate, prestige. Alger and Brams (1967 and 2967) calculated the number of diplomats each nation sends abroad, the number of diplomats it hosts in its capital, the difference between the two figures, and the average size of a nation's embassy abroad (Alger and Brams 1967, 646). While Alger and Brams did not calculate prestige per se, they did attempt to calculate the importance of a nation to the exchange of information among diplomats, and subsequently, to the international system. Notably, Small and Singer (1973) argue that the number of embassies based in a capital represents "some consensus as to how important the recipient state is to all" other states in the international system (ibid, 578).

Alger and Brams (1967, 654) further postulate that prestige lies in the "balance" between how much the world reports on a given state and how much that state reports to the world. Prestige thus relates to the world's interest in a specific state. Similarly, Kinne (2014) argues that diplomatic networks form around nations that are deemed as salient in the international community. Network hubs are considered prestigious as they act as centres for the exchange of information, ideas, and resources. As such, prestige arises from perception as one state is recognised by all others as an important source of information.

Harold Nicolson's classic definition of prestige from 1937 identifies an additional component, and that is reputation. Prestigious countries' reputations are "derived from previous character, achievements or associations; or especially from past success (Nicolson, 1937)." Nicolson asserts that prestige also stems from the influence of reputation on perceptions of power as well as a sense of historical romance that generates glamour.

To summarise, previous studies have conceptualised prestige through three parameters: *Centrality* to information exchange, *Presence* or interest in a nation, and *Reputation* emanating from the perceived salience of a nation to the international system.

Neumayer (2008) examined why nations establish embassies in some states but not others. Using statistical analysis, Neumayer found that nations are more likely to be represented among their closest neighbours, among nations with greater economic or military power, and thus perceived international importance, and among nations who share their ideology. These all attest to *Presence*, or the world's relative interest in a state. Maliniak and Plouffe (2011) found that nations open embassies given the desire to join an extensive diplomatic network. Using network analysis, the authors found that nations open embassies in capitals that already host many diplomats, thus gaining accesses to an important player in the international system while also engaging with many other actors. In other words, *Centrality* influences the number of embassies hosted in a capital.

The aforementioned studies offer initial insight into how online and offline prestige may be measured. First, through Hard Power rankings such as economic power (e.g., GDP Per Capita). Second, through the level of interest from one's peers. Online prestige can also be measured through the language that diplomats employ on social media as this attests to ideology and cultural proximity within the digital realm. Lastly, online centrality may be measured through levels of interest from epistemic communities (Mai'a 2013) or stakeholders that are associated with diplomacy. Studies have found that when communicating online, diplomats prioritise four target audiences, or epistemic communities: media institutions, think tanks, policy makers, and the diplomatic milieu including multilateral institutions (Cassidy and Manor 2016; Bjola 2019).

While *Reputation* is less quantifiable, terms such as "attraction" and "reputation" have been used in policy reports that convey a similar idea to prestige. The *Soft Power Index*, first published in 2010, uses 66 metrics to rank the Soft Power of states, or their ability to obtain foreign policy goals through attraction and persuasion (Nye 1990). The metrics include government, culture, education, global engagement, and digital. *The Good Country Index*, first published in 2014, measures the contribution of each country to the global community. It offers measurements in seven categories including science and technology, culture, international peace and security, world order, plants and climate, prosperity and equality, and health and well-being. Together, these indices which cover aspects of reputation, attraction, and perceived goodness, may be synonymous with the perception-based aspects of prestige first addressed by Nicolson (1937).

The studies reviewed thus far support a conceptualisation of prestige that centres on a) relative *Presence*, or interest within the international community, b) *Centrality* in terms of information exchange, and c) *Reputation* or one's attractiveness among one's peers. Notably, while *Presence* or interest in a state may stem from its Hard Power resources, *Reputation* is more dependent on Soft Power resources such as the perceived goodness of a state. This chapter focuses its analysis on these three factors as they can all be operationalised and measured. In the offline realm, *Presence* can be calculated through the number of embassies deployed to a state's capital, and the number of embassies that same state deploys abroad. In the online realm, *Presence* can be calculated by the number of peers an MFA attracts on Twitter, and the number of peers it follows in return. The online *Centrality* of an MFA or UN Mission among a network of its peers may be measured using network analysis while online and offline *Reputation* may be measured through the Good Country Index.

However, the online realm does not necessarily mirror the offline one. For instance, the UN Mission of a state that hosts few embassies may become central to online exchanges of information by disseminating information from the network's core to its periphery. In this way, a state may perform an act of upward prestige mobility enabling it to overcome prestige deficits. On the other hand, the Mission of a nation with abundant Hard Power resources may fail to publish information online thus attracting very few peers. In this case, the state in question has performed an act of downward prestige mobility while failing to convert offline influence to online interest and centrality.

In addition, prestige functions differently in different diplomatic forums. Alger and Brams (1967) found that membership in IOs provides greater opportunities for states with limited resources to play an important role in international diplomacy, as opposed to the bilateral system. They thus confirm that niche venues create opportunities for upward prestige mobility. UN forums may be of particular interest as they create a level playing field as each state counts for one vote. When investigating the work of permanent representatives to the UN, Pouliot (2011) found that diplomats from states with limited resources can become important players if they position themselves as brokers between blocs of states. Such brokers pass information between blocs and facilitate negotiations. In other words, the UN enables more peripheral states to obtain influence through information exchange.

2015 analysis

James Pamment and I conducted the first large-scale analysis of online and offline prestige. Our work was guided by five hypotheses. First, based on the existing literature, we assumed that states which host many embassies in their capitals also deploy many embassies abroad. Hosting many embassies is a signifier of prestige as it attests to the importance of a state. Moreover, states that host many embassies serve as hubs around which diplomatic network coalesce. Yet we also assumed that influential states that host many embassies will deploy many embassies abroad given a desire to maximise information-gathering and disseminating capacities. While numbers of physical embassies may determine offline prestige, the number of peers an MFA or UN Mission attracts on Twitter may be the equivalent of online prestige. Thus, we assumed that MFAs and UN Missions that attract many of their peers will also follow many peers in return, again maximising information-gathering and disseminating capacities. Notably, these hypotheses rested on the dimension of *Presence*, or interest.

Prestige has also been conceptualised as *Centrality* in information exchanges. Our second hypothesis examined whether MFAs and UN Missions with the most extensive online Presence are also the most central to online information exchange. This hypothesis therefore examined whether MFAs or UN Missions that attract many peers on Twitter become information hubs around which Twitter networks coalesce.

Online prestige differs from offline prestige as important diplomatic institutions may also attract followers from epistemic communities, or stakeholders that are relevant to diplomacy including journalists, media institutions, and multilateral institutions such as UN-related bodies. We therefore assumed that the higher the prestige of MFAs or UN Missions in terms of offline diplomatic representation, the higher their prestige in terms of followers from epistemic communities.

Finally, prestige has been conceptualised as being dependent on *Reputation*. Both Kinne (2014) and Neumayer (2008) assert that ideological and reputational factors may shape the salience of diplomatic actors in information exchange. We therefore hypothesised that MFAs and UN Missions with high prestige will be from countries that rank high on reputational indices and which have an abundance of Hard Power resources.

It should be noted that our analysis also examined digital strategies. For instance, the language used by diplomats online may influence their ability to attract their peers. Accounts that tweet in English are more likely to amass peers than accounts that tweet in Arabic or Spanish. Similarly, accounts that tweet often are more likely to attract their peers as online activity breeds followers (Kampf, Manor, and Segev 2015).

2015 sample

To test our hypothesis, we created a sample of 67 MFAs that are active on Twitter. This sample was diverse with regard to geographic location, as it included MFAs from Asia (e.g., Azerbaijan, India, Israel), Africa (e.g., Egypt, Ethiopia), Western Europe, Eastern Europe, North America, South America (Brazil, Venezuela), and Australia and New Zealand. Next, we compiled a sample of 33 UN Missions that were active online in both NY and Geneva. We decided to focus on NY and Geneva as in 2015 the number of Missions in Vienna or Rome that were active on Twitter was quite small. Importantly, the sample of the MFAs and UN Missions were also diverse in terms of culture, language, levels of economic prosperity, and diffusion of ICTs (Hilbert 2011). For a full list of each sample see Appendices 1 and 2.

2015 methods

Open source databases were used to calculate the number of physical embassies to and from each nation in the sample. The Visone network analysis software (Brandes and Wagner 2004) was used to calculate two parameters. The first was the Indegree Centrality, or the number of peers that an MFA/UN Mission attracts. The higher the Indegree Centrality of an MFA or UN Mission, the greater the level of interest in that MFA or UN Mission. Second, Betweenness Centrality measures the extent to which a network relies on an MFA or UN Mission to circulate information. Put differently, MFAs or UN Missions with high Betweenness scores are the most central nodes in a network.

Examining the role of epistemic communities was achieved by creating a sample of 540 news outlets including global news agencies (e.g., CNN, Reuters), major newspapers throughout the world (e.g., *New York Times*, Kenya's *Daily Nation*), diplomatic correspondents, and editors. This sample was compiled using open source databases listing the most influential news organisations in each nation around the world. Additionally, a sample was compiled of 43 UN-related organisations that were active on Twitter in 2015 including the UN Environment Program, the World Trade Organization, the UNHCR, and more.

New analysis in 2020

This chapter offers a new analysis of prestige mobility. To do so, the chapter returned to the sample of 33 UN Missions in January of 2020. Its main objective was to examine differences in the networks of UN Missions in NY and in Geneva in terms of network density. The past five years have seen the rapid digitalisation of diplomatic institutions around the world. While in 2015 MFAs were still adapting to digital surroundings, by 2020 many have mastered the use of social media. MFAs around the world now also offer diplomats social media training while publishing manuals with best practices for social media activities (Manor 2016). It was thus assumed that both the NY and Geneva networks had grown in density as UN Missions more eagerly followed their peers on Twitter.

Moreover, the new 2020 analysis investigated whether additional nations had attained upward prestige mobility while others may have lagged behind, performing downward prestige mobility. It is possible that over the past five years new nations have become central to online information exchange while others have neglected their digital accounts, or failed to keep up with the pace of digitalisation.

Finally, the new 2020 analysis sought to include two additional parameters into the analysis of online prestige. The first was whether being an avid follower of one's peers increases a UN Mission's centrality. Recent studies suggest that MFAs that follow their peers become more central to online networks as they are able to disseminate information from the network's periphery to its core (Manor and Segev 2020). The 2020 analysis thus included a measurement of Outdegree centrality, or the extent to which a UN Mission is an avid follower of its peers. Second, the new 2020 analysis evaluated the possible impact of digital savviness on a UN Mission's centrality. This was achieved by taking into account each nation's level of internet penetration. It is possible that a diplomat who migrated online in 2008 is more familiar with, and more adept at using, social media than one that just recently migrated online.

In summary, the variables explored in this section include Hard Power resources, namely GDP Per Capita and population size with data gathered from the CIA Factbook. The section also examined Soft Power resources through the use of the Good Country Index. Digital strategies that were evaluated included the number of tweets published in 2015, the language used on Twitter (i.e., English or other), and Outdegree centrality, or eagerly following one's peers. Finally, digital savviness was explored using internet penetration levels, which were gathered from the Internet World Stats webpage.

2015 results

In order to test our first research hypothesis, a statistical analysis examined the Pearson correlation coefficient between the number of embassies to and from each nation in our sample. Within the sample of 67 MFAs, we found a significant positive and substantial correlation ($r=0.87$, $p\leq0.01$) indicating that countries which host many embassies also deploy many embassies abroad. This was also the case with the sample of 33 UN Missions ($r=0.92$, $p\leq0.01$). Online results mirrored those of the offline analysis as MFAs and UN Missions that attracted the most interest from their peers also expressed reciprocal interest in their peers. In the MFA sample we found a significant positive correlation ($r=0.58$, $p\leq0.01$) as was the case with the UN in NY ($r=0.63$, $p\leq0.01$) and Geneva ($r=0.47$, $p\leq0.01$). Notably, the correlations from the online analysis were somewhat weaker than those obtained from the analysis of the offline, brick and mortar system. This could suggest that online diplomatic reciprocity is less binding than offline reciprocity.

Additionally, we found a significant statistical correlation between a nation's offline prestige and its MFA's ability to attract followers from epistemic communities, namely media institutions, UN-related organisations, and one's peers

($r=0.41$, $p\leq0.01$). In other words, MFAs that attracted the most epistemic followers tended to be from countries that host many embassies. This suggests a certain degree of prestige transference from the offline realm to the online one as *Presence* and *Reputation*, or perceived importance, lead to online interest. This analysis also supported our conceptualisation of online prestige as being determined by epistemic communities. Similar results were obtained from the UN in the NY sample ($r=0.40$, $p\leq0.01$) and in Geneva ($r=0.40$, $p\leq0.01$).

Finally, we employed linear regression models to explain variation in offline and online prestige. In the MFA sample, we sought to explain variation in the number of embassies hosted in a capital. The initial model included GDP Per Capita, Population Size, and Good Country Index Scores. The Good Country Index Scores did not have a significant contribution. In the final model, both GDP Per Capita and Population Size had a significant contribution. As such, offline prestige seems to rest mostly on Hard Power resources. Conversely, online prestige, measured by the numbers of peers each MFA attracts, as well as its following from epistemic communities, was explained by Good Country Index Scores, Population Size, and Language, where each had a significant contribution. Thus, variations in online prestige are influenced by Hard Power resources (population size), reputational factors (Good Country Index), and online strategies (tweeting in English). The fact that GDP Per Capita did not explain variations in online prestige suggests that reputational factors may help counterbalance limited Hard Power resources thereby enabling upward prestige mobility.

When analysing variations in the online prestige of UN Missions in Geneva, measured by the number of peers following each mission and followers from epistemic communities, Population Size did not have a significant contribution. Moreover, Good Country Index Scores were omitted from the model as they had no correlation with the online prestige of Geneva-based Missions. The final model included GDP Per Capita and Number of Tweets, which both had a significant contribution. These results indicate that online prestige in Geneva is explained by both Hard Power resources (GDP Per Capita) and digital strategies (Number of Tweets). These results indicate that online strategies, such as sharing pertinent information with one's peers, can counterweight limited Hard Power resources, thus enabling states to perform upward prestige mobility.

When analysing variations in the online prestige of UN Missions in NY, measured by the number of peers following each mission and followers from epistemic communities, the initial model included the following: GDP Per Capita, Number of Tweets, and Good Country Index Scores. GDP Per Capita did not have a significant contribution. Both Number of Tweets and Good Country Index Scores had a significant contribution. Unlike the Geneva and the MFA sample, Hard Power resources did not explain variation in the online prestige of NY Missions. Thus, this UN forum offers greater possibilities for upward prestige mobility

The aforementioned results offer three important conclusions. First, the offline and online realms of diplomacy are not entirely separate. States that attract offline interest are also likely to attract online interest. However, offline prestige is not directly transferable online. First, reciprocal following online is less binding than in the offline system of embassies. Second, online prestige is not determined solely by Hard Power resources but by a combination of Hard Power resources, Soft Power, or perceived goodness and digital strategies. This suggests that nations can use the online realm to counterweigh offline prestige deficits. Lastly, Good Country Index scores were most influential in the UN in NY while Number of Tweets was influential in both UN forums. This was not the case with the MFA sample. Thus, UN forums may serve as niche venues in which nations may overcome Hard Power or prestige deficits.

However, the 2015 analysis also suffered from several limitations. Chief among these is the fact that it was based on data from 2015. Yet in digital terms, five years is an eternity. It is possible that since 2015 more nations have incorporated social media into their diplomatic toolkit while others have developed new digital capabilities. Additionally, the analysis did not account for digital savviness, which may be an important factor. Diplomats who are more accustomed to social media may be more willing to share relevant information online thereby increasing the number of peers they attract. Third, it is possible that the networks evaluated in 2015 have grown denser over time as each Mission follows, and is followed, by a greater number of peers. This might limit a nation's ability to perform prestige mobility. To assess the manner in which the UN networks have evolved over time, this chapter returns to the NY and Geneva samples in 2020. The results of this new, updated analysis are presented in the following section.

2020 results

The 2020 analysis began by comparing the 2015 and 2020 UN networks. This comparison may be seen in Table 8.1. The NY network of Missions has grown considerably denser. In 2015, the average NY Mission attracted 23.9 of its peers out of a possible 32, while in 2020 that number rose to 29.5. This is a substantial increase considering that the sample size was 33. Additionally, in 2015, the US Mission to NY boasted the most followers with 30 out of a possible 32 peers.

TABLE 8.1 Density of NY and Geneva samples in 2015 and 2020

New York			
Year	Average Number of Peers (out of 32)	Highest Number of Peers (out of 32)	Lowest Number of Peers (out of 32)
2015	23.9	30	14
2020	29.5	32	27
Geneva			
2015	22.7	29	8
2020	25.7	30	14

In 2020 a number of Missions obtained the maximum number of 32 followers including Canada, Denmark, France and Germany. Finally, in the 2015 network Latvia attracted the smallest number of peers – 14 out of 32. In 2020, Uganda attracted the smallest number of peers – 27 out of a possible 32.

Similar yet more modest results were obtained in Geneva as each Mission gained an average of 3 peers. While in 2015 the US and Australian Missions attracted the most peers, 29 out of 32; in 2020 the UK was the only Mission to attract 30 out of a possible 32. Finally, while in 2015 Ethiopia attracted the smallest number of peers (8), in 2020 the EU attracted the smallest number of peers (14). These results indicate that while both networks have grown denser, they still differ from one another as Geneva Missions seem less likely to follow their peers on Twitter.

Moving from averages to a nation-specific analysis, Table 8.2 presents the gap between the number of peers each Mission attracted in 2015 and 2020. Positive gaps indicate that Missions have been able to attract new peers while negative gaps suggest that Missions have lost peers. Missions coloured in grey attracted the highest number of new peers.

As can be seen, with the exception of Azerbaijan, all NY Missions attracted new peers in 2020. Azerbaijan was the only Mission to lose peers since 2015. Missions that attracted the most peers were Bahrain, Iceland, India, Latvia, and the Maldives. These results are indicative of upward prestige mobility as the Missions who gained the most new peers tended to have limited offline prestige, both in terms of GDP and in terms of numbers of embassies posted to their capitals. India was the only nation to make substantial gains in both forums. The Missions that attracted the most peers in Geneva were Azerbaijan, Chile, and Finland, again nations with limited offline prestige.

While the highest gain in NY was +14 (Latvia), the highest gain in Geneva was +9 (India). Notably, two Missions in Geneva lost followers, Russia and Latvia. The Russian Mission in Geneva is demonstrative of downward prestige mobility given that Russia is a dominant world power which hosts 147 embassies in Moscow. In this case, Russia was unable to transfer offline prestige to the online realm. The aforementioned results further demonstrate that the NY network of Missions has grown denser while the density of Geneva has moderately increased. However, in both networks, nations with limited offline prestige were able to make considerable gains in terms of peers.

To further analyse the Geneva and NY samples, a linear regression model was used to identify which factors contribute to variance in Betweenness centrality. As mentioned earlier, Betweenness measures a node's centrality to exchanges of information. Several parameters were taken into account including: GDP Per Capita, Internet Penetration Rates, Outdegree centrality or the extent to which a Mission is an avid follower of its peers, and Good Country Index Scores.

Geneva centrality had a significant correlation with GDP Per Capita ($r = 0.434$, $p \leq 0.012$), Internet Penetration Rates ($r = 0.372$, $p \leq 0.033$), Outdegree centrality

TABLE 8.2 Number of peers attracted by UN Missions in 2015 and 2020

	New York Sample			Geneva Sample		
	2015	2020	Gap	2015	2020	Gap
Albania	23	30	+7	19	25	+6
Australia	26	30	+4	29	29	0
Azerbaijan*	16	10	−6	18	25	+7
Bahrain	20	29	+9	17	22	+5
Brazil	22	30	+8	18	23	+5
Canada	24	32	+8	23	27	+4
Chile	24	29	+5	15	22	+7
Denmark	27	32	+5	27	29	+2
Ethiopia	22	29	+7	8	14	+6
European Union	27	31	+4	27	28	+1
Finland	26	32	+6	19	27	+8
France	25	30	+5	27	29	+2
Georgia	25	31	+6	22	27	+5
Germany	28	32	+4	24	28	+4
Iceland	21	32	+11	23	27	+4
India	17	28	+11	16	25	+9
Italy	25	30	+5	20	25	+5
Israel	21	25	+4	21	25	+4
*Latvia	14	28	+14	25	24	−1
Maldives	16	28	+12	15	20	+5
Mexico	20	28	+8	21	23	+2
Netherland	27	32	+5	28	28	0
New Zealand	28	31	+3	26	29	+3
Norway	26	31	+5	27	29	+2
Poland	27	32	+5	25	28	+3
Rwanda	28	30	+2	20	23	+3
*Russia	25	28	+3	23	22	−1
Sweden	28	31	+3	28	29	+1
Switzerland	24	31	+7	24	29	+5
UAE	24	31	+7	23	24	+1
Uganda	25	27	+2	21	25	+4
United Kingdom	27	31	+4	29	30	+1
United States	30	31	+1	27	29	+2

*Missions that lost followers

($r=0.664$ $p\leq0.001$), and Good Country Index scores ($r=0.516$ $p\leq0.002$). GDP was highly correlated with Internet Penetration Rates ($r=0.853$) hence due to multicollinearity only one of these variables was included in the model. A regression model was built with GDP Per Capita, Outdegree centrality and Good Country Index scores as explanatory variables. GDP Per Capita was not significant in this model and the final model included Outdegree centrality (standardised beta 1.236, $p\leq0.001$) and Good Country Index scores (standardised beta

0.023, $p \leq 0.028$). The model had R^2 of 0.525. Using Internet Penetration Rates instead of GDP Per Capita yielded similar results. Thus, online prestige in the Geneva forum rests *not* on Hard Power resources (GDP Per Capita) but on Soft Power resources such as perceived goodness, and on digital strategies, namely following one's peers on Twitter. These results indicate that as was the case in 2015, so in 2020 digital diplomacy may help nations overcome prestige deficits. Moreover, unlike the 2015 analysis, the 2020 analysis suggests that digital savviness may play a role in enabling upward prestige mobility as evident from the correlation with Internet Penetration Rates.

NY centrality had a significant correlation with GDP Per Capita ($r=0.560$, $p \leq 0.001$), Internet Penetration Rates ($r=0.452$, pU0.008), Outdegree centrality ($r=0.875$, $p \leq 0.001$), and a borderline significant correlation with Good Country Index scores ($r=0.325$ $p \leq 0.065$). A regression model was built with GDP Per Capita, Outdegree centrality, and Good Country Index scores as explanatory variables. Good Country Index scores was not significant in this model and the final model included Outdegree centrality (standardised beta 2.746, $p \leq 0.001$) and GDP Per Capita (standardised beta 0.035, $p \leq 0.008$). The model had R^2 of 0.55. Using Internet Penetration Rates instead of GDP Per Capita yielded similar results.

In both the NY and Geneva samples, Outdegree centrality, or being an avid follower of one's peers, accounted for variations in Betweenness centrality. This could be explained from a networked perspective as centrality relates to one's ability to disseminate information from the network core to its periphery, and vice versa. Thus, in the online sphere, being interested in others is more prestigious than obtaining interest given that centrality is an important marker of prestige. These results suggest that offline prestige is not directly transferable online as online networks function differently from offline ones. Online, prestige stems from facilitating information exchange and not just gaining many followers.

The results of the NY analysis differ from those in Geneva as variability in network centrality in NY was not explained by reputational indices such as the Good Country Index. Moreover, variance was explained by Hard Power Resources (GDP Per Capita). This may stem from the fact that prestige in NY emanates from membership in elite forums such as the UN Security Council, which are based on Hard Power resources. Yet as was the case in Geneva, digital strategies such as following many peers and digital savviness may help limit the influence of Hard Power resources in online prestige.

Table 8.3 compares the NY Missions that had the highest and lowest Betweenness centrality score in 2015 and 2020. The table offers several insights given that, with exception of the UAE, none of the Missions that were central to information exchanges in 2015 remained central in 2020. This suggests that over a five-year period the NY network underwent significant changes. Of the seven Missions that were most central to information exchanges, or had the highest Betweenness centrality scores in 2020, Georgia, Iceland, Norway, and the UAE are examples of upward prestige mobility. They obtained online

TABLE 8.3 NY Missions to score high and low on Betweenness Centrality in 2015 and 2020

New York					
Rank	Betweenness Centrality High 2015	Number of Embassies Hosted in Capital	Rank	Betweenness Centrality High 2020	Number of Embassies Hosted in Capital
1	United States	176	1	Canada	129
2	United Arab Emirates (UAE)	106	2	Iceland	14
3	Australia	104	3	Norway	68
4	Germany	158	4	Sweden	106
5	European Union	74	5	Georgia	33
6	Poland	96	6	Switzerland	123
7	New Zealand	44	7	United Arab Emirates (UAE)	106
Rank	Betweenness Centrality Low 2015	Number of Embassies Hosted in Capital	Rank	Betweenness Centrality Low 2020	Number of Embassies Hosted in Capital
1	Bahrain	37	1	Azerbaijan	62
2	Azerbaijan	62	2	Israel	86
3	Russia	147	3	Latvia	35
4	Mexico	87	4	Maldives	6
5	Latvia	35	5	Uganda	44
6	India	156	6	Albania	38
7	Georgia	33	7	Rwanda	26

centrality while in the offline realm they have little prestige owing to a small number of embassies hosted in their capital. For instance, Iceland hosts only 44 embassies as opposed to the USA, which hosts 176. Yet Iceland is more central to the network than the USA. Notably, of the seven most central Missions in 2020, none are members of the Security Council demonstrating that Hard Power resources can be overcome through digital diplomacy even in the NY forum.

When examining the Missions that were least central to exchanges of information, or that received the lowest Betweenness centrality scores in 2015, one can find many instances of downward prestige mobility. Such is the case with India, Mexico and Russia who failed to translate offline prestige, measured by number of embassies hosted in a capital, to the online realm. Yet none of these nations appear in the 2020 ranking suggesting, again, that the NY network had been reconfigured over a five-year period.

Table 8.4 offers a similar analysis of the Geneva sample. As can be seen, France, Georgia, Sweden, and the USA were central to online exchanges of

TABLE 8.4 Geneva Missions to score high and low on Betweenness Centrality in 2015 and 2020

Geneva Rank	Betweenness Centrality High 2015	Number of Embassies Hosted in Capital	Rank	Betweenness Centrality High 2020	Number of Embassies Hosted in Capital
1	United Arab Emirates (UAE)	106	1	United Kingdom	164
2	Sweden	106	2	Sweden	106
3	France	157	3	France	157
4	United States	176	4	Australia	104
5	Georgia	33	5	United States	176
6	Germany	158	6	Georgia	33
7	Switzerland	123	7	New Zealand	44
Rank	Betweenness Centrality Low 2015	Number of Embassies Hosted in Capital	Rank	Betweenness Centrality Low 2020	Number of Embassies Hosted in Capital
1	Ethiopia	102	1	Brazil	131
2	Brazil	131	2	Ethiopia	102
3	Bahrain	37	3	Uganda	44
4	Uganda	44	4	Russia	147
5	Canada	129	5	Rwanda	26
6	Italy	139	6	Bahrain	37
7	Rwanda	26	7	Finland	63

information in both 2015 and 2020. Similarly, five Missions that received low Betweenness centrality scores in 2015 also received low scores in 2020. This further demonstrates that the Geneva network has undergone fewer changes than the NY network. Only two Missions in 2020 performed upward prestige mobility – Georgia and New Zealand. By contrast, three Missions performed downward mobility including Brazil, which hosts 131 embassies; Ethiopia, which hosts a 102 embassies; and Russia, which hosts 147 embassies. Upward prestige mobility may thus be more limited in the Geneva forum.

Finally, Table 8.5 identifies the seven Missions to receive the highest Indegree Betweenness scores, or that attracted the most interest from their peers. Missions coloured in grey also ranked high on Indegree Betweenness scores in 2015.

In the NY sample, only three Missions attracted large numbers of peers in both 2015 and 2020: Germany, the Netherlands, and Poland. In Geneva, five Missions attracted large numbers of peers in both 2015 and 2020, again attesting to the differences between the two networks. In the NY forum, Denmark, Finland, Iceland, and Poland performed upward prestige mobility, outperforming all Security Council members except Germany. These Missions also represent states with limited economic or military power as none of them are members in the G7 or the G20 clubs of nations. By contrast, in the Geneva sample only

TABLE 8.5 UN Mission to score high Indegree Betweenness scores in 2020

New York			Geneva		
Rank	Indegree Centrality High 2020	Number of Embassies Hosted in Capital	Rank	Indegree Centrality High 2020	Number of Embassies Hosted in Capital
1	Poland	96	1	United Kingdom	164
2	Netherlands	108	2	United States	176
3	Iceland	14	3	Switzerland	123
4	Germany	158	4	Sweden	106
5	Finland	63	5	Norway	68
6	Denmark	74	6	New Zealand	44
7	Canada	129	7	Australia	104

two Missions exhibit upward prestige mobility – New Zealand and Norway, as the UK, the USA, and Australia are all members of the G20 and host many embassies. Notably, in both samples, financial powerhouses and military powers such as India, Japan, Mexico, and Russia failed to translate offline prestige to online interest.

Discussion and conclusions

This chapter sought to examine whether online, or digital, diplomacy can help nations overcome the limitations of offline diplomacy. Imbued within the digital diplomacy research corpus is the assumption that digital diplomacy is a "game changer," which reconfigures power relations and offers peripheral nations the ability to challenge the dominance of nations with robust Hard Power resources (Manor and Pamment 2019). Additionally, the chapter aimed to demonstrate that the emergence of digital diplomacy offers scholars the opportunity to reconceptualise traditional concepts in diplomacy such as prestige. Finally, the chapter examined possible changes in online networks of diplomatic institutions over a five-year period. The chapter focused on UN forums as IOs have been shown to create a more levelled playing field in which Hard Power resources do not solely determine power relations.

Previous studies have conceptualised prestige through three parameters: *Presence*, or the world's interest in state (Alger and Brams 1967; Small and Singer 1973); *Centrality*, or a capital's position as a hub of information and resources (Kinne 2014); and *Reputation*, or the influence of reputation on perceptions of power (Nicolson 1937). This chapter adopted the same parameters while adapting them to online environments. Following Neumayer (2008) and Maliniak and Plouffe (2011), network analyses and statistical modelling were used to measure online prestige.

The 2015 analysis found that in both the offline and online realms, nations that attract interest from their peers are also likely to express reciprocal interest in their peers. Moreover, the 2020 analysis found that being an avid follower of one's peers on Twitter explained variability in UN Missions' network centrality. These findings suggest that offline prestige is not entirely transferable online. In the offline world, nations that *attract* the most interest obtain the highest prestige. On Twitter, nations that *give* the most interest obtain the highest prestige.

In 2020, nations that hosted a small number of embassies were able to generate considerable interest from their peers, demonstrating a form of upward prestige mobility. The UN Missions of Denmark, Finland, Iceland, New Zealand, Norway, and Poland were amongst the most followed on Twitter despite hosting few embassies. These examples demonstrate that IOs, including UN forums, do offer nations the opportunity to overcome offline limitations, in this case prestige deficits.

This is also evident from the statistical modelling. In the 2015 analysis, MFAs' offline prestige emanated solely from Hard Power resources while online prestige rested on reputational factors such as the Good Country Index scores. Similarly, the 2015 analysis found that UN Missions' online prestige rested on Hard Power, reputational factors, and online strategies such as posting many tweets and tweeting in English. Thus, online strategies can help nations perform upward prestige mobility. This manifested itself in 2020 when examining those Missions that obtained the highest Betweenness and Indegree centrality scores.

The NY sample exhibited greater changes over a five-year period as well as higher levels of prestige mobility. This may be counterintuitive as the NY forum rests on Hard Power resources as is the case with the UN Security Council. Yet it is possible that nations can obtain upward prestige mobility in NY as Twitter is more central to Missions' work. In the USA, Twitter is extensively used by both the general public and elites such as journalists, editors, policy makers, and diplomats. This is not the case in Switzerland.

Importantly, this chapter demonstrates that digital diplomacy can help states overcome an additional limitation – lack of diplomatic representation abroad. Nations with limited diplomatic networks may use Twitter networks to gather information from their peers, thus anticipating policy changes or shocks to the international system. Moreover, nations may attract many of their peers on Twitter enabling them to assess possible objections to their own policy agenda.

It is important to note that the results of this chapter may indirectly strengthen the credibility of IOs. This is important as IOs have come under attack from social movements, political parties, and leaders looking to benefit from the rebuke of globalisation and the resurgence of nationalism. In 1967, Alger and Brams found that membership in IOs offers greater opportunities for states with limited resources to play an influential role in international diplomacy. This was also evident in the new 2020 analysis. States such as Azerbaijan, Chile, and Finland attracted more peers than G7 states, while Georgia, Iceland, New Zealand, Norway, and Sweden were more central to online UN networks than most G7 and G20 states. Prestige mobility thus creates a more levelled playing field as peripheral states can exert influence on international affairs.

The fact that peripheral states can obtain influence through prestige mobility realises the vision of many IOs which seek to create an international community. A community that tackles shared challenges, addresses shared threats, and achieves shared prosperity. As such, prestige mobility may indirectly restore the credibility of IOs while preventing additional states from exiting the international community, as was the case with the UK.

As opposed to 2015, the 2020 analysis showed that online prestige in both UN forums is also dependent on internet penetration rates. This further suggests that digital savviness, and digital strategies can aid nations looking to overcome offline prestige deficits. However, both the NY and Geneva networks have grown denser over the past five years. This could hamper the ability to perform upward prestige mobility. In a dense network, where everyone follows everyone else, it is harder to become a central node. Thus, nations seeking upward prestige mobility may look to other niche venues.

An analysis conducted for this chapter suggests that the network of Missions to UNESCO has yet to take shape as most Missions do not follow their peers. UNESCO may thus serve as a new venue for prestige mobility. The same may be true of capitals that host many UN organisations including Addis Ababa, Nairobi, Rome, and Vienna. Future studies may choose to examine the density of such networks, as well as nations' ability to overcome prestige deficits be it by attracting many peers or becoming central to exchanges of information. Scholars may also examine whether those nations that perform prestige mobility offer their diplomats digital training, thus equipping them with digital strategies. Finally, studies may explore whether prestige mobility is possible in other IOs such as NATO or the African Union.

Appendix 1: sample of 67 MFAs

Afghanistan
Albania
Argentina
Armenia
Australia
Austria
Azerbaijan
Bahrain
Belarus
Belgium
Brazil
Bulgaria
Canada
Chile
Colombia
Croatia
Cuba
Cyprus

Dominican Republic
Ecuador
Egypt
Ethiopia
EU
Finland
France
Georgia
Germany
Greece
Iceland
India
Iraq
Ireland
Israel
Italy
Japan
Jordan
Kazakhstan
Kenya
Kosovo
Kuwait
Latvia
Mexico
Moldova
Netherland
Norway
Pakistan
Peru
Poland
Qatar
Romania
Russia
Rwanda
Serbia
Singapore
South Korea
Slovakia
Slovenia
Spain
Sweden
Thailand
Trinidad and Tobago
Turkey
UAE
UK
Ukraine
United States of America
Venezuela

Appendix 2: sample of 33 UN Missions

Albania
Australia
Azerbaijan
Bahrain
Brazil
Canada
Chile
Denmark
Ethiopia
European Union
Finland
France
Georgia
Germany
Iceland
India
Italy
Israel
Latvia
Maldives
Mexico
Netherland
New Zealand
Norway
Poland
Rwanda
Russia
Sweden
Switzerland
UAE
Uganda
United Kingdom
United States of America

References

Alger, Chadwick F., and Steven J. Brams. "Patterns of Representation in National Capitals and Intergovernmental Organizations." *World Politics* 19, no. 4 (1967): 646–63. doi:10.2307/2009718.

Archetti, Cristina. "The Impact of New Media on Diplomatic Practice: An Evolutionary Model of Change." *The Hague Journal of Diplomacy* 7, no. 2 (2012): 181–206. doi:10.1163/187119112X625538.

Bjola, Corneliu. "Digital Diplomacy 2.0: Trends and Counter Trends." *Revista Mexicana de Politica Exterior* no. 113 (2019): pp. 1–14.

Bjola, Corneliu, Jennifer Cassidy, and Ilan Manor. "Public Diplomacy in the Digital Age." *The Hague Journal of Diplomacy* 14, no. 1–2 (2019): 83–101. doi:10.1163/1871191X-14011032.

Bjola, Corneliu, and Marcus Holmes. *Digital Diplomacy: Theory into Practice*. Oxon: Routledge, 2015.

Brandes, Ulrik, and Dorothea Wagner. "Analysis and Visualization of Social Networks." In *Graph drawing software*, edited by Michael Jünger and Petra Mutzel, 321–40. Berlin, Heidelberg: Springer, 2004.

Cassidy, Jennifer, and I. Manor. "Crafting Strategic MFA Communication Policies During Times of Political Crisis: A Note to MFA Policy Makers." *Global Affairs* 2, no. 3 (2016): 331–43. doi:10.1080/23340460.2016.1239377.

Crilley, Rhys, Marie Gillespie, and Alistair Willis. "Tweeting the Russian Revolution: RT's# 1917LIVE and Social Media Re-Enactments as Public Diplomacy." *European Journal of Cultural Studies* (2019). 1367549419871353. doi:10.1177/1367549419871353.

Hilbert, Martin. "The End Justifies the Definition: The Manifold Outlooks on the Digital Divide and Their Practical Usefulness for Policy-Making." *Telecommunications Policy* 35, no. 8 (2011): 715–36. doi:10.1016/j.telpol.2011.06.012.

Hocking, Brian, Jan Melissen, Shaun Riordan, and Paul Sharp. "Futures for Diplomacy: Integrative Diplomacy in the 21st Century." *Working Paper, Netherlands Institute of International Relations' Clingendael'*, 2012.

Kampf, Ronit, Ilan Manor, and Elad Segev. "Digital Diplomacy 2.0? A Cross-National Comparison of Public Engagement in Facebook and Twitter." *The Hague Journal of Diplomacy* 10, no. 4 (2015): 331–62. doi:10.1163/1871191X-12341318.

Khatib, Lina, William Dutton, and Michael Thelwall. "Public Diplomacy 2.0: A Case Study of the US Digital Outreach Team." *The Middle East Journal* 66, no. 3 (2012): 453–72. doi:10.3751/66.3.14.

Kinne, Brandon J. "Dependent Diplomacy: Signaling, Strategy, and Prestige in the Diplomatic Network." *International Studies Quarterly* 58, no. 2 (2014): 247–59. doi:10.1111/isqu.12047.

Mai'a k, Davis Cross. "Rethinking Epistemic Communities Twenty Years Later." *Review of International Studies* 39, no. 1 (2013): 137–60. doi:10.1017/S0260210512000034.

Maliniak, Daniel, and Michael Plouffe. "A Network Approach to the Formation of Diplomatic Ties." In *APSA 2011 Annual Meeting Paper*.

Manor, I. *Are we there yet: Have MFAs realized the potential of digital diplomacy?: Results from a cross-national comparison* (pp. 1–110). Brill, 2016.

Manor, Ilan. "America's Selfie–Three Years Later." *Place Branding & Public Diplomacy* 13, no. 4 (2017): 308–24.

Manor, Ilan. *The Digitalization of Public Diplomacy*. Switzerland: Springer International Publishing, 2019.

Manor, Ilan, and James Pamment. "Towards Prestige Mobility? Diplomatic Prestige and Digital Diplomacy." *Cambridge Review of International Affairs* 32, no. 2 (2019): 93–131. doi:10.1080/09557571.2019.1577801.

Manor, Ilan, and Elad Segev. "Social Media Mobility: Leveraging Twitter Networks in Online Diplomacy." *Global Policy* 11, no. 2 (2020): 233–44. (Forthcoming).

Manor, I. and M. Holmes. "Palestine in Hebrew: Overcoming the Limitations of Traditional Diplomacy." *Revista Mexicana de Politicia Exterior*, 133, 1–17, May-August 2018.

Metzgar, Emily T. "Is It the Medium or the Message? Social Media, American Public Diplomacy & Iran." *Global Media Journal* 12, no. 21 (2012): 1.

Murti, Bhattiprolu, and R. S. Zaharna. "India's Digital Diaspora Diplomacy: Operationalizing Collaborative Public Diplomacy Strategies for Social Media." *Exchange: Journal of Public Diplomacy* 5, no. 1 (2014): 3.

Natarajan, Kalathmika. "Digital Public Diplomacy and a Strategic Narrative for India." *Strategic Analysis* 38, no. 1 (2014): 91–106. doi:10.1080/09700161.2014.863478.

Neumann, Iver B. *Diplomatic Sites: A Critical Enquiry*. New York: Columbia University Press, 2012.

Neumayer, Eric. "Distance, Power and Ideology: Diplomatic Representation in a World of Nation-States." *Area* 40, no. 2 (2008): 228–36. doi:10.1111/j.1475-4762.2008.00804.x.

Nicolson, Harold. *The Meaning of Prestige*. Cambridge: Cambridge University Press, 1937/2014.

Nye, Joseph S. "Soft Power." *Foreign Policy* 80, no. 80 (1990): 153–71. doi:10.2307/1148580.

Pamment, James. *New Public Diplomacy in the 21st Century: A Comparative Study of Policy and Practice*. Oxon: Routledge, 2012.

Pouliot, Vincent. "Diplomats as Permanent Representatives: The Practical Logics of the Multilateral Pecking Order." *International Journal* 66, no. 3 (2011): 543–61. doi:10.1177/002070201106600302.

Seib, Philip. *Real-Time Diplomacy: Politics and Power in the Social Media Era*. New York: Palgrave Macmillan, 2012.

Seib, Philip. *The Future of Diplomacy*. Cambridge: John Wiley & Sons, 2016.

Seo, Hyunjin, and Dennis F. Kinsey. "Three Korean Perspectives on US Internet Public Diplomacy." *Public Relations Review* 39, no. 5 (2013): 594–6. doi:10.1016/j.pubrev.2013.06.006.

Small, Melvin, and J. David Singer. "The Diplomatic Importance of States, 1816–1970: An Extension and Refinement of the Indicator." *World Politics* 25, no. 4 (1973): 577–99.

Spry, Damien. "Facebook Diplomacy: A Data-Driven, User-Focused Approach to Facebook Use by Diplomatic Missions." *Media International Australia* 168, no. 1 (2018): 62–80. doi:10.1177/1329878X18783029.

9

THE (UN)MAKING OF INTERNATIONAL ORGANISATIONS' DIGITAL REPUTATION

The European Union, the "refugee crisis," and social $_m$edia

Ruben Zaiotti

> Reputation, reputation, reputation! O! I have lost my reputation. I have lost the immortal part of myself, and what remains is bestial. My reputation, Iago, my reputation!
>
> (Cassio, in Shakespeare, *The Tragedy of Othello, the Moor of Venice*, Act II. Scene III, 262–264).

Introduction

As a hybrid and ever-evolving political entity in a world still dominated by states, the European Union is continuously striving to gain greater recognition as an independent and effective actor in global affairs. These efforts at strengthening its presence on the world stage have been at the centre of the organisation's activities since foreign policy officially became an area of EU competence in the 1990s (White 2017). Since then, the EU has substantially expanded the scope and size of its diplomatic capabilities and activities. The EU currently boasts a dedicated diplomatic corps with a capillary presence across the globe, and it is active in numerous military and civilian missions around the world (Carta 2013). The EU has also become more active in the realm of "public diplomacy" (Cross and Melissen 2013). The emphasis on public diplomacy stems from the recognition that, in order to project a more appealing image to the rest of the world, the EU has to win the "hearts and minds" of foreign populations, and it can accomplish this goal by building on one of the EU's self-proclaimed major assets, namely its image as "force for good" promoting democracy, human rights, and the rule of law. The EU has deployed more resources for these public relations efforts, supporting cultural and outreach events and "people to people" activities that showcase Europe and its member states beyond Europe. The Union has also embraced more eagerly public communication using both traditional and "new" media (European Commission 2013, 2016)

These efforts' stated goal is to improve perceptions of the EU (European Commission 2016). Nevertheless, there are challenges to build a coherent and inspiring narrative about what the EU is and stands for that resonate with foreign publics. Some of these challenges are structural, and have to do with the peculiar "postmodern" (i.e., complex, unfinished, contested) nature of the EU project, a feature that affects the type of content to be diffused and the ability of non-European publics to "get" what the EU represents. These challenges are compounded by the still underdeveloped and chaotic features of EU structures that should manage the narrative (i.e., competing actors and interests in EU public diplomacy, lack of coordination, limited resources). Besides these long-term challenges, there are also short-term ones, which are more contingent, less predictable, but with the same potential to destabilise the EU's image. These situations originate from events beyond EU control and whose implications undermine the EU official narrative about itself. In the last decade, these events have taken the form of a series of political "crises" (Castells et al. 2018; Dinan et al. 2017), which have seriously put to the test the EU's status as a competent, coherent, and progressive political entity. One of these events is the so-called "refugee crisis" (Nedergaard 2019). The term describes the series of circumstances stemming from the sudden surge in migration flows around Europe's south-eastern borders in the summer of 2015 due to the worsening of the civil conflict in Syria and the ensuing displacement of its citizens in neighbouring countries.

Pundits and EU officials agree that this event, and the manner in which the EU has handled it, has negatively affected how the EU is perceived around the world (Nedergaard 2019; Georgiou and Zaborowski 2017). At the height of the refugee crisis, for instance, European Commission President Juncker was quite blunt in his assessment of its impact: "EU's reputation is being damaged worldwide by the failure of member countries to manage the refugee crisis."[1] Along similar lines, then High Representative for Foreign Affairs and Security Policy of the EU, Federica Mogherini, stated that EU action on the issue of the refugee crisis "greatly weakens our [the EU's] credibility abroad."[2] These claims, however, are based on anecdotal evidence, and they lack clarity on what "EU reputation" consists of, who is influencing it, and the mechanism linking crises and EU's reputation. As a result, the assessments provided are superficial, incomplete, and possibly skewed.

The present chapter seeks to provide a systematic and empirically grounded answer to the question of the impact of the refugee crisis on the EU's reputation as international organisation. Theoretically, this paper builds on the literature that focus on EU's "international identity" and external perceptions (Cederman 2001; Lucarelli 2013; Lucarelli and Manners 2006) and expands on this body of work to include insights drawn from the field of organisational communication (Miller 2008). The premise of the proposed argument is that reputation is a dialogical process, characterised by an ongoing communicative exchange between a reputation-seeking entity and reputation-builders. The dialogical nature of reputation has been recognised in the EU literature; yet, when examining the EU's reputation-making process, the focus has tended to be on the first component of this dyadic relation, namely what the EU as organisation is doing to build its reputation, and especially its communication strategies (Elgström 2007). To analyse the content and impact of these "image building" exercises, scholars have relied on EU official public relations practices (e.g., external communication and media relations efforts, EU institutions, and individual officials' presence on mass media) and on traditional media as main platforms where these communicative practices take place (Brüggemann 2010; Laursen and Valentini 2013; Valentini and Nesti 2010; Valentini and Laursen 2012; Martins, Lecheler, and de Vreese 2012). In order to rebalance the over-emphasis on EU official channels, this paper adopts what in organisation theory is called an "outside in" approach (Manning et al. 2012; Hurley 2002). In this perspective, the emphasis is on individuals not affiliated with the organisation under consideration that through their feedback (or "customer experience") contribute to the organisation's reputation building. These experiences, in turn, shape reputation depending on the actors, situation, issue, and temporal framework involved, in recognition of the multifaceted nature of this phenomenon. To redress the reliance on traditional media as data source (see for instance, Georgiou and Zaborowski 2017), the chapter explores how the European Union's reputation is built and evolves on social media. This form of communicative technology has not been extensively used to study perceptions of the EU abroad[3]; social media analysis nonetheless has the potential to offer a more comprehensive and textured picture of EU reputation in world affairs.

Empirically, this chapter assesses the impact of the refugee crisis on EU reputation by examining the online activities of private individuals expressing their opinions on the EU and its handling of the crisis on the social media platform Twitter during the height of the crisis (July 2015- June 2016). As the focus is on the EU's "international" reputation (i.e., beyond Europe), the study covers the opinions communicated via tweets by individuals based outside the EU. The dataset created for this project is then analysed through a combination of content and sentiment analysis to determine relevant themes and trends characterising the collected material.

The findings of this study confirm that the refuge crisis has indeed affected the EU's reputation. However, its impact is more nuanced than it has been presented in existing accounts. First, the EU reputation has only been marginally tarnished, if at all; second, the assessment of EU performance during the crisis does not substantially differ from that of the EU member states most directly involved in the crisis (Germany, Italy, Greece, France), thus showing that the tensions that these set of events created within the EU were not reflected in the way these actors were blamed (or praised) for their response. Third, the crisis, while challenging the Union's reputation, has simultaneously increased the organisation's global visibility and salience, thus contributing to the strengthening of its identity as an independent actor. Crucially, this outcome has occurred *despite* the lack of efforts on the part of the EU to proactively manage its reputation online. The case study examined in this chapter also provides relevant insights and lessons into how international organisations can manage critical situations, and how these experiences can inform IOs' digital diplomacy.

The chapter is organised as follows. The first section examines the concept of reputation and how it can be applied to the study of international organisations such as the European Union. The second section outlines the methodology used to collect and analyse the data, while the third section presents the study's main findings. The concluding section addresses the implications of these findings for the EU and its efforts at reputation management.

On organisations and their reputation

Reputation is a term drawn from social psychology that has been extensively applied to the study of corporate entities, including political ones (Mercer 1996). The primary function of reputation is symbolic – to prove external entities with an efficient mechanism for identifying and categorising an organisation (Martins 2005). As it is the case for individuals, an organisation's reputation is not a predefined condition; instead, it is a socio-cognitive phenomenon involving a group of individuals and an entity that is the object of their observation (Fombrun and Rindova 1998; Barnett et al. 2006). This observation is not passive; it is evaluative, as it emerges from observers' collective *judgments* about the organisation. These judgements are about the organisation's identity (what it is) is and its performance (what it does; Foreman et al. 2012, 185; Dhalla 2007, 247). As these assessments are conducted over time and constantly re-elaborated, an organisation's reputation is a cumulative and open-ended process (Barnett et al. 2006; Fombrun and Rindova 1998).

The sources of reputation stem from stakeholder experiences of an organisation. These experiences are influenced by an organisation's activities and the "noise" in the system, such as the media and interpersonal exchanges. Organisations are not passive while their reputation is constructed. They strive to communicate with external actors in an effort to shape their impressions. This process of image management or "corporate branding" (Kowalczyk and Pawlish 2002) feeds into external actors' perceptions of the organisation. In this sense, reputation contributes to an organisation's identity-making process (Foreman et al. 2012). Stakeholders then decode these signals and information, and, together with information they garner from other sources such as media, make assessments and form their perceptions about the organisation (Fombrun and Shanley 1990).

There is a tendency in the political science literature to treat reputation as a monolithic category. In the organisation literature, however, it is becoming common to add qualifiers to the reputation construct (Lang et al. 2011). Lange et al. (2011), for instance, distinguish "being known" from the more specific "being known for something" and the more general "favorability." Reputation is also contingent. There is variation in terms of stakeholders' perceptions of an organisation's actions and how well they are consistent with the organisation's specific mandate (Bromley 2002). Similarly, reputation may change depending on not just what the organisation does but also on the evolving societal norms and the different cultural contexts it is exposed to (Vidaver-Cohen 2007, 278). The medium and methods through which reputation is assessed (be it a personal experience, focus group, survey, online, prompted or unprompted) can have an impact too, as each mode has its peculiar features, biases, and constraints.

Reputation's contingent nature is heightened by the fact that it is sensitive to external events, such as a crisis (Coombs and Holladay 2006). In organisational theory, a crisis is defined as "a significant threat to operations that can have negative consequences if not handled properly" (Barton 1993). In crisis manage-ment, the threat is the potential damage a series of unforeseen circumstances can inflict on an organisation. Reputational loss is one of the main threats a crisis can unleash. Indeed, all crises threaten to tarnish an organisation's reputation. Crises, however, also offer opportunities to demonstrate competence and reinforce one's core values. The overall impact of a crisis on an organisation's reputation is thus open-ended.

Because of its ephemeral nature (it cannot be observed directly), reputation is difficult to measure. The organisation theory literature has sought to refine measurement techniques that apply to private and public organisations, includ-ing political ones (see Helm 2005; Money and Hillenbrand 2006). Reputation is operationalised by considering the degree of admiration or respect, trust, and good feeling observers experience for the organisation, as well as their perception of the organisation's level of overall public esteem. These categories are deter-mined by a series of "predictors." The Reputation Institute, for instance, looks at organisational performance, service quality, leadership practices, governance procedures, citizenship activities, workplace climate, and approach to innovation (Vidaver-Cohen 2007, 280). The methods used to measure reputation reflect the particular nature of reputation, namely that it is contingent (it can only be determined data a particular point in time) and cumulative (depends on evalu-ations developed over time). Moreover, while reputation measurement is based on respondents' beliefs about an organisation, which can be gauged through ethnographic analysis or direct questioning (Bromley 2002), an organisation's overall reputation is determined by the collective ("meta") evaluation of these responses. When this assessment is based on stakeholders' experiences in the digital world, the collection of relevant data for the purpose of determining an organisation's reputation is accomplished through *social media monitoring* (SMM), a method used in consumer research involving an "observational, passive and quantitative approach" to collect information generated by new media platforms (Gillen and Merchan 2013).

In the European Union literature, reputation is treated, albeit in passing, as part of the broader discussion about the EU identity's external dimension. The

EU "international identity," or how the EU defines itself in world politics, has received academic attention since the EU became active in foreign affairs in the 1990s. Since then, this attention has ebbed and flowed in parallel to the (limited) successes and (numerous) failures of EU foreign policy. As mentioned in the introduction, most of the work on EU external identity has focused on how the organisation has tried to build and project its image as an actor in world affairs, using EU's official foreign policy documents or policy statements to study these efforts (e.g., Cederman 2001; Lucarelli 2013; Lucarelli and Manners 2006).

When the role of the external environment and actors has been considered, the focus has been on these actors' "expectations" (Hill 2005) or "perceptions" (Chaban and Holland 2014; Lucarelli 2013; Larsen 2014). These studies have typically relied on elites' interviews (public officials, experts, journalists; see for instance, Elgström 2007) or content analyses of traditional media (Meyer 1999; Van Noije 2010; Georgiou and Zaborowski 2017) as main data collection techniques. These choices, however, raise the issue of selection bias (respondents having pre-conceived notions of the organisation), thus providing a narrow perspective on what reputation is. Research that has sought to capture the perceptions of a wider population raises the question of salience. Survey-based analyses (see, for instance, Valentini 2013; AA.VV. 2015) tend to focus on how individuals perceive the EU in abstract, not the impact on reputation per se, as the general population, especially outside Europe, tend to have limited knowledge of the EU and what it does.

This work seeks to bridge the gap in the existing literature by empirically examining the EU's reputation on social media. The choice of social media as data collection source from both theoretical and methodological considerations. The theoretical reasons for using Twitter to study reputation stem from the discursive, dialogical, public, and networked nature of social media (Humphreys 2016; Gillen and Merchan 2013), all central features in reputation-building. Social media platforms such as Twitter represent platforms on which communication among individuals (and organisations they represent) takes place. Communicative practices (e.g., tweets) are prerequisites to build reputation, as evaluations of an entity have to be expressed publicly in order to contribute to an organisation's reputation. These communicative practices are dialogical, as they entail exchanges between users, and these interactions, in turn, create networks of individuals who share common interests (an "imaged community"; Grudz et al. 2011).

Methodologically, social media as a source of data is consistent with an outside in approach, for it encompasses views of a potentially large section of the population over a particular subject or organisation. It is also unprompted (hence avoiding selection bias and salience of subject) and unfiltered. It is also free to use, public, multicast (i.e., many to many), interactive, and networked. Twitter as data collection tool is used extensively in consumer research, but less so in EU research, and its potential has not been fully exploited.

Assessing the EU reputation during the refugee crisis: methodological issues

The analysis of the EU reputation is based on a dataset generated for this project. The dataset consists of information extrapolated from the social media platform Twitter between July 2015 and June 2016.[4] This data consists of tweets in English and Spanish that contain a set of keywords related to the refugee crisis ("Europe/Europa," "EU/UE," "border/frontera," "migration/migracion," "refugee/refugiado," "Schengen"). This textual data was filtered to include tweets from private users (i.e., no news media or official accounts) located outside Europe.

The assessment of the EU's reputation was conducted through a combination of sentiment and content analysis. Sentiment analysis is a text classification method that measures a text's subjectivity and opinion (or "semantic orientation") by focusing on a text's "polarity" – i.e., whether a word, phrase, or sentence contains positive, negative, or neutral content – and its intensity (i.e., the strength of the evaluations towards a subject topic, person, or idea; Taboada 2016). In this project, sentiment scoring involves the detecting of sentiment-bearing terms, the determination of their polarity and intensity, and then the calculation of an aggregate value for the message or sentiment object of interest. The rating scale used to calculate the scoring is a 5-point Likert scale (from −2 as "very negative" to +2 as "very positive" and 0 as "neutral"). For the purpose of this study, reputation is thus operationalised in terms of collective sentiment towards the EU as organisation as it emerged and developed during the refugee crisis.

The coding of the textual data (tweets) entailed the tagging of relevant signifiers of emotions (adjectives, nouns, verbs, adverbs)[5]. Captured signifiers that refer to the same phenomena were grouped by meaning (thus creating a semantic field). Attention has been paid to intensifiers ("contextual valence shifters"; Polanyi and Zaenan 2006), which could have an impact in determining the strength of a text. In this context, the reposting of a message (retweet) is treated as evidence of endorsement of opinion or emotion (Lee and Ma 2012). In this project, data coding has been processed manually. To increase reliability, the analysis has relied on inter-rater agreement involving two reviewers per tweet, with the final sentiment determined by the average between the two reviewers' assessments.

Sentiment analysis was complemented with content analysis of the collected Twitter-generated textual data. This analysis was deployed to measure the frequency of occurrence in the data set (i.e., "salience") of the issues, events, and actors involved in the refugee crisis and to assess the strength and variation of EU reputation during the period under consideration.[6] The information extrapolated from sentiment and content analysis was then examined to find patterns and possible overarching narratives connecting these patterns.[7]

The impact of the refugee crisis on EU reputation: findings[8]

Figure 9.1 visualises the aggregate data on the salience of the refugee crisis during the period under consideration (August 2015–June 2016). The number of tweets sent by non-affiliated users based outside Europe and containing references to the crisis is just under 4,000 (3,936), of which 12% are in Spanish. The crisis's global digital salience (calculated in terms of tweets per day) consistently grew from the late summer 2015, before decreasing in the early summer 2016. The peaks in terms of online discussion of the crisis were reached in concomitance with major policy events (e.g., Chancellor Merkel's decision to open Germany's borders to refugees in September; Paris terrorist attacks in November; EU–Turkey refugee deal in March). As expected, given the higher Twitter penetration and the relevance of the topic for local audiences, the majority of tweets outside Europe came from North America (the USA and Canada). However, social media activity in other parts of the world (especially Asia) was robust as well (see Figure 9.2). The European Union – whether as a corporate entity or as represented by its main institutions (European Commission and European Council) and leaders (Commission President Juncker and Council President Tusk) was the most cited policy actor (1,204 or 33% of total tweets), followed at a distance by EU member states (Germany, France, Greece, and Italy) and their leaders (e.g., German Chancellor Merkel; see Figure 9.3). References to the EU increased consistently in the first part of the period under consideration before subsiding after March 2016 (see Figure 9.4). For member states, these peaks occurred at different times (for Germany, September; for France, November; for Greece and Italy, January). Being the most prominent policy actor during the crisis, the EU faced the most scrutiny, and, with it, the possibility of a greater impact on its reputation.

When it comes to users' reaction to the refugee crisis, sentiment analysis of Twitter activity beyond Europe indicates an overall neutral or mildly positive (score between 0 and +1 on the sentiment scale) assessment of the event throughout the period under consideration (see Figure 9.5). The trend is consistent with the crisis salience's trajectory noted above, with an increase in positive evaluations from the summer of 2015 up until the spring of 2016, before turning to neutral at the beginning of the summer. In the initial stages of the crisis, users' feelings ranged from astonishment ("Schengen being suspended wow") to concern ("Migrant crisis is threatening the foundation of Europe EU") to outright pessimism ("imo Schengen is dead"). The mood became more positive and optimistic in the following months, with terms such as "hope," "good," "possible" appearing more frequently (e.g., "I really hope Schengen area won't collapse the freedom to travel between countries is what makes Europe great").

If we consider users' assessment of individual policy actors and their performance, the data points to similar trends characterising the crisis as a whole. The reputation of the European Union fluctuated in the first months of the crisis, from slightly negative (−0.4) to neutral, before consistently improving in the new year, reaching a peak in the spring of 2016 (+0.4), and then becoming neutral at the beginning of the summer (see Figure 9.6). These trends have been consistent across different geographical locations (see Figure 9.7). The upward trends characterising the EU reputation were replicated in the other policy actors' data, with the initial negative assessment (Germany −0.6; France −1; Greece −1.1; Italy −0.4) moving into positive territory in the following months (with peaks of +0.6 for Germany, Greece and Italy; and +0.2 for France). During the crisis, the European Union was not, therefore, a target of the "Brussels blame game" (i.e., using the EU as a scapegoat for EU member states' political failures)

The consistency in the assessment of the EU and member states' performance suggests that no single policy actor stood out in terms of perceptions of the handling of the crisis. The European Union, however, is arguably the entity that gained the most from the crisis in terms of international image. In sharing their views of EU's performance during the crisis, Twitter users highlighted the organisation's agency and authority, as exemplified by the recurrent association with action verbs such as "planning," "proposing," "making," "protecting," "imposing" (e.g., "The EU's *plans* to save Schengen the future of Schengen and the unity of the EU are at stake"; emphasis added).

The overall results of Twitter's sentiment analysis suggest that the EU's digital reputation during the refugee crisis was not undermined, as its critics suggested. More generally, the crisis did not raise the type of negative commentary among the non-European public that might have been expected, given the nature of the event. The trends characterising Twitter users' views of the EU's performance are also consistent with the degree of salience that the EU maintained during the crisis. Thus the greater attention and scrutiny that these events brought did not lead to a deterioration of the EU's reputation. On the contrary, the evaluations of the EU's performance improved.

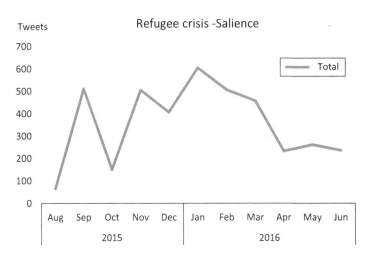

FIGURE 9.1   Overall salience

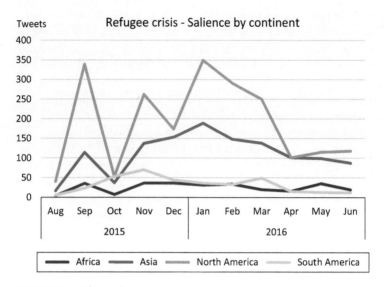

FIGURE 9.2   Salience by continent

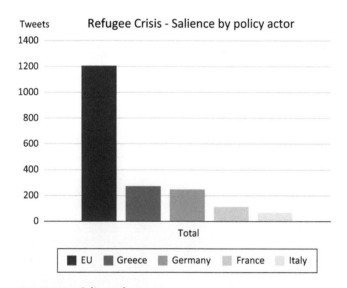

FIGURE 9.3   Salience by actor

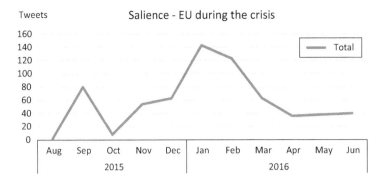

FIGURE 9.4   Salience – EU

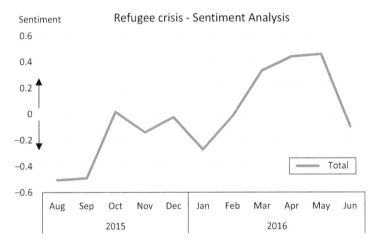

FIGURE 9.5   Overall sentiment

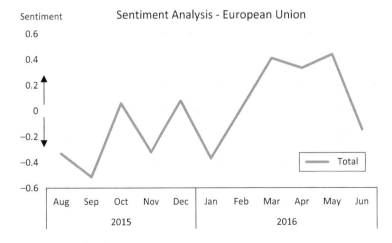

FIGURE 9.6   Sentiment

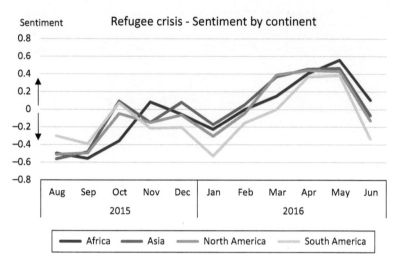

FIGURE 9.7 Sentiment by continent

Conclusions

> Reputation is an idle and most false imposition; oft got without merit, and
> lost without deserving: you have lost no reputation at all, unless you repute
> yourself such a loser.
>
> (Iago, in Shakespeare, *The Tragedy of Othello,*
> *the Moor of Venice*, Act II. Scene III, 265–268)

The present chapter has provided an empirical contribution to the study of reputation in contemporary global affairs, using the European Union and the online assessment of its handling of the refugee crisis as a case study. As Jervis (1970, 6) argued, in International Relations a country's positive evaluation can be "of greater use than a significant increment of military or economic power." Reputation's main asset is that it provides a measurement of reliability and predictability in an anarchical world (Mercer 1996). Reputation, however, is not just valuable because it smooths relations among states. As the organisational theory literature has shown, reputation plays an essential role in connecting an organisation with its external stakeholders and strengthening their relationship (Fombrun 2015). This "social" dimension of reputation has gained prominence in organisations' life because of the growing importance of social media, which have rendered organisations much more visible and accountable (Schlipphak 2013). In turn, social media offer a way for organisations to manage their image more proactively, thanks to their ability to engage directly with the public. The growing importance of the public dimension in organisations' daily activities is reflected in the realm of international affairs, as online reputation-management has become a core component of contemporary diplomacy (Bjola and Holmes 2015).

This study has provided evidence to support the claim that the refugee crisis, despite putting the organisation under considerable stress, did not substantially dent the European Union's global reputation during this event, as EU officials and commentators had assumed. The greater exposure that this event provided to the organisation also had the (unintentional) effect of raising the EU's profile on the world stage. One of these findings' most intriguing implications is that the crisis, rather than undermining it, might have actually helped the EU's ongoing reputation-building effort. As the organisational literature suggests, reputation-building is premised on an organisation's greater external recognition, here understood as the public acknowledgement of one's status or merits (Gehring et al. 2013). Recognition is in turn necessary for an organisation to develop a personal identity, as organisations – like persons – fundamentally depend on the feedback of other subjects in order to properly function in a community (Greenhill 2008). Being recognised also denotes an organisation's degree of integration in a given community. When it comes to public organisations such as IOs, this community includes both peers (i.e., other organisations and states) and external stakeholders (NGOs, individual citizens). For IOs, external stakeholders' recognition is typically low, as these organisations are less directly involved with the general public. Highly contentious and publicised circumstances, such as humanitarian crises or conflicts, provide opportunities to increase IOs' public acknowledgement of their presence and roles in world politics. Crucially, this recognition occurs even if the assessment of IOs performance in these situations is neutral or even negative. There is a tendency in public commentaries to consider a "bad reputation" as weakening an organisation's corporate identity. Yet, in terms of projecting one's power on the world stage, being acknowledged at all among members of the public is preferable to being completely ignored.

This assessment of the impact of the refugee crisis points to potential lessons that IOs can learn on how to use new media to manage their international reputation. First, it suggests that a low-key digital strategy in dealing with a politically charged issue might be a sound approach. Whether because of lack of planning and resources or because of the fear of damaging further one's reputation, the EU and its surrogates (i.e., EU delegations around the world) avoided explicitly to address the refugee crisis on its digital platforms. While successful in the short term, this passive approach to digital diplomacy might have deleterious effects on organisations in the long run (Wang 2006). Critical situations can, in fact, highlight gaps between the image the organisation is trying to project to the outside world and its reputation among key stakeholders. The organisational literature has defined this gap as "dissonance," a condition that if not adequately addressed can threaten an organisation's success (Alsop 2004; Vidaver-Cohen 2007, 280; Borgerson, Magnusson, and Magnusson 2006; Hatch and Schultz 2002; Cornelissen et al. 2007, 7). Organisations can tackle this challenge through reputation management. At its core, reputation management is a practice aimed at aligning public perceptions and expectations of an organisation with the perceptions and expectations that the organisation ought to communicate about itself

(Eisenegger and Imhof 2008). These strategies – also referred to as "bridging" and "buffering" (Meznar and Nigh 1995), "mimicking" (Whetten and Mackey 2002), "expressing," and "mirroring" (Hatch and Schultz 2002) seek to help an organisation to (re)gaining a degree of consonance between its internal identity (as expressed by those working for the organisation), its corporate identity (i.e., the organisation's projected image), and its corporate reputation (i.e., collective beliefs about organisation held by external stakeholders; Orlitzky et al. 2003).

These efforts at aligning organisations' identities nowadays occur more and more online. IOs have mimicked states in deploying digital diplomacy at the forefront of this strategy. In their efforts to achieve consonance in their online messaging, however, IOs such as the EU have typically adopted an *inside out* strategy, whereby an organisation seeks to review one's capabilities and strengths, to use existing resources more efficiently. As this study has suggested, more and more of an international organisation's success is based on its external digital reputation. This state of affairs points to the importance of an *outside in* strategy that emphasises the centrality of stakeholders and the need to engage them more proactively, taking their perspectives seriously into account and incorporating their ideas into the organisation's narrative about itself. This approach requires a rethinking of the perception of insiders on how the organisation is viewed and perceived by external constituencies (Dutton and Dukerich 1991). In the literature on EU identity, the reciprocal relationship between organisational identity and image has been recognised (see Lucarelli 2013); to date, however, limited empirical analysis of how outsiders' perceptions influence the self-representation processes within the organisation has been carried out. Given their ability to directly connect organisations and the public, social media platforms such as Twitter provide a powerful tool to monitor and possibly manage these identity-making dynamics. A more proactive reputation-management approach in times of crisis would not change overnight how an international organisation such as the EU is perceived by the outside world. Nevertheless, such a stance would go far in proving wrong Iago's quip about reputation being "idle and false"; it would also give an opportunity to an international organisation to prove that it actually deserves the kind of reputation that at any given time it holds among members of the international community and the public.

Notes

1 "Refugee crisis has hurt EUs reputation Juncker admits," *Daily Sabah*, January 16, 2016. Available at https://www.dailysabah.com/europe/2016/01/16/refugee-crisis-has-hurt-eus-reputation-juncker-admits
2 "Mogherini: EU will lose its reputation because of refugee crisis," *Meta MK*, 25 September 2015. Available at http://meta.mk/en/mogerini-eu-go-gubi-ugledot-poradi-begalskata-kriza/
3 In Bain and Chaban's (2017) work on EU perceptions abroad, a section is dedicated to the analysis of Twitter in selected countries. The focus, however, is on official EU accounts and EU-sponsored events.

4 The collection of tweets was conducted through a Python data mining programme.
5 The focus is on opinionated texts where the authors do explicitly express their sentiment. A combination of source and intent analysis was conducted to detect the appropriate type of text (opinion vs news and marketing).
6 On the concept of "salience" and its application to the study of organisations, see Van Dick et al. 2005.
7 The mixed-method approach used to collect and analyse social media data seeks to provide a comprehensive and detailed picture of the complex phenomenon under consideration. There are nonetheless limitations resulting from the reliance on this approach. In terms of data collection, despite the broad scope of the analysis, the data is not representative of all views and locations. The results are based only on one – albeit popular – social platform. Digital reputation does not represent the totality of the EU's reputation, which is to a large extent still built and sustained in the "real world." Because of technical glitches in the Python twitter data mining programme during the ten months collection period, some tweets might not have been captured in the final dataset. In terms of analysis, there is ambiguity in the reading of textual content, albeit it is mitigated by human analysis as opposed to machine reading. The focus on only two (Western) languages, while capturing a large part of comments on the subject, are still short of a truly "global" perspective.
8 Special thanks go to Nafisa Abdulhamid and Yannick Marchand for their work in collecting and analyzing the data presented in this chapter.

References

AA.VV.. *Analysis of the perception of the EU and of EU's policies abroad.* Vilnius: Public Policy and Management Institute (PPMI), 2015. Available at https://ec.europa.eu/fpi/sites/fpi/files/eu_perceptions_study_executive_summary.pdf.

Alsop, Ronald J. "Corporate Reputation: Anything but Superficial-the Deep but Fragile Nature of Corporate Reputation." *Journal of Business Strategy* 25, no. 6 (2004): 21–9.

Bain, Jessica, and Natalia Chaban. "Emerging EU Strategic Narrative? Twitter Dialogues on the EU's Sustainable Energy Week." *Comparative European Politics* 15, no. 1 (2017): 135–55.

Barnett, Michael J., John M. Jermier, and Barbara A. Lafferty. "Corporate Reputation: The Definitional Landscape." *Corporate Reputation Review* 9, no. 1 (2006): 26–38.

Barton, Laurence. *Crisis in Organizations: Managing and Communicating in the Heat of Chaos.* Cincinnati, OH: South-Western Publishing Company, 1993.

Bjola, C., and M. Holmes. *Digital diplomacy: Theory and practice.* London: Routledge, 2015.

Borgerson, J. L., M. E. Magnusson, and F. Magnusson. "Branding Ethics." In *Brand Culture,* edited by J. Schroder, and M. Salzer-Morling, 171–85. London: Routledge, 2006.

Bromley, Dennis B. "An Examination of Issues that Complicate the Concept of Reputation in Business Studies." *International Studies of Management & Organization* 32, no. 3 (2002): 65–81.

Brüggemann, Michael. "Public Relations Between Propaganda and the Public Sphere: The Information Policy of the European Commission." In *Public Communication in the European Union. History, Perspectives and Challenges,* edited by Chiara Valentini, and Giorgia Nesti, 67–91. Newcastle upon Tyne, UK: Cambridge Scholars Publishing, 2010.

Carl-Göran, Heidegren. "Review Essay Recognition and Social Theory." *Acta Sociologica* 47, no. 4 (2004): 365–73.

Carta, Caterina. *The European Union Diplomatic Service: Ideas, Preferences and Identities.* New York: Routledge, 2013.

Castells, Manuel, Oliver Bouin, Joao Caraça, Gustavo Cardoso, John Thompson, and Michel Wieviorka, eds. *Europe's Crises.* Cambridge: John Wiley & Sons, 2018.

Cederman, Lars-Erik, ed. *Constructing Europe's Identity: The External Dimension.* Boulder, CO: Lynne Rienner Publishers, 2001.

Chaban, Nathan, and Martin Holland, eds. *Communicating Europe in Times of Crisis – External Perceptions of the European Union.* Basingstoke UK: Palgrave MacMillan, 2014.

Coombs, W. Timothy, and Sherry J. Holladay. "Unpacking the Halo Effect: Reputation and Crisis Management." *Journal of Communication Management* 10, no. 2 (2006): 122–37.

Cornelissen, Joep P., Haslam S. Alexander, and John M. T. Balmer. "Social Identity, Organizational Identity and Corporate Identity: Towards an Integrated Understanding of Processes, Patterns and Products." *British Journal of Management* 18, no. 1 (2007): 1–16.

Cross, Maia, and Jan Melissen. *European Public Diplomacy: Soft Power at Work.* New York US: Palgrave Macmillan US, 2013.

Dhalla, Rumina (2007). "The Construction of Organizational Identity: Key Contributing External and Intra-Organizational Factors." *Corporate Reputation Review* 10 (4): 245–60.

Dinan, Desmond, Neill Nugent, and Willam E. Paterson. *The European Union in Crisis.* London UK: Macmillan International Higher Education, 2017.

Dutton, Jane E., and Janet M. Dukerich. "Keeping an Eye on the Mirror: Image and Identity in Organizational Adaptation." *Academy of Management Journal* 34, no. 3 (1991): 517–54.

Eisenegger, Mark, and Kurt Imhof. "The True, the Good and the Beautiful: Reputation Management in the Media Society." In *Public Relations Research: European and International Perspectives and Innovations,* edited by Ansgar Zerfass, Betteke van Ruler, and Krishnamurthy Sriramesh, 125–46. Wiesbaden: VS Verlag Für Sozialwissenschaften / GWV Fachverlage, Wiesbaden, 2008.

Elgström, Ole. "Outsiders' Perceptions of the European Union in International Trade Negotiations." *JCMS: Journal of Common Market Studies* 45, no. 4 (2007): 949–67.

European Commission. "Principles of Online Communication" [WWW], 2013. http://ec.europa.eu/ipg/basics/web_rationalisation/principles_en.htm.

European Commission. *Strategic Plan 2016 – 2020 – DG Communication.* 1853065 – 19/04/2016.

European Commission. *Towards an EU strategy for international cultural relations. Joint Communication to The European Parliament and The Council,* 2016. Brussels, 8.6.2016 JOIN (2016) 29 final

Fombrun, C. Reputation. *Wiley encyclopedia of Management.* Hoboken: Wiley, 2015.

Fombrun, Charles J., and Violina Rindova. "Reputation Management in Global 1000 Firms: A Benchmarking Study." *Corporate Reputation Review* 1, no. 3 (1998): 205–12.

Fombrun, Charles, and Mark Shanley. "What's in a Name? Reputation Building and Corporate Strategy." *Academy of Management Journal* 33, no. 2 (1990): 233–58.

Foreman, Peter O., David A. Whetten, and Alison Mackey. "An Identity-Based View of Reputation, Image, and Legitimacy: Clarifications and Distinctions Among Related Constructs." In *The Oxford Handbook of Corporate Reputation,* edited by

Michael L. Barnett, and Timothy G. Pollock. Oxford: Oxford University Press, 2012.

Gehring, Thomas, Sebastian Oberthür, and Marc Mühleck. "European Union Actorness in International Institutions: Why the EU Is Recognized as an Actor in Some International Institutions, but Not in Others." *JCMS: Journal of Common Market Studies* 51, no. 2 (2013): 849–65.

Georgiou, Myria, and Rafai Zaborowski. *Media Coverage of the "Refugee Crisis": A Cross-European Perspective.* Strasbourg, France: Council of Europe, 2017.

Gillen, Julia, and Guy Merchan. "Contact Calls: Twitter as a Dialogic Social and Linguistic Practice." *Language Sciences* 35, no. C (2013): 47–58.

Greenhill, Brian. "Recognition and Collective Identity Formation in International Politics." *European Journal of International Relations*, 14, no. 2 (2008): 343–68.

Gruzd, Anatoliy, Barry Wellman, Yuri Takhteyev, and Edward A. Tiryakian. "Imagining Twitter as an Imagined Community." *American Behavioral Scientist* 55, no. 10 (2011): 1294–318.

Hatch, Mary Jo, and Majken Schultz. "The Dynamics of Organizational Identity." *Human Relations* 55, no. 8 (2002): 989–1018.

Helm, Sabrina. "Designing a Formative Measure for Corporate Reputation." *Corporate Reputation Review* 8, no. 2 (2005): 95–109.

Hill, Christopher. "Closing the Capabilities-Expectations Gap?" In *A Common Foreign Policy for Europe?* edited by John Peterson, and Helene Sjursen, 35–56. London: Routledge, 2005.

Humphreys, Ashlee. *Social Media: Enduring Principles.* Oxford; New York: Oxford University Press, 2016.

Hurley, Robert F. "Putting People Back into Organizational Learning." *Journal of Business & Industrial Marketing* 17, no. 4 (2002): 270–81.

Jackson, Kevin T. *Building Reputational Capital: Strategies for Integrity and Fair Play That Improve the Bottom Line.* Oxford UK: Oxford University Press, 2004.

Jain, Rajendra Kumar, and Shreya Pandey. "The Public Attitudes and Images of the European Union in India." *India Quarterly* 68, no. 4 (2013): 331–43.

Jervis, Robert. *The Logic of Images in International Relations.* Princeton, NJ: Princeton, 1970.

Jørgensen, Knud Erik, ed. *The European Union and International Organizations.* London: Routledge, 2009.

Kowalczyk, S. J., and Pawlish, M. J. "Corporate Branding through External Perception of Organizational Culture." *Corporate Reputation Review* 5, no. 2–3 (2002): 159–74.

Lange, Donald, Peggy M. Lee, and Ye Dai. "Organizational Reputation: A Review." *Journal of Management* 37, no. 1 (2011): 153–84.

Larsen, Henrik. "The External Perceptions Literature and the Construction of Gaps in European Union Foreign Policy." *International Politics Reviews* 2, no. 1 (2014): 11–8.

Laursen, Bo, and Chiara Valentini. "Media Relations in the Council of the European Union: Insights into the Council Press Officers' Professional Practices." *Journal of Public Affairs* 13, no. 3 (2013): 230–8.

Lee, Chei Sian, and Long Ma. "News Sharing in Social Media: The Effect of Gratifications and Prior Experience." *Computers in Human Behavior* 28, no. 2 (2012): 331–9.

Lievrouw, Leah A., and Sonia Livingstone. *The Handbook of New Media.* London, Thousand Oaks, CA and New Delhi: Sage publications, 2006.

Lindemann, Thomas, and Erik Ringmar, eds. *The International Politics of Recognition.* London: Paradigm Publications, 2011.

Longo, Michael, and Philomena Murray. "No Ode to Joy? Reflections on the European Union's Legitimacy." *International Politics* 48, no. 6 (2011): 667–90.

Lucarelli, Sonia. "Perceptions of the EU in International Institutions." In *Routledge Handbook on the European Union and International Institutions: Performance, Policy, Power,* edited by Knud Erik Jørgensen, and Katie Verlin Laatikainen. Abingdon: Routledge, 2013.

Lucarelli, S. and Manners, I., eds. *Values and Principles in European Union Foreign Policy.* London: Routledge, 2006.

Manning, Harley, Kerry Bodine, Josh Bernoff, and Mel Foster. *Outside In: The Power of Putting Customers at the Center of Your Business.* New York: Forrester Research, 2012.

Martins, Ana Isabel, Sophie Lecheler, and Claes H. De Vreese. "Information Flow and Communication Deficit: Perceptions of Brussels-Based Correspondents and EU Officials." *Journal of European Integration* 34, no. 4 (2012): 305–22.

Martins, Luis L. "A Model of the Effects of Reputational Rankings on Organizational Change." *Organization Science* 16, no. 6 (2005): 701–20.

Mercer, Jonathan. *Reputation and International Politics.* Ithaca, NY: Cornell University Press, 1996.

Meyer, C. "Political Legitimacy and the Invisibility of Politics: Exploring the European Union's Communication Deficit." *Journal of Common Market Studies* 37, no. 4 (1999): 617–39.

Meznar, Martin B., and Douglas Nigh. "Buffer or Bridge? Environmental and Organizational Determinants of Public Affairs Activities in American Firms." *Academy of Management Journal* 38, no. 4 (1995): 975–96.

Miller, K.I. "Organizational Communication." In *The International Encyclopaedia of Communication,* edited by W. Donsbach. London UK: Wiley Publishing, 2008.

Money, Kevin, and Carola Hillenbrand. "Using Reputation Measurement to Create Value: An Analysis and Integration of Existing Measures." *Journal of General Management* 32, no. 1 (2006): 1–12.

Murthy, Dhiraj. "Digital Ethnography: An Examination of the Use of New Technologies for Social Research." *Sociology October* 42, no. 5 (2008): 837–55.

Nedergaard, Peter. "Borders and the EU Legitimacy Problem: The 2015–16 European Refugee Crisis." *Policy Studies* 40, no. 1 (2019): 80–91.

O'Neill, Shane, and Nicholas H. Smith, eds. *Recognition Theory as Social Research: Investigating the Dynamics of Social Conflict.* Basingstoke: Palgrave Macmillan, 2012.

Orlitzky, Marc, Frank L. Schmidt, and Sara L. Rynes. "Corporate Social and Financial Performance: A Meta-Analysis." *Organization Studies* 24, no. 3 (2003): 403–41.

Polanyi, Livia, and Annie Zaenen. "Contextual Valence Shifters." In *Computing Attitude and Affect in Text: Theory and Applications,* edited by James G. Shanahan, Yan Qu, and Janyce Wiebe, 1–10. Dordrecht: Springer, 2006.

Schlipphak, Bernd "Action and Attitudes Matter: International Public Opinion Towards the European Union." *European Union Politics* 14, no. 4 (2013): 590–618.

Taboada, Maite. "Sentiment Analysis: An Overview from Linguistics." *Annual Review of Linguistics* 2, no. 1 (2016): 325–47.

Turner, John C., Penelope J. Oakes, Alexander S. Haslam, and Craig McGarty. "Self and Collective: Cognition and Social Context." *Personality & Social Psychology Bulletin* 20, no. 5 (1994): 454–63.

Valentini, Chiara. "Political Public Relations in the European Union: EU Reputation and Relationship Management Under Scrutiny." *Public Relations Journal* 7, no. 4 (2013).

Valentini, Chiara, and Bo Laursen. "The Mass Media: A Privileged Channel for the EU's Political Communication." In *The European Public Sphere – From Critical Thinking to Responsible Action,* edited by Luciano Morganti, and Leonce Bekemans, 129–46, Brussels, BE: P.I.E.-Peter Lang, 2012

Valentini, Chiara, and Giorgia Nesti, eds. *Public Communication in the European Union. History, Perspectives and Challenges.* Newcastle upon Tyne, UK: Cambridge Scholars Publishing, 2010.

Van Dick, Rolf, Ulrich Wagner, Jost Stellmacher, and Oliver Christ. "Category Salience and Organizational Identification." *Journal of Occupational & Organizational Psychology* 78, no. 2 (2005): 273–85.

Van Noije, Lonneke. "The European Paradox: A Communication Deficit as Long as European Integration Steals the Headlines." *European Journal of Communication* 25, no. 3 (2010): 259–72.

Vidaver-Cohen, Deborah. "Reputation Beyond the Rankings: A Conceptual Framework for Business School Research." *Corporate Reputation Review* 10, no. 4 (2007): 278.

Wang, Jian. "Managing National Reputation and International Relations in the Global Era: Public Diplomacy Revisited." *Public Relations Review* 32, no. 2 (2006): 91–6.

Whetten, David A., and Alison Mackey. "A Social Actor Conception of Organizational Identity and Its Implications for the Study of Organizational Reputation." *Business & Society* 41, no. 4 (2002): 393–414.

White, Brian. *Understanding European Foreign Policy.* London UK: Macmillan International Higher Education, 2017.

PART IV

International organisations and contestation

10

DIPLOMAT OR TROLL? THE CASE AGAINST DIGITAL DIPLOMACY

Tobias Lemke and Michael Habegger

Introduction

The rapid diffusion of social media platforms and messaging services such as Twitter, WhatsApp, and Instagram, along with the proliferation of internet-connected devices, is fundamentally changing aspects of human life. Increasingly, everyday life takes place online. From interpersonal communication, banking, shopping, and dating – activities and everyday practices that were previously conducted offline – have in a few short years, become partly – and in some cases almost fully – mediated by digital technology. There has been no shortage of popular and scholarly work investigating the implications of this transition. According to some, we are now living in a "network society" (Castells 2011), driven by the libertarian dream of crowdsourcing (Shirky 2008; Bollier 2009), and marked by a condition of media hybridity (Chadwick 2013). On the one hand, this has created extraordinary political space for marginalised voices (Almeida and Lichbach 2003; Fraser 2009; Bennett and Segerberg 2013). On the other hand, people are subject to unprecedented levels of capital concentration and state surveillance (Morozov 2011; Tufekci 2017).

The changes wrought by the digital revolution are not confined to the domestic level. Increasingly, digital technology is changing the way collectivities, including states, relate to one another (e.g., Hanson 2008; Sassen 2008; Lemke and Habegger 2018). One particular area of interest has been the advent of so-called digital diplomacy (e.g., Bjola and Holmes 2015; Manor 2016). There are now more than 200 Ministries of Foreign Affairs (MFAs) and foreign ministers active on Twitter, in addition to hundreds of heads of state and missions to UN institutions (Twiplomacy 2018). The power of digitally mediated social media is said to be especially ground-breaking in the realm of public diplomacy, where statespersons are now capable of connecting with foreign publics instantaneously and over great distances (Hallams 2010).[1] Hayden, for example, suggests that in the fragmented media ecology of the 21st century, the goal of public diplomacy is transformed from the mere transmission of information to the interactive construction and leveraging of long-lasting relationships with foreign publics (2012, 3). Likewise, Pamment (2013) focuses on the two-way street of new public diplomacy that stresses engagement and listening over the one-sided transfer of information. Kampf and her co-authors (2015) investigate the extent to which the adoption of social media can help states to communicate with audiences dialogically, a relationship said to be more meaningful in its ability to engage interlocutors in a two-sided transfer of information and opinion.[2] Correspondingly, the difference between traditional forms of public diplomacy and the new digital diplomacy is that the latter envisions a more egalitarian and reciprocal dialogue between the diplomat and her audience. In contrast, traditional diplomacy is largely characterised as authoritative, hierarchical, and one-directional (Melissen 2005; Cowan and Arsenault 2008).

However, the oft-praised merger of diplomatic practice and digital technology is not without its challenges and limitations. For one, much of the discussion surrounding the power of digital diplomacy is primarily concerned with theory building rather than testing. The few empirical studies that exist tend to find little evidence that digital diplomacy is living up to its promise, and suggest that IOs and MFAs are struggling to facilitate a more dialogic communication style (e.g., Vance 2012; Kampf et al. 2015, 360–2; Berglez 2016; Manor 2016). For example, Michal Krzyżanowski's (2018, 299–300) examination of the European Commission's use of Twitter as a tool for public communication finds that much of the its online communication resembles pre-digital communication strategies: it remains strictly elitist, largely autopoietic and forgoes many opportunities to engage in more meaningful political or democratic engagement with web users. Echoing this assessment, Manor finds that foreign ministries utilise social media mainly to influence elite audiences rather than to foster dialogue with foreign populations and fail to collaborate with non-state actors or use social media as a source of information for policy makers (2016, 93). Another obstacle in the way of mainstreaming digital diplomacy is that the use of social media necessitates the formulation of best practices for employees tasked with directing digital outreach operations. Yet, training ambassadors may prove a substantial drain on resources, especially when staff members are unfamiliar with digital environments (McNutt 2014).

This raises questions about the fundamental compatibility of digital media and established patterns of international relations and order, including the prospects of developing digital diplomacy strategies that operationalise the affordances of social media platforms to enhance the communicative capacities of IOs and MFAs in the global public sphere.[3] Is digital diplomacy the new frontier in diplomatic studies or should scholars and practitioners of the diplomacy field be more sceptical of the integration of digital media and diplomatic practice?

In this paper, we caution against an overly optimistic reading of the digital turn in diplomatic studies and argue that the merger of diplomatic practice and digital technology may present more challenges than benefits for diplomats who seek to connect with international audiences via digital media. How so? The problem, we suggest, is structural in kind. Specifically, we argue that the open and unrestricted media environment that characterise today's social media networking sites is in many ways incompatible to the practice of traditional diplomacy, understood as a centuries-old system of rules, norms, and rituals to organise the peaceful interaction of states or state-like units. Simply put, the formalised and consensus-oriented communicative style of diplomacy does not mix well with the radically open and attention-oriented communication style pervading social media platforms.

To draw out this distinction, this paper develops an ideal-typical classification of traditional diplomacy (understood in its pre-digital state) and digital communication (understood through the predominant ways in which people engage with social media platforms today). Each ideal-type is structured along three dimensions that shape the overall flow and purpose of communication: (1) *scope*, (2) *process*, and (3) the underlying *logic of communication*. Diplomacy rests on the idea that a limited number of vetted actors (scope) interact over an extended period of time while following a strict set of behavioural rules to manage said interaction (process). The primary purpose of diplomacy is the amelioration of conflict between states by peaceful means – convergence and compromise (logic). In contrast, the realm of digital communication includes nearly countless actors, many of whom are anonymous and interact irregularly and without much oversight or rules to guide their interactions. This includes engaging with the community of practice called the internet, writ large, where the practices associated with "trolling" and "*pwning*" are the quite successful at sustaining engagement through the conjuring of outrage on the part of (imagined) audiences (i.e., what we in the past have called "potentially-interested others," see Lemke and Habegger 2018). The result is a communicative logic that stresses radicalisation, polarisation, and ultimately divergence rather than convergence. The relationship is depicted in Table 10.1.

Based on this differentiation, we suggest that the merger of diplomatic and digital practices may not only prove ineffective but can potentially be perilous. At best, IOs and MFAs will find it difficult to promote and achieve their diplomatic goals through the integration and adoption of digital communication

TABLE 10.1 Ideal-typical classification of traditional diplomacy and digital communication

Ideal-typical Dimension	Traditional Diplomacy	Digital Politics
Scope	Contraction	Expansion
Process	Deceleration	Acceleration
Logic	Convergence	Divergence

practices. At worst, the attempt may distort and perhaps even undermine the primary function of diplomacy by providing a strategic opening for less savoury and disruptive bad faith actors to exploit the affordances of digital media for their own ends.

The remainder of the paper begins with a review of the historical development of diplomacy as an institution of international politics and its constitution as an ideal-type. In the next section, we do the same for digital communication by first walking through its historical emergence before focusing on key attributes that allow us to typologise it as an ideal-type. Importantly, our classification suggests that there is an inherent discrepancy between the communicative logics that drive diplomacy and digital communications, respectively. As a result, we conceive of "digital diplomacy" as a contradiction in terms.

We illustrate these claims by analysing the digital communications behaviour of NATO's official Twitter account (@NATO) over the course of a one-month period (March 2019). We employ a qualitative grounded theory methodology to identify prominent themes in @NATO's messaging and comment on its overall communication style. We then compare our findings with the feed activity of another Twitter account, Russia's Embassy in the United Kingdom (@RussianEmbassy). We find that the communicative style of each account differs significantly and in important ways. In the case of @NATO, an international organisation, tweets are mainly used to make official announcements and link to press releases. Overall, this suggests NATO remains committed to the communicative logic of diplomacy and that digital platforms are used as a way to broaden the dissemination of NATO's standard public outreach content – with the obvious downside that the content generated little traction on the platform. In contrast, @RussianEmbassy, a different kind of institution – namely, an MFA – with a different kind of diplomatic mission and political orientation, utilises a distinctly more digital communication style, which is more contentious and antagonistic. We even find some evidence that @RussianEmbassy engages in transgressive digital practices with the apparent goal of undermining and ridiculing potential geopolitical competitors, including NATO. Together, the embassy's digital outreach strategy seems to be more focused on generating attention through affective content. While this appears more effective in terms of garnering public engagement on the platform, it has little to do with traditional notions of diplomatic practice. We conclude our comparison with a brief discussion.

The development of traditional diplomatic relations

The development of diplomacy as an international institution has been discussed in great detail elsewhere (e.g., Anderson 1993; Reus-Smit 1999) and it will suffice to cover the major institutional developments. Following the decline of the Roman Empire, Europe and its many principalities were little more than a loose conglomeration of states. By the onset of the Hundred Years

War, the picture changed as the rivalry between the Plantagenets of England and the French King brought the states of Western Europe into more regular political and military contact with each (Anderson 1993, 2). Continuing processes of state-centralisation also meant that rulers now asserted their dominance over domestic rivals and emerged as singular and continuous representatives of their territories (Kienast 1936). A diplomatic system recognizable to contemporary onlookers emerged around the 15th century in the Italian peninsula. Here, an environment of near-constant power-political competition put a premium on the acquisition of information about the potential actions of competitors (Mallett 1981). Against this backdrop, two modern principles of diplomacy gradually emerged. First, states began to regularly send and receive diplomatic representatives. Second, rulers established permanent embassies in foreign territories for the purpose of gaining reliable information about political developments (Mattingly 1955, 108–118). This proto-diplomatic network spread northwards across the Alps in the 16th century before spreading eastwards to encompass the many states of Eastern Europe and the Russian Empire (Anderson 1993, 70).

The volume of diplomatic conduct precipitated the institutionalisation of diplomatic relations, leading to the first foreign offices and state departments. While these tended to be small, their formation brought a formalisation to a still-relatively ad hoc diplomatic system. The year 1773 saw the creation of the *Staats und Reichskanzlei* as the administrative centre of foreign policy-making in the Austrian Empire. However, France went furthest in establishing a well-organised foreign ministry machinery of a recognizably modern bent (Anderson 1993, 76–80). The gradual institutionalisation of the diplomatic service went in hand-in-hand with its piecemeal professionalisation. Throughout the nineteenth century, foreign ministries became more systematic and meritocratic, promoting the acquisition of practical experience through travel and academic study. This led to the notion that diplomacy constituted a distinct professional field run by a *corps diplomatique* (Holsti 2004, 189). In this respect, diplomacy became more modern and independent of the fixtures of inherited rank and social status that dominated old regime society (Anderson 1993, 123).

By the turn of the 20th century, the growing importance of public opinion – at least in the constitutional democracies of the Western *Entente* powers – signalled a shift from a diplomacy based on dynastic concerns to one that reflected the interests of a popularly governed bureaucratic state (Reus-Smit 1999, 87–121). This opening of diplomacy accelerated after the First World War with the emergence of the League of Nations system (Holsti 2004, 195–6). While these developments did little to prevent the diplomatic blunders of the interwar period, innovations in communications technology continued the trend towards open diplomacy after the Second World War. The 20th century saw the complete transformation of diplomacy from its ad hoc, secretive, and elite-based beginning to a new highly formalised, open, and "democratic" conception of international relations (Nicholson 1961) – one that required substantial public explanation and openness despite its growing complexity and technical sophistication.

Diplomacy as ideal-type

For an ideal-typical classification of diplomacy, we focus on three core characteristics of diplomatic practice (Table 10.2). The first is diplomacy's historical tendency to limit the number of legitimate actors during diplomatic negotiations. We call this the *scope* of diplomatic communications. The second is the prevalence of ritual and precedence that streamlines and decelerates diplomatic relations along a strict behaviour code (i.e., diplomatic etiquette). We call this the *process* of diplomatic communications. Together, scope and process coalesce into a third dimension, the overall logic of diplomatic practice: the convergence of inter-state interests and amelioration of international conflict by peaceful means.

A word of caution regarding our methodology. According to Max Weber, ideal-types serve as analytical measuring sticks that help researchers capture the most salient and essential components of any social thing (1999, 191). Ideal-types can be developed genealogically through careful historical analysis or by the application of a more classificatory and deductive mode of thinking that considers the logical functions of the object in question. We combine both approaches. However, ideal-types have limitations as well. They constitute abstractions located at the poles of variation. That is, they attempt to capture the essence of a thing in its purest form. Consequently, ideal-types are rarely found in real life, and complex empirical actuality will almost always deviate from the most essential characteristics one identifies in an ideal-type. Nonetheless, we argue that the ideal-type allows us to engage the issue of digital diplomacy from a theoretical vantage point by comparing how the essential characteristic of traditional diplomatic practice and digital communications match up *in theory*.

The scope of diplomacy

One of the primary characteristics of modern diplomacy is the deliberate reduction of the number of legitimate actors that can participate in the formalised practice of inter-state relations. This deliberate lessening of interlocutors is driven

TABLE 10.2 Traditional diplomacy as ideal-type

Ideal-typical Dimensions	
Scope	*Concentration;* few-to-few communication; limited number of legitimate interlocutors
Process	*Deceleration;* streamlining and ordering of the diplomatic process through the imposition of standardized behavioural rules
Logic	*Convergence;* amelioration of inter-state conflict through peaceful means

by two related historical processes. The first deals with the *recognition of* official representatives. In the Middle Ages, all sorts of principals sent diplomatic agents to various recipients (Queller 1967, 11). For example, it was not uncommon for a group of merchants to send representatives to the rulers of a foreign territory to negotiate terms of trade. Anderson argues these "plebeian" origins of diplomatic representation persisted until the 17th century when the titles "ambassador" and "procurator" were used widely and interchangeably (1993, 4).

From the end of the 15th century onwards, Europe's rulers became less inclined to allow their subjects this freedom and the idea that *only* sovereigns could conduct diplomacy crystallised (Anderson 1993, 6). The right to send ambassadors was denied to rulers whose sovereignty was limited by any kind of feudal tie or pledge of subjection to a liege lord (Krauske 1885, 155–6). By the beginning of the 1700s, it was clear that representation was prerogative of sovereigns alone. Correspondingly, a clear system of hierarchy emerged within the diplomatic branch, accompanied by the development of a distinct professional group of diplomats who adhered to their own traditions and standards.

A second process involved the gradual *hierarchisation* of diplomatic relations along a great-power/lesser-power continuum that, over time, concentrated a significant amount of diplomatic capital among a small number of great powers in the international system (Bull 1977; Reus-Smit 2005, 90). Some English School (ES) scholars have theorised this idea through the concept of collective hegemony; authoritative control was not exercised necessarily by a single state but could be collective, coalitional, or inclusive in character (Clark 2011, 9–10; see Webster 1934, 153). Accordingly, the hierarchisation of power and influence at the top of the international totem pole increased the efficiency of diplomacy considerably.

A potential proxy measure of this concentration of diplomatic power is the number of key negotiating states and signatories during landmark treaties throughout early-modern and modern diplomatic history. Although there is some variance in numbers over several conferences, from the Peace of Westphalia in 1646–1648 to the Potsdam and Yalta Conference, the number of delegations involved in negotiations was reduced from 190 to just three. While many of these negotiations were attended by delegations as numerous or larger than those at Westphalia, the influence of lesser powers decreased markedly over time. Even today, with a record United Nations membership of some 190 states and countless intergovernmental and non-governmental organisations crowding the global diplomatic field, a disproportional amount of diplomatic power remains concentrated among the five veto-wielding powers of the UN Security Council. Moreover, the growing popularity of face-to-face diplomacy among heads of state (Riordan 2003), especially during high-profile summit meetings, has led to a decline of the ambassadorial role as the main conduit of communication between governments. Today, diplomatic influence and power are pooled at the very top of the international political hierarchy.

The process of diplomacy

The second key attribute of the diplomatic ideal-type is the *process* of communication. This includes the tendency of diplomacy to streamline and order relations along a standardised communicative pathway. We think of this as a form of strategic *deceleration*: diplomacy seeks to slow down relations among states by creating standards of conduct, formal rules, and a clear hierarchy of participants, all with the goal of producing reciprocal resolutions to international problems.

This tendency to formalise and streamline the process is observable in a number of ways. One is the key role of ceremony and ritual in the conduct of diplomatic affairs. From its earliest beginnings, religious ceremony was an important ingredient in the conduct of relations between rulers, and negotiations were often begun with prayers and agreements signed in churches or abbeys. For example, it was common for parties to a negotiated treaty to take a solemn and public oath of observance, almost always in a church and sworn on some particularly venerated relic (Anderson 1993, 5). The same tendency towards greater formality and display can be seen in the growing importance of ceremonial orations usually given by a representative in their first formal audience by the ruler to whom he had been sent. Because 15th-century Italian humanists championed the art of rhetoric and the ability to mould words, Italian Renaissance diplomacy was particularly taken to the practice of commencing negotiations with tediously verbose displays of rhetoric (Reus-Smit 1999, 73).

A clear hierarchy of diplomatic rank emerged over time as the controversial question of precedence, the formal ranking of diplomats during official state function, was settled. By the 18th century, the titles of "extraordinary" and "minister plenipotentiary" became the most common ranks in the diplomatic service below that of the resident ambassador (Krauske 1885, 150–86). Relatively new categories of *charge d' affaires*, secretary of embassy and legation, were appearing to fill in the lower ranks – all of which gave structure to the diplomatic process. Even modern diplomacy, much less concerned with the projection of social status, still follows clear lines of precedent and hierarchy. More importantly, diplomacy (especially when it is exercised publicly) continues to show a proclivity towards ritualism. Official state visits are almost always accompanied by opulent displays of ceremony, including military parades, colour guards, military bands, and sundry of nation-state panoply. Even if this only captures the public face of diplomacy, it is telling that politicians continue to observe these standards in an effort to set the stage for the more political and technical negotiations that follow.

The logic of diplomacy

If the scope and process of diplomacy push the practice towards fewer numbers of interlocutors who interact in an increasingly organised, rigid, and rule-based environment, what does this tell us about the overall logic of diplomatic practice? Although diplomacy fulfils a variety of functions in international relations (e.g., ceremony, management, information-exchange, communication, negotiation, and the creation of rules as international law), its core function, we suggest, remains a normative commitment to the creation and maintenance of international order, primarily through the creation of universal rules (i.e., international law) and the peaceful settlement of inter-state conflict (Barston 2013, 3).

This does not preclude the fact that, at a substantive level, much of the business of diplomacy is concerned with the management of routine issues, including relatively mundane activities such as coordination, consultation, lobbying, and adjustments to the agenda of official or private visits. The everyday conduct of diplomacy may seem low profile, tedious, and even overly bureaucratic. However, the machinery of diplomacy does not diminish the fact that – at an abstract level – diplomacy is concerned with reducing tension, the clarification of arguments, and the quest for acceptable solutions to inter-state disputes. This notion is shared by many in the field. Adam Watson argues that the "central task of diplomacy" is "the management of change and the maintenance by continued persuasion of order in the midst of change" (Watson 1992). Accordingly, the gradual evolution of diplomacy went hand in hand with the idea that relations among states can be ameliorated by continuous and intelligent diplomacy (Reus-Smit 1999, 149) and put on a "more stable and peaceful footing than they would otherwise be" (Sharp 2009, 11).

Of course, diplomacy can be put towards other, more sinister, ends. In a Clausewitzian sense, diplomacy frequently serves as an extension of political conflict, and even war. The practice of counter-diplomacy or coercive diplomacy are two prominent examples.[4] Still, the development of diplomacy as an institution demonstrates a general cross-case willingness of political units to work within a framework of rules even when the character of diplomacy varies from one international system to another. Two particular mechanisms are worth highlighting. The first is *negotiation*, defined as an attempt to explore and reconcile conflicting positions in order to reach an acceptable outcome (Barston 2013, 51). What makes negotiation especially salient for our discussion is that regardless of the nature of the outcome of any negotiation episode (which may actually favour one party over another), the purpose of negotiation is the identification of areas of common interest and conflict (Iklé 1964). During negotiations, parties seek compromises in order to narrow gaps between positions until a point of convergence is reached (Zartman 1975, 71–2). Accordingly, successful negotiation usually includes substantial *convergence* over areas of common interest.

Closely related to negotiation is the mechanism of *mediation*. One of the central tasks of diplomacy is contributing to the pacific settlement of disputes between states and other actors. Traditionally, the methods used for this include mechanisms such as conciliation, arbitration, and mediation. These methods received formal recognition in both the League of Nations Covenant and United Nations Charter (Article 12 of the League of Nations Covenant and Chapter 6, Article 33 of UN Charter). Whereas conciliation relates to the clarifying of positions and arbitration is generally conducted juridically, mediation, either directly or indirectly, attempts to promote a temporary or permanent solution based on a conception of outcomes likely to "receive joint or widespread acceptance by the parties in dispute" (Barston 2013, 262). As Kissinger put it, "the utility of a mediator is that, if trusted by both sides, he can soften the edge of controversy and provide a mechanism for adjustment on issues of prestige" (1982, 883). Again, we note diplomacy's fundamental concern with choreographing *convergence* through *compromise*.

The development of digitally mediated communications

The historical development of digital communication is key for explaining the exponential growth in global interaction capacity between non-state actors (e.g., Christakis and Fowler 2009; Lemke and Habegger 2018). Accordingly, the current era of digital communication is in many ways a continuation of the information revolution begun some 25 years ago. The expansion of computerised communicative forms through the use of fax machines, modems, and email familiarised people with frequent communication with more widely dispersed others. The arrival of "Web 2.0" in the mid-aughts made the means to publish information online more broadly accessible. People were increasingly able to post their opinions and experiences, and comment on and appropriate the work of their peers online without the explicit intervention of traditional gatekeepers. However, doing so still required a substantial amount of technical know-how and access to expensive internet-connected computers. Accordingly, it was the creation and diffusion of social media networks across platforms and devices, especially smartphones, that truly expanded interaction capacity by substantially increasing the number of people who could participate in digital communication on a daily basis. Today, people use the knowledge they gather through everyday experience to act creatively and take advantage of the communicative opportunities provided by the affordances of digital media.

The development of specific social technologies also expanded the space for political expression and contention, partly due to choices made by big tech companies and the character of the algorithms that govern information flows, but also due to the creativity of regular people encountering the technologies on their own (e.g., della Porta 2007; Earl and Kimport 2011; Castells 2012, 58). Innovations such as the inclusion of hashtags in social media posts, subscribing to newsletters, sharing photos and videos, following or friending political advocacy groups, and participating in political blogging communities may all broadly be characterised as variations on the fundamental practices of digital communication. These involve the ubiquitous, frequent, and lightweight practices of receiving and sending information, images, and videos, as well as friending, following, and sharing. These practices tend to produce a distinct political dynamic usually referred to as the politics of outrage (e.g., Sobieraj and Berry 2011). Actors promote normative agendas such as liberal human rights and the rule of law, but also disseminate ideological content oriented towards recruiting others susceptible to messages meant to attack liberal institutions and ideology. Instead of depending on diplomatic efforts employing the diplomatic logic at the state level, today, individuals and groups communicate across borders autonomously. In sum, the development of digital communications technology created a relatively horizontal and open space prone to activism and contention.

Digital communication as ideal-type

We have argued diplomacy rests on the notion that a limited number of vetted actors interact with one another while following a strict set of behavioural rules to manage said interaction. In contrast, digital communication is driven by almost countless actors – many of whom remain anonymous – that interact irregularly and without much official oversight or rules to guide their interactions. The inherent and ambiguous ubiquity of the internet presents problems for the creation of a common code of behavioural standards. Thus, the establishment of a streamlined and ordered process of communication might prove more difficult in the digital vis-à-vis the analogue realm. Finally, we highlighted that what individuals and groups of people do online on a day-to-day basis contributes to the formation of a particular kind of communicative logic that seeks the attraction of attention, oftentimes through the dissemination of affective content that is more outrageous, contentious, and radical than the rest. The result is divergence rather than convergence (see Table 10.3).

The scope of digital communication

In contrast to the diplomatic field, digital communication and associated technologies have vastly reduced the opportunity costs traditionally associated with collective mobilisation. Based in part on the arguments made by scholars of contentious politics who view the emergence of digital media as a turning point in the trajectory of collective action (Almeida and Lichbach 2003; Bennett and Segerberg 2013), we argue contemporary networks of activists and participants are no longer tied to one another by geographic proximity. Today, episodes of collective action and protest can be global in scope even as they unfold hundreds or even thousands of miles apart. More importantly, the arrival of consumer-oriented social media platforms opened avenues for communication and participation in a digital public sphere to those otherwise

TABLE 10.3 Digitally mediated communications as ideal-type

Ideal-typical Dimensions	
Scope	*Expansion*; many-to-many communication; potentially unlimited number of interlocutors
Process	*Acceleration*; abundance of information and users pressures content to become more extreme to capture attention; quest for immediacy; lack of gatekeepers
Logic	*Divergence*; radicalisation and polarisation; development of outrage culture; emergence of trolling practices as modus operandi

unfamiliar with the technical aspects of the internet (Bohman 2004; Dahlgren 2005; Shirky 2008). Thus, it requires little training or expertise to become an effective organiser in the 21st century. Social media has democratised political action by removing much of the power of traditional gatekeepers and subsequently allowed for the unhindered evolution and expansion of democratic values (e.g., Karagiannopoulos 2012).

Nowadays, the skyrocketing rates of ownership of smartphones, the use of communication applications, and the increasing sophistication of web platforms undergird the reality of a constant connectedness to information. As such, social media and connected devices, apps, and web platforms put (potential) actors in touch with one another and increase the frequency of interaction between actors and ideas. Digital communications networks have also fragmented the traditional (mass) media system, effectively empowering "new" actors and multiplying the number of centres of power (Chadwick 2013). The social ties that constitute these new configurations, supported by the mundane activities of friending, following, and sharing, contribute to the ongoing instability of established networks of authority and rule as well as the availability of new allies and coalition partners (Tilly 2015, 60). The increasing number of linkages enables the bundling together of various grievances into novel identity categories (McAdam, Tarrow and Tilly 2001, 138), and the prevalence of weak ties gives activists the opportunity to extend their messages to a broader audience (Bennett, Bruening, and Givens 2008; Velensuela, Arriagada, and Scherman 2014). While initial access to these technologies was enjoyed by relatively wealthy actors from the West who marshalled resources to local like-minded activists, digital technologies are much more widely available, meaning that many more people, groups, and ideas are vocalised. A side-effect of this development is that an increasing number of vocal counter-progressive actors are now finding their home in the discourse of what we have traditionally considered as the liberal Western world (e.g., Phillips and Milner 2018). These arguments are well-established in the political communication and Science and Technology Studies (STS) literatures, but there remains a need for diplomatic studies scholars to decouple digital communications technologies from Western cultural frames. The notion that "the West" developed these technologies, and, therefore, they will be inherently useful for the promotion of liberal agendas, is unrealistic.

In sum, the scope of digital communication, in its ideal-typical form, is distinct from diplomacy. The substantial number of actors that can (if they wish) participate in communication across borders, as well as their relatively horizontal arrangement, marks digital communication. The affordances of social media networks in use today (at least) ostensibly promote an equality of voices and configurations of actors, no matter their power-political position or ideological commitments. The increasing interaction capacity allows for the participation of various novel configurations of actors with (potentially) divergent and varied agendas. Thus, no one, and no topic, is truly off the table – even by custom.

The process of digital communication

Social media (i.e., their affordances) support particular kinds of social interaction and, depending on the platform, have a particular kind of collective action baked in (Milan 2015b, 4). First, consider the immediate and straightforward ways in which participants can gain access to information. Social media enable a near-constant connectedness to information, allowing for large numbers of people to react to news events and political developments in essentially real time. Of course, much of the information they see is tailored to their interests (or their consumer tastes) due to sorting behaviour when it comes to enrolment in different information networks. However, this state of informational and communicative connectedness lends itself to the acceleration of the conversation, no matter the topic.

The resulting acceleration of information diffusion can create a lack of coherence in messaging. Necessity explains part of this as the affordances of social media encourage the rapid sharing of information in order to garner attention. In today's participatory and fragmented media ecology, actors can broadcast to immense publics while citizen journalists and social entrepreneurs can document newsworthy events and generate viral "memes" and moments that often affect national conversations. Simultaneously, this proliferation of digital conversation and interaction has added to the glut of available information and hence has made the procurement of attention crucial (Tufekci 2013, 850). As Simon noted before, "the wealth of information means a dearth of something else: a scarcity of whatever it is that information consumes. What information consumes is rather obvious: It consumes the attention of its recipients. Hence a wealth of information creates a poverty of attention" (1971, 40). Attention is the lifeblood of digital communications.

Moreover, the structure of social media platforms generally only allows for the publication of short messages and small collections of images rather than nuanced essays, well-reasoned speeches, etc. If someone wants to promote a particular message on social media, it should be short, sweet, and quick. The trade-off is that people who may be interested in passing along the information or adding on to it will not be as easily able to ascertain the larger programme or goal underlying the original message. The result is a lack of coherence: NATO might share a message commemorating the signing of a treaty, but its brevity and lack of context may only serve to dilute the message or confuse the imagined audience.

On the other hand, these same affordances can lead to extreme message coherence but a dearth of nuance and sophistication (i.e., clear but shallow political content). Short and simple messages may rapidly diffuse without the meaningful creative participation of an imagined audience. Thus, the process of digital communication may be marked by large numbers of coherent but shallow bits of information. A cursory look at the Russian Embassy in the UK's tweets shows this very phenomenon: it frequently publishes tweets leveraging existing sentiment on social media sarcastically denouncing NATO as "bad," but this is about the end of it – at least for the typically politically unsophisticated Twitter user.

What techniques do invested actors use to promote their agendas onto imagined audiences? One popular, familiar, and easy technique is to use the retweet and quote-tweet functions of Twitter to draw attention to particular ideas and topics (e.g., Yardi and Boyd 2010). This is a way to expand political discourse. Activists may use the quote-tweet function to augment the existing information in an attempt to extend and evolve the narrative frames that serve to sustain a movement or policy (Theocharis et al. 2015, 216). Other common linguistic conventions found on Twitter, such as hashtags, shortened links to external content, likes, retweets, and lists constitute just a few of the large catalogue of practices available to digital communication participants that have significant structuring consequences for the political discourse and everyday conversation (Milan 2015a, 890). These techniques are becoming intuitive, and, at least on Twitter, help constitute the process of digital communication.

Another pertinent example is the creative use of memes across social media and internet messaging platforms where images can be easily published and shared. Memes are small units of culture that spread from person to person by copying or imitation (Dawkins 1976). Memes today are most commonly located in digital space, diffusing from person to person (or post to post), although they frequently "scal[e] up" (Shifman 2014, 18) into a shared social phenomenon that shapes, represents, and reconstitutes shared understandings and "general mindsets" (2014, 4). A meme "connect[s] across contingency ... [and] through its circulation, the meme connects a group of people which are otherwise dispersed and unconnected" (McDonald 2015, 973; see also Knuttila 2011). Importantly, memes are useful for the generation of virality – the rapid spread of a single relatively unchanging cultural artifact – and diffusion, which involves complex forms of cultural agency and local adaptation (Shifman 2014, 157).

Together, these processes guarantee that memes not only quickly spread across networks, but their potential effects on digital conversations and dialogue remain unpredictable and volatile. The meme of Pepe the Frog reputedly assisted Donald Trump's election campaign for President, in part because its simplicity and relative shallowness was able to link disparate groups together in support of a populist candidate and campaign. The images of the character, V, from *V for Vendetta*, were useful in the process of quickly linking various opposition groups together in Egypt in 2011 (e.g., Herrera 2015; Gerbaudo 2015). The ubiquitous practice of posting images of cute cats was employed by ISIL to recruit people to their cause and humanise masked militants. The practice of sharing memes may be appropriated by activists as expressions of dissent (Pfaff and Yang 2001). All this, perhaps, begs the question – what memes do IOs have that might lend themselves to the process of digital communication?

It is what people actually do with social media, in combination with the platforms' affordances, that drives the process of digital communication. The rapid process of aggregating voices into an environment promotes immediacy, acceleration, and adaptation. It is in this way that we can speak of actor constitution on digital platforms. The process of aggregating voices rapidly into various configurations occurs in an environment where there is little need to engage in persuasion let alone deliberation. There is no requirement that there be a coherent agenda behind the information that one comes across on social media before he or she (unconsciously) passes it along. As we will discuss in the following section, disruption, not coherence, is the endgame.

The logic of digital communication

Defining the scope and process of digital communication allows for the synthesising of a *logic* of digital communication – one that is highly contentious and can feed on the generation of outrage and radical content to attract attention. How so? The multitude of actors and the speed by which the social media platforms are populated with content create a digital environment rich in information. This wealth of information makes the procurement of attention all the more important. In turn, the fundamental practices associated with digital communication – sending and receiving information, images, and videos – are ubiquitous, frequent, and lightweight and produce a distinct political dynamic that is often related to the economy of outrage (Berry and Sobieraj 2014; Castells 2015). Posting emotionally laden content is an effective way to enrol potentially interested others into a misinformation campaign. It is this logic that primarily informs the constitution of (politically oriented) entities online. Social media technologies are crucial in determining the character of collective subjects and the role that they play in how those entities become self-conscious.

In turn, the gratification felt by participants in social media conversations, quantified in likes, retweets, and replies, creates a particular mechanism that explains the constitution of the logic of digital communication. On the one hand, the affect experienced through social media participation can produce a spiral of radicalisation, an increasing contradiction between prevailing claims, programmes, self-descriptions, and descriptions of entities and individuals (McAdam et al. 2001, 161). The incentives for radicalisation, due in large part to the vast number of potential audience members, are such that the more extreme the viewpoint, the more attention a user will receive. More attention means more gratification for users and an increased likelihood they will return to the source of content.

A drive towards radicalisation can also manifest itself in the application of individual-level activities, such as *pwning* practices.[5] *Pwning*, in this context, is doing or saying anything online that is perceived to upset an imaginary set of political centrists. Engaging in *pwning* is one way in which to foster collective identity across networks and borders (Bennett 2003; Della Porta and Mosca 2005). In-group identity is strengthened by likes and friendly replies to the messages imagined as "owns" while references to those being "owned" strengthen a sense of in-group and out-group identities (Yardi and Boyd 2010). It takes a lot of discursive, technical, and tedious work to create a sense of shared experience necessary for the generation of an identity. Not only this, but it breeds an additional sense of competition for attention, driving further a culture of the extreme. Any collectivity emerging from a particular social media site will be marked by its extreme attributes.

On the other hand, the acceleration encouraged by social media affordances can lead to a spiral of mundanity, where relatively vapid or meaningless bits of information or opinion can receive lots of attention exactly because they are easy to understand (e.g., "dunking" by saying one word on a quote tweet). This can lead to a divergence between configurations of entities and individuals as simple bits of information become a kind of cultural currency making little sense to others. The enclaves these spirals produce, however, are not impenetrable. Rather, it is the very shallowness of the content produced and shared in the radical and mundane spirals that allows for members of one fluid configuration to (accidentally) find themselves enrolled in another's political project. That is, groups and communities are formed almost accidentally – unconsciously at first – through the discovery of common interests (both political and recreational) or involvement in particular social or political projects. This could very well occur through the constant encounter with others in networks linked through global communications networks and the social practices that follow (e.g., hashtags, message boards, Facebook groups, or comments on blog and local newspaper items). Facebook, among others, encourages the "sharing or linking and participating in predetermined protest actions" (Agarwal et al. 2014b, 336–7). Individual participants are generally acting on their learned predispositions to share information they "like" on social media, and not purposefully adhering to or challenging diplomatic protocols or the larger liberal order. People experience the collective individually, and the lack of principled commitments lowers the stakes involved with sharing (counter)productive information.

Together, the logic of digital communication can lead to the formation of a segment of international actors – fluidly situated between the diplomatic and civil society realms – who engage politically, on social media. As these entities engaging in digital communication on social media coalesce into collectivities with comprehensive political agendas, they challenge our neat analytical distinctions between diplomacy, public diplomacy, soft power, and civil society and interest group advocacy. IOs could find themselves here. But in engaging in digital diplomacy – the hybrid form – they will end up constituting themselves through disruptive digitally mediated practices such as *meming* and *pwning*. Engaging in these communication practices means (at best, tacitly) accepting the presence of an almost ideological commitment to transgression that is bound up in the logic of digital communication. This (negative) agency without a desire for (positive) agency undermines the extant geopolitical order in ways that, without the affordances and ubiquity of social media, would be impossible.

Methods

We illustrate our argument by analysing and comparing a corpus of tweets from the official Twitter accounts of NATO (@NATO) and the Russian Embassy in the UK (@RussianEmbassy) with the purpose of locating their communicative logic along the diplomatic-digital spectrum developed. We chose these accounts specifically based on their comparatively high profile and frequent use of the social media platform. They also "fit the bill," in the sense that they represent an IO and MFA, respectively – the usual targets of research on digital diplomacy. Our analysis should be interpreted in strictly exploratory terms and future research should expand its scope to address issues of case selection and comparability. For now, we are simply interested in two broad questions. First, what are international actors such as NATO, and MFAs such as the Russian Embassy in the UK, actually tweeting about? Second, does their Twitter behaviour match the communicative logic of ideal-typical diplomatic communication, digital communication, or both?

For the purpose of our present discussion, we employ a sequential mixed methods design (Creswell 2014; Murthy 2018) that begins with a quantitative analysis of a large corpora of tweets before conducting a qualitative analysis of individual tweets following the grounded theory approach (Corbin and Strauss 2015). We begin with the compilation of a dataset of 3,200 tweets from each account structured along several automated coding categories. This helps us to discuss general differences in activity and engagement between each set of tweets (i.e., retweets and likes as a proportion of the number of each account's respective followers) and provides a general picture of the Twitter usage of each handle.

For the qualitative element of our study, we hand-coded a smaller dataset of 98 tweets – published within the month of March 2019 – which we created by randomly selecting 49 from each account. There exists a variety of methods to code tweets and their users (e.g., Dann 2010; Honeycutt and Herring 2009), however, hand-coding is considered the gold standard (e.g., Hughes et al. 2014). Thus, for each tweet, we asked what the tweet is about (i.e., subject area) and who the tweet is for (i.e., audience). To ensure intercoder reliability, we took turns interpreting the tweet corpora. Each author analysed each tweet – which were arranged non-sequentially – using the Status URL so as to maintain the context by which people would encounter them on their own devices. Although we entered the coding phase with some preconceived notions of what we expected to find (i.e., evidence of specific communicative logics), we followed a grounded theory approach by engaging each tweet individually and on its own terms. Accordingly, our concepts and categories should be derived from data collected during the research process and not chosen prior to beginning the research (Corbin and Strauss 2015, 7). This approach is particularly suitable for dealing with complexity by directing us to locate action in context. For this reason, employing emergent coding methods – though it is time-consuming – presents tremendous opportunities to understand tweets individually and collectively (Murthy 2018).

After doing this we matched our findings with the categories developed in the ideal-type face with the intention of identifying patterns. In this sense, our methodology follows a four-stage model of (1) category development (ideal-types), (2) quantitative analysis (large dataset analytics), (3) grounded theory approach (individual hand-coding of tweets), and (4) deductive analysis (comparison of ideal-type categories with hand codes).

Results

We begin with a general overview of the Twitter activity of @NATO and @RussianEmbassyUK. After weighting the retweets and likes of the @RussianEmbassyUK by a factor of approximately 7.25 to make up the difference between its number of followers (84,568) and @NATO's (614,203), we can see some significant differences between the engagement that each account receives. The average NATO tweet in our sample received 12.23 favourites ($SD = 55.01$), while the average Russian Embassy tweet received 282.52 ($SD = 365.98$). The difference between the two samples is highly significant ($p < 0.0001$, $t = 5.1974$, $SE = 52.01$, $CI = 165.73$ to 374.86). The average NATO tweet received 74.02 retweets ($SD = 59.80$), while the average Russian Embassy tweet earned 262.21 ($SD = 248.48$). The difference between these two samples, again, is highly significant ($p < 0.0001$, $t = 5.0399$, $SE = 35.442$, $CI = 116.93$ to 259.46). Together, this preliminarily indicates we are observing two different kinds of accounts with different kinds of practices, audiences, and content.

Qualitative results

For the second stage of the project, we approached each individual tweet asking: (1) what is the subject or function of this tweet and (2) who is the tweet addressed to? Following the grounded theory approach, each author hand-coded all 98 tweets individually before we merged our analysis around several prominent themes and concepts. For the @NATO corpus, we identified four separate categories for question one and five categories for question two (see Table 10.4).

Much of the @NATO dataset is dominated by commemorative tweets highlighting the anniversaries of Eastern European member states joining the Alliance. Oftentimes, these tweets also signal NATO's values.

TABLE 10.4 @NATO Twitter content analysis summary

Subject and Function of Tweet	Audience of Tweet
Commemoration of historical event	General public
Member state ascension	Specific member state
Signalling of NATO values & alliance affirmation	Specific non-member state
Information	Secretary-General
Press release & announcement	Specific institution (i.e., US Congress)
	NATO personnel

Relatively generic press announcements and tweets providing additional information about past and future events are also common. Many contain links to other websites.

There are few surprises regarding audience type. Most of @NATO's tweets are directed at a general audience, although the value-laden tone of the corpora suggest the account is talking to an audience who is already sympathetic to the organisation and will respond positively to frequent value signalling. In some instances, tweets address specific actors, including Member States, non-Member States, the Secretary-General, and members of the organisation. There are no tweets in our dataset to address actors that could be considered "competitors" or "enemies" of the alliance and only one retweet suggests an engagement with a more contentious political issue – terrorism.

Jens Stoltenberg ✔
@jensstoltenberg

Three years ago, terrorism struck in Brussels.
Two years ago, in London. One week ago, in
Christchurch. Terrorism comes in many forms
& may hide behind religion or ideology. But it
always attacks our freedom & our values. Let
our answer be to stand up against hate –
every time.

Our analysis of the @RussianEmbassy Twitter corpus yielded quite different results during the hand-coding stage. Following the same procedure as before, we developed a concept inventory that includes seven topics for question one and six for question two (see Table 10.5).

At first glance, we notice some overlap. The @RussianEmbassy feed produces a significant number of tweets dealing with the commemoration of historical events, often through the use of the #OTD ("on this date") hashtag.

TABLE 10.5 @RussianEmbassy Twitter content analysis summary

Subject and Function of Tweet	Audience of Tweet
Commemoration of historical event #OTD	General public
Economic opportunity framing & prestige strategies	Individual states (antagonists)
Press release & announcement	International organizations (antagonists)
Information & cultural framing	Politicians, leaders, & spokespersons
Value signalling (e.g., stability, sovereignty, non-intervention)	Individuals
Disinformation & fake news	News organisations (antagonists)
Political crisis & blame attribution	

Likewise, we find relatively generic information bites and press releases, as well as a significant level of "cultural framing" ostensibly designed to attract tourism to parts of Russia or simply to underscore the "natural beauty" of the landscape.

There are significant differences, however. For one, the account frequently draws attention to ongoing crises around the world. Many of these tweets are framed to highlight the positive role Russia plays ameliorating these conflicts while shifting blame towards Western actors, including the United States and NATO. The sample is much more contentious and antagonistic than its @NATO counterpart.

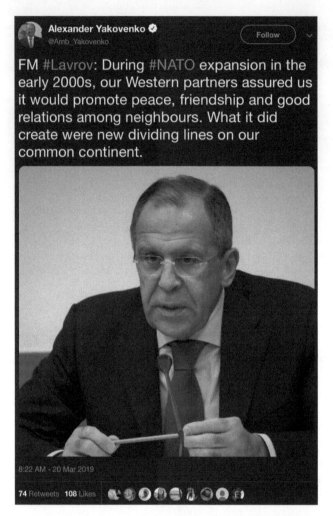

This more antagonistic framing falls in line with the dataset's general disposition to depict the world in competitive zero-sum terms. An ongoing concern with underscoring Russia's international prestige and influence is one aspect of this. We also note frequent recourse to what we have labelled "opportunity frames," which are frequent assurances that Russia's economy is doing exceptionally well and worthy of attracting foreign investment.

Another noteworthy element in the sample is a consistent engagement with the concept of "fake news" and the distribution of alleged dis- or mis-information. One element of this is the dissemination of the Kremlin's pro-separatist Ukraine narrative. Repeatedly, the account pushes the legitimacy of the ongoing separatist war effort in Eastern Ukraine and even goes so far as to support the outcome of the controversial 2015 referendum generally believed to have been staged by Russian-backed separatist groups. Finally, the account draws from another well-worn tactic of the fake news and outrage repertoire: alleging voter fraud.

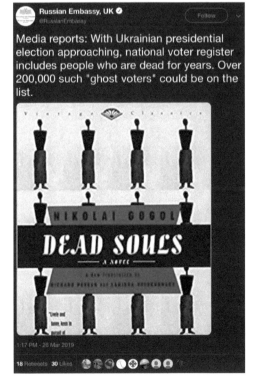

In some cases, the handle directly attacks several Western news organisations, accusing them of false or biased reporting in sarcastic tones.

Deductive analysis (ideal-types)

What about the concepts and categories we identified in our ideal-typical classification? A few observations stand out. For one, our preliminary analysis suggests that @NATO's Twitter activity coheres with the communicative logic of
traditional diplomacy. We see this in the way tweets are generally addressed to
other alliance members (though not exclusively) and the importance of historical commemoration and value signalling. The frequent use of flag emojis could
be interpreted as a digital adoption of an integral part of traditional diplomatic
practice: the importance of ceremony, precedent and ritual, all of which overlaps
with the scope and process orientation of the traditional ideal-type.

We reach a similar verdict regarding the ideal-typical logic of diplomatic communication. Tweets that affirm membership, commemorate member ascension,
and signal allies can certainly be interpreted as attempts towards convergence
around common goals. Overall, @NATO seems focused on projecting an image
underscoring the commitment and solidarity of the alliance. This appears "diplomatic" enough. At the same time, the limited audience scope (i.e., general public, NATO personnel, and Member States) limits the reach of the organisation's
digital messaging – despite their more than 600,000 followers. This corroborates
findings across the field that point to the lack of dialogic communication in the
digital communication practices of most IOs and MFAs. @NATO's imagined
audience is limited to an elite network.

Is there evidence of a drive towards compromise? Not really. Of course, this may be more of a function of the limited scope of @NATO's engagement online than a misappropriation of diplomatic communication. To compromise requires interaction with a party that holds at least partly divergent views, preferences, or incentives. One close case is one tweet in which the account addresses an ongoing international conference with Jordan in London to underscore the importance of continued NATO-Jordanian cooperation. But even here, it is unclear whether the goal is to facilitate compromise between parties in dispute. In this sense, @NATO falls short of one critical aspect of diplomatic communication.

The results of our @RussianEmbassy analysis look different. Although the embassy's digital staff is similarly engaged in the dissemination of what one might consider routine diplomatic communication, the overall tone of the corpus is more antagonistic and contentious than @NATO's. In this alone, @RussianEmbassy is shifting away from the ideal-typical logic of diplomatic communication.

Regarding scope, we already noted the MFA's sample addresses a greater variety of actors, including direct communication with news organisations. Although one may consider this an elite audience, it suggests that @RussianEmbassy seeks interaction with a variety of users. If nothing else, directly engaging with contentious public issues speaks to a willingness to escalate and accelerate the communicative process. Relatedly, the peddling of what many would consider conspiracy theories (e.g., the legitimacy of the Ukrainian referendum and the illegitimacy of Ukrainian general election) is a contentious exercise aimed at drawing attention through affective appeals.

The attribution of blame is another contentious move. In a series of tweets, @RussianEmbassy accuses Washington and its allies of being responsible for the crises in Eastern Ukraine and Syria. However, it is the open engagement with the issue regarding disinformation and "fake news" – as well as attacks on mainstream media sources – that likely is the strongest indication for the embrace of the digital logic. The account's direct mention of the *London Times* Twitter account, @thetimes, is an example of trolling. This is not to say that @RussianEmbassy ceases to fulfil a diplomatic function in the ideal-typical sense. These practices speak not only to a willingness to forgo compromise for the sake of "scoring points" on Twitter with an imagined audience, but to a recognition that digital communication unfolds along a culturally contingent logic. More importantly, in this saturated information environment, attention is valuable.

Discussion

We began this paper with a discussion of digital diplomacy and the potential challenges associated with its practical emergence in world politics. We then argued that the merger between diplomatic practice and digital communications may be more problematic than previously thought, given their reliance on divergent, and in some ways, counteracting communication logics. We suggested that while diplomacy seeks to ameliorate conflict through convergence and compromise, the communicative logic of digital communication amplifies contention by pushing users to diverge and radicalise. Social media, it turns out, is an environment ill-suited for the good-faith efforts that exemplify traditional diplomatic practice. To test these claims, we analysed the Twitter activity of NATO and the Russia embassy in the UK. Not only are @NATO and @RussianEmbassy engaged in quite distinct activities online, but the latter's tendency to espouse a much more contentious and outrageous style of communication suggest that Russian digital staff recognise the peculiarity of the digital communication environment and is willing to take full advantage of it despite (or maybe because of) the damage it can do to diplomatic relations.

Where does this leave digital diplomacy? For one, it urges scholars and practitioners to seriously consider the issue of *hybridity*. Diplomatic and digital practice will continue to merge in unpredictable ways and produce unexpected outcomes. The affordances of social media themselves encourage this behaviour (Brassi and Trere 2012; Kavada 2015). Future research must pay attention to the emergent unintended consequences of technical design and digital culture. Second, we caution against an overly optimistic and liberal-triumphalist reading of digital diplomacy. To be sure, many continue to see the spread of digital connectivity as a means to extend the global appeal and reach of liberal-democratic values. However, states like Russia, China, and Turkey increasingly restrict internet access under the slogan of "digital sovereignty." Dangers include the appropriation of digital media and their affordances for less sanguine purposes such as online recruitment by transnational terrorist networks and the spread of bigoted, racist, and hateful content. Moreover, the use of social media *itself* has become an important focus of attention. Engaging in not-ideal-typical diplomacy becomes noteworthy *simply because it occurs on social media*. Perhaps one of the most important takeaways, then, is that because social media *may* be used towards "good" ends (e.g., the promotion of human rights, government accountability, and democracy), it does not follow that this is its primary function in global politics. In fact, our discussion suggests the communicative logic of digital politics makes this an unlikely outcome.

Lastly, our discussion urges agents of (digital) diplomacy to consider how they appropriate social media. Of course, adapting to new media practices will be difficult – especially for states and IOs pursuing diplomatic, liberal, and cooperative pursuits. Time invested may not pay off, especially if the public reach of these campaigns remains limited. Conversely, digital outreach strategies that may gain more public traction can run counter to the values some IOs and MFAs wish to promote. IOs and MFAs that are unwilling to go down the rabbit hole of digital online polemics are better served to abstain from public outreach on social media platforms, or at least curb their expectations. Losing out on the reach of social media might be worth it if the alternative is to regularly get *pwned* by actors highly proficient in weaponising digital media for trolling or other nefarious purposes. To be diplomat or to be a troll, that is the question before us.

Notes

1 Roberts (2007) defines public diplomacy as foreign policy activities aimed at creating a positive climate among foreign publics in order to facilitate the acceptance of another country's foreign policy.
2 Kent and Taylor (1998) define dialogic communication to be the product of two-way symmetrical communication.
3 We follow Phillips and Milner's typology of social media affordances that includes (1) modifiability, (2) modularity, (3) accessibility, and (4) achievability (2018).
4 Counter-diplomacy seeks the continuation or extension of a conflict and facilitation of parallel violence, while coercive diplomacy aims to compel changes in behaviour using threats, sanctions, and the withdrawal or denial of rewards (Barston 2013, 5, 48).
5 *Pwning* is a purposeful misspelling of "owning."

References

Aflano, Mark, Carter Adam, and Marc Cheong. "Technological Seduction and Self-Radicalization." *Journal of the American Philosophical Association* 4, no. 3 (2018): 298–322.

Agarwal, Sheental D., Michael L. Barthel, Caterina Rost, Alan Borning, W. Lance Bennett, and Courtney N. Johnson. "Grassroots Organizing in the Digital Age: Considering Values and Technology in Tea Party and Occupy Wall Street." *Information, Communication & Society* 17, no. 3 (2014): 326–41. doi:10.1080/1369118x.2013.873068.

Almeida, Paul D., and Marc I. Lichbach. "To the Internet, from the Internet: Comparative Media Coverage of Transnational Protest." *Mobilization* 8, no. 3 (2003): 249–72.

Anderson, Matthew Smith. *The Rise of Modern Diplomacy, 1450–1919*. London: Routledge, 1993.

Barassi, Veronica and Emiliano Trere. "Does Web 3.0 Come after Web 2.0? Deconstructing Theoretical Assumptions Through Practice." *New Media & Society* 14, no. 8 (2012): 1269–85.

Barston, Ronald P. *Modern Diplomacy*. 4th ed. London: Routledge, 2013.

Behr, Ines von, Anaïs Reding, Charlie Edwards, Luke Gribbon, Rand Europe, and United Kingdom. "Radicalisation in the Digital Era: The Use of the Internet in 15 Cases of Terrorism and Extremism." 2013. https://www.ncjrs.gov/App/Publications /abstract.aspx?ID=266610.

Ben-David, A., and A. Matamoros-Fernandez. "Hate Speech and Covert Discrimination on Social Media: Monitoring the Facebook Pages of Extreme-Right Political Parties in Spain." *International Journal of Communication* 10 (2016): 1167–93.

Benkler, Yochai. *The Wealth of Networks: How Social Production Transforms Markets and Freedom*. New Haven, CT: Yale University Press, 2006.

Benkler, Yochai, Robert Faris, and Hal Roberts. *Network Propaganda: Manipulation, Disinformation, and Radicalization in American Politics*. New York: Oxford University Press, 2018.

Bennett, William. "Communicating Global Activism." *Communication & Society* 6, no. 2 (2001): 143–68.

Bennett, W. Lance, and Alexandra Segerberg. "The Logic of Connective Action: Digital Media and the Personalization of Contentious Politics." *Information, Communication & Society* 15, no. 5 (2012): 739–68. doi:10.7551/mitpress/9970.003.0006.

Bennett, W. Lance, and Alexandra Segerberg. *The Logic of Connective Action*. New York: Cambridge University Press, 2013.

Bennet, L., C. Breunig, and T. Givens. "Communication and Political Mobilization: Digital Media and the Organization of the anti-Iraq War Demonstrations in the U.S." *Political Communication* no. 25 (2008): 269–89.

Berglez, Peter. "Few-to-Many Communication: Public Figures' Self-Promotion on Twitter Through 'Joint Performances' in Small Networked Constellations." *Annales: Series Historia et Sociologia* 26, no. 1 (2016): 171–84.

Berry, Jeffrey and Sarah Sobieraj. *The Outrage Industry*. New York: Oxford University Press, 2014.

Bjola, Corneliu, and Marcus Holmes. *Digital Diplomacy: Theory and Practice*, 163–72. London: Routledge, 2015.

Blaya, C. "Cyberhate A Review and Content Analysis of Intervention Strategies." *Aggression and Violent Behavior* 45 (2019): 163–72.

Bohman, James. "Expanding Dialogue: The Internet, the Public Sphere and Prospects for Transnational Democracy." In *After Habermas: New Perspectives on the Public Sphere*, edited by Nick Crossley, and John Michael Roberts. Malden, MA: Blackwell Publishing, 2004.

Bollier, David. *Viral Spiral: How the Commoners Built a Digital Republic of Their Own*. New York: The New Press, 2009.

Bull, Hedley. *The Anarchical Society: A Study of Order in World Politics*. New York: Columbia University Press, 1977.

Bull, Hedley, and Adam Watson. *The Expansion of International Society*. Oxford: Clarendon Press, 1984.

Burnap, P., and M.L. Williams. "Cyber Hate Speech on Twitter: An Application of Machine Classification and Statistical Modeling for Policy and Decision Making." *Policy & Internet* 7, no. 2 (2015): 223–42.

Butterfield, Herbert. "Balance of Power." In *Diplomatic Investigations: Essays in the Theory of International Politics*, edited by Herbert Butterfield and Martin Wight. Cambridge, MA: Harvard University Press, 1966.

Buzan, Barry, and Richard Little. *International Systems in World History: Remaking the Study of International Relations*. New York: Oxford University Press, 2000.

Castells, Manuel. *The Rise of the Network Society, with a New Preface: The Information Age: Economy, Society, and Culture*. Hoboken, NJ: Wiley, 2009.

Castells, Manuel. *The Rise of the Network Society*. Hoboken, NJ: Wiley, 2011.

Castells, Manuel. *Networks of Outrage and Hope: Social Movements in the Internet Age*. Malden, MA: Polity Press, 2012.

Castells, Manuel. *Networks of Outrage and Hope: Social Movements in the Internet Age*. Malden, MA: Polity Press, 2015.

Causey, C., and P.N. Howard. "Delivering Digital Public Diplomacy." In *Relational, Networked and Collaborative Approaches to Public Diplomacy: The Connective Mindshift*, edited by R. S. Zaharna, A. Arsenault, and A. Fisher, 144–56. Oxon: Routledge, 2013.

Chadwick, Andrew. *The Hybrid Media System: Politics and Power*. New York: Oxford University Press, 2013.

Christakis, Nicholas A. and James H. Fowlder. *Connected: The Surprising Power of our Social Networks and How They Shape Our Lives*. New York: Little, Brown Spark, 2009.

Clark, Ian. *Hegemony in International Society*. New York: Oxford University Press, 2011.

Corbin, J., and A. Strauss. *Basics of Qualitative Research: Techniques and Procedures for Developing Grounded Theory*. 4th ed. Thousand Oaks, CA: SAGE, 2015.

Cottey, Andrew, and Anthony Forster. *Reshaping Defence Diplomacy*. London: Oxford University Press, 2004.

Cowan, G., and A. Arsenault. "Moving from Monologue to Dialogue to Collaboration: The Three Layer of Public Diplomacy." *The Annals of the American Academy of Political & Social Science* 616, no. 1 (2008): 10–30. doi:10.1177/0002716207311863.

Creswell, John. *A Concise Introduction to Mixed Methods Research*. Thousand Oaks, CA: SAGE, 2014.

Dahlberg, Lincoln. "The Internet and Democratic Discourse: Exploring the Prospects of Online Deliberative Forums Extending the Public Sphere." *Information, Communication & Society* 4, no. 4 (2001): 615–33. doi:10.1080/13691180110097030.

Dahlgren, Peter. "The Internet, Public Spheres, and Political Communication: Dispersion and Deliberation." *Political Communication* 22, no. 2 (2005): 147–62.

Dann, Stephen. "Twitter Content Classification." *First Monday* 15, no. 12 (2010).

Dawkins, R. *The Selfish Gene*. New York: Oxford University Press, 1976.

della Porta, Donatella, ed. *The Global Justice Movement: Cross-National and Transnational Perspectives*. Boulder, CO and London: Paradigm Publications, 2007.

Deuze, Mark. *Media Work*. Boston, MA: Polity Press, 2007.

Della Porta, Donatella and Lorenzo Mosca. "Global-net for Global Movements? A Network of Networks for a Movement of Movements." *Journal of Public Policy* 25, no. 1 (2005.): 165–90.

Earl, Jennifer, and Katrina Kimport. *Digitally Enabled Social Change: Activism in the Internet Age*. Cambridge, MA: MIT Press, 2011.

Feenberg, Andrew, and Darin David Barney. *Community in the Digital Age: Philosophy and Practice*. Lanham, MD: Rowman & Littlefield Publishing Group, 2004.

Forestal, Jennifer. "The Architecture of Political Spaces: Trolls, Digital Media, and Deweyan Democracy." *American Political Science Review* 111, no. 1 (2017): 149–61. doi:10.1017/s0003055416000666.

Fraser, Nancy. *Scales of Justice: Reimagining Political Space in a Globalizing World*. New York: Columbia University Press, 2009.

Gerbaudo, Paolo. *Tweets and the Streets: Social Media and Contemporary Activism*. London: Pluto Press, 2012.

Gerbaudo, Paolo. "Protest Avatars as Memetic Signifiers: Political Profile Pictures and the Construction of Collective Identity on Social Media in the 2011 Protest Wave." *Information, Communication & Society* 18, no. 8 (2015): 916–29. doi:10.1080/1369118x.2015.1043316.

Hallams, E. "Digital Diplomacy: The Internet, the Battle for Ideas & US Foreign Policy." *CEU Political Science Journal* 4 (2010): 538–74.

Hanson, Elizabeth C. *The Information Revolution and World Politics*. Lanham, MD: Rowman & Littlefield Publishing Group, 2008.

Hayden, C. "Social Media at State: Power, Practice, and Conceptual Limits for US Public Diplomacy." *Global Media Journal-American Edition* 11, no 21 (2012): 1–21.

Herrera, L. *Revolution in the Age of Social Media: The Egyptian Popular Insurrection and the Internet*. New York: Verso, 2014.

Holsti, K.J. *Taming the Sovereigns: Institutional Change in International Politics*. New York: Cambridge University Press, 2004. doi:10.1017/cbo9780511491382.

Honeycutt, Courtenay, and Susan C. Herring. "Beyond Microblogging: Conversation and Collaboration via Twitter." *Proceedings of the 42nd Hawaii International Conference on System Sciences*, 2009.

Howard, Philip N. *The Digital Origins of Dictatorship and Democracy: Information Technology and Political Islam*. New York: Oxford University Press, 2010.

Iklé, Fred Charles. *How Nations Negotiate*. New York: Harper and Row, 1964.

Kampf, Ronit, Ilan Manor, and Elad Segev. "Digital Diplomacy 2.0? A Cross-National Comparison of Public Engagement in Facebook and Twitter." *The Hague Journal of Diplomacy* 10, no. 4 (2015): 331–62. doi:10.1163/1871191x-12341318.

Karagiannopoulos, Vasileios. "The Role of the Internet in Political Struggles: Some Conclusions from Iran and Egypt." *New Political Science* 34, no. 2 (2012): 151–71. doi:10.1080/07393148.2012.676394.

Kavada, Anastasia. "Creating the Collective: Social Media, the Occupy Movement and Its Constitution as a Collective Actor." *Information, Communication & Society* 18, no. 8 (2015): 872–86.

Kent, Michael L., and Maureen Taylor. "Building Dialogic Relationships Through the World Wide Web." *Public Relations Review* 3, no. 24 (1998): 321–34. doi:10.1016/s0363-8111(99)80143-x.

Kienast, Walter. "Die Anfänge des europäischen Staatensystems im späteren Mittelalter." *Historische Zeitschrift* cliii (1935–36) (1936): 229–71. doi:10.1524/hzhz.1936.153.jg.229.

Kissinger, Henry. *Years of Upheaval*. Boston, MA: Little, Brown and Co, 1982.

Knuttila, L. "User Unknown: 4chan, Anonymity, and Contingency." *First Monday* 16, no. 10 (2011).

Krauske. *Die Entwicklung der ständigen Diplomatie vom fünfzehnten Jahrhundert bis zu den Beschluessen von 1815 und 1818*. Leipzig: Otto, 1885.

Krzyżanowski, Michał. "Social Media In/and the Politics of the European Union." *Journal of Language & Politics* 2 (2018): 281–304.

Lemke, Tobias, and Michael W. Habegger. "A Master Institution of World Society? Digital Communications Networks and the Changing Dynamics of Transnational Contention." *International Relations* 32, no. 3 (2018): 296–320. doi:10.1177/0047117817747666.

Little, Richard. "Neorealism and the English School: A Methodological, Ontological, and Theoretical Assessment." *European Journal of International Relations* 1, no. 1 (1995): 9–34. doi:10.1177/1354066195001001002.

Mallett, M. "Diplomacy and War in Late Fifteenth-Century Italy." *Proceedings of the British Academy* lxvii (1981): 268–9.

Manor, Ilan. "Are We There yet: Have MFAs Realized the Potential of Digital Diplomacy?." *Brill Research Perspectives in Diplomacy & Foreign Policy* 1, no. 2 (2016): 1–110. doi:10.1163/9789004319790_002.

Mattingly, Garrett. *Renaissance Diplomacy.* Boston, MA: Houghton Mifflin, 1955.

McAdam, Doug, Sidney Tarrow and Charles Tilly. *Dynamics of Contention.* New York: Cambridge University Press, 2001.

McDonald, Kevin. "From Indymedia to Anonymous: Rethinking Action and Identity in Digital Cultures." *Information, Communication & Society* 18, no. 8 (2015): 968–82. doi: 10.1080/1369118x.2015.1039561.

McNutt, K. "Public Engagement in the Web 2.0 Era: Social Collaborative Technologies in a Public Sector Context." *Canadian Public Administration* 57, no. 1 (2014): 49–70. doi:10.1111/capa.12058.

Melissen, J. "The New Public Diplomacy: Between Theory and Practice." In *The New Public Diplomacy: Soft Power in International Relations*, edited by J. Melissen, 3–27. New York: Palgrave Macmillan, 2005. doi:10.1057/9780230554931_1.

Milan, Stefania. "From Social Movements to Cloud Protesting: The Evolution of Collective Identity." *Information, Communication & Society* 18, no. 8 (2015a): 887–900. doi:10.1080/1369118x.2015.1043135.

Milan, Stefania. "When Algorithms Shape Collective Action: Social Media and the Dynamics of Cloud Protesting." *Social Media & Society* (2015b): 1–10. doi:10.1177/2056305115622481.

Murthy, Dhiraj. *Twitter: Social Communication in the Twitter Age.* 2nd ed. Malden, MA: Polity Press, 2018.

Silber, Mitchell D., Arvin Bhatt, and Senior Intelligence Analysts. "Radicalization in the West: The Homegrown Threat." 2007. http://moonbattery.com/graphics/NYP D_Report-Radicalization_in_the_West.pdf.

Morozov, Evgeny. *The Net Delusion: The Dark Side of Internet Freedom.* New York: PublicAffairs, 2011.

Munn, L. "Alt-Right Pipeline: Individual Journeys to Extremism Online." *First Monday* 24, no. 6 (2019).

Nicholson, Harold. "Diplomacy Then and Now." *Foreign Affairs* 40, no. 1 (1961): 39–49.

Nicolson, Harold. *Diplomacy.* London: Oxford University Press, 1963.

Ociepka, B. "Impact of New Technologies on International Communication: The Case of Public Diplomacy." *Information Science* 59 (2012): 24–36.

Pamment, James. *New Public Diplomacy in the Twenty-First Century: A Comparative Study of Policy and Practice.* New York: Routledge, 2013.

Pfaff, Steven, and Guobin Yang. "Double-Edged Rituals and the Symbolic Resources of Collective Action: Political Commemorations and the Mobilization of Protest in 1989." *Theory & Society* 30, no. 4 (2001): 539–89.

Phillips, Whitney, and Ryan M. Milner. *The Ambivalent Internet: Mischief, Oddity, and Antagonism Online.* Cambridge: Polity Press, 2018.

Queller, D.E. *The Office of Ambassador in the Middle Ages.* Princeton, NJ: Princeton University Press, 1967.

Reus-Smit, C. *The Moral Purpose of the State: Culture, Social Identity, and Institutional Rationality in International Relations.* Princeton, NJ: Princeton University Press, 1999.

Reus-Smit, Christian. "The Constructivist Challenge After September 11." In *International Society and Its Critics*, edited by Alex J. Bellamy. Oxford: Oxford University Press, 2005. doi:10.1093/0199265208.003.0005.

Riordan, Sian. *The New Diplomacy*. Cambridge, MA: Polity Press, 2003.

Rizk, Nagla, Lina Attalah, and Nadine Weheba. "The Networked Public Sphere and Civic Engagement in Post-2011 Egypt: A Local Perspective." http:// www.arabnps .org/egypt/.

Roberts, William R. "What Is Public Diplomacy? Past Practices, Present Conduct, Possible Future." *Mediterranean Quarterly* 18, no. 4 (2007): 36–53. doi:10.1215/10474552-2007-025.

Sassen, Saskia. *Territory, Authority, Rights: From Medieval to Global Assemblages*. Princeton, NJ: Princeton University Press, 2008.

Seib, P. *Real-Time Diplomacy: Politics and Power in the Social Media Era*. New York: Palgrave Macmillan, 2012.

Shane, Peter M. *Democracy Online: The Prospects for Political Renewal Through the Internet*. New York: Psychology Press, 2004.

Sharp, Paul. *Diplomatic Theory of International Relations*. New York: Cambridge University Press, 2009.

Shiffman, Denise. *Age of Engage: Reinventing Marketing for Today's Connected, Collaborative, and Hyperinteractive Culture*. Ladera Ranch, CA: Hunt Street Press, 2008.

Shifman, Limor. *Memes in Digital Culture*. Cambridge, MA: MIT Press, 2014.

Shirky, Clay. *Here Comes Everybody: The Power of Organizing Without Organizations*. New York: Penguin, 2008.

Simon, H. "Designing Organizations for an Information-Rich World." In *Computers, Communications and the Public Interest*, edited by M. Greenberger, 37–72. Baltimore, MD: Johns Hopkins University Press, 1971.

Simpson, Gerry. *Great Powers and Outlaw Sates: Unequal Sovereigns in the International Legal Order*. New York: Cambridge University Press, 2004.

Singer, Peter Warren, and Emerson T. Brooking. *LikeWar: The Weaponization of Social Media*. Boston, MA: Mariner Books, 2018.

Sobieraj, Sarah, and Jeffrey Berry. "From Incivility to Outrage: Political Discourse in Blogs, Talk Radio, and Cable News." *Political Communication* 28, no. 1 (2011): 19–41. doi:10.1080/10584609.2010.542360.

Sotiriu, S. "Digital Diplomacy: Between Promises and Reality." In *Digital Diplomacy*, edited by C. Bjola, and M. Holmes. New York: Routledge, 2015.

Stein, J.G. "Introduction." In *Diplomacy in the Digital Age*, edited by J.G. Stein. Toronto, ON: McClelland & Stewart, 2011.

Tapscott, Don, Anthony D. Williams, and Dan Herman. "Government 2.0: Transforming Government and Governance for the Twenty-First Century." *New Paradigm*, 2007. http://mobility.grchina.com/innovation/gov_transforminggovernment.pdf.

Theocharis, Yannis, Will Lowe, Jan W. van Deth, and Gema Garcia-Albacete. "Using Twitter to Mobilize Protest Action: Online Mobilization Patterns and Action Repertoires in the Occupy Wall Street, Indignados, and Aganaktismenoi Movements." *Information, Communication & Society* 18, no. 2 (2015): 202–20. doi:10.1 080/1369118x.2014.948035.

Tilly, Charles. *Identities, Boundaries and Social Ties*. New York: Routledge, 2015.

Tufecki, Zeynep. "The Medium and the Movement: Digital Tools, Social Movement Politics, and the End of the Free Rider Problem." *Policy & Internet* 6, no. 2 (2014): 202–8. doi:10.1002/1944-2866.poi362.

Tufekci, Zeynep. "'Not this One': Social Movements, the Attention Economy, and Microcelebrity Networked Activism." *American Behavioral Scientist* 57, no. 7 (2013): 848–70.

Tufekci, Zeynep. *Twitter and Tear Gas: The Power and Fragility of Networked Protest*. New Haven, CT: Yale University Press, 2017.

Twiploamcy. https://twiplomacy.com/blog/twiplomacy-study-2018/, 2018.

Valenzuela, S., A. Arriagada, and A. Scherman. "Facebook, Twitter, and youth Engagement: A Quasi-Experimental Study of Social Media Use and Protest Behavior Using Propensity Score Matching." *International Journal of Communications* 8 (2014): 2046–70.

Vance, A.M. "Post-9/11 US Public Diplomacy in Eastern Europe: Dialogue via New Technologies or Face-To-Face Communication?" *Global Media Journal – American Edition* 11, no. 21 (2012): 1–19.

Watson, Adam. *The Evolution of International Society: A Comparative Historical Analysis*. London: Routledge, 1992.

Weber, Max,. "Die 'Objectivitaet' Sozialwissenschaftlicher und Sozialpolitischer Erkenntnis." In *GEssamelte Aufsaetze zur Wissenschaftslehre*, edited by Elizabeth Flitner, 146-214. Postdom: Internet Ausgabe, 1999. www.uni-potsdam.de/u/paed/Flitner/F litner/Weber/. Accessed April 1, 2019.

Webster, Charles. K. *The Foreign Policy of Castlereagh, 1815–1822*. London: Bell and Sons, 1934.

Wight, Martin. *Power Politics*. New York: Holmes & Meier, 1978.

Yardi, S., and D. Boyd. "Dynamic Debates: An Analysis of Group Polarization Over Time on Twitter." *Bulletin of Science, Technology & Society* 30, no. 5 (2010): 316–27.

Zartman, I. William. "Negotiation: Theory and Reality." *Journal of International Affairs* 29, no. 1 (1975): 71–2.

11

COPING WITH DIGITAL DISINFORMATION IN MULTILATERAL CONTEXTS

The case of the UN Global Compact for Migration

Corneliu Bjola

Introduction

The adoption of the UN Global Compact for Safe, Orderly, and Regular Migration by 164 governments at an international conference in Marrakesh on December 10, 2018, was expected to be a cause of celebration for the global efforts seeking to recognise the plight of the people forced to flee their countries. The timing of the event made the issue even more relevant since it coincided with the 70th anniversary of the Universal Declaration of Human Rights. It was therefore rather surprising to see the UN Secretary-General, António Guterres, introducing the compact at the opening intergovernmental session in a rather apologetic manner, by defending its aspirations against "many falsehoods" and seeking to dispel the "myths" about its implications for the migration policies of the Member States (UN News 2018).

The Global Compact hardly stated any ambition to overrule Member States on the crucial issue of migration. It was instead designed to provide a menu of policy actions and best practices, from which governments could draw to implement their national migration policies (Carrera et al. 2018, 3). As it soon became clear, Guterres' concerns about the compact being subject to an intense campaign of disinformation were not unfounded (Slocum 2018). A number of Western countries, including the United States and several European governments, most of them ruled or politically pressured by populist parties, decided to abstain or vote against the agreement (Gotev 2018). The case is emblematic for the topic of digital disinformation examined in this chapter for two reasons.

On the one hand, it shows that disinformation is not just a bilateral issue, by which countries may seek to undermine the informational environment of their competitors in pursuit of political or geostrategic goals (Bjola and Pamment 2018; Pomerantsev and Weiss 2014). It also has a growing and sophisticated multilateral dimension, albeit largely overlooked, which in the context of international organisations could be even more toxic as it may affect the fate of a larger number of issues and actors. While motivations for using disinformation in national (Bandeira et al. 2019) and multilateral contexts (Fidler 2019) are quite different, the results could be nevertheless equally damaging for the already thinning fabric of the international order (Bradshaw and Howard 2019).

On the other hand, the UN Global Compact case reveals the informational vulnerability of IOs in the current post-truth environment and raises legitimate questions about their ability to carry out their functions in a suitable manner. Unlike states, IOs are generally more constrained in their capacity to adapt themselves to the imperatives of the digital age (Ecker-Ehrhardt 2018), leaving them with no good options for responding to new challenges other than to become more innovative in their efforts to enhance their digital institutional resilience. These preliminary remarks point to a timely and important question that this chapter aims to address: *what risks do IOs face if they fail to contain the ramifications of digital disinformation?*

Focusing on the specific situation of the United Nations and drawing on theories of (de)legitimation of power and prestige orders (Berger et al. 2006), this chapter argues that the potential challenge that digital disinformation pose to international organisations is "manufactured delegitimation." Inherent tensions between IOs and member states could be digitally exploited in a manner that is qualitatively distinct from the usual process of political contestation, hence the focus on the notion of "manufactured delegitimation." The set of constitutive rules legitimating the power position of the UN vs Member States could therefore be disturbed by disinformation to the point that the organisation may find itself in the situation of not being able to fulfil key functions that it has been mandated to perform.

The theoretical implications of this argument will be examined using the UN Global Compact for Migration (UNGCM) as a case study for unpacking the possible mechanisms by which digital disinformation may undermine the legitimacy of the UN. Drawing on Twitter data collected between September 2018 and January 2019, the study will examine the pattern, intensity, and impact of the digital disinformation campaign against UNGCM and explore its implications for the policy agenda of 73rd session of the UN General Assembly (UNGA). The chapter will be structured as follows. The first part will review the context and drivers of the rising digital disinformation disorder and explain their relevance for the activity of international organisations. The second part will introduce the logical model of (de)legitimation of international organisations and contextualise it to the challenge of digital disinformation. The third section will return to the case of the UN Global Compact on Migration and empirically probe three propositions about the pathways by which digital disinformation may affect UN's legitimacy. The chapter will conclude with a set of recommendations about how the UN could improve its resilience to digital disinformation.

The digital disinformation disorder

The rise of echo chambers, fake news, and the deliberate weaponisation of information by state and non-state actors in the recent years has fuelled fears about digital technologies potentially reaching the point of undermining the very fabric of the post-Second World War liberal international order (Bennett and Livingston 2018; Diamond et al. 2016; Pomerantsev 2015). Taking note of this, the academic literature on digital disinformation has pursued two general lines of inquiry. The first one has focused on *state actors and their strategic use of digital disinformation as a foreign policy tool*. Following the surprising results of the US presidential elections in 2016, questions about patterns and implications of digital electoral interference have dominated the academic research in the field. By deploying armies of "trolls" and "bots" (Howard et al. 2018; Jamieson 2018) to create epistemic confusion and political polarisation (Bjola 2018; Richey 2018; Tucker et al. 2018, 28), Russia has been identified, for instance, to be one of the most active state actors to use digital disinformation for influencing the results of elections in Western democracies. Other countries, such as China (Drun 2018; Packham 2019) and Iran (Tabatabai 2018), have been also seeking to develop capacity for conducting similar operations, but the results have been apparently much less convincing thus far.

An additional use of digital disinformation as a foreign policy tool includes sophisticated (hybrid) methods of deterrence by which the target country is pressured not to pursue a certain course of action, or by case to reverse it, due to the perceived detrimental effects it may have on the interests of a rival state. This was the case, for instance, with the Russian opposition to the Swedish–NATO host agreement in 2015 (Kragh and Åsberg 2017, 798), to the Finnish's similar attempt to strengthen their relationship with NATO in 2016 (Bjola and Papadakis 2020), or to the Dutch referendum on the trade agreement between the European Union and Ukraine in 2016 (Higgins 2017). The ongoing dispute in the Middle East between Qatar and Saudi Arabia follows the same pattern as each country has been involved in organising complex digital disinformation campaigns with the goal to alter the foreign policy behaviour of the other (Pinnell 2018; Wood 2018). The mechanism by which digital disinformation is supposed to work in all these cases is similar. Digital disinformation is expected to generate offline results in two steps: first by undermining the political standing of the target government in front of its own population or of the international community, and second, by using the weakened position of the government to extract political concessions.

A second body of literature has called attention to *the role of non-state actors in promoting disinformation* and for good reasons. While state actors' contribution to the global digital disinformation disorder is clearly significant, it cannot fully explain, however, the vast amount of disinformation that is being produced every day around the world. According to the 2019 Digital News Report, concern about misinformation and disinformation remains high despite recent efforts by social media platforms to build public confidence. In Brazil, 85% agree with a statement that they are worried about what is real and fake on the internet. Concern is also high in the UK (70%) and the USA (67%), but much lower in Germany (38%) and the Netherlands (31%) (Newman et al. 2019, 9). Evidence suggests that organised social media manipulation campaigns took place in 70 countries in 2019, up from 48 countries in 2018 and 28 countries in 2017. Most importantly, in each country, researchers have found at least one political party or government agency using social media to shape public attitudes domestically (Bradshaw and Howard 2019, i).

In the 30 countries that held elections or referendums between June 2018 and May 2019, the Freedom House has found that domestic actors have abused information technology to subvert the electoral process via three distinct forms of digital election interference: *informational measures*, by which online discussions are surreptitiously manipulated in favour of the government or particular parties; *technical measures*, which are used to restrict access to news sources, communication tools, and in some cases the entire online network; and *legal measures*, which authorities apply to sanction and punish regime opponents and chill political expression (Shahbaz and Funk 2019). Other studies have confirmed these findings, by pointing out how the use of computational propaganda by domestic actors has succeeded in re-shaping the media ecosystems of various countries (Woolley and Howard 2018), primarily by amplifying the power of agenda setting, priming, and framing of the more vocal or radical groups (Benkler et al. 2018).

According to these two bodies of literature, motivation is the key factor in explaining the eagerness with which digital disinformation has been embraced by both state and non-state actors. From a prospect theory perspective (Vis and Kuijpers 2018), the issue is hardly a puzzle. Simply put, the perceived gains of engaging in digital disinformation relative to the status quo (e.g., doing nothing) far outweigh any possible losses. For state actors, the costs are minimal relative to other options, and the potential losses are negligible, especially for large countries, as involvement in digital disinformation could be easily camouflaged and by extension denied. However, as the Russian examples of election interference and foreign policy deterrence have shown, the potential gains could be significant. Similarly, for non-state actors, such as governments or political parties, the risk of punishment for violating election rules is simply negligible relative to the potential gains to be made through the political exploitation of digital disinformation, as the case of the VoteLeave campaign during the Brexit Referendum in U.K. has shown (Graham-Harrison 2018). In other words, unless the cost of losses could be substantially increased, for instance, via international sanctions or cyber deterrence in the case of state actors, or by legal sanctions in the case of non-state actors, the incentives for resorting to digital disinformation in pursuit of political goals will likely remain strong.

That being said, the relevance of these theoretical implications for the study of digital disinformation in the context of international organisations is rather marginal. IOs do not have foreign policy ambitions similar to states', nor do they elect their leaders by popular vote. Therefore, the incentive for state and non-state actors to use digital disinformation to extract political concessions from IOs or to attain control over their levers of power is much more muted. This observation does not preclude the idea of digital disinformation being deployed against IOs, but it suggests that the underlying motivations of state and non-state actors to engage in such actions might be different, and by extension the patterns of disinformation and political consequences could depart as well from the existing models. This is an important gap in the literature, which the next section will seek to address by explaining why legitimacy is the main asset that international organisations should seek to protect against digital disinformation campaigns.

The legitimacy blind spot

As a fundamental asset that permits IOs to properly function, legitimacy – understood as the belief about how power is exercised by IOs with respect to certain ends, processes, and structural designs (Zaum 2013, 10) – is a key concept to examine in order to understand IOs' potential vulnerability to digital disinformation. From a functionalist perspective, legitimacy shapes IOs' ability to stay relevant as the focal arenas for states' efforts to coordinate policies and solve problems, to improve their capacity to develop new rules and norms, and to secure compliance with international rules and norms (Coicaud and Heiskanen 2001; Tallberg and Zürn 2019, 582). From a normative perspective, legitimacy calls attention to IOs' constitutive role in global ordering (Clark 2003; Claude 1966): do IOs mainly serve as instruments of the strong to project their influence around the world (Mearsheimer 1994, 13), or as elements of "constitutional orders" that operate to allocate rights and limit the exercise of power (Ikenberry 2001, 29)?

To be sure, the legitimacy stakes for IOs have always been high. As Buchanan and Keohane bluntly put it, "if one is unclear about the appropriate standards of legitimacy or if unrealistically demanding standards are assumed, then public support for global governance institutions may be undermined and their effectiveness in providing valuable goods maybe impaired" (Buchanan and Keohane 2006, 407). Academic research suggests that the causes of decline and death of IOs primarily relate to pre-digital structural factors such as the geopolitical context and/or accumulating institutional dysfunctions (Eilstrup-Sangiovanni 2018; von Borzyskowski and Vabulas 2019). However, if we take seriously the literature on disinformation, we also need to consider the possibility that well-targeted digital disinformation campaigns could turn legitimacy into a major vulnerability of IOs.

The theory of legitimation and delegitimation of power and prestige orders (PPO) developed by Berger et al. (2006) offers an innovative framework for approaching the non-"organic" dimension of IOs' potential decline. PPO theory represents a refinement of the expectations states theory (EST), an influential sociological theory developed by Berger and his colleagues two decades earlier, and which has later became an influential anchor for a vibrant research program in Social Psychology (Chizhik et al. 2003; Correll and Ridgeway 2003; Kalkhoff and Thye 2006). EST sought to explain the patterns by which status hierarchies would form in situations where actors were oriented towards the accomplishment of a task or a collective goal (Berger et al. 1974, 1977). Most interestingly, it has found that pre-existing social inequalities serve as cues from which members of the group form expectations concerning each other's task abilities. These expectation states determine the power and prestige order of the group (Knottnerus 1988, 421).

PPO has taken the EST's argument a step further by seeking to elucidate how the assignment of task success or failure to members affects power and prestige orders via processes of legitimation and delegitimation (Berger et al. 2006, 381). In essence, these processes involve a careful calibration between normative prescriptions (what P owes to O) and performance expectations (what O owes to P). According to Berger et al., when we say that the order between any two actors, P and O, has become legitimated it means three things (Berger et al. 2006, 385). First, that expectations for valued status positions that P holds for O have become normatively prescriptive, that is, P not only anticipates deferring to O for accomplishing the task, but it is normatively required to do so. Second, that P applies these normative prescriptions with the understanding that O will meet the performance expectations needed to accomplish the task. Third, P assumes that its conditional deferential behaviour towards O will have collective support by virtue of the fact that others in the group hold the same normative prescriptions.

The key point that these three provisions advance is that the pattern of convergence/divergence between normative prescriptions and performance expectations determines the scope of PPO legitimacy. If performance evaluations of task success or failure assigned to P and O are consistent with the order of valued status positions, then the legitimacy of the power and prestige order between O and P is safely reproduced. By contrast, if these evaluations are inconsistent with the ordering of P and O, then the probability of delegitimation of the said order increases (Berger et al. 2006, 394). It is this insight that makes the PPO theory particularly valuable for theorising conditions of legitimation and delegitimation of international organisations. If we consider P to represent the member states and O to stand for the international organisation, then questions regarding the process of (de)legitimation of IOs could be conceptualised in terms of how well O meets P's expectations regarding task performance and to what extent P may decide to revise, and by case weaken, its normative prescriptions toward O in case these expectations are consistently subpar.

Drawing on the PPO theory, a three-stage logical model (structure, process, outcome) could be designed for assessing processes of (de)legitimation of IOs (see Figure 11.1). The IO structure is defined by the set of rules and norms that members states have negotiated prior to the establishment of the organisation. The foundational charter or treaty stipulates the objectives the organisation is

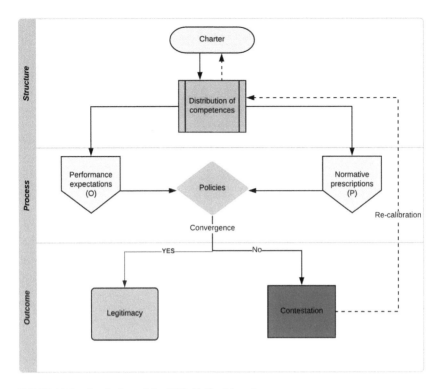

FIGURE 11.1 Logical model of IO (de)legitimation

supposed to accomplish as well as the distribution of competences and responsi-bilities between MS and IO bodies, which can vary significantly. In some organ-isations like NATO, member states have the upper hand in decision-making, while in others like the EU, member states have accepted to "pool" their sover-eignties and share or even concede specific policy competences to supranational bodies (Peterson 1997). Rules are always tested in practice and in the case of IOs this takes place via international law and politics (Hurd 2019). As IOs set out their policies, questions invariably arise about whether these policies are effective in delivering global public goods and in line with the mandate of the organisa-tion, hence the debate about IOs' "output legitimacy" (Steffek 2015).

At the same time, they also call attention to the responsibilities that member states have in terms of assisting the organisation in fulfilling its tasks even when that might conflict with their own interests (Harris 2007). It is this particu-lar tension between the performance expectations of the IO and the normative prescriptions of its members that can plant the seed for the delegitimation and eventual collapse of the organisation. The case of the League of Nations, which proved unable to reconcile its ambition to eradicate war with the structural flaws of its institutional design, offered a vivid historical illustration of this tension (Smith 1976). However, not all cases of contestation may lead to the demise of the organisation as institutional tensions could be also productive and force the organisation to re-calibrate its constitutive rules as circumstances evolve. Peacekeeping, for instance, had no explicit reference in the UN Charter, but its legal basis was rather firmly established by the International Court of Justice (ICJ) through the doctrine of implied powers in 1970 (White 2007).

The logical model thus offers an analytically coherent framework for studying the conditions by which digital disinformation could facilitate non-organic forms of delegitimation of IOs. The central argument of the logical model is that consistent divergence between performance expectations and normative prescriptions could trigger a legitimacy crisis. Such forms of divergence are hardly unusual (see Table 11.1) as endogenous and exogenous factors, such as financial pressures, normative transformations, and disaster imperatives, often force IOs to change and adapt (Nayyar 2011, 350). The issue could arguably become more problematic if the situation persists with no credible solution in sight (Eilstrup-Sangiovanni 2018). From a digital disinformation perspective, the key question we need to ask is whether a legitimacy crisis could be artificially manufactured by actors seeking to amplify negative perceptions of IOs' performance and to encourage disruptive repudiations of MS' normative prescriptions.

The crucial difference between *manufactured delegitimation* and conventional, "business as usual" processes of IO delegitimation stems from the fact that in the first case institutional tensions are being misleadingly magnified, and by case engineered, through the systematic, targeted (and concealed) deployment of digital disinformation, while in the second case, these tensions evolve organically as a result of the inability of the organisation to adapt to changing circumstances. The difference is empirically subtle, but nevertheless important. It involves the systematic presentation of an issue, via digital channels, in an inaccurate fashion, with little or no connection to the available facts of the case. This calls attention to the need for clear benchmarks by which the contribution of digital disinformation to deepening the divide between performance expectations and normative prescriptions could be reasonably separated from that generated through regular channels of political contestation.

TABLE 11.1 Patterns of legitimacy crisis formation

Performance expectations	Normative prescriptions	Example
+	+	*No crisis*; IO functions as expected (WTO) - before 2016
−	+	*Latent crisis*; IO may underperform but MS remain largely supportive (UN)
+	−	*Emerging crisis*; IO performs reasonably well, but some MS are critical of the broader implications of this performance (EU before Brexit)
−	−	*Terminal crisis*; IO consistently underperforms and MS turn against it (the League of Nations)

To explore possible patterns by which manufactured legitimation could be initiated and developed, the study advances three testable propositions on the relationship between digital disinformation and political discourse in the context of (organic) political contestation of the legitimacy of international organisations:

P1: Political contestation may deform the online space in which IOs' performance expectations are discussed. *Digital disinformation may aggravate this process by resorting to tactics that seek to corrupt the channels by which messages are disseminated.*

P2: Political contestation may weaken the epistemic basis for assessing the gap between IOs' performance expectations and member states' normative prescriptions. *Digital disinformation may aggravate this process by using polarised messages to reframe the discussion of substantive issues.*

P3: Political contestation may hinder institutional re-calibration of the relationship between IOs and member states. *Digital disinformation may aggravate this process by lowering the bar for the escalation of negative assessments of IO/MS relationship.*

Each proposition covers a specific pattern by which tensions between the IO and member states could be digitally exploited. These patterns are qualitatively distinct from the usual process of political contestation. The deployment of corrupting tactics for the purpose of deforming the online space of discussion, the use of polarised themes to generate epistemic confusion, and facilitation of the escalation of negative assessments of the relationship between IOs and member states are distinctive methods by which digital disinformation may contribute to the process of manufactured delegitimation. It is also important to note that the validation of these propositions does not imply that the organisation has been depleted of its legitimacy, but rather that the organisation experiences a crisis of legitimacy and that digital disinformation is a major enabling factor in this process.

Case study: the UN Global Compact for Migration

Following the European migrant crisis in 2015 (BBC 2015), the UN General Assembly decided in September 2016 to develop a global compact for safe, orderly, and regular migration (UNGCM). After 18 months of consultation and six rounds of negotiation, the UN Member States finalised the text for the Global Compact in July 2018. The agreement was subsequently adopted by 164 states at the Intergovernmental Conference in Marrakesh, Morocco on December 11, 2018 and endorsed by the General Assembly a week later. The final text included 23 objectives aiming to facilitate better international cooperation and management of transnational migration challenges at the local, national, regional, and global levels (United Nations 2018). Despite its non-binding legal character (Peters 2018), the compact provoked a severe political backlash, especially in Europe (Peel 2018). It stoked fears that it would trample on the rights of the Member States, regardless of the fact that "respect for national sovereignty" was enshrined in three places in the document itself (Banulescu-Bogdan 2018).

UNGCM represents an interesting case study for exploring the role of digital disinformation as a possible vector of political contestation of the UN for several reasons. First, it speaks to an issue of great contemporary relevance with significant implications for the UN transformative agenda in the 21st century. The 2030 Agenda has recognised migration as a core development consideration, and this marks the first time that migration has been explicitly integrated into the global development agenda (Sonya 2018, 13). Second, the political backlash that the compact triggered in Europe, the USA, and Australia signalled the development of a potentially structural divide between the stated expectations of the UN in the field of migration and the normative prescriptions of the Member States, a divide that requires closer inspection. Third, there is substantial evidence to suggest that disinformation played a significant role in mobilising political support against UNGCM (Rasche and Paul-Jasper Dittrich 2019). What is less understood are the repercussions that digital disinformation might have had on public perceptions of UN legitimacy and the solutions that could be deployed in the future to prevent similar situations from happening again.

Methodologically, the study draws on a mixed method approach combining qualitative and quantitative research methods. In a first step, a data set containing five collections of tweets were extracted using the Interactive Network Graph tool made available by the Observatory on Social Media (OSoMe) at the Indiana University (OSoMe 2020). The five collections included tweets posted worldwide in the months of September 2018–January 2019 based on co-occurrences with the following hashtags: #UNGA, #UNGA73, #GlobalGoals, #Youth2030, #ClimateAction, #A4P, #MigrationsPakt. The first six represented the official hashtags the UN's social media team promoted online before the start of the 73rd session of the UN General Assembly on September 18, 2018 to highlight key themes of discussion during UNGA73. #GlobalGoals referred, for instance, to the UN's support for the sustainable development goals; #ClimateAction focused on climate change; #Youth2030 covered strategies of youth empowerment, development, and engagement; while #A4P stood for the "Action for Peacekeeping" initiative. The last one, #MigrationsPakt, is a German hashtag associated with the online protests against UNGCM that originated in Austria and Germany in August–September 2018 (Murdoch 2018).

The goal of the data collection was two-fold: first, to capture the possible interaction between the themes promoted by the UNGA, on the one hand, and the populist critics, on the other hand, hence the inclusion of the #MigrationsPakt in the search alongside the six UNGA official hashtags; second, to longitudinally trace this interaction for the duration of the crisis (September 2018–January 2019), hence the breakdown of the data set into five monthly collections. In a second step, the five collections were processed in Excel and then imported into the Polinode

A. Aggregate number of references for each topic

B. Evolution of public interest on each topic

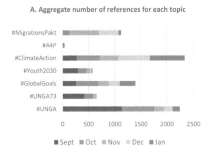

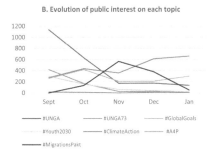

FIGURE 11.2   Breakdown of conversation topics

software for visual and social network analysis. The objective in this case was to obtain a more granular view of the underlying patterns of conversation, especially of the issues surrounding the three propositions described in the previous section: how digital disinformation may shape the online space in which the UN performance is discussed, how it may frame perceptions of the UN's relationship with Member States, and how it may hinder conditions for institutional recalibration.

The descriptive analysis of the trending topics of conversation during the selected period shows that online users hardly voiced any concerns about the migration compact in September 2018. Their interest in the topic peaked in October and November, only to recede after the UNGA endorsement of the agreement in December 2018 (see Figure 11.2A and B). The two dedicated hashtags (#UNGA, UNGA73), which were used for branding the 73rd session, dominated the conversation in September and early October. This is hardly unusual as one would expect them to be more frequently referenced during the UNGA General Debate when the heads of states were invited to formally deliver their speeches (September 25–October 1, 2018). With the exception of #A4P, the other topics promoted by the UNGA continued to attract the attention of the online public, especially #ClimateAction and #GlobalGoals, but they were clearly overshadowed by #MigrationsPakt in the month of November.

While descriptive analysis can prove useful for monitoring progress and evaluating the results of digital campaigns (e.g., whether their messages resonate or not with the online public), it does not say much about how competing campaigns may interact and influence each other. Social network analysis (SNA) can bridge this gap and untangle these connections by revealing the intensity with which certain topics are discussed by the online public and the pathways of influence they may exercise on other topics. As Figure 11.3 shows, the clusters of online conversation inspired by the agenda of the 73rd session of the UNGA changed dramatically between October 2018 and January 2019. Anti-migration sub-topics (#migrationpakt) started to rapidly multiply in October 2018 and to form a dense and active cluster of political discontent, which basically deformed the online space covering the UN agenda in the months of November and December 2018.

Oct 2018   *Nov 2018*

Dec 2018   *Jan 2019*

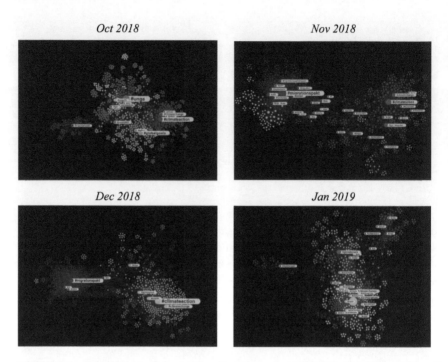

FIGURE 11.3 Breakdown of the topics of conversation related to the 73rd session of the UNGA

Social network analysis also provides visual support to the idea that the process of deformation of the online space does not take place abruptly, but in stages. *Incubation*, the first stage, refers to the method by which a theme is implanted and nurtured online so that it can reach a critical mass of adherence and influence as it happened with the anti-migration discourse in October 2018. Once this critical point is reached, the second stage, *interference*, becomes possible either by calling attention to the promoted theme of the anti-migration cluster or by discouraging public consideration of important issues on the UN agenda. The size of the clusters of UN promoted hashtags was, for instance, about 25–30% smaller in November and December than in the months of October and January.[1] By contrast, the size of the anti-migration cluster increased by roughly 80% in the months of November and December, compared to October and January.[2] In other words, people posted 80% more comments online on anti-migration topics and 25–30% less on UN-related issues in the months of November and December compared with the months of October 2018 and January 2019.

Our first proposition about the process by which political contestation may contribute to IO delegitimation receives, therefore, reasonable empirical support. By shifting the discussion away from the UN thematic agenda, the anti-migration discourse significantly deformed the online space of conversation concerning UN's performance expectations. However, these findings cannot validate, solely by themselves, the conclusion that the deformation of the online space was the result of digital disinformation as opposed to legitimate political contestation. A third stage, *hijacking*, could have confirmed the latter and further deepened the deformation process, but this outcome lacked enough empirical support in this case. That would have implied a deliberate and controversial use of UN-promoted hashtags for promoting anti-migration messages and therefore a more systematic effort of coordination than the current evidence suggests. The difference in the language of communication (German vs English) could have also discouraged users from embracing hijacking as a tactic for corrupting the channels by which anti-UNGCM messages could be disseminated.

Political contestation arguably weakens conditions for constructive political dialogue due to the partisan frames that actors develop and deploy in support of their positions on issues. Concerns for reputation and for setting unhelpful precedents may prevent UN diplomats from adopting hyper partisan positions in their interactions with each other (Johnstone 2003), but this constraint does not necessary apply to online users, since engagement in the digital medium is mainly driven by emotions, in general (Bjola et al. 2019, 6), and by negative emotions in particular (Fan et al. 2014). Empirical studies have shown, for instance, that anger encourages partisan, motivated evaluation of uncorrected misinformation (Weeks 2015) and that engagement with polarised messages increases the negativity of the discussion (Zollo et al. 2015). As a result, one would expect digital disinformation campaigns to both feed and be fed by negative emotions, which can be accomplished by attaching negative emotional frames to issues of interest. As data in Figure 11.4 suggests, this pattern is, in fact, empirically traceable in our case study as well,[3] thus validating our second proposition.

The overall negative profile of the subtopics connecting the nodes in the anti-migration cluster (Figure 11.4A) is primarily due to the use of a broader range of polarising messages, such as mentions of various cases of violence attributed to refugees in Germany (#chemitz, #freiburg, #messerattacke, #susannaf), praise of violent protests (#giletsjaunes, #gelbwesten) or harsh political criticism of the German government or the UN (#merkelmussweg, #migrationspaktstoppen). While the hashtags criticising the German and UN positions regarding

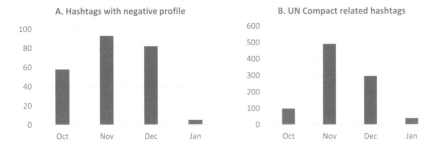

FIGURE 11.4   Breakdown of anti-migration subtopics by emotion and issue-relevance

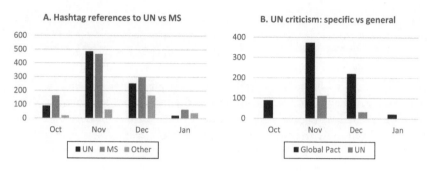

FIGURE 11.5 Breakdown of anti-migration subtopics by criticism target and type

the Global Compact could normally be viewed as part of the regular process of political contestation, the fact that they were interlaced with highly polarised messages with no connection to the substance of the Global Compact would place them in the category of digital disinformation. Furthermore, as Figure 11.4B suggests, negative emotions largely frame the discussion of compact-related hashtags, especially in the month of November, thus creating an epistemically confusing background for the discussion of these topics.

Turning to our third proposition, it is also important to know whether online discussions regarding the Global Compact could hinder potential efforts of institutional re-calibration by undercutting MS' commitments to the organisation. As Figure 11.5A indicates, the conversation in the anti-migration cluster did unfold in a binary pattern with most of the hashtags in each month focusing on migration themes related to either the UN or to national authorities (government, parliament, political parties). The remaining category ("other") was significantly smaller and included a few references to other governments, such as that of France, or to the European Union. These findings demonstrate, as suggested by the logical model, that political contestation of the UNGCM reflected growing perceptions of the UN presumably exceeding its competences in the policy area of migration and mounting dissatisfaction with the German government for failing to "correct" the alleged overreach.

At the same time, one should take note of the fact that online criticism of the UN primarily focused on the Global Compact and did not expand to other areas for the duration of the campaign (see Figure 11.5B), despite the intensity of the negative emotional framing of UNGCM-related hashtags discussed above. This finding is important as it suggests that the reputational setback arising from such circumstances for the UN would be rather limited, with minimal prospects of evolving in a more serious legitimacy crisis. However, as many of the assumptions informing the criticism of the Global Compact were based on false or misleading information, one should also qualify this finding by pointing out that disinformation actually lowered the bar for the escalation of negative assessments of the relationship between the UN and national governments thus increasing the chances of triggering a potential legitimacy crisis.

To conclude, the empirical analysis has provided nuanced support for the three propositions examining the conditions by which digital disinformation could have manufactured a legitimacy crisis for the UN following the online campaign organised against the Global Compact on Migration in August–December 2018. The campaign significantly deformed the online space of discussion regarding UN's performance expectations by shifting attention to the anti-migration theme and by discouraging public consideration of important issues on the UN agenda. The analysis also revealed that the campaign relied on polarising messages for reframing the discussion on UNGCM thus increasing epistemic confusion about the substantive issues on migration that the Global Compact sought to address. Finally, while the campaign made easier for negative and largely misleading assessments of the relationship between the UN and the German government to escalate, these messages stayed focused on issues related to the Global Compact and refrained from a more systematic criticism of the organisation.

Conclusion

In the past decade, digital disinformation has become the tactic of choice for many state and non-state actors simply because the gains of engaging in such practice are perceived to far outweigh any possible risks. State actors have discovered, for instance, that digital disinformation could be useful for influencing foreign elections or deterring foreign governments from pursuing certain policies. Non-state actors have also been using social media to shape public attitudes domestically and sustain political support for various leaders and parties, especially on the authoritarian side of the spectrum. Amidst these developments, a glaring gap of significant relevance for the already besieged liberal international order continues to be overlooked in the academic literature: the use of digital disinformation in multilateral contexts, especially against international organisations. To bridge this gap, this chapter has drawn on the case of the disinformation campaign against the UN Global Compact for Migration and argued that the potential challenge international organisations may face as result of digital disinformation is manufactured delegitimation.

The empirical analysis has shown that the disinformation campaign against the Global Compact has been successful in shifting public attention away from the UN agenda, increasing epistemic confusion about the objectives and provisions of the Global Compact, but without causing a negative escalation of attacks on the UN institution as a whole. While the legitimacy of the UN in this case suffered only a minor setback, one should not understate the cumulative effect of multiple disinformation campaigns in the long term. The study also exposed the empirical difficulties researchers may face when trying to distinguish between legitimate political contestation and disinformation, hence the need for identifying reliable metrics (e.g., corrupted tactics, polarised themes, toxic escalations) for unpacking the unique pathways by which digital disinformation may help engineer legitimacy crises for international organisations. Since the study has focused on a single case study, one should keep in mind that the conclusions presented in this chapter are primarily intended to demonstrate the feasibility of the conceptual framework for understanding the risk that digital disinformation can pose to international organisations.

Given the threat of manufactured delegitimation, what IOs can then do to protect themselves against the corrosive effects of digital disinformation? A close reading of the empirical findings in this chapter can helps us identify several methods by which IOs can stay ahead of potential attacks to their reputation and legitimacy. *Monitoring* the online space is definitely a first good step as it can help identify potential disinformation campaigns while they are still in the incubation period. Obviously, there is no need to track and respond to every single manifestation of political contestation, but those clusters of users that appear to rely on corrupted tactics of communication and have a message that rapidly grows and advances to the centre of the conversation need to be taken seriously. Once this stage is reached, *debunking* becomes critically necessary for reducing the potential of falsehoods to "stick" to the public agenda and to deform the online space of conversation. Debunking requires, however, a robust response capacity but also a good understanding of the contextual elements that would allow the discussion to be steered back to issues relevant for the UN agenda. Providing people with sources that share their point of view, introducing facts via well-crafted visuals, and offering an alternate narrative rather than a simple refutation may help dilute the effect of disinformation, alas not eliminate it completely (Bjola 2019).

As polarised messages draw their energy from antagonistic engagements, the response message should also carefully seek to remove, or at least not to add, negative emotions to the context of the conversation. This is why digital emotional intelligence that is, the ability to read, interpret, and manage emotions inhabiting the digital medium (Bjola et al. 2019, 88), may prove critical for the success of *emotional framing* as a counter-tactic necessary for improving epistemic clarity around the substantive issues that are being discussed online. Last but probably most importantly, the best way to prevent disinformation campaigns from undermining the legitimacy of the organisation is to act proactively. This will require the organisation to constantly explain to the online public how it contributes to solving collective problems in close collaboration with the member states. The goal in this case to establish a robust *"reputational shield"* for the organisation, which should be able to withstand potential disinformation attacks.

Notes

1 The total number of nodes in the UN-related clusters in October and January was 1,615, compared to 1,186 in November and December (26.56% difference). Similarly, the total number of edges in the UN-related clusters in October and January was 11,133, compared to 7,683 in November and December (30.98% difference).

2 The total number of nodes in the anti-migration cluster in November and December was 482, compared to 124 in October and January (74.28% difference). Similarly, the

total number of edges in the anti-migration cluster in November and December was 4,329 compared to 727 in October and January (83.20% difference).

3 The analysis was based on a sample drawing on the top 20 most frequently used hashtags in the anti-migration cluster in each of the four months. Political criticism without a call to action has been excluded from the emotional profile.

References

Bandeira, L., D. Barojan, R. Braga, and J.L. Penarredonda. *Disinformation in Democracies: Strengthening Digital Resilience in Latin America – ProQuest*, 2019. https://search.proqu est.com/docview/2218043131/?pq-origsite=primo.

Banulescu-Bogdan, N. *The Backlash Against the Global Compact on Migration Is a Blow for Multilateralism*. Emerging Europe, 2018. https://emerging-europe.com/voices/the-b acklash-against-the-global-compact-on-migration-is-a-blow-for-multilateralism/.

BBC. *Migrant Crisis: One Million Enter Europe in 2015*. BBC News, 2015. https://www .bbc.co.uk/news/world-europe-35158769.

Benkler, Y., R. Farris, and H. Roberts. *Network Propaganda*. Oxford University Press, 2018. doi:10.1093/oso/9780190923624.001.0001.

Bennett, W.L., and S. Livingston. "The Disinformation Order: Disruptive Communication and the Decline of Democratic Institutions." *European Journal of Communication* 33, no. 2 (2018): 122–39. doi:10.1177/0267323118760317.

Berger, J., T.L. Conner, and M.H. Fisek. *Expectation States Theory: A Theoretical Research Program*. Cambridge, MA: Winthrop, 1974.

Berger, J., M.H. Fisek, R.Z. Norman, and J. Morris Zelditch. *Status Characteristics in Social Interaction: An Expectation States Approach*. New York: Elsevier, 1977.

Berger, J., C.L. Ridgeway, M.H. Fisek, and R.Z. Norman. "The Legitimation and Delegitimation of Power and Prestige Orders." *American Sociological Review* 63, no. 3 (2006): 379. doi:10.2307/2657555.

Bjola, C. "Propaganda as Reflexive Control: The Digital Dimension." In *Countering Online Propaganda and Extremism: The Dark Side of Digital Diplomacy*, edited by C. Bjola, and J. Pamment, 13–27. London and New York: Route, 2018.

Bjola, C. *The "Dark Side" of Digital Diplomacy: Countering Disinformation and Propaganda*. Real Instituto Elcano, 2019. http://www.realinstitutoelcano.org/wps/portal/riel cano_en/contenido?WCM_GLOBAL_CONTEXT=/elcano/elcano_in/zonas _in/ari5-2019-bjola-dark-side-digital-diplomacy-countering-disinformation-pro paganda.

Bjola, C., J. Cassidy, and I. Manor. "Public Diplomacy in the Digital Age." *The Hague Journal of Diplomacy* 14, no. 1–2 (2019): 83–101. doi:10.1163/1871191X-14011032.

Bjola, C., and J. Pamment. *Countering Online Propaganda and Extremism: The Dark Side of Digital Diplomacy*. London and New York: Routledge, 2018.

Bjola, C., and K. Papadakis. "Digital Propaganda, Counterpublics and the Disruption of the Public Sphere: The Finnish Approach to Building Digital Resilience." *Cambridge Review of International Affairs* (2020): 1–29. doi:10.1080/09557571.2019.1704221.

Bradshaw, S., and P.N. Howard. *The Global Disinformation Order 2019*, 2019. https://co mprop.oii.ox.ac.uk/wp-content/uploads/sites/93/2019/09/CyberTroop-Report19.pdf.

Buchanan, A., and R.O. Keohane. "The Legitimacy of Global Governance Institutions." *Ethics & International Affairs* 20, no. 4 (2006): 405–37. doi:10.1111/j.1747-7093.2006.00043.x.

Carrera, S., K. Lannoo, M. Stefan, and L. Vosyliūtė. *Some EU Governments Leaving the UN Global Compact on Migration: A Contradiction in Terms?* Vol. 15, 2018. www.ceps.eu.

Chizhik, A.W., M.G. Alexander, E.W. Chizhik, and J. A. Goodman. "The Rise and Fall of Power and Prestige Orders: Influence of Task Structure." *Social Psychology Quarterly* 66, no. 3 (2003): 303–17.

Clark, I. "Legitimacy in a Global Order." *Review of International Studies* 29, no. S1 (2003): 75–95.

Claude, I.L.J. "Collective Legitimization as a Political Function of the United Nations." *International Organization* 20, no. 3 (1966): 367–79.

Coicaud, J.-M., and V.C.N.-K.L. Heiskanen. *The Legitimacy of International Organizations*. Tokyo: United Nations University Press, 2001. L. 2001 341.

Correll, S.J., and C.L. Ridgeway. "Expectation States Theory." In *Handbook of Social Psychology*, edited by J. Delamater, 29–51Boston, MA: Springer, 2006.

Diamond, L., M.F. Plattner, and C. Walker. "Authoritarianism Goes Global: The Challenge to Democracy." In *Authoritarianism Goes Global: The Challenge to Democracy*, 2016. doi:10.1080/10220461.2018.1500304.

Drun, J. *Taiwan's Social Media Landscape: Ripe for Election Interference?* Center for Advanced China Research, 2018. https://www.ccpwatch.org/single-post/2018/11/13/Taiwans -Social-Media-Landscape-Ripe-for-Election-Interference.

Ecker-Ehrhardt, M. "International Organizations "Going Public"? an Event History Analysis of Public Communication Reforms 1950–2015." *International Studies Quarterly* 62, no. 4 (2018): 723–36. doi:10.1093/ISQ/SQY025.

Eilstrup-Sangiovanni, M. "Death of International Organizations. The Organizational Ecology of Intergovernmental Organizations, 1815–2015." *Review of International Organizations* (2018). doi:10.1007/s11558-018-9340-5.

Fan, R., J. Zhao, Y. Chen, and K. Xu. "Anger Is More Influential than Joy: Sentiment Correlation in Weibo." *PLoS One* 9, no. 10 (2014). doi:10.1371/journal. pone.0110184.

Fidler, M. *Disinformation Colonialism and African Internet Policy | Council on Foreign Relations*. Council on Foreign Relations, 2019. https://www.cfr.org/blog/disinforma tion-colonialism-and-african-internet-policy.

Freedom House. *Freedom on the Net: The Crisis of Social Media*, 2019. https://www.fre edomonthenet.org/sites/default/files/2019-11/11042019_Report_FH_FOTN_2019 _final_Public_Download.pdf.

Gotev, G. *Nine EU Members Stay Away from un Migration Pact*. EurActiv, 2018. https:// www.euractiv.com/section/global-europe/news/nine-eu-members-stay-away-from -un-migration-pact/.

Graham-Harrison, E. "Vote Leave Broke Electoral Law and British Democracy Is Shaken." *The Guardian*, 2018. https://www.theguardian.com/politics/2018/jul/17/ vote-leave-broke-electoral-law-and-british-democracy-is-shaken.

Harris, P.G. "Collective Action on Climate Change: The Logic of Regime Failure." *Natural Resources Journal* 47, no. 1 (2007): 195–224. doi:10.2307/24889135.

Higgins, A. "Fake News, Fake Ukrainians: How a Group of Russians Tilted a Dutch Vote." *The New York Times*, 2017. https://www.nytimes.com/2017/02/16/world/ europe/russia-ukraine-fake-news-dutch-vote.html.

Howard, P.N., S. Woolley, and R. Calo. "Algorithms, Bots, and Political Communication in the US 2016 Election: The Challenge of Automated Political Communication for Election Law and Administration." *Journal of Information Technology & Politics* 15, no. 2 (2018): 81–93. doi:10.1080/19331681.2018.1448735.

Hurd, I. "Legitimacy and Contestation in Global Governance: Revisiting the Folk Theory of International Institutions." *Review of International Organizations* 14, no. 4 (2019): 717–29. doi:10.1007/s11558-018-9338-z.

Ikenberry, G.J. *After Victory: Institutions, Strategic Restraint, and the Rebuilding of Order After Major Wars.* Princeton, NJ: Princeton University Press, 2001.

Jamieson, K.H. *Cyberwar: How Russian Hackers and Trolls Helped Elect a President: What We Don't, Can't, and Do Know.* New York: Oxford University Press, 2018.

Johnstone, I. "Security Council Deliberations: The Power of the Better Argument." *European Journal of International Law* 14, no. 3 (2003): 437–80. doi:10.1093/ejil/14.3.437.

Kalkhoff, W., and S.R. Thye. "Expectation States Theory and Research." *Sociological Methods & Research* 35, no. 2 (2006): 219–49. doi:10.1177/0049124106290311.

Knottnerus, J.D. "A Critique of Expectation States Theory." *Sociological Perspectives* 31, no. 4 (1988): 420–45. doi:10.2307/1388969.

Kragh, M., and S. Åsberg. "Russia's Strategy for Influence Through Public Diplomacy and Active Measures: The Swedish Case." *Journal of Strategic Studies* (2017). doi:10.1080/01402390.2016.1273830.

Mearsheimer, J.J. "False Promise of International Institutions," *International Security*, Vol. 19, Issue 3. (1994; 95): 5–26.

Murdoch, S. *The Far Right Targets the UN Migration Pact.* HOPE Not Hate, 2018. https://www.hopenothate.org.uk/2018/12/07/far-right-target-un-migration-pact/.

Nayyar, D. *Governing Globalization.* Oxford and New York: Oxford University Press, 2011.

Newman, N., W. Richard Fletcher, A. Kalogeropoulos, and R. Kleis Nielsen. *Reuters Institute Digital News Report*, 2019. https://reutersinstitute.politics.ox.ac.uk/sites/default/files/2019-06/DNR_2019_FINAL_0.pdf.

OSoMe. *Interactive Network Graph*, 2020. http://osome.iuni.iu.edu/tools/networks/.

Packham, C. *Australia to Probe Foreign Interference Through Social Media Platforms.* Reuters, 2019. https://uk.reuters.com/article/uk-australia-politics/australia-to-probe-foreign-interference-through-social-media-platforms-idUKKBN1Y90E5.

Peel, M. "European States Reject Divisive UN Compact on Migration." *Financial Times*, 2018. https://www.ft.com/content/00624c22-f176-11e8-ae55-df4bf40f9d0d.

Peters, A. "The Global Compact for Migration: To Sign or Not to Sign?" *EJIL: Talk!* 2018. https://www.ejiltalk.org/the-global-compact-for-migration-to-sign-or-not-to-sign/.

Peterson, J. "The European Union: Pooled Sovereignty, Divided Accountability." *Political Studies* 45, no. 3 (1997): 559–78. doi:10.1111/1467-9248.00096.

Pinnell, O. "The Online War Between Qatar and Saudi Arabia." *BBC News*, 2018. https://www.bbc.co.uk/news/blogs-trending-44294826.

Pomerantsev, P. "Authoritarianism Goes Global (II): The Kremlin's Information War." *Journal of Democracy* 26, no. 4 (2015): 40–50. doi:10.1353/jod.2015.0074.

Pomerantsev, P., and M. Weiss. *The Menace of Unreality: How the Kremlin Weaponizes Information, Culture and Money.* Institute of Modern Russia, 2014. http://imrussia.org/media/pdf/Research/Michael_Weiss_and_Peter_Pomerantsev__The_Menace_of_Unreality.pdf.

Rasche, L., and Paul-Jasper Dittrich. (2019). *Interpretation and Truth. How Right-Wing Populist Disinformation Informs the Debate on Migration.*, Jacques Delors Institute Berlin, Policy Paper, https://www.hertie-school.org/fileadmin/user_upload/20190911_Desinformation_Migration_EN_Dittrich_Rasche.pdf

Richey, M. "Contemporary Russian Revisionism: Understanding the Kremlin's Hybrid Warfare and the Strategic and Tactical Deployment of Disinformation." *Asia Europe Journal* 16, no. 1 (2018): 101–13. doi:10.1007/s10308-017-0482-5.

Shahbaz, A., and A. Funk. *Digital Election Interference.* Freedom House, 2019. https://www.freedomonthenet.org/report/freedom-on-the-net/2019/the-crisis-of-social-media/digital-election-interference.

Slocum, J. *The Global Compact for Migration: International Cooperation Amidst a Nationalist Disinformation Campaign*. Chicago Council on Global Affairs, 2018. https://www.the chicagocouncil.org/blog/global-insight/global-compact-migration-international-co operation-amidst-nationalist.

Smith, M. "The League of Nations and International Politics." *Journal of International Studies* 2, no. 3 (1976): 311–23. doi:10.1017/S0260210500116754.

Sonya, I. *Migration and the 2030 Agenda A Guide for Practitioners*, 2014. www.iom.int.

Steffek, J. "The Output Legitimacy of International Organizations and the Global Public Interest." *International Theory* 7, no. 2 (2015): 263–93. doi:10.1017/S1752971915000044.

Tabatabai, A.M. "A Brief History of Iranian Fake News: How Disinformation Campaigns Shaped the Islamic Republic." *Foreign Affairs* 97, no. 4, (2018). https ://www.foreignaffairs.com/articles/middle-east/2018-08-24/brief-history-ira nian-fake-news.

Tallberg, J., and M. Zürn. "The Legitimacy and Legitimation of International Organizations: Introduction and Framework." *Review of International Organizations* 14, no. 4 (2019): 581–606. doi:10.1007/s11558-018-9330-7.

Tucker, J.A., A. Guess, P. Barberá, C. Vaccari, A. Siegel, S. Sanovich, D. Stukal, and B. Nyhan. *Social Media, Political Polarization, and Political Disinformation: A Review of the Scientific Literature*, 2018. Hewlet Foundation, https://www.hewlett.org/wp-content/uploads/2018/03/Social-Media-Political-Polarization-and-Political-Disinformation-Literature-Review.pdf

UN News. *Governments Adopt UN Global Migration Pact to Help Prevent Suffering and Chaos*, 2018. https://news.un.org/en/story/2018/12/1028041.

United Nations. *Global Compact for Migration*. Refugees & Migrants, 2018. https://re fugeesmigrants.un.org/migration-compact.

Vis, B., and D. Kuijpers. "Prospect Theory and Foreign Policy Decision-Making: Underexposed Issues, Advancements, and Ways Forward." *Contemporary Security Policy* 39, no. 4 (2018): 575–89. doi:10.1080/13523260.2018.1499695.

von Borzyskowski, I., and F. Vabulas. "Hello, Goodbye: When Do States Withdraw from International Organizations?" *Review of International Organizations* 14, no. 2 (2019): 335–66. doi:10.1007/s11558-019-09352-2.

Weeks, B.E. "Emotions, Partisanship, and Misperceptions: How Anger and Anxiety Moderate the Effect of Partisan Bias on Susceptibility to Political Misinformation." *Journal of Communication* 65, no. 4 (2015): 699–719. doi:10.1111/jcom.12164.

White, N.D. *International Peacekeeping the un Charter and Peacekeeping Forces: Constitutional Issues*, 2007. doi:10.1080/13533319608413639.

Wood, J. *How a Diplomatic Crisis Among Gulf Nations Led to Fake News Campaign in the United States*. GlobalPost, 2018. https://www.pri.org/stories/2018-07-24/how-di plomatic-crisis-among-gulf-nations-led-fake-news-campaign-united-states.

Woolley, S.C., and P.N. Howard. *Computational Propaganda: Political Parties, Politicians, and Political Manipulation on Social Media*. New York: Oxford University Press, 2018.

Zaum, D. "International Organizations, Legitimacy, and Legitimation." In *Legitimating International Organizations*, Dominik Zaum (ed.). Oxford: Oxford University Press, 2013: 3–25

Zollo, F., P. Kralj Novak, M. DelVicario, A. Bessi, I. Mozetič, A. Scala, G. Caldarelli, and W. Quattrociocchi. "Emotional Dynamics in the Age of Misinformation." *PLoS One* 10, no. 9 (2015): 1–22. doi:10.1371/journal.pone.0138740.

12

RETHINKING INTERNATIONAL ORGANISATIONS IN THE DIGITAL AGE

Corneliu Bjola and Ruben Zaiotti

IOs' digital turn

Academic research exploring the transformative role of digital technologies in international affairs has mostly focused on the use of social media by ministries of foreign affairs and embassies in their work (Bjola and Holmes 2015), especially on their digital efforts to refine and enhance their public diplomacy strategies (Manor 2019; Spry 2019; Strauß et al. 2015). As a result, the potential contributions that these technologies could make, as well as the challenges they pose, to multilateral diplomacy through the work of international organisations have been largely neglected in academic inquiry, an omission that the present volume has promised to address. In fact, this is the first volume to examine, in a theoretically informed and empirically systematic fashion, the broader ramifications of the use of social media on the internal dynamics, multilateral policies, and strategic engagements of international organisations.

To this end, the volume has brought together a multidisciplinary group of scholars and practitioners to discuss the evolving relationship between digital technologies and IOs from four distinct perspectives: the nature of the IOs' "digital universe," which reflects on the added value of digital tools to IOs' communication strategy and diplomatic practices; the role of social media in shaping IOs' autonomy as actors on the international stage; the contribution of digital platforms to enhancing IOs' legitimacy and the challenges the latter may face in this process; and finally, the impact of digital contestation on IOs' authority and on their ability to conduct and implement policies in a context dominated by the rise of post-truth politics and disinformation, which the digital medium has been credited to have ushered in (Bjola and Pamment 2018). Each chapter in the volume has offered a distinct theoretical viewpoint to these four themes and has also generated an impressive assortment of empirical findings.

On the question of whether the evolving digital context has changed how IOs now define their policy priorities and conduct their activities, the evidence seems to be mixed. According to Matthias Ecker-Ehrhardt, against the backdrop of recurring political crises and the growing pressure on IOs to manage external contestation, self-legitimation has emerged as the primary driver of social media integration into IOs' communication strategies. This motivation is closely followed by considerations of using digital monitoring and communication for improving the effectiveness of multiple policy programs on the ground. At the same time, digital tools appear, in some cases, to reinforce pre-digital patterns of communication rather than disrupt them. Michał Krzyżanowski shows, for instance, that social media helped sustain some of the deep-seated dispositions of EU communicative and organizational practices by remaining enclosed within the EU politico-institutional realm and evading connections with the wider European citizenry.

The relationship between IOs and member states is also going through a process of organisational restructuring as digital integration leans towards the breaking down of institutional barriers and the disruption of traditional boundaries of power, authority, and hierarchy. Caroline Bouchard has found that digital ICTs, particularly social media platforms, have led to the redefinition of the UN's external communications strategies. In addition, the impact of the diffusion of new digital ICTs has also been visible in internal communication processes, especially with respect to the UN rules of procedures, strategic interactions, and informal relationships. Recalling the process of digital reform that the Commonwealth Secretariat has embarked on since 2015, Nabeel Goheer shows how the organisation has managed to transform itself from a rigid bureaucracy to a value-creating network by unleashing the digital power of the organisation in the form of data, display, delivery, and discovery. Natalia Grincheva's study of the International Commission of Museums also lays bare the internal tensions that digital platforms may provoke by creating a conducive context for the decentralisation of power and by reconfiguring the channels of institutional influence.

As Ecker-Ehrhardt has demonstrated in his chapter, legitimation concerns constitute the main reason for which IOs seek to develop and deploy digital capabilities in their work. The assumption is that social media make IOs more vulnerable to public scrutiny and, therefore, they need to make extra efforts to engage with the online public and to explain their policies and actions. Interestingly, Matthias Hofferberth has found little evidence of such strategy being deployed in the case of the UN. Neither institutional nor individual UN handles have shown an inclination for self-criticism or for engaging in deliberation with the online public. Thus, as it stands, the UN *Twittersphere* does not constitute a tool of discursive engagement, but it rather serves as an organizational "echo chamber" of validation and promotion. In the same vein, Ilan Manor has found that UN forums offer Member States the opportunity to use digital tools to overcome the limitations of offline diplomacy by increasing their digital influence and prestige. That being said, prestige mobility may indirectly contribute to boosting the legitimacy of IOs by maintaining the vision of an international community that tackles shared challenges, addresses shared threats, and achieves shared prosperity. Challenging common expectations, Ruben Zaiotti shows that even a badly managed crisis could end up having a positive impact on the legitimacy of an organisation. For example, while challenging the European Union's reputation, the refugee crisis in 2015 has simultaneously increased the organization's global visibility and salience, thus contributing to the strengthening of its identity as an independent actor.

Part of the reason why IO self-legitimacy strategies tend to remain undeveloped also relates to the conflict-prone nature of the digital medium, which can be easily leveraged into a toxic form of digital contestation. As Lemke and Habegger have shown in their chapter, unlike traditional diplomacy, which generally aims at mitigating conditions for conflict and at improving long-term stability, digital communication, in contrast, thrives on short-term effects and negative emotions. This explains why, according to them, the contentious and outrageous style of communication of the Twitter account of the Russian Embassy in London has captured the attention of the online public despite the damage it has produced to Russian-UK bilateral relations. Similarly, IOs find themselves at a disadvantage when they seek to promote policies to a controversy seeking and emotionally hungry online public. As shown by Bjola, an emotionally charged disinformation campaign against the UN Global Compact for Migration has managed to shift public attention away from the UN agenda and increase epistemic confusion about the UNGCM's objectives and provisions. While the legitimacy of the UN, in this case, has suffered only a minor setback, Bjola argues that the cumulative effect of multiple disinformation campaigns could be quite damaging for IOs in the long term, by eventually creating the conditions for "manufactured delegitimation."

The conclusions reached by the various chapters in the volume paint a complex picture of the evolving process of adaptation and transformation of IOs in the digital age. They suggest that IOs do perceive digital technologies as a potential "game-changer" for both internal (power disruption) and external reasons (accountability pressure). They also reveal that IOs' efforts to integrate the new technologies into their work remain suboptimal, as the ambition to build and expand their digital presence has not yet been matched by a coherent approach that can help them transform into digitally engaging and institutional resilient organisations. While a lack of resources and the weaponised toxicity of the digital medium are generally offered as plausible explanations for this disconnection, the more structural cause may actually hide in plain sight. More specifically, IOs' efforts to integrate 21st century technologies into their 20th century design may be hindered by their institutionally path-dependent outlook of their role and functions as multilateral institutions. If so, then we need to take a closer look at what types of digital blind spots may affect IOs, whether they can be removed, and, if so, with what effect.

Digital Blind Spots

As a distinct analytical entity, the concept of blind spot has surprisingly received scant attention in IR scholarship, despite the occasional reference in the literature exploring the role of cognitive biases in foreign policy decision making (Janis, 1982; Jervis 2017; McDermott 2004). Blind spots are generally understood as a form of hidden bias that influences people's perceptions of the social reality but without them exercising a conscious, intentional control over how this happens (Banaji and Greenwald 2013). The term has been used by IR scholars, mainly in a metaphorical way, for describing cultural biases, primarily Western, informing social scientific inquiry (Bilgin 2010; Colgan 2019), theoretical limitations in realist thought concerning sources of international conflict (Ayoob 2016), persistent flaws in the US foreign policy in the Middle East (Elgindy 2019), or implicit biases which may influence the shapes of international law and its scholarship (Kanetake 2018). In short, a blind spot is viewed in IR scholarship as one of the many types of cognitive biases that foreign policy-makers experience, but without a clearly defined profile.

Approaching the issue from the perspective of formal logic, Sorensen offers a more tangible definition of the concept with credible analytical value. He argues that a "proposition p is an *epistemic blindspot* for person a (at time t) if and only if p is consistent, while Kap (for a knows that p) is inconsistent" (Sorensen 2006, 131). For example, the proposition "the coffee is strong" is an epistemic blind spot for a given individual (Bob) if that individual cannot possibly comment on the taste of the coffee (e.g., Bob has no sense of taste) even if that proposition is true. What constitutes, therefore, an epistemic blind spot is not the validity of p (whether the coffee is sweet or sour), but the fact that the validity of p remains inaccessible to Bob (condition #1), although not necessarily to others, who might be able to confirm or refute it (condition #2). In other words, reliable knowledge is possible (condition #2), but not accessible to Bob for certain reasons (condition #1). These reasons may relate to Bob's socially and culturally situated position (Button 2011, 698), but also to the means by which he reaches the said proposition, his cognitive profile, or to the time at which he tries (Sorensen 2017).

Epistemic blind spots pose a problem for decision-making as they imply that certain courses of action could hypothetically be taken without us being able to assess the full implications of the available information. While such omissions might not necessarily lead to bad decisions, it is reasonable to assume that blind spots are more likely to increase the propensity for making mistakes. More specifically, they may help explain why decision-makers may miss important signals, form a distorted view of the unfolding events, delay their reactions, or draw the wrong lessons from their experience. The good news, one may argue, is that according to condition #2, blind spot prevention is actually possible since others should have access to the type of knowledge that one misses. The bad news is that the knowledge required to prevent blind spots often reveals itself clearly only in retrospect. In other words, while it might be difficult to completely remove epistemic blind spots, one may argue that the ambition should be more limited in scope: to develop methods for identifying them so that their potential negative implications could be timely addressed and minimised.

Applied to the case of International Organizations, the analytical value of Sorensen's definition stems from the formal method if offers for identifying epistemic blind spots that IOs may develop in the context of digital integration. More specifically, it puts forward the thesis that *digital blind spots* are likely to arise from knowledge that may assist the functioning of IOs (condition #2), yet this knowledge could be reasonably overlooked by their leadership (condition #1). In the context of the themes discussed in this volume, it would be thus important to understand the potential blind spots that IOs may form in relation to their position on issues concerning the digital universe they operate in, the level of autonomy from member states, the ability to protect their legitimacy, as well as to the challenge that digital contestation may pose to their authority. In sum, the interesting question to ask is *what type of knowledge would be important for IOs to possess in relation to these four topics, yet that they may not be able to properly recognise and absorb?*

The answer to this question may embrace two forms: *weak* vs *strong* blind spots. The difference between them lies with an IO's ability to locate knowledge relevant for its digital integration efforts. Weak blind spots would thus refer to situations in which IOs should normally be able to accomplish this task with minimal efforts, while strong blind spots would involve unusual hardship in the pursuit of the same goal, despite the availability of information. One would reasonably expect, for instance, that IOs should face minor difficulties in following the evolution of the digital landscape, especially of new technological developments and trends. Such information is widely available and therefore it can be normally accessed by any organisation with a minimal interest in the topic. However, IOs may find it more challenging to recognise and understand the broader ramifications of this transformation and the potential contribution that new digital developments can make to their activities. While the information may be available, lack of expertise or institutional constraints may prevent IOs from discerning and absorbing relevant knowledge for their activities.

Let us consider four distinctive features (data, intensity, speed, sustainability) that drive and shape the process of digital transformation and examine how they may inform the formation of weak vs blind spots for IOs. To start with, the exponential growth of the global data sphere (163 zettabytes by 2025, ten times more than in 2016) has turned *Big Data*, the "bloodstream" of the digital revolution, into the most valuable commodity of our age. To put things into perspective, every two days we create as much information, the former Google CEO Eric Schmidt once claimed, as we had done from the dawn of civilisation up until 2003, roughly five exabytes of data (or 0.005 ZB) (Siegler 2010). One interesting implication of this process is that information could become a strategic resource. As argued by Rosenbach and Mansted (2019), technological advancements have ushered in a new era of information geopolitics, which is bound to change how states define their national interests and strategic priorities, and how they project power onto the world stage. In particular, the belief that the data-driven economy is a winner-takes-all environment could see states and their domestic tech industry develop much closer relationships together, a situation which is already evident in China, but also emergent in Europe and the United States. Digital protectionism is not inevitable (Fan and Gupta 2018), but, if it happens, it could have important implications for IOs as well.

A weak blind spot could be the result, for instance, of taking for granted the "participatory culture" of previous digital eras (Jenkins and Deuze 2008; Karpf 2019) under the assumption that the push for the "democratization" of digital content production and distribution will continue unencumbered. If this understanding is replaced by a government-driven approach that sees data and/or its underlying architecture in more strategic terms (Kennedy and Lim 2018), then IOs may actually find themselves in the position to enhance their autonomy. They may need to acquire new competencies in order to negotiate and coordinate new global digital cooperation mechanisms and even a "Digital Commons Architecture" (United Nations 2019) by which to overcome the risk of digital fragmentation and address emerging global challenges. A stronger blind spot could, however, develop from IOs assuming that states' interest in facilitating digital cooperation may moderate their appetite for digital mercantilism and strategic zero-sum game with respect to the acquisition and use of data. In the latter case, IOs' autonomy will likely suffer as member states will conceivably find their brokerage services redundant.

Second, the *intensity* of the process of digital transformation reflects itself in the way in which values, norms, and interests are being reshaped by the attributes of the new technologies. As mentioned elsewhere (Bjola et al. 2019), the cognitive heuristics that online users have developed in reaction to information overload aim to mitigate the challenge of conducting effective communication in the digital space. The transition from textual to visual communication is favoured, for example, by the intense competition for attention in the online space coupled with the ability of images to pack a large amount of information in an easily absorbable format. Emotional framing adds a powerful new layer to digital communication by highlighting the significance of users' moods and feelings in shaping the scope and scale of online engagement. Algorithms complete the picture as their crucial role in filtering, processing, and interpreting relevant data turn them into influential, yet opaque, tools of agenda-setting. In sum, visual enhancement, emotional framing, and algorithmic-driven engagement have become critical ingredients of meaning generation and social identity development, and by extension of foreign policy decision making.

One common blind spot that applies to IOs as well is the tendency to overlook the combined effect of these three elements (visuals, emotions, algorithms) and to focus on their separate implications. As Bennett and Segerberg (2012) have shown, digital communication follows a connective logic, according to which taking public action becomes less an issue of demonstrating support for generic goals, and more an act of personal expression and self-validation achieved by sharing ideas online, negotiating meanings, and structuring trusted relationships. Personalised engagement is, therefore, the critical ingredient of successful online communication and the three elements discussed above, visuals, emotions, algorithms, play a key role in shaping it. This line of reasoning has two implications for IOs. From a "digital universe" perspective, this could translate into a weak blind spot for IOs, as their mode of engagement involves statements and actions of a general not personal interest. From a disinformation perspective, personalisation favours the formation of a strong blind spot as digital contestation becomes more effective via micro-targeting (Youyou et al. 2015), but also more difficult to detect and, therefore, to counter.

Third, the *speed* by which new digital technologies now enter the global market and the swiftness by which they are mass adopted is also unprecedented. It took, for instance, the telephone 75 years to reach 100 million users, but only three years for Facebook and only one year for WeChat to achieve the same performance (Dreischmeier et al. 2015). Staying ahead of the technological curve thus requires a cognitive shift from following to anticipating and possibly pushing new trends. Consider, for instance, the case of artificial intelligence. As the pace of digital change increases, conceptions of decision-making in international affairs are being also recast as algorithms and machines acquire a critical and increasingly dominant role in this process. It is increasingly expected, for instance, for AI to undertake more complex tasks that require cognitive capabilities such as making tacit judgements, sensing emotion, and driving processes that previously seemed impossible (Duan et al. 2019, 67). Technical conditions are not yet in place to make it possible for AI to assist decision-makers in prescribing a course of action in a non-deterministic fashion, by automatically adapting its recommendations based on continuous description, diagnostic, prediction, and action loops (Bjola 2020, 17–18). However, efforts are being done to scale up research of relevance for IOs by using AI to improve the security of diplomatic missions and to maximise the effectiveness for international humanitarian operations (Horowitz et al. 2018, 12–13).

The speed of the process of digital transformation may catch IOs off-guard primarily because of their digitally asynchronous organisational culture. Real-time management, transparency, decentralization, informality, and interactivity are critical norms to inform the effectiveness of digital activity. However, they may not necessarily sit culturally well with IOs' institutionally entrenched preferences for incrementalism, confidentiality, hierarchy, and top-down decision-making (Bjola 2017, 9). Organisational cultures do change but generally in a slow and often uneven fashion (Schein 2004). Drawing again on the AI example, one could argue that the success of machine learning integration in the activity of international organisations is also a blind spotting issue. On the "weak" side, IOs' proclivity to react rather than anticipate challenges would likely prompt them to look for AI solutions to the problem of the day (e.g., data management) and overlook the likely pressures they may increasingly face in the future (e.g., disorder containment). On the "stronger" side of the blind spotting problem, it would be also essential to understand how AI integration may affect IOs' sphere of autonomy. AI may help transform IO from actors mainly catering to the interests of the member states to those of the broader international community. The costs of this transformation for IOs' legitimacy should be also carefully considered.

Finally, the *sustainability* of the process of digital innovation may also complicate efforts seeking to facilitate IOs' institutional adaptation and strategic planning. With the arrival of the 5G technology in the next decade, a fresh stream of digital technologies (extended reality, artificial intelligence, blockchain, digital twinning) is expected to become widely available and to accelerate the pace of information exchange, global interaction, policy innovation, and strategic engagement (Lewis 2018). Advanced technologies are deemed to facilitate a qualitative leap from the current process of digitisation (i.e., conversion of traditional content and services into a digital format) to a more holistic form of digital transformation, which according to the European Commission would involve the "fusion of digital and key enabling technologies (KETs), and the integration of physical and digital systems" (European Commission 2019). The word "fusion" carries particular analytical weight as it speaks to the qualitative difference that advanced technologies could make to the way in which organisations operate as the process of digital transformation evolves. More specifically, the digital technology will no longer work as a mere appendix to traditional IO processes by providing logistical and decision-making support. It will instead become a core component of the organisation's mission, design, and policies to the extent that every singly activity of the organisation will have to meet conditions for digital integration in order to be adopted.

The interesting question is, of course, whether IOs may overlook or misread some important technological developments that the next stage of the process of digital transformation could make available for them. For example, extended reality (AR and VR), which blends real and virtual worlds, could theoretically prove beneficial for IOs' outreach activities or even their ability to conduct negotiations remotely. Similarly, digital twinning could offer a real-time comprehensive linkage between IOs' physical and digital operations ranging from improving internal communication flows to humanitarian aid delivery and disaster response coordination. A weak blind spot may arise from narrowly focusing on the potential benefits of the emerging technologies without paying due attention to the scale and reliability of the digital ecosystem in which these technologies will operate. This may lead to a situation in which the adopted technologies will fail to transform the IOs' "digital universe" as the broader ecosystem is not strong enough to sustain it yet. A stronger blind spot may follow from assuming that advanced technologies are ethically neutral and hence they can be safely deployed with little concern for the reputation and legitimacy of the organisation. However, the idea that values may be embodied in technical systems and devices has taken root in a variety of disciplinary approaches to the study of technology and society (Flanagan et al. 2008) and, therefore, the ethical implications surrounding the adoption of advanced technologies will have to be carefully considered as well.

From digital diplomacy to digital international organisations?

What if international organisations manage to overcome their blind spots? One possibility resulting from the "digital disruption" (McQuivey 2013) that new communication technologies have brought to the realm of diplomacy and international relations is a radical transformation of IOs into full-fledged "digital organizations" (Smart et al. 2017). These organisations' design is based on the same core principles that underlie digital technologies themselves. First, a digital IO is built around personnel with the ability to self-manage and to operate within a non-hierarchical chain of command (Lee and Edmondson 2017). Second, the organisation relies on resources that are collectively owned and shared among its members (Hess 2012). Third, the organisation establishes rules and infrastructures that encourage connections and collaboration among its members, both internally and externally (Camarinha-Matos and Afsarmanesh 2004). The technological instruments supporting this newly re-designed organisation include cloud computing, big data analytics, cognitive computing, and collaboration platforms (Smart et al. 2017).

One of the most significant implications of a move towards digital IOs is the reformulation of power dynamics within these organisations. The visibility of the information circulating on social platforms creates a channel for employees to signal the possession of knowledge, and with it, the ability to influence the decision-making process (Treem and Leonardi, 2013). The use of digital collaborative platforms can, therefore, have a democratising effect on knowledge contributions. Members of a digital organisation can also increase their network within the organisation, obtain greater access to individuals higher up in the hierarchy, and thus increase their social capital. Moreover, they can more effectively participate in the discursive practices that contribute to the definition of the organisation's narrative about itself.

IOs' digitalisation would also transform how these organisations relate to the outside world. This process could lead, for instance, to the upgrading of the "networked diplomacy" that IOs are already performing today (Hocking et al. 2012). This form of diplomatic practice encourages the engagement with non-traditional actors (e.g. NGOs), work on cross-sectoral policy agendas, and the establishment "horizontal" relationships with stakeholders (Melissen and Hocking 2015, 27). A digital IO could provide organisational structure and resources more suitable to a networked diplomacy in the digital age. It would be in a better position to more efficiently engage with a broader set of constituencies, establish more transparent relations with them, and favour openness in the sharing of information. It could also provide the platform and support for citizens' direct participation in global governance (Steffek et al. 2008).

The move towards a digital IOs world would not be exempt from challenges and controversy. This radical organisational transformation would question taken-for-granted notions that continue to define contemporary international relations and diplomacy, from hierarchy as organising principle to the reliance on top-down communication and the emphasis on secrecy (Melissen and Hocking 2015). The ubiquity of digital tools could also accentuate some of the problematic aspects of the digital revolution affecting IOs today. A fully developed digital public space within which IOs operate, for instance, might not lead to a more open and democratic organisation after all; instead, it might create pressure for conformity, whereby members of the organisation merely reproduce the norms and practices spearheaded by the organisations' leadership. The same can be said for external stakeholders, whose contributions to debates about matters of IOs' policy and vision might be used to legitimise pre-existing agendas. More ominously, digital IOs could expand and strengthen their surveillance capacity. The ubiquity of social media as a communicative tool, coupled with the ease in storing the digital traces left on online platforms, would allow organisations to monitor and track more closely and efficiently the practices of their workers and stakeholders (Zhang and Vos 2014). In turn, those participating in digital exchanges involving IOs might become reluctant to express their opinions because of the fear of surveillance and possible reprisal (Bekkers et al. 2013).

These challenges and controversies raise the question of how the transition to a new digital organisational model might occur in the first place. In the realm of foreign affairs, the pressure to become more digitised is less pronounced than for their domestic or private counterparts, as they are less involved in service delivery and face less political or market-driven demands for change (Melissen and Hocking 2015, 24). The process of digitalisation is also likely to be uneven among and within IOs. Depending on their mandate and resources, some international organisations might transition to the digital world more quickly and extensively than others, with particular units (e.g., those dealing with public diplomacy) leading the way (Melissen and Hocking 2015, 23). The path to the creation of digital IOs, therefore, will not be linear. Indeed, whether IOs will become digital in full or in part (or at all), which organisation will get there or not, or at what pace, will not be decided solely by IOs themselves, but also by factors beyond their direct control. This transformation's trajectory is thus consistent with the one envisioned in "chaos theory," an analytical approach that scholars of Public Administration and International Relations have borrowed from the natural sciences to study organisational change (Keyes and Benavides 2018; Bousquet and Curtis 2011).

This model's key insight is to consider private and public organisations as part of a dynamic network of actors analogous to ecological systems in nature. These systems can experience surprise or uncertainty ("noise") as a result of events ("attractors" or "stressors") originating from the context in which organisations are inserted (e.g., a financial crisis, a natural disaster; Koehler 1997). Organisations then process the positive and negative feedback they gather from the noise around them and try to formulate appropriate responses to the new environment. The outcome of this process is the creation of a new order, also referred to as an organisation's "co-evolution" (Porter 2006). The ensuing new arrangements of interaction and patterns of behaviour, spurred by radical policy decisions, may lead to a disruption of the entire system. The path leading to change is characterised by complexity, with phenomena of "punctuated change," "bifurcations," "phase shifts," and "feedback loops" affecting the decision-making process (Klijn 2008).

The context within which IOs currently operate is characterised by a high volume of "noise." The rise of populist and nationalist movements among IOs' leading member states is eroding the consensus over the multilateralist principles that have undergirded the international order since the Second World War. IOs' budgets are increasingly under strain, leaving IOs with limited scope for maintaining, let alone expanding, their operations. The rapid advances in technology, especially with regards to communication, have provided opportunities but also challenges to these organisations, reducing their control over events and policy agendas. Global crises are also becoming more complex and difficult to manage, as exemplified by COVID-19, the global pandemic that hit the world in the first part of 2020. While they represent a serious threat to the established order, these trends also provide fertile terrain for a radical transformation of IOs.

Some of these changes are already occurring. As a response to the spread of the COVID-19 virus, international organisations, like other private and public entities at a domestic and international level, have ordered most of their employees to work from home and transferred the core of their operations online. While it has been a temporary measure in the face of an impending crisis, the unprecedented move offered a glimpse of how a digital organisation can be set up and operate, and this experiment – and the lessons learnt from it – will loom large in future blueprints of IOs. Some international organisations also grasped this unique opportunity to increase their profile in the digital world. The World Health Organization (WHO), for instance, was criticised for its handling of the Ebola outbreak in West Africa in 2014 (Kamradt-Scott 2016). One area that came under particular scrutiny was the WHO's bungled public relations response (Guidry et al. 2017).[1] By the time the COVID-19 virus became a global crisis half a decade later, the organisation had upgraded its digital communication strategy. Thanks to a sophisticated social media campaign during the crisis, the WHO has consolidated its reputation and leadership on health-related matters, and for some commentators it reached the status of "the planet's most important social influencer" (Brown 2020). One of its main achievements was its successful engagement with younger audiences (16–24 years old), a category typically out of reach of international organisations, through its active presence on platforms such as TikTok and viral campaigns such as the Safe Hands Challenge. The WHO also collaborated closely with social media organisations to counter the spread of disinformation (Convertino 2020). Despite all the challenges IOs are facing today, the WHO case shows how IOs can still be central actors in world politics, if these organisations are able and willing to adapt to the new digital era.

To conclude, the nature and scope of the digital transformation remain elusive as the micro-level effects of digital technologies follow a complex pattern of conversion into broader macro-level ramifications for global ordering processes. International organisations sit, however, at the centre for this process and their ability not only to react but also to shape the direction in which digital technologies develop is likely to have major implications for the reconfiguration of the global order and politics in the coming decades. The conceptual benchmarks we have provided in this volume are designed to facilitate this transition by encouraging IOs to be more reflective about the "digital universe" they generate, the digital parameters of their autonomy as actors on the international stage, the contribution that digital platforms can make to enhancing their legitimacy, and the challenges that post-truth politics and digital contestation may bring to their authority and ability to pursue and protect multilateralism in the digital age.

Note

1 During the height of the Ebola crisis, the WHO spokesperson entered into a public spat – played out on social media – with a leading health NGO, Médecins Sans Frontières (MSF), which claimed that WHO had underplayed the crisis.

References

Ayoob, M. *Realism's Gaping Blind Spots—And How to Fix Them*. National Interest, 2016. https://nationalinterest.org/blog/the-buzz/realisms-gaping-blind-spots—-how-fix-them-17306?page=0%2C1.

Banaji, M.R., and A.G. Greenwald. *Blindspot: Hidden Biases of Good People*. New York: Delacorte Press, 2013.

Bekkers, V., A. Edwards, and D. de Kool. "Social Media Monitoring: Responsive Governance in the Shadow of Surveillance?" *Government Information Quarterly* 30, no. 4 (2013): 335–42.

Bennett, W. L., and A. Segerberg. "The Logic of Connective Action." *Information, Communication & Society* 15, no. 5 (2012): 739–68. doi:10.1080/1369118X.2012.670661.

Bilgin, P. "The 'Western-Centrism' of Security Studies: 'Blind Spot' or Constitutive Practice?" In *Security Dialogue*, Vol. 41, 615–622. Sage Publications, Ltd, 2010. doi:10.2307/26301701.

Bjola, C., and M. Holmes. "Digital Diplomacy: Theory and Practice." In *Digital Diplomacy: Theory into Practice*, 2015. doi:10.4324/9781315730844.

Bjola, Corneliu. *Adapting Diplomacy to the Digital Age: Managing the Organisational Culture of Ministries of Foreign Affairs*, Vol. 2017, 2017. https://www.swp-berlin.org/fileadmin/contents/products/arbeitspapiere/WP_Diplomacy21_No9_Corneliu_Bjola_01.pdf.

Bjola, Corneliu. *Diplomacy in the Age of Artificial Intelligence*, 2020. http://eda.ac.ae/.

Bjola, Corneliu, J. Cassidy, and I. Manor. "Public Diplomacy in the Digital Age." *The Hague Journal of Diplomacy* 14, no. 1–2 (2019): 83–101. doi:10.1163/1871191X-14011032.

Bjola, Corneliu, and J. Pamment. *Countering Online Propaganda and Extremism: The Dark Side of Digital Diplomacy*. London and New York: Routledge, 2018.

Bousquet, A., and S. Curtis. "Beyond Models and Metaphors: Complexity Theory, Systems Thinking and International Relations." *Cambridge Review of International Affairs* 24, no.1 (2011): 43–62.

Brown, Abraham. "Coronavirus: The World Health-Organization Is Becoming the World's Most Important Social Media Influencer." *Forbes Magazine*, March 16, 2020. https://www.forbes.com/sites/abrambrown/2020/03/16/coronavirus-the-world-health-organization-is-becoming-the-worlds-most-important-social-media-influencer/#1011e61a5321.

Button, M.E. "Accounting for Blind Spots: From Oedipus to Democratic Epistemology." *International Political Theory* 39, no. 6 (2011): 695–723.

Camarinha-Matos, L. M., and Afsarmanesh, H. *Collaborative Networked Organizations. A Research Agenda for Emerging Business Models*. New York: Springer, 2004.

Colgan, J.D. "American Perspectives and Blind Spots on World Politics." *Journal of Global Security Studies* 4, no. 3 (2019): 300–9. doi:10.1093/jogss/ogz031.

Convertino, Jesse. "Social Media Companies Partnering with Health Authorities to Combat Misinformation." *ABC News*, March 5, 2020. https://abcnews.go.com/Technology/social-media-companies-partnering-health-authorities-combat-misinformation/story?id=69389222.

Cianni, M., and S. Steckler. "Transforming Organizations to a Digital World." *People & Strategy* 40, no. 2 (2017): 14–20.

Dreischmeier, R., K. Close, and P. Trichet. *The Digital Imperative*, Vol. 2017, 2015. https://www.bcgperspectives.com/content/articles/digital_economy_technology_strategy_digital_imperative/.

Duan, Y., J.S. Edwards, and Y.K. Dwivedi. "Artificial Intelligence for Decision Making in the Era of Big Data – Evolution, Challenges and Research Agenda." *International Journal of Information Management* 48 (2019): 63–71. doi:10.1016/j.ijinfomgt.2019.01.021.

Elgindy, K. *Blind Spot America and the Palestinians, from Balfour to Trump*. Washington, D.C.: Brookings Institution Press, 2019.

European Commission. *Advanced Technologies*, 2019. https://ec.europa.eu/growth/industry/policy/advanced-technologies_en.

Fan, Z., and A. Gupta. "The Dangers of Digital Protectionism." *Harvard Business Review*, 2018. https://hbr.org/2018/08/the-dangers-of-digital-protectionism.

Flanagan, M., D.C. Howe, and H. Nissenbaum. "Embodying Values in Technology: Theory and Practice." In *Information Technology and Moral Philosophy*, edited by J. van den Hoven, and J. Weckert, 322–53. Cambridge University Press, 2008, doi:10.1017/CBO9780511498725.017.

Guidry, Jeanine P.D., Yan Jin, Caroline A. Orr, Marcus Messner, and Shana Meganck. "Ebola on Instagram and Twitter: How Health Organizations Address the Health Crisis in Their Social Media Engagement." *Public Relations Review* 43, no. 3 (2017): 477–86.

Hocking, B., and J. Melissen. *Diplomacy in the Digital Age*. Clingendael, Netherlands Institute of International Relations, 2015. https://www.clingendael.org/sites/default/files/pdfs/Digital_Diplomacy_in_the_Digital%20Age_Clingendael_July2015.pdf.

Hocking, B. L., J. Melissen, S. Riordan, and P. Sharp. *Futures for Diplomacy: Integrative Diplomacy in the 21st Century*. Netherlands Institute of International Relations' Clingendael', 2012. https://www.clingendael.org/publication/futures-diplomacy-integrative-diplomacy-21st-century#:~:text=Clingendael%20authors%20Brian%20Hocking%2C%20Jan,tackling%20a%20broad%20international%20agenda.

Horowitz, M.C., G.C. Allen, E. Saravalle, A. Cho, K. Frederick, and P. Scharre. *Artificial Intelligence and International Security*, 2018. https://www.cnas.org/publications/reports /artificial-intelligence-and-international-security.

Huang, J., J. Baptista, and R.D. Galliers. "Reconceptualizing Rhetorical Practices in Organizations: The Impact of Social Media on Internal Communications." *Information & Management* 50, no. 2–3 (2013): 112–24.

Janis, I. L. *Groupthink. Psychological Studies of Policy Decisions and Fiascoes.* Boston: Houghton Mifflin, 1982.

Jenkins, H., and M. Deuze. "Convergence Culture." *Convergence: The International Journal of Research into New Media Technologies* 14, no. 1 (2008): 5–12. doi:10.1177/1354856507084415.

Jervis, R. "Perception and Misperception in International Politics." In *Perception and Misperception in International Politics*. Princeton University Press, 2017. doi:10.2307/j. ctvc77bx3.

Kamradt-Scott, A. "WHO's to Blame? The World Health Organization and the 2014 Ebola Outbreak in West Africa." *Third World Quarterly* 37, no. 3 (2016): 401–18.

Kanetake, M. "Blind Spots in International Law." *Leiden Journal of International Law* 31, no. 2 (2018): 209–18. doi:10.1017/S0922156518000109.

Karpf, D. "Two Provocations for the Study of Digital Politics in Time." *Journal of Information Technology & Politics* (2019). doi:10.1080/19331681.2019.1705222.

Kennedy, A.B., and D.J. Lim. "The Innovation Imperative: Technology and US–China Rivalry in the Twenty-First Century." *International Affairs* 94, no. 3 (2018): 553–72. doi:10.1093/ia/iiy044.

Keyes, Laura M., and Abraham David Benavides. "Chaos Theory, Uncertainty, and Organizational Learning." *International Journal of Organization Theory & Behavior* 21, no. 4 (2018): 226–41.

Klijn, E. H. "Complexity Theory and Public Administration: What's New? Key concepts in Complexity Theory Compared to their Counterparts in Public Administration Research." *Public Management Review* 10, no. 3 (2008): 299–317.

Koehler, Gus A.. *What Disaster Response Management Can Learn from Chaos Theory: Conference Proceedings.* Sacramento, CA: DIANE Publishing, 1997.

Lee, M.Y., and A.C. Edmondson. "Self-Managing Organizations: Exploring the Limits of Less-Hierarchical Organizing." *Research in Organizational Behavior* 37 (2017): 35–58.

Lewis, J.A. "How 5G Will Shape Innovation and Security: A Primer." In *Center for Strategic and International Studies*, 2018. https://www.csis.org/analysis/how-5g-will -shape-innovation-and-security.

Liu, B.F., and J.D. Fraustino. "Beyond Image Repair: Suggestions for Crisis Communication Theory Development." *Public Relations Review* 40, no. 3 (2014): 543–6.

Manor, I. "The Digitalization of Public Diplomacy." In *The Digitalization of Public Diplomacy*, Palgrave Macmillan, 2019. doi:10.1007/978-3-030-04405-3.

McDermott, R. *Political Psychology in International Relations.* Ann Arbor: The University of Michigan Press, 2004.

McQuivey, J. *Digital Disruption: Unleashing the Next Wave of Innovation.* Las Vegas: Forrester Research Inc, 2013.

Porter, T. B. "Co-Evolution as a Research Framework for Organizations and the Natural Environment." *Organization Environment* 19 (2006): 479–504.

Rosenbach, E., and K. Mansted. *The Geopolitics of Information*, 2019. www.belfercenter .org/D3P.

Schein, H.E. *Organisational Culture and Leadership.* Hoboken: John Wiley & Sons, 2004.

Siegler, M. G. *Eric Schmidt: Every 2 Days We Create as Much Information as We Did up to 2003*, Vol. 2018. 2010. Techcrunch. https://techcrunch.com/2010/08/04/schmidt -data/.

Snow, C. C., Ø. D. Fjeldstad, and A. M. Langer. "Designing the Digital Organization." *Journal of Organization Design* 6, no. 1 (2017): 2–13.

Sorensen, R.A. "Conditional Blindspots and the Knowledge Squeeze: A Solution to the Prediction Paradox." *Australasian Journal of Philosophy* 62, no. 2 (2006): 126–35. doi:10.1080/00048408412341321.

Sorensen, R.A.. *Epistemic Paradoxes*. Stanford Encyclopedia of Philosophy Stanford Encyclopedia of Philosophy, 2017. doi:10.1111/1467-9973.00225.

Spry, D. "More than Data: Using the Netvizz Facebook Application for Mixed-Methods Analysis of Digital Diplomacy." In *More than Data: Using the Netvizz Facebook Application for Mixed-Methods Analysis of Digital Diplomacy*, 2019. doi:10.4135/9781526465641.

Steffek, J., and P. Nanz. "Emergent Patterns of Civil Society Participation in Global and European Governance." In *Civil Society Participation in European and Global Governance. Transformations of the State*, edited by J. Steffe, C. Kissling, and P. Nanz. London: Palgrave Macmillan, 2008.

Strauß, N., S. Kruikemeier, H. van der Meulen, and G. van Noort. "Digital Diplomacy in GCC Countries: Strategic Communication of Western Embassies on Twitter." *Government Information Quarterly* 32, no. 4 (2015): 369–79. doi:10.1016/j.giq.2015.08.001.

Treem, J.W., and P.M. Leonardi. "Social Media Use in Organizations: Exploring the Affordances of Visibility, Editability, Persistence, and Association." *Annals of the International Communication Association* 36, no. 1 (2013): 143–89.

United Nations. *The Age of Digital Interdependence Report of the UN Secretary-General's High-Level Panel on Digital Cooperation*, 1–47, 2019. https://digitalcooperation.org/wp -content/uploads/2019/06/DigitalCooperation-report-for-web.pdf.

Youyou, W., M. Kosinski, and D. Stillwell. "Computer-Based Personality Judgments Are More Accurate than Those Made by Humans." *Proceedings of the National Academy of Sciences of the United States of America* 112, no. 4 (2015): 1036–40. doi:10.1073/pnas.1418680112.

Zhang, B., and M. Vos. "Social Media Monitoring: Aims, Methods, and Challenges for International Companies." *Corporate Communications: an International Journal* 19, no. 4 (2014): 371–83.

INDEX

Printed in Poland
by Amazon Fulfillment
Poland Sp. z o.o., Wrocław